Kevin D. Ray

Romans

Romans

An Exposition of Chapter 8 : 5–17
The Sons of God

D. M. Lloyd-Jones

ZONDERVAN
PUBLISHING HOUSE

OF THE ZONDERVAN CORPORATION | GRAND RAPIDS, MICHIGAN 49506

To the faithful and enthusiastic Friday-nighters at Westminster Chapel 1955–68

ROMANS: THE SONS OF GOD
© D. M. Lloyd-Jones 1974

First published 1974

First Zondervan printing 1975
Seventh printing 1981
ISBN 0-310-27920-8

Printed in the United States of America

Contents

[vii]

Contents

Contents

[ix]

Contents

Preface

This further series of sermons on the Epistle to the Romans was preached in Westminster Chapel between March 1960 and April 1961. Our Friday evening sessions were held from the beginning of October to the end of May each year.

This volume deals with momentous questions such as the doctrine of Sanctification and the baptism with the Holy Spirit. It, therefore, deals with matters which are not only crucial in the living of the Christian life, but also highly controversial.

I have tried to state fairly views which have been very popular but which I have felt compelled to reject. We can all thank God that we are not saved by our understanding; nevertheless, the Scriptures were written for our instruction, and it is our business to grapple with them. The greater our understanding the greater will be our enjoyment of this new 'life in the Spirit'.

I do not apologize for summarizing so frequently the main thrust of the Apostle's majestic argument, for the greatest danger is to 'miss the wood because of the trees'. The same applies to my constant endeavour to compare 'Scripture with Scripture'.

Whatever the reader may feel, I have to confess that the preaching of these sermons gave me greater joy than anything in my long experience as a preacher. I thank God that I have experienced something of this again in preparing them for publication. God grant a like experience to others.

As usual I am deeply indebted to all who have helped and encouraged me in the work – especially Mrs E. Burney, Mr S. M. Houghton and my wife.

November 1974   D. M. LLOYD-JONES

One

*

For they that are after the flesh do mind the things of the flesh; but they that are after the Spirit the things of the Spirit.
For to be carnally minded is death; but to be spiritually minded is life and peace.
Because the carnal mind is enmity against God: for it is not subject to the law of God, neither indeed can be.
So then they that are in the flesh cannot please God.

Romans 8: 5–8

It can be argued, as I have suggested in a previous volume, that the message of this great and most eloquent chapter really begins at verse 5. The first four verses sum up the argument of chapter 7; and here we have a new section which runs from the 5th verse to the end of the 13th verse.

Let us remind ourselves that the object of the entire chapter, and therefore the object of every subsidiary section, is really to prove the contention of verse 1, namely, that 'There is therefore now no condemnation to them which are in Christ Jesus'. That is the fundamental proposition. The Apostle's purpose is to show the absolute certainty and finality of the full and complete salvation of all who are 'in Christ Jesus' – in other words, of all who are in the realm of the Spirit, and in whom the Holy Spirit of God dwells. Of course this has its negative side – that this salvation only applies to such people as have been set free from 'the law of sin and death' by 'the law of the Spirit of life in Christ Jesus'. They are the only people for whom there is no condemnation and to whom, therefore, this certainty of final and complete salvation applies. The Apostle has been reminding us in verses 3 and 4 of the way in which believers have been put into that position and thereby set free from the Law and all its demands, and all that it does to those who are unregenerate and 'in the flesh'.

Having done that, Paul can proceed to prove that it is essential that we should be 'in Christ', and in the realm of the Spirit, before this can possibly happen to us. He has made his great asseveration in verses 1 and 2; then in verses 3 and 4 he shows us how we get into that position. Now he wants to establish the fact that it is only to such people that this full and final salvation is guaranteed and is absolutely certain. We can put it in this way, that the object of verses 5 to 13 is to prove the contention of verse 4 in particular, and especially its second statement. He has told us that the object of salvation is 'that the righteousness of the law might be fulfilled in us'. But, he says, 'the righteousness of the law' is only fulfilled in those 'who walk not after the flesh, but after the Spirit'. Now he proceeds to show why he speaks in this way, why it is that only in those who walk 'after the Spirit' and not 'after the flesh' can 'the righteousness of the law' be fulfilled.

A general analysis of this sub-section, verses 5 to 13, I suggest, is the following: Verses 5 to 8 give us a picture of the contrast between the Christian and the non-Christian, with the special object of showing that 'the righteousness of the law' cannot possibly be fulfilled in the non-Christian but only in the Christian. In verses 9 to 11 Paul applies this to the Roman Christians. He says: 'But ye are not in the flesh, but in the Spirit, if so be that the Spirit of God dwell in you. Now if any man have not the Spirit of Christ, he is none of his' – that is to say, he is not a Christian at all. As far as they are concerned he knows that they are 'in the Spirit' and not 'in the flesh'. So he shows them what their present position is in the light of that fact, and what their future glory is going to be as its outcome. Then in verses 12 and 13 he gives them a practical exhortation because of all that is true of them. 'Therefore, brethren, we' – of whom all this is true – 'we are debtors, not to the flesh, to live after the flesh; for if ye live after the flesh, ye shall die: but if ye through the Spirit do mortify the deeds of the body, ye shall live.'

Two things, therefore, stand out very clearly here. The first is that in verses 1 to 4, as I have been careful to stress all along, the Apostle is describing and writing about all Christians, not merely some Christians. He gives no indication whatsoever that there are two classes of Christians. A popular teaching says that there are 'carnal' Christians and 'spiritual' Christians, and that here Paul is talking only about the 'spiritual' Christians. This section will confirm and prove to the hilt our contention that in verses 1 to 4 the Apostle has been talking about all Christians, not certain special Christians only, not only Christians who have received some second experience. That 'there is therefore now no condemnation to them which are in Christ Jesus' is true of every Christian. This is quite basic because it determines, as we have seen, our view of sanctification. Verses 5 to 13 will prove that to us quite clearly and put it beyond any doubt whatsoever.

The second principle that verses 5 to 13 bring out clearly is that a complete change in us is absolutely essential to salvation. If a man does not undergo a radical change, if he does not enter into the realm of the Spirit, 'the righteousness of the law' can never be fulfilled in him. Christianity, as the Apostle has told us so often, involves a complete, a radical change in the nature of the human being.

These, then, are the two great principles on which we must keep our eyes. They stand out very clearly in the first sub-section of this section, verses 5 to 8. It is quite clear, I repeat, that here the Apostle is comparing and contrasting not two types of Christians but the non-Christian with the Christian. They that are 'after the flesh' are the non-Christians; they that are 'after the Spirit' are the Christians. It is a wrong interpretation to say that 'they that are after the flesh' are the so-called 'carnal' Christians; for we shall see that the Apostle says something about them which makes it impossible that they should be Christians at all. We must keep this particularly in view because the Apostle's whole object is to show how utterly impossible it is to say of any man as he is by nature that to him there is 'no condemnation' or that 'the righteousness of the law' will be fulfilled in him. On the other hand, the moment a man is delivered from the condemnation of the law, and is changed, and in this new realm, his hope is certain, and nothing can ever rob him of it.

That, then, is the theme we are going to consider. But instead of taking the passage verse by verse, and drawing out the contrast between the two types of persons verse by verse, it seems to me to be more advantageous to consider first of all what the Apostle tells us about the non-Christian; and afterwards to look at the

Christian positively as a whole. This method will help us to follow the Apostle's argument.

We take first what Paul says here about the man who is not a Christian. His general description of him is that he is 'after the flesh'. What does he mean by this? We have earlier explained that the word 'flesh' means fallen human nature, human nature as it is before the Spirit of God begins His work in a person. It is man left to himself, man born, developing and growing in life in this world outside the activity of God upon him. The non-Christian is 'after the flesh'. The word 'after' is interesting. Some would translate it as 'according to the flesh', but the best translation is 'under the flesh'. The word the Apostle uses carries the idea of being 'under' something else, under authority in particular. So we are told that the non-Christian is one who is habitually dominated by the nature with which he was born. Chapter 5 has already told us in a most amazing manner – and Paul has worked it out in detail in chapters 6 and 7 – that we are born like this because of our connection with Adam and because of Adam's sin. Everyone born subsequent to Adam has been born 'after the flesh'; we are born under the power, the domination of this fallen human nature which we inherit. The Apostle adds that it is something that is continuous – 'they are after the flesh'. They are born in sin, they exist in sin, in sin they go on living.

How does that show itself, and to what does it lead? The first thing is that such a man 'minds' certain things. 'They that are after the flesh do *mind* the things of the flesh.' That is a most interesting expression. In the Epistle to the Philippians the Apostle uses exactly the same expression several times. He says: 'Let us therefore, as many as be perfect, be thus *minded*: and if in any thing ye be otherwise *minded*, God shall reveal even this unto you' (3: 15). Verse 16 has the same word: 'Nevertheless, whereto we have already attained, let us walk by the same rule, let us *mind* the same thing.' Then Paul introduces it negatively in verse 19, where he is talking about people 'whose end is destruction, whose God is their belly, and whose glory is in their shame, who *mind* earthly things'. 'To mind' is a term with which we are familiar, an expression that is quite commonly used. If a man is a busybody and puts too many questions to you and shows too great an interest in your affairs, you say to him ,'Mind your own business'. The expression means, therefore, the deliberate action of your mind on certain objects. That is why you say to the busybody, 'Do not train your mind on me and on my affairs, switch it to your own affairs, mind your own business'.

But the term includes not only thought and understanding, it includes the affections, the emotions, the desires and the objects of pursuit. In other words, it is a comprehensive term. 'To mind earthly things' not only means that non-Christians think about them occasionally, but that these are the things which they think of most of all; these are the things of which they think habitually, the trend or the bent of their thinking is toward them. 'Earthly things' are the things that please them most of all, the things that give them greatest satisfaction; and therefore the things which they seek after most of all. The term is comprehensive, and we must not limit it merely to the intellectual aspect. It is much wider than the interests of the mind, and takes in the whole personality. The Apostle John, in his First Epistle (chapter 2, verses 15 to 17) has the same idea though he uses a different term. He says: 'Love not the world, neither the things that are in the world.' He might equally well have said, '*Mind* not the world, neither the things that are in the world'.

The first thing about the non-Christian, therefore, is that because he is dominated by his fallen human nature, he is a man who is deliberately interested in, and concerned about 'the things of the flesh'. Once more we have to be careful that our understanding of this expression is sufficiently comprehensive. What are 'the things of the flesh'? The danger is to limit the term to sensual pleasures and to the sins that belong only to the body. The term 'the flesh' tends to make us think immediately of physical sins, sins which belong primarily to the realm of our animal being. They are certainly included, but it is important for us to realize that the term is very much more comprehensive in its use, as we find when we turn to the Epistle to the Galatians chapter 5, verses 19 to 21. 'Now the works of the flesh are manifest, which are these; adultery, fornication, uncleanness, lasciviousness'. Yes, but also 'Idolatry, witchcraft, hatred, variance, emulations, wrath, strife, seditions, heresies, envyings, murders, drunkenness, revellings, and such like'. We see that the notion is indeed a very wide one. Or go back again to the First Epistle of John, chapter 2, verses 15 to 17: 'Love not the world, neither the things that are in the world'. What are they? The Apostle lists them as 'the lust of the flesh, and the lust of the eyes, and the pride of life'. 'The flesh, is a big term, a widely inclusive one.

What then does 'the flesh' mean? In a word it means 'worldly-mindedness'. That is a term which John Bunyan uses, and it is the term that some people would use here. 'Worldly-mindedness'! It includes everything which is opposed to 'the mind' and 'the life' of the Holy Spirit. Another way of putting it is to say that 'the things of the flesh' means every aspect of life without God, everything in life from which God is excluded. It refers, in other words, to the life of this world only; it denotes a complete severance from all that is spiritual. It concentrates on the visible, the seen, and has nothing at all to do with the unseen. Or again, we can say that it means the temporal only, this world of time only; it has nothing to do with the eternal. Its reference is to life in this world only, to life bounded by the body and the various qualities and attributes of the fleshly mind, but to the exclusion of the spiritual element.

The tragedy of the matter is that many people think that this description – 'they that are after the flesh do mind the things of the flesh' – applies only to open, obvious, profligate sinners, on the streets and in the public houses of great cities; the fact being that it includes also very highly intellectual people, very moral people, and people whom the world would describe as very noble. To 'mind the things of the flesh' includes political interests without God, social interests without God, cultural interests without God. That is what the expression means. Paul has in mind man's highest pursuits, his philosophy, his art, his culture, his music, that never get beyond the flesh. God is outside it all, He is excluded from it; there is nothing spiritual about it. Men may write very cleverly, and in a very learned and interesting and entertaining manner about social conditions; they can tell us how to ameliorate bad conditions, how to improve them; they can write eloquently about forming some sort of Utopia, they can produce masterpieces of art and of literature and of music; but there is no soul there, there is no God there, no Spirit there. It is all 'after the flesh'.

How important it is to realize the truth of this matter! That is why that list in Galatians 5 is so important. Paul does not stop at drunkenness and adultery and murder and things of that type. He goes to the realm of the inner man; and there you find that his list is all-inclusive. So what the Apostle is really saying about the non-Christian is that it does not matter where he fits in this gamut of possible interests and behaviour and conduct, he is still only *minding* 'the things of the flesh.' It is because the world does not understand this that it is not interested in the Gospel. The world's good, moral people are admired so much today; and yet the Apostle's words describe exactly where they stand. They are as much 'after the flesh' and they as much 'mind the things of the flesh' as does the man who falls into drunkenness or gives rein to his passions and lusts. It is purely a difference of degree. There is no essential difference at all.

The good, cultured well-spoken moral man is as devoid of the Spirit as the most obvious and profligate sinner; he is outside the life of God as much as the other. He hates to be told this, of course; that is why he is the typical Pharisee. And that is why the Pharisees crucified the Lord Jesus Christ. He convinced them of being 'after the flesh' and 'minding' only the things of the flesh. What a terrible state this is! and how alarming it is to realize that people can be in it without ever imagining it! They draw many distinctions and divisions; but there are none in reality. The only difference between the obvious so-called 'sinner' and the highly cultured good moral man is purely a social difference, a superficial one. Let me go a little further; it is perhaps a difference in the skin; the second man keeps his skin a little cleaner than does the first man. The first man has mud and filth and mire about him in abundance, the other takes baths very frequently, so his skin looks very white. But the difference is skin-deep only. In their inner beings, as men, and in their relationship to God, there is not the slightest difference between them; they both together *mind* the things of the flesh. All their thinking, all their interests, all their pursuits are entirely outside the realm of the spiritual and of God. That is what the Apostle tells us about them.

The next thing the Apostle says about them is found in verse 6, where we find the words, 'To be carnally minded is death'. The translation in the Authorized Version is most unfortunate; the expression should not have been changed. It should read, 'The mind of the flesh is death' or, 'To have the mind of the flesh is death'. He has already said that non-Christians *mind* the things of the flesh; now he is saying that the people who do *mind* the things of the flesh, and have the sort of mind that does that, are dead.

[7]

Here Paul is describing the quality, or the state of mind of people who only *mind* the things of the flesh. It is, he says, nothing else but sheer death.

Our Lord gives us the best understanding of this in what He said to Peter on that occasion at Caesarea Philippi when the Apostle made his great confession in reply to our Lord's question 'Who do ye say that I am?' Matthew records the matter in his 16th chapter. Peter said, 'Thou art the Christ, the Son of the living God'. But a few minutes later, when our Lord began to tell the disciples about His approaching death, Peter said, 'Be it far from thee, Lord'. Our Lord rebuked him severely and said, 'Get thee behind me, Satan, for thou savourest not the things that be of God, but the things that be of men'. The word translated 'savourest', really means 'to think' – 'thou thinkest not the things that be of God'. Indeed, it is the very word which is used in this sixth verse of Romans 8. 'The trouble with you, Peter,' said our Lord in effect, 'is that your whole mentality is wrong, your whole way of thinking is wrong; you are not thinking the things of God, you are thinking the things of man.' 'Peter', He seems to say, 'what is the matter with you? You have just made your great confession, and I told you that "flesh and blood had not revealed it unto you, but my Father which is in heaven". Now you are proving that I was right, because when I go on to make a great spiritual statement to you, you turn and say "That be far from thee, Lord". Peter, the trouble with you is that you are now thinking, not after God, but after men; your whole outlook, your whole mentality, your whole process of thinking is sadly astray.' That is the idea in the phrase 'The mind of the flesh is death'.

Let me illustrate this further, by what the Apostle tells us in the twelfth chapter of this Epistle in the second verse: 'Be not conformed to this world: but be ye transformed.' How? 'By the renewing of your mind.' It is absolutely essential that the mind be renewed. In the absence of a renewal of the mind man is entirely hopeless. You will find the same in Ephesians 4, verses 17 to 24, and also in the second chapter of the First Epistle to the Corinthians: 'The natural man receiveth not the things of the Spirit of God.' Why not? 'Because they are foolishness unto him: neither can he know them.' Why not? 'Because they are spiritually discerned. But he that is spiritual judgeth all things, yet he himself is judged of no man' (1 Corinthians 2: 14, 15).

[8]

The statement that 'The mind of the flesh is death' means that the natural man is in a state of spiritual death. That is what the Apostle says everywhere about the unbeliever, about the man who is not a Christian. We find it mentioned at the beginning of the second chapter of Ephesians: 'You hath he quickened, who were dead in trespasses and sins.' 'Dead'! He repeats it again in verse 5: 'Even when we were dead in sins, he hath quickened us together with Christ.' The Apostle is saying the same thing here. The man who is 'under the flesh', and governed and controlled by his fallen human nature, not only *minds* the things of the flesh – those worldly things out of which God is shut – but he does so because he is spiritually dead. He is alive physically, he exists, but spiritually he is a dead man.

The Apostle's statement means that the man is dead to God, he lives as if there were no God. Some of your greatest moral men, some of your most cultured men in the world are in that position. They are very able, very cultured, very much interested in life, they never get drunk, they are not guilty of adultery. . . . 'Ah', you say, 'you cannot say that such a man "minds the things of the flesh".' I do just that! God is not in all his thoughts, he is completely dead to God, he is living as if there were no God. That is what is meant by spiritual death. Spiritual death is to be outside the life of God. Our Lord has settled the matter for us. In John's Gospel, chapter 17, verse 3, we read: 'And this is life eternal, that they might know thee, the only true God, and Jesus Christ whom thou hast sent.' The man who has not got eternal life does not know God, he is outside the life of God; and that means that he is dead. The spiritual realm does not exist for him, he scoffs at it; spiritual realities mean nothing whatsoever to him; he is dead to them all. Ask him to read the New Testament, and he says that it is 'nonsense'; draw his attention to spiritual things and he does not know what you are talking about.

There is a well-known story which seems to me to supply a perfect illustration of this point. It concerns two great men, William Wilberforce the leader in the movement for the abolition of slavery, and William Pitt the Younger, one time Prime Minister of Britain. They were both brilliant men, they were both politicians, and they were very great friends. But William Wilberforce was converted and became a Christian, while William Pitt, like so many others, was but a formal Christian. William Wilberforce was very much concerned about his friend. He loved him as a man and was greatly concerned about his soul. He was most anxious therefore that Pitt should go with him to listen to a certain preacher, a London clergyman of the Church of England named Richard Cecil. Cecil was a great evangelical preacher, and Wilberforce delighted in his ministry, so he was ever trying to persuade Pitt to go with him to listen to Cecil. At long last Pitt agreed to do so. Wilberforce was delighted and they went together to a service. Richard Cecil was at his best, preaching in his most spiritual and elevated and exalted manner. Wilberforce was enjoying himself, and feeling lifted up into the very heavens. He could not imagine anything better, anything more enjoyable, anything more wonderful; and he was wondering what was happening to his friend William Pitt, the Prime Minister. Well, he was not left long in a state of uncertainty as to what had been happening, because, before they were even out of the building Pitt turned to Wilberforce and said, 'You know, Wilberforce, I have not the slightest idea what that man has been talking about'. And he hadn't, of course. As a man can be tone deaf to music, all who are not Christians are tone deaf to the spiritual. That which was ravishing the mind and the heart of Wilberforce conveyed nothing to Pitt. He was bored, he could not follow it, he could not understand it, he did not know what it was about. A man of great brilliance, a man of great culture, a man of great intellectual ability, but all that does not help! 'The natural man receiveth not the things of the Spirit of God, for they are foolishness unto him; neither can he know them, because they are spiritually discerned' (1 Corinthians 2:14). Richard Cecil might as well have been preaching to a dead man. The dead cannot appreciate these things, neither could William Pitt. He himself confessed it. It is not what Wilberforce says about him; it is what he said about himself.

There are such people. They come to a place of worship, they listen to things that ravish the hearts of believers, but they see nothing in it at all. There are many such people in the churches now, as there always have been. They want whist drives and dances, entertainments and socials, and to meet one another socially. That is because they are not alive to spiritual things. They are dead, dead to God, dead to the Lord Jesus Christ, dead to the realm of the spiritual and all spiritual realities, dead to their own soul and spirit and their everlasting and eternal interests. They never think about such matters at all. That is their trouble. That is what the Apostle says here about them. This mind of the flesh shuts them out from the life of God and from all the interests that emanate from the life of God. The trouble with the unbeliever, the non-Christian, is that he is in a living death, he is merely existing. He is shut out from the life of God; and if he dies in that condition he will continue to all eternity shut out from the life of God. Nothing more terrible can be contemplated. That is the meaning of spiritual death.

The Apostle then goes on to say another thing about the non-Christian in verse 7: 'Because the carnal mind is enmity against God.' Here, again, it is unfortunate that we have this translation in the Authorized Version, for in the original it still is, 'the mind of the flesh'. 'Because the mind of the flesh is at enmity against God.' This explains why 'the mind of the flesh' is death. If a man is at enmity against God he is obviously outside the life of God; and that means that he is dead. Here we have one of our striking proofs that the Apostle is not comparing and contrasting two types of Christians, but is comparing and contrasting the non-Christian and the Christian. You cannot say of any man who is a Christian that he is at enmity against God; it is impossible. A man cannot be at enmity against God and be a Christian at the same time. Why is he a Christian at all? Because he wants to be right with God. Why does he believe on the Lord Jesus Christ? Because he believes that the Lord Jesus Christ puts him right with God. Why did he ever want that blessing? Because he sees the consequences of being an enemy of God. So here the Apostle depicts a man who is at enmity against God. This is not a so-called 'carnal' Christian; there is no such thing. This is the non-Christian, this is a man who is not a Christian in any true sense, and this is the man Paul has been describing all along. He is contrasting the non-Christian with the Christian, any Christian.

The Apostle says the same thing in many other places. In Colossians 1 : 21, for instance, we have: 'You that were sometime' – once upon a time – 'alienated and enemies in your mind by wicked works.' They were once in that condition, but now it is no longer the case. Why so? Because they have become Christians. In other words, the contrast is between the non-Christian and the Christian. But let me emphasize once more that this state of enmity is that of every person who is not a Christian. 'Ah but,' you say, 'I know certain people who say, "I would not like to say that I am a Christian, but I believe in God"; what about them?' The simple truth about them is this, that they are at enmity against God. 'But,' you say, 'they are interested in God, they believe in God, they read books about God, and they talk and argue about God.' No, they do not ! 'But how can you say that so dogmatically?' I do so for this reason: they think they are interested in God, but their interest is not in God, it is in some figment of their own imagination, it is some product of their own philosophy and their own thoughts. 'But why do you say even that?' asks someone. I answer, the way to prove that such persons are not true Christians is quite simple. Say to them, 'Do you believe in God?' They reply, 'Of course we believe in God; we have always believed in God'. Next confront them with the God of the Bible, who is not only love but also justice and righteousness; confront them with the God who not only shows mercy and compassion but also wrath; and you will find that they snarl their teeth at you. They will say that they do not believe in such a God! Of course they do not; they have never truly believed in God. What they believe in is a god whom they have constructed for themselves. They have made a god of their own, and for this they have no authority whatsoever, except that it fits in with their thoughts. They say, 'The God I believe in is a God who is entirely a God of love'. Wrath? Of course not! Impossible! But what is their authority for speaking in this fashion? They have none at all. It is simply that they, and people like them, agree in saying these things.

The only true knowledge that we have of God is to be found in the Bible. God has revealed Himself. No man can know God of himself – 'no man can see God, or has seen God, at any time'. If a man could understand God with his own mind he would be equal to God, if not greater. By definition God is absolute and infinite and eternal in all His attributes and qualities. We cannot arrive at Him of ourselves; He must reveal Himself. He has done so, in the Scriptures and in the Lord Jesus Christ. And the Lord Jesus Christ has taught us about the wrath of God, about the judgment of God, and about hell. Yes, but the moment these people who say they believe in God hear such things, they become furious and remonstrate against it; they hate it. Indeed, they hate

God; as Paul tells us, this 'mind of the flesh is enmity against God'. It wants a god after its own image, and it hates the God of the Bible, the God and Father of our Lord Jesus Christ, the God preached by this Apostle Paul and all the other apostles. This is the all-too-common state of things today; alas, you find it in so-called Christian pulpits and churches. In the name of God and of Christ men are showing their enmity and their hatred of God, the living God, 'the only true God'. Let us not therefore be misled or deluded by people who say that they believe in God; the question is, Do they believe in the God who has revealed Himself, who is the only God? All natural men, all who are not Christians, are 'at enmity against God'.

The fifth thing Paul tells us about non-Christians is that 'they are not subject to the law of God'. What he means is that they do not submit themselves to it. How can they? If they hate Him why should they subject themselves to Him? Instead of submitting themselves as a soldier does to his commanding officer, to the General set over him, they rebel, they are antagonistic. They do not care what God has said; they do what they want to do. They are not taking orders, they are following out their own minds, and their own likes and dislikes, and their own understanding. Man by nature is an enemy of God, he is a rebel against God, he flouts the commandments of God. 'All we like sheep have gone astray, we have all gone after our own devices.' That is true of all men who are not Christians. They are trampling and spitting upon the Ten Commandments, and the moral law, and all the sanctities. Of course they are! They are haters of God, and they hate His law; they abominate it; 'they are not subject to the law of God'.

Next the Apostle adds, 'Neither indeed can be.' 'This mind', he says, 'is not subject to the law of God, neither indeed can be.' Here we have a basic statement about the unbeliever. The unbeliever, says Paul, is not only like that, but he cannot do anything about it. 'His mind is not subject to the law of God, neither indeed can be.' We find exactly the same idea in 1 Corinthians 2: 14: 'The natural man receiveth not the things of the Spirit of God, for they are foolishness unto him, neither can he know them.' He cannot know them. Why? 'Because they are spiritually discerned.' A man who is tone deaf to music cannot create a delight in music in himself. He may desire it, but he cannot attain to it; it is impossible. What the Apostle is saying is that

[13]

this natural man, this non-Christian, not only hates God, and is not subject to the law of God; but he cannot desire to love God, he cannot desire to obey Him. He cannot choose to do so, he is totally incapable of any spiritual effort. I am not saying this; it is the Apostle Paul who says it. The popular teaching which says that we have to preach the Gospel to the natural man as he is, and that he, as he is, decides to believe on the Lord Jesus Christ; and that then, because he has believed, he is given new life, is regenerated, – this, I say, is a complete denial of what the Apostle teaches here. The natural man, this man after the flesh, this unbeliever, cannot believe in God; he cannot believe in and on the Lord Jesus Christ. He is 'at enmity' against Him; he hates Him, he is altogether opposed to Him. He is shut out from His life, he lacks a spiritual faculty, he is incapable of spiritual good – 'neither indeed can be'. He is completely helpless; he cannot choose to love God. You cannot love God and hate Him at the same time. Why should a man who is at enmity to, and a hater of God, decide suddenly to love Him? There is no reason; his whole nature is against Him, his whole bias, his whole bent, everything in him is opposed to God; he is in complete and entire helplessness; he is dead. And there is nothing more final than that!

The man who is spiritually dead hates God, rebels against Him, and can do no other, for 'the natural man receiveth not the things of the Spirit of God, for they are foolishness unto him, neither can he know them, for they are spiritually discerned'. And if you have not got the spiritual faculty you cannot discern them. If that is lacking in a man, and he is completely dead, how can he discern them? He cannot; and, of course, the world is proving that very thing today. Total inability!

What is the result of all this? It is stated in the eighth verse, 'So then' – here is the conclusion, the thing the Apostle was really setting out to prove – 'so then, they that are in the flesh' – they are the same people, they are 'after the flesh', they are governed by 'the mind of the flesh' – 'so then, they that are in the flesh cannot please God'. His displeasure is upon them; they can do nothing at all about pleasing Him. They cannot bring forth any fruit unto God. As Paul has already said in chapter 7, verse 5, the righteous demands of the law cannot be fulfilled in them. 'In the flesh', 'after the flesh', governed by 'the mind of the flesh', they are entirely and altogether outside God and His life; and there is nothing in them or about them that recommends them to God. Such are the unbelievers.

How then does anyone become a believer? The answer has already been given in verse 2, and we shall proceed to work it out. 'The law of the Spirit of life in Christ Jesus hath set me free.' I have not done it; it has been done to me. It is God's action. 'By grace are ye saved through faith; and that not of yourselves: it is the gift of God.' 'We are His workmanship' (Ephesians 2: 8–10). We can do nothing, it is all of God. And let us thank God that it is so, for it is because it is all of God that it is certain, it is safe, it is sure. We are not just believers, we have been 'made anew', born again; we are in the realm of the spiritual, we have been put there, we are 'in Christ', the Spirit of God has incorporated us into Him. It is His action.

Thus far we have been looking at the negatives; and how important it is that we should do so! We shall never realize what we are as Christians until we first realize what we were as non-Christians, and what was absolutely essential before we could ever become Christians. If God had not quickened us we should still be dead. A dead man cannot give himself life. God quickened us, and because God has put life into us we are alive in Christ Jesus, and in the realm of the Spirit.

Two

*

For they that are after the flesh do mind the things of the flesh; but they that are after the Spirit the things of the Spirit.
For to be carnally minded is death; but to be spiritually minded is life and peace.
Because the carnal mind is enmity against God; for it is not subject to the law of God, neither indeed can be.
So then they that are in the flesh cannot please God.

Romans 8: 5–8

Having looked negatively at the difference between the non-Christian and the Christian we now come to the positive aspect. Here the Apostle puts before us a very remarkable picture and description of the Christian man. We shall look at it not only in order to grasp the Apostle's argument but also because there is no better way of discovering our own state, and where we stand, than by examining ourselves in the light of this kind of statement. We must also bear in mind the fact that the Apostle's ultimate objective is to establish the certainty of the final and full salvation of all who are 'in Christ'. That is his fundamental proposition: 'There is therefore now no condemnation to them that are in Christ Jesus' – there never will be, there never can be. That is what he is proving, and we have here one of his subsidiary proofs. The man who is 'in Christ' is safe, eternally safe, because these things are true of him.

We should all be concerned about our assurance of salvation, because if we lack assurance we lack joy, and if we lack joy our life is probably of a poor quality. 'The joy of the Lord is your strength' (Nehemiah 8: 10). It is important from two standpoints, therefore, that we should consider this description of the Christian. We must be quite sure that we are in this position, and that we are not still 'after the flesh'. But it is still more important that we should have the assurance which results from the 'minding the things of the Spirit,' as here spoken of by the Apostle. I stress once more the point that what the Apostle says here applies to every Christian, and not only to certain special Christians who have had some kind of second experience. You cannot be a Christian if you do not 'mind the things of the Spirit.' That is finally put beyond any doubt by the statement of the ninth verse where Paul begins to apply his teaching and says: 'But ye are not in the flesh, but in the Spirit, if so be' – which means 'assuming what I know to be true of you' – 'that the Spirit of God dwell in you'. And then, to make it doubly certain: 'Now if any man have not the Spirit of Christ he is none of his', that is, he is not a Christian at all. He does not say that if he has not the Spirit of Christ he is a poor Christian or a so-called 'carnal' Christian. He says he is not a Christian. We really must get rid of the notion that in this chapter the Apostle is comparing two types of Christians. He is contrasting the non-Christian with any Christian, with all Christians rightly so-called.

What then are the characteristics of the Christian? May God the Holy Spirit grant us understanding here, not only that we may derive assurance, but that we may see something of the glory of being a Christian, the wonder of it all, the amazing thing that God has done for us in Christ Jesus. What is a Christian? It is obvious that he is the exact opposite of the non-Christian, the man we have already considered. But that is not a good way of describing a Christian, although it is done far too often. The Christian's position is essentially positive; and we must follow the Apostle as he puts it in positive terms. The Christian is not merely a man who no longer does what he used to do. Of course that is true of him, but that is the very least you say about him; that is introduction, that is preamble. What we have to say about the Christian is essentially positive, gloriously positive. God forbid that we should be giving the world the impression that we are mere negations, that we are simply people who do not drink, who do not go to cinemas, who do not smoke, and do not do this and that. What a travesty of Christianity that is, and especially in the light of all the glorious positives that the New Testament puts before us.

The first thing the Apostle tells us about the Christian is that he is one who is 'after the Spirit'. 'They that are after the Spirit mind the things of the Spirit.' At this point let us remember that the word 'after' carries the same weight and the same shade of meaning as it did in the case of the man who 'walks after the flesh'. The suggestion is that he is 'habitually dominated by' the Spirit. To be dominated habitually by the Spirit characterizes the trend and tenor of his life. And by 'the Spirit' Paul means the 'Holy Spirit', so we spell the word with a capital 'S'. He does not mean the human spirit. Certain people have gone astray at this point, assuming that when the Apostle described the other man as 'after the flesh' he was only referring to certain physical sins, or sins committed by the body, various types of debauchery or open, flagrant, obvious sins. So they assume that by 'the Spirit' he means the life of the mind, the intellect, the ability of man to appreciate poetry and art – the spirit of man in contradistinction to his body, his flesh. But we have already shown conclusively that 'the flesh' means not simply the body, the animal part, but the whole of a man's life, man in his fallen state and uninfluenced by the Spirit of God. So here the Apostle is contrasting the kind of life which is 'after the flesh' with this other life which is dominated by, controlled by, regulated by, determined by the Holy Spirit of God. That is the first thing that is true of every Christian. You cannot be a Christian at all unless this is true of you. The Apostle will say later, in verse 14, the same thing in a different way: 'For as many as are led by the Spirit of God, they are the sons of God'; and that is true of all Christians. If you are a Christian you are a son of God. And if you are a son of God you are 'led', Paul says, 'by the Spirit of God'. This is simply another way of saying that the Christian's life is under the charge of the Holy Spirit, the third Person in the blessed Holy Trinity.

The next step is that, as a person controlled by the Holy Spirit, he 'minds the things of the Spirit'. The word 'minds', as we saw in the case of the non-Christian, carries the notion of setting the mind upon something. There is also the element of deliberation, and furthermore, the action is voluntary. So the man who is dominated by the Spirit 'sets' his mind in a certain direction. But it is a comprehensive term, as we saw, and it does not stop at the intellect. It includes the emotions, the desires, and the feelings, and so it is indicative of a man's total interests. It tells us about the things which attract him, which interest him, the things which he desires, the things which he pursues.

Once again, for an exposition of the theme we turn to the
First Epistle to the Corinthians, the second chapter, and especially
from verse 6 to the end. As we saw, the non-Christian, when
these things are put before him, regards them as foolishness; and
that is true of all who are not Christians. But they are not foolish
to the Christian; he 'minds' them, he desires them, he follows
after them. This is now his first and greatest interest, this is the
matter which to him is of chief concern. I emphasize this because
it is not the case that the Christian comes to these things as a
matter of duty or of habit or of custom. No, he 'minds' them,
sets his mind upon them, pursues them; they represent his chief
interest. We must give full value to the word 'minds'; otherwise
it can almost be misleading for us.

Here then is the Christian; he is a man who 'minds the things of
the Spirit'. What are these? I start once more with a negative.
They are not merely things that belong to the realm of the
intellect. Neither, I venture to add, does the Apostle simply
mean that the Christian is 'interested in religion'. To be interested
in religion and to be interested in the things of the Spirit are not
the same thing. There are many who are 'interested in religion'
who are actually antagonistic to 'the things of the Spirit'. The
history of every great movement of the Spirit proves that abundantly. The bitterest opponents of our Lord were the Pharisees,
the religious people. And so it has continued to be. The people
who have been interested in religion have generally persecuted
Reformers; they have been much more hostile to Reformers than
the outsiders, the uninterested and unconcerned. And this has
been still more obvious in the case of revivals. So if we desire to
know whether we 'mind the things of the Spirit' or not, it is not
enough to say that we are interested in religion; it is not enough
even to say that we are members of churches. You can be a member of a church and hotly resent 'the things of the Spirit'. You
may be very interested in religious organizations, in religious
activities, in denominations, in activities of your particular church,
and so on, but it may have nothing to do with 'minding the things
of the Spirit'. Indeed, as I say, it can be the greatest enemy of such
things.

I go a step further. To 'mind the things of the Spirit' does not
mean an interest even in theology as an end in itself, for a man
can be interested in theology and Christian doctrine and yet not

'mind the things of the Spirit.' A man can take up theology as a subject. Many have done so, and have made a career of it. They have enjoyed it, have been expert in it; but it may have nothing at all to do with 'the things of the Spirit'; indeed, again, it may be extremely hostile to them. In other words, it is possible for a man with his natural mind to grasp a theological system in an intellectual way only. That may be of no spiritual value to him at all; it can even be the cause of his damnation. A man can approach Christianity as an intellectual system, as a philosophy; and if he has a certain type of mind he can be greatly interested in it. I have known men of whom that is true. Theology was their hobby, the subject they enjoyed reading. As other men have their various hobbies and pursuits, this happened to be theirs; and it can be one of the most fascinating intellectual pursuits that a man can take up. But a man can be interested and immersed in it, and spend his life at it, and yet remain spiritually dead. Now, of course, as I am about to show, the man who 'minds the things of the Spirit' in the right way is obviously interested in theology and doctrine and in religion. All I am saying at the moment is that a mere interest in religious pursuits does not establish the fact that we are 'minding' the things of the Spirit.

Similarly, to 'mind the things of the Spirit' means much more than an interest in religious phenomena. Certain people suppose that because they are interested in religious phenomena they are thereby 'minding the things of the Spirit', and this becomes a snare to them. I refer to the cult of 'experiences'. There is a type of mind that is very interested in experiences; and again I would add that there is nothing that is more interesting or fascinating. There is great interest at the present time in extra-sensory phenomena. People are interested in human psychology, in the working of the human mind, in human behaviour, in different types of human personality. It is a fascinating study; and in the realm of religion, remarkable things have often happened. We read the lives of the saints, of great religious characters, and find that they have had particular experiences. It is an interesting study; but it can be pursued with a purely secular mind, with the 'mind of the flesh'. Various people have written books and articles along this line who were not interested in the truth of God so much as in phenomena – acts and experiences, miracles, healings and things of that kind. The cults batten on such things, and are really kept going by them. And when this is done in terms of Christian terminology or in a kind of spiritual atmosphere, where you are no longer dealing with physical healing in the usual manner, but are invoking the unseen world and powers and forces that cannot readily be explained, many assume that they are already in the realm of the truly spiritual. In the same way mysticism can even become at times the greatest enemy of Christian truth and of the Christian faith. To 'mind the things of the Spirit' does not mean any of those things in and of themselves. As long as they are the concomitants of the pursuit of the true faith, all may be well, but if a person stops at them he may still be far from 'minding the things of the Spirit.'

What then is the test? The things of the Spirit are the things to which the Spirit, the Holy Spirit, always draws attention. In the First Epistle to the Corinthians chapter 2, verse 11, the Apostle describes them as 'the things of God': 'For what man knoweth the things of a man, save the spirit of man which is in him? even so the things of God knoweth no man, but the Spirit of God'. In the same context the Apostle also calls them 'a hidden mystery'. 'We speak the wisdom of God in a mystery, even the hidden wisdom' (I Corinthians 2 : 7). These are 'the things of the Spirit'; They are completely hidden from the world. The man who is 'after the flesh' knows nothing about them, and does not understand them; they are 'foolishness' to him. It matters not how nice a man may be, nor how superficially godly he may seem to be, nor how religious; these things are 'foolishness' to him. 'Neither can he know them', says Paul, to make it still more certain. These things are hidden mysteries, 'hidden wisdom', altogether outside him; he is living in a different realm from that to which the Christian belongs. The Christian is a man who has been awakened to truly spiritual things; 'God hath revealed them unto us by His Spirit'. We see them, they are no longer a mystery to us. 'Mystery', as used in the New Testament, does not mean something mysterious, vague, nebulous, indefinite. It means something that is inaccessible to the natural mind, but which God in His grace has revealed to the Christian by the Spirit. It is no longer a mystery to the Christian; he now possesses an understanding. And that is why he is interested in these things and wants them. These are the things that he 'minds'.

What are these things? It is not at all easy to determine the best

[21]

order; but I will start from the experimental standpoint. Christians are interested in themselves as 'souls'. Are you interested in yourself as a soul primarily, or are you interested in yourself as a member of your profession, or as a husband, or as a wife, or as parents, or as children? Or does your interest lie in your business, your work, your occupation, your leisure, your hobbies? What is your view of yourself? How do you think of yourself? What significance do you attach to yourself? The first thing that is true about a Christian is that he is concerned about himself as a soul. No one else has that interest; but the Christian always has it. That is why I was emphasizing that the Christian is never interested in truth in an abstract manner – never! I have known men who have studied, and even taught the Bible as if it were on a par with Shakespeare. A Christian is not like that. A Christian can never be detached and objective. He is concerned as a person; his soul is in his pursuits; he is concerned primarily about his soul; he has this living interest in himself as a soul, as a spirit.

I hasten to add that it is of course himself in relation to God. This is the Christian's supreme interest – God and himself and the relationship between them. This is the thing that he 'minds'. His mind always comes back to it; this is the centre of his life; this is the real soul of his whole being and existence. He does many other things; he is a husband, a father, a professional man or a man engaged in business. But these do not come first; this man's centre is just this – God and himself, his soul and God and their relationship. This is the Christian's prime interest even when theology is involved. To him theology is not just a subject, a detached interest. The same applies to phenomena and experiences and all else. His concern is not primarily even to be a better man or a different man. It is always his relationship to God. He was not concerned about this before; he was at enmity against God. The things of God were foolishness to him, he never thought about them, he did not want to think about them; they were outside him, and he was outside them. That is no longer true.

And of course he is interested in relating what he 'minds' to his life in the here-and-now. He is concerned about his soul and his relationship to God in this life and in this world; he does not postpone such considerations to the next world. Certainly he is interested in his final destiny; but he is also interested in life here and now. He wants to be rightly and truly related to God now;

and he is ill at ease if anything clouds or disturbs that relationship. This is the thing that he 'minds'; this is the thing that he is 'after', this is the thing he is pursuing, his 'pursuit of God'. Dr A. W. Tozer has used the expression appropriately as the title of one of his books, *The Pursuit of God*. This is the thing that the Christian man pursues; he wants this relationship to be right now and in eternity. Indeed, this is so true of this man that we are entitled to say of him that everything else becomes relatively unimportant to him. I do not hesitate to put it as strongly as that. If you cannot say quite honestly that everything else becomes relatively unimportant to you in comparison with this, I do not see that you have any right to call yourself a Christian. In other words, this is the thing that establishes that we are Christians. Everything else falls into position because this now is the thing that matters centrally. And if it means that I have to give up everything else in order that this may be right, I am prepared to do it.

> *Perish every fond ambition,*
> *All I've thought, and hoped, and known;*
> *Yet how rich is my condition,*
> *God and heaven are still mine own.*

Have you got this great concern? Can you say that what matters to you above everything else is your soul? Can you say that it matters more to you than your position, your profession, your money, your husband, wife, children, family, prospects, and everything else? Does it come first? Our Lord has said that 'He that loveth father or mother more than me is not worthy of me; and he that loveth son or daughter more than me is not worthy of me' (Matt. 10: 37).

Because the soul interest is the supreme interest, the Christian is aware of and is concerned about his sinfulness. He knows what it is to be in trouble about his soul. He is aware of his weakness, and he spends much of his time thinking about these things. Of course, when he was in the old state, in a mechanical manner he may have got on to his knees by the side of his bed at night to say his prayers, but he rarely if ever stopped to consider his soul truly, and his relationship to God, and his eternal destiny. He wanted God to bless him, of course; he thought that might help him, so he said his prayers mechanically and may have offered up a few petitions; but he never had a concern about himself, he never hated himself because of his sin and his failure and his rebellion against God, and his lack of love. These things had never concerned him. But a man who is a Christian not only is concerned about them, he cannot get away from them; in a sense they obsess him. Something has happened to this man; and the Apostle is about to tell us what it is. But here he shows us the effect, as it were, first. He starts in verse 5 with the man in action and in practice, and says 'he minds the things of the Spirit'.

What are the things of the Spirit? They include the soul and its relationship with God, its distance from God by reason of sin, its shame and folly and weakness and inability. These are the things that concern the Christian man. He 'minds' them; but he goes further, for the Spirit does not leave a man there. Thank God He does not. He starts with us in that way, but He does not leave us there. The chief work of the Spirit, after all, is to glorify the Lord Jesus Christ. 'He shall glorify me', says our Lord about Him. That is what He is engaged to do. Let me interject a warning at this point. Beware of regarding anything as the work of the Spirit in you, no matter how striking the phenomena may be, if it has not led you to the Lord Jesus Christ in a way that you have never known before. Our great enemy tries to counterfeit these things, and he can produce phenomena; but he never leads to the Lord Jesus Christ. But the Spirit has been sent to glorify Jesus Christ the Lord, and He will always lead us to Him. The Apostle, of course, in that second chapter of First Corinthians makes a very big point of this. He says about the non-Christians, 'None of the princes of this world knew him, for had they known him they would not have crucified the Lord of glory'. They did not know Him because they lacked the Spirit. 'But God hath revealed [the truth] unto us by his Spirit: for the Spirit searcheth all things, yea, the deep things of God.'

What does the Spirit reveal about Christ? He reveals His Person – 'The Lord of glory'. The Christian has no doubt about the Person of Jesus Christ; the Spirit has revealed Him to him in the depth of his being, his mind, his heart – 'The Lord of glory'. The Christian is not in trouble about the two natures in the one Person. He does not understand, but he believes; nothing else is adequate to explain this Person. He sees He is truly man, he sees equally that He is truly God; he knows that the Babe of Bethlehem is the 'Lord of glory' who has come down on earth to dwell. The

Spirit has revealed it. There is no question in the believer's mind as to the Person of the Lord Jesus Christ. But he is equally clear about His work, and especially His atoning work. The Christian has no trouble about this. It is the people who bring their natural minds and philosophy to these matters who are in trouble and say that they cannot understand, and that substitutionary atonement almost seems immoral to them. Of course it does! The princes of this world did not know Him, and the preaching of the Cross has been 'foolishness' to them always; they have always ridiculed it, they are still doing so. Why? Not only because they have never truly seen themselves as sinners, and have never seen the glory and the holiness of God and their need of salvation; they have never had this work of the Spirit in them, a work that opens a man's understanding to see that there is only one way whereby a man can be reconciled to God, and that is, that God should 'lay on Him the iniquity of us all', and 'make Him to be sin for us, who knew no sin'; that God should smite Him with the stripes that we deserve, as the Spirit has revealed through the various writers in the Scripture. The Christian, the man who is 'after the Spirit', delights in these things, and rejoices in them. They are not boring to him, they are life to him. He says with Isaac Watts, 'When I survey the wondrous Cross'. He does not merely take a casual glance at it now and again at a Communion Service. He 'surveys' it, he contemplates it, he stands in amazement before it, and meditates upon it. It is to this he gives his time; this is where his heart is drawn; this is the thing that grips him and moves him, the thing he wants to understand more and more, and can never understand sufficiently. He 'minds' it, he is 'after' it. This has been true of Christians throughout the centuries, and, thank God, it is still true.

In the same way the Christian man is concerned about the way of salvation. We are told frequently today that people are no longer interested in such terms as justification and sanctification, and their like. But when has man in his natural state ever been interested in justification and sanctification? When has man ever desired to know the meaning of these terms? These are spiritual matters. The trouble with modern men is not they they do not understand the terminology of the Authorized Version of the Bible, it is that they are spiritually dead. Give it to them in other translations and it will still mean nothing to them. They may be interested in it as literature; but it is not mere literature, it is the Word of God. Here is something which is only 'spiritually discerned', and the man who has been convicted by the Spirit and who sees himself as a soul before God, wants to know how a man can be just with God and reconciled to God. And if there is one thing he rejoices in more than anything it is 'justification by faith only'. He does not have to go into a monastery and become a monk or a hermit, or take up a great programme of fasting and penances. No, he believes, and in a moment he is declared just and reconciled to God. There is nothing so thrilling to the Christian, nothing so marvellous as that! Here the romantic element of the Gospel comes in – 'the fool who came to scoff remains to pray'. He glories in the Gospel, he rejoices in it. He does not stumble at it; he thanks God for these great resounding terms, and he wants to go on repeating them. Oh yes! he is interested and fascinated by the terminology of salvation, as well as by the thing itself.

'Union with Christ'! 'What are you talking about?' says the natural man, 'I do not understand you.' Of course he does not; how can he? 'Neither can he', says Paul in 1 Corinthians 2: 14, as he says here in Romans 8: 7. Of course he cannot! Try as he will, he cannot. I do not blame the man who comes to me and says, 'I see nothing in your New Testament'. I am sorry for him for this reason – he is a man who has not been enlightened by the Spirit. But the moment he is enlightened by the Spirit he will be very anxious to know what 'union with Christ' means, what sanctification means, what all these glorious terms mean.

These truths are the interest of the Christian; these are the things in which he revels, on which he dwells; this is his life, his world, his all. Communion with God! He is more concerned to have a true and a living and a real communion with God than anything else. There was a time, perhaps, when his supreme ambition was to enter Buckingham Palace or to get into certain select clubs and circles in the City of London. He would now give them all up gladly if only he could know God in a more intimate manner, and have real communion and fellowship with Him. Am I describing you? This is the man who is 'after the Spirit'; these are the things that matter to him. He would give up everything for just one moment of knowing himself dealing directly with God, and of God being real to him, in a living fellowship.

Prayer is another subject that concerns the Christian man. He wants to know more about it; he would like to pray in a more diligent and thorough manner. Then add to that the fellowship of God's people. 'We know that we have passed from death to life, because we love the brethren', because we are attracted by God's people and like meeting them, and can never meet them too frequently. We are ready to let the world go by with its society and so-called pleasure; our desire is to talk to simple souls who know the Lord and who can tell us about the Lord's dealings with them. We feel then that the feast is rich, the company is glorious. They are God's children, and there is no one on earth to compare with them. 'Iron sharpeneth iron'; these things unite us; deep calls to deep as heart unites with heart.

But I must add a further word. The Christian is not only interested in his own soul, he is also concerned about the whole state of the world. It is a libel on us to say that we are not interested in the state of the world. But we are not interested as the non-Christian man is interested. He is interested only politically, socially, and so on. We are interested as we see the world in the grip of the devil. We alone, as Christians, understand what is wrong with the world. We see 'powers' and 'principalities', 'the rulers of the darkness of this world', behind the visible and seen phenomena, and we see perplexed politicians trying to deal with the problems, and failing. We know they must fail because they do not see what is at the back of it all. We see it as the conflict between heaven and hell. So we have a concern about these things, we have a 'mind' for these things, a spiritual concern. We say, 'This is the victory that overcometh the world, even our faith'. Nothing else will do so, nothing else can do so. There is no hope of improving the world apart from this, that individuals become Christian, and if large numbers do so, a Christian period or era in history ensues. So we have an insight and an understanding in that respect that the non-Christian cannot claim.

What I am really saying is that the man who is 'after the Spirit' minds the things of the Spirit. In other words, the Bible is his Book. Here is his interest, here is his life; he wants to know this, he wants to understand it. And, let me repeat, he wants to do it in the right way. Certain people seem to be able to gallop through a book of the Bible in one night. That is not studying the Bible in a spiritual manner. It is not just a matter of headings and classifications and divisions. It is the spiritual content that matters;

God's mind is revealed in Scripture. We must seek it there, and not just skim lightly over the surface, imagining that we have 'done' one book of Scripture, and then take up the next. No! Here are 'the riches of God's grace' and glory and wisdom; and the Christian is the man who wants to understand the Bible in that sense, and not merely to have a superficial academic acquaintance with the mere letter of the Scriptures.

Speaking about the Christian, Paul says: 'He that is spiritual judgeth all things, yet he himself is judged of no man.' He has an understanding of all things, the world included. The unbeliever fails to understand him, but of him it can be said: 'For who hath known the mind of the Lord, that he may instruct him? But we have the mind of Christ' (I Corinthians 2: 14–16). Paul does not mean that we have that mind in its fulness, but that we have it as regards the character or nature of our minds. If you are a Christian you have a new understanding, 'old things are passed away; behold, all things are become new'. You also have new desires. Lest I depress some soul, especially some young Christian, let me make it clear at this point that I am not asserting that the man who is 'after the Spirit', and who 'minds the things of the Spirit', understands all these matters fully, to his complete satisfaction. Of course he does not! 'We see now through a glass darkly'. But the thing I emphasize is that we do *see* now. The unbeliever sees nothing. We do see, and though it be through a glass darkly, 'through a riddle in an enigma', thank God, what I see is of more value to me than the whole universe. My sight is dim, but I thank God for what I am seeing. I am seeing 'things that eye hath not seen, nor ear heard', 'things which have not entered into the heart of man', 'things which God hath prepared for them that love him'. 'Now we have received, not the spirit of the world, but the Spirit that is of God, that we might know the things that are freely given to us of God.'

I am not asking whether you see truth in all its glory and in its absolute perfection. I know you do not; no one does. But what I am asking is this, Have you got a taste for these things? At the risk of being misunderstood, I will even put it like this: Do you enjoy what I have been saying? I venture to assert, in all humility, that if you have not been enjoying what I have been saying, I doubt whether you are 'after the Spirit' at all. But if you can say, 'Well, I do not understand it all, and very much of it is beyond me;

but I feel attracted by these things more than anything else. These are what I want to know, I wish I knew more, I am like a new-born babe, I desire "the sincere milk of the word, that I may grow thereby"; that is all I ask.' Have you got a taste for these things? Are these the things that are beginning to 'hold' you, and to interest you, to fascinate and to thrill you, more than anything else you have ever known or heard? If so, however young you may be in the faith, however small and weak your faith, however ignorant you may be, I have authority to tell you that you are 'after the Spirit', you are a child of God, and therefore an heir of glory.

Three

*

For they that are after the flesh do mind the things of the flesh; but they that are after the Spirit the things of the Spirit.

For to be carnally minded is death; but to be spiritually minded is life and peace.

Because the carnal mind is enmity against God: for it is not subject to the law of God, neither indeed can be.

So then they that are in the flesh cannot please God.

Romans 8: 5–8

We continue our study of this statement which presents us with the contrast between the non-Christian and the Christian. The one is entirely different from the other. The Christian is not merely a man who believes and remains where he was; he is a man who has been entirely changed, his whole position has been moved. The difference between the Christian and the non-Christian is both radical and complete. God has done something to the Christian that makes him altogether different from the man who is not a Christian. The Christian is 'in Christ', he has a new life, and in this new life he is dominated by, and led by, the Holy Spirit. The Apostle announces this as the fundamental thesis: 'The law of the Spirit of life in Christ Jesus hath made me free from the law of sin and death.'

We are now looking positively at the Christian. We have already seen that the first thing that is true of him is that he 'minds the things of the Spirit'. But, says the Apostle in verse 6, another thing is true about him; the man who follows 'the mind of the flesh' is in a state of spiritual death; but the man who is 'after', and is governed by, the mind of the Spirit has 'life and peace'. The relationship between the 6th verse and the 5th verse is interesting and important. Each of the two verses leads to another, for they have a kind of reciprocal relationship. What the Apostle is saying essentially and primarily is that the Christian minds the things of the Spirit because he is alive. In other words verse 6 supplies the explanation of verse 5. But it is equally true to say that as a man minds the things of the Spirit he has an ever-increasing measure of life. When we were looking at the other side of the matter we said similarly that the non-Christian minds the things of the flesh because he is spiritually dead; and it is equally true to say that to mind the carnal things, the things of the flesh, leads to death. It is a reciprocal relationship. And it is exactly the same here as we look at the positive side.

The first thing the Apostle tells us is that to be spiritually minded, or to have the mind of the Spirit, is 'life'. It is a proof of the fact that we have life, spiritual life. We saw that the other man has no interest in spiritual things because he is dead. You preach to him, you get him to read the Scriptures, but it makes no impression upon him. Why? Because he is dead; it is as if he were not there at all. He hears the same truth as the Christian who glories in it, but this man sees nothing in it. It does not move him, or affect him, or rouse him, or please him. He is dead to it. But the Christian minds the things of the Spirit, and is interested in them for this one reason, he is alive, and life always shows itself. Now the Apostle started with the manifestation of life but he is careful to show that that is the result and product of life – 'To be spiritually minded is life.' I am very concerned to bring out this point because I have been suggesting ever since the 10th verse of chapter 5 that this is really the key to the understanding of the whole of chapters 5, 6, 7 and 8. My suggestion was that until the end of chapter 4 the Apostle was proving and elaborating his great doctrine of justification by faith only, and that then he begins to apply the doctrine in the 5th chapter by showing its consequences. And what he emphasizes immediately is this question of life.

Consider the matter once more in the light of chapter 5, verse 10: 'For if, when we were enemies, we were reconciled to God by the death of his Son, much more, being reconciled, we shall be saved in his life.' There we have the first mention of this great theme which the Apostle elaborates at such length, and which, as I understand it, is the whole secret of what he is saying in this 8th chapter. The Christian is not merely a man who believes in the

Lord Jesus Christ. Of course he believes in Him, but that is not the most important thing to say about him. The great thing to say about the Christian is that he is alive in Christ, and that the life of Christ is in him. We are in the life of Christ; that is the basis of assurance, of final certainty; and that is, as I have suggested, the great theme of this 8th chapter.

Let me demonstrate this clearly. The Apostle starts there in the 10th verse of chapter 5. Then he repeats the matter quickly in verse 12 of that chapter: 'Wherefore, as by one man sin entered into the world, and death by sin; and so death passed upon all men, for that all have sinned.' That is what Adam did to us. Adam killed us. What does Christ do? He gives us life. It is implied there in verse 12. You have it again in the 15th verse: 'Not as the offence, so also is the free gift. For if through the offence of one many be dead, much more the grace of God, and the gift by grace, which is by one man, Jesus Christ, hath abounded unto many'. In what respect? Well, the opposite of death is 'life'. There it is once more. But look at it in verse 17: 'For if by one man's offence death reigned by one; much more they which receive abundance of grace and the gift of righteousness shall reign in life by one, Jesus Christ'. And then still more specifically in verse 18: 'Therefore as by the offence of one judgment came upon all men to condemnation; even so by the righteousness of one the free gift came upon all men' – Unto what? – 'unto justification of life'. He brings them together: 'justification' and 'life'. You cannot be justified without receiving this life also. So there Paul brings the two terms together.

Again, in chapter 6, Paul elaborates the matter at great length: 'Therefore we are buried with him by baptism into death: that like as Christ was raised up from the dead by the glory of the Father, even so we also should walk in newness of life' (v.4). That is a kind of suggestion, a foretaste, of what the Apostle is saying in the 6th verse of this 8th chapter. We are walking in a new life, in a new way. Then in verse 5 of chapter 6: 'For if we have been planted together in the likeness of his death, we shall be also in the likeness of his resurrection.' Verse 8: 'Now if we be dead with Christ we believe that we shall also live with him.' The same truth appears in verse 10: 'For in that he [Christ] died, he died unto sin once: but in that he liveth, he liveth unto God.' Then verse 11: 'Likewise reckon ye also yourselves to be dead indeed unto sin, but alive unto God through Jesus Christ our Lord.' That we are alive unto God is the fact that we must realize. We were 'dead', but we are 'alive.' We are to 'reckon' this, we are to lay hold upon it, we are to believe this, we are to live in the light of it, to realize that we are no longer 'dead' but 'alive unto God'. But the Apostle continues: 'But now being made free from sin, and become servants to God, ye have your fruit unto holiness, and the end everlasting life. For the wages of sin is death; but the gift of God is eternal life through Jesus Christ our Lord' (vv. 22 and 23). We do not have to wait for eternal life until we are dead; we have it now. If you are a Christian you have already received it – 'eternal life through Jesus Christ our Lord'.

Chapter 7 repeats the same emphasis upon life. In verse 4 we read: 'Wherefore, my brethren, ye also are become dead to the law by the body of Christ; that ye should be married to another, even to him who is raised from the dead, that we should bring forth fruit unto God.' And, as we have seen, in the 2nd verse of this 8th chapter Paul repeats the truth again in that resounding statement: 'The law of the Spirit of life in Christ Jesus hath made me free from the law of sin and death.'

This is clearly the Apostle's major theme; and if we fail to grasp this we are missing his most essential argument. The Christian is one who is 'alive from the dead', 'alive unto God', 'married to the Lord Jesus Christ' who is alive from the dead for evermore, and therefore the Christian, married to Him, and one with Him, is also alive for evermore. Such is the argument. Or, as Paul puts it in Ephesians 2: 1: 'And you hath he quickened who were dead.' You have been raised with Christ out of death, you are alive with Christ, you are seated with Christ even in the heavenly places at this moment. Or, as Peter says: 'We have been made partakers of the divine nature' (2 Peter 1: 4). That is the position of the Christian. He has a new life, a new disposition, a new power, a new energy – it is life from Christ and life in Christ.

In many ways this is the major theme of the New Testament; everything, including justification, leads up to it, and centres in it. The doctrine of regeneration is absolutely foundational. It is because so many do not realize this that they have a wrong view of evangelism, and become interested overmuch in decisions, and then believe that people can fall away after they have become Christians. It is all because of a failure to understand the idea of

[33]

regeneration and of life, that we really are born again as the result
of the operation of the Spirit, and are made 'partakers of the
divine nature.' Our Lord Himself preached this more clearly than
anyone else. We find it near the beginning of the Gospel according
to St John, in the famous incident concerning the woman of
Samaria in chapter 4 verse 14: 'Whosoever drinketh of the water
that I shall give him shall never thirst; but the water that I shall
give him shall be in him a well of water springing up into everlasting life.' There can be no greater statement of the matter
than that. We find a similar statement in the 5th chapter of
St John's Gospel in verse 24: 'Verily, verily, I say unto you, He
that heareth my word, and believeth on him that sent me, hath
everlasting life.' He has it; it is not merely that he will receive it at
a future date – 'hath everlasting life, and shall not come into
condemnation; but is passed from death unto life'. The same
truths appear, though in the reverse order, here in Romans 8,
where we read: 'There is therefore now no condemnation to them
that are in Christ Jesus', and that is because they have life; in
John 5 we are told that the believer 'hath everlasting life', and
that in consequence he shall not come into condemnation. Again,
in the 6th chapter of John's Gospel, verse 35: 'Jesus said unto
them, I am the bread of life: he that cometh to me shall never
hunger; and he that believeth on me shall never thirst.' And
again in verses 50 to 58: 'This is the bread which cometh down
from heaven, that a man may eat thereof, and not die' – and so on.
But turn to the 10th chapter, verse 10, of that Gospel: 'The thief
cometh not, but for to steal, and to kill, and to destroy: I am
come that they might have life, and that they might have it more
abundantly.' Here we have a glorious statement of this same
doctrine. He has come not merely to give us forgiveness, not
merely to reconcile us to God, but to give us life, and to give it
more abundantly. Then, still in the same Gospel, in the opening
verses of chapter 17, we find our Lord saying that he has been
sent into the world for this reason: 'Thou hast given him power
over all flesh, that he should give eternal life to as many as thou
hast given him'; and then follows the definition of eternal life,
'that they might know thee the only true God, and Jesus Christ,
whom thou hast sent'. Thus this is a doctrine which is taught
everywhere in the New Testament. The Apostle sums it all up in
a very wonderful statement in 1 Corinthians 15:45: 'The first
man Adam was made a living soul; the last Adam was made a

quickening spirit.' The Lord Jesus Christ quickens us, and gives us this life about which the Apostle is speaking.

But what is the meaning of this term 'life' which we find in so many different places? This is again a very important test which we must apply to ourselves; it is a very important check, so to speak, on what we considered in verse 5 of our chapter. It is possible for a man to simulate being a Christian, to take up many Christian duties, and to do many things that a Christian does. The way to distinguish between the two is to apply this test of life. I will explain how it operates. According to New Testament teaching the Christian is a person who is no longer dead, or, at least, he is no longer dying. He is aware within himself of an ability to respond to God. Previously we dealt with the matter in terms of what he does in practice when he sets his mind upon spiritual things. We are now looking at it from a slightly different angle. 'Like attracts like.' There is affinity between the iron filings and the magnet. The life that is in the Christian has the same characteristic; he is no longer dead or dull when you put these things before him. Even when the Christian is at his very worst and lowest there is always this evidence of life. Let me remind you of the Apostle Peter's statement in his First Epistle, chapter 2, verse 2: 'As newborn babes, desire the sincere milk of the word, that ye may grow thereby.' It is because the child is alive – no matter how young or however much an infant he may be – that he desires the milk; and the fact that he desires the milk is a proof of life. This is a vital fact about the Christian. Every born-again person knows it, though perhaps he cannot state it very clearly. It is the difference between having something inside you and something outside you. Many religious people are not born again; their religion is outside them, they carry it, as it were, in a bag. The Christian knows that it is inside him. It may be very weak and feeble, but it is there, and he knows it; there is a liveliness and a life of which he was not conscious before. And this of course affects everything he does. The author of the Epistle to the Hebrews tells us that one of the sad things about the non-Christian is that all his works are of no value, because they are 'dead works'. He says in chapter 9, verse 14: 'How much more shall the blood of Christ, who through the eternal Spirit offered himself without spot to God, purge your conscience from dead works to serve the living God?' 'Dead works'! They may be very good works according to the standard of the world; they may be religious, they may be moral; but they are dead. There is no life in them, and they cannot put life into anyone else. But the moment a man becomes a Christian everything he does has life in it; his poorest works have this quality of life. It is the same difference as exists between an almost perfectly constructed artificial flower, and a natural living flower. The artificial flower may actually look much better than the living one, which may be drooping. But it is dead, lifeless, changeless. The living flower may be drooping, but if you give it water and nourishment it will lift up its head and open out, and appear again in all its glory and beauty. The two flowers illustrate the difference between dead works and live works.

Another way in which we can put it is to say that the activities of the Christian are never superimposed, they are never added on. Let me venture on another illustration. The difference between the non-Christian and the Christian is the difference between a Christmas-tree on which people hang presents, and a living tree that bears fruit. They have to put them on the Christmas tree; it does not and cannot produce anything. But in the case of the growing tree it produces fruit. The fruit is no longer imposed from outside; it is something produced from the life, the sap and the power that are in the living tree. Or, to put it in yet a different way, what the Christian does is not merely a matter of duty; it is the spontaneous expression of what he feels within. That is the deciding point, it seems to me, between the man who is trying to make himself a Christian, and one who is a Christian. The man who is not a Christian feels it is right for him to go to church, to read the Scriptures, and to pray; it is a matter of duty, and he has to force himself to do it. But when a man becomes spiritually alive there is the spontaneity that you see in a child who desires milk, and who 'makes for it', stretches out his hand for it because he wants it.

Our Lord dealt with the same matter in the Sermon on the Mount as recorded in the 7th chapter of Matthew's Gospel, in verse 15: 'Beware of false prophets, which come to you in sheep's clothing.' You look at these men and you say, 'Sheep'. They look like sheep in every way. Ah, 'but inwardly they are ravening wolves.' Again, 'Ye shall know them by their fruits. Do men gather grapes of thorns, or figs of thistles? Even so, every good tree bringeth forth good fruit; but a corrupt tree bringeth forth evil fruit. A good tree cannot bring forth evil fruit, neither can a corrupt tree bring forth good fruit. Every tree that bringeth not forth good fruit is hewn down, and cast into the fire. Wherefore by their fruits ye shall know them.' Our Lord's argument is that what is inside must come out. If there is no life within it cannot come out; it is artificial, counterfeit, superimposed, added. It lacks the genuineness that is always the indication of life. Our Lord was clearly very much concerned about this. He says a similar thing at the end of the 12th chapter of Matthew's Gospel, in verse 33: 'Either make the tree good, and his fruit good; or else make the tree corrupt, and his fruit corrupt: for the tree is known by its fruit.' Again He says: 'O generation of vipers, how can you, being evil, speak good things? for out of the abundance of the heart the mouth speaketh.' It all comes from the inside; it is out of the heart. 'A good man out of the good treasure of his heart bringeth forth good things; an evil man out of the evil treasure bringeth forth evil things.' The characteristic of the Christian is that all that he does comes in this way out of the heart. Or, to go back to our Lord's statement to the woman of Samaria, it is like 'a fountain'. The Christian's life is comparable to a fountain, not to a trough, not to a cistern. You look at a cistern and the water in it; and though you take out of it, it still seems fairly full. That is because water flows into it; it is a matter of replenishment. But if the inflow stops it becomes empty. How different is a cistern from a fountain which bubbles up from depths that no one can fathom or can find. There is some inner power, some generating force in it, and it bubbles up year in year out. Take of its water and it still looks the same. On and on it flows; and when cistern waters fail or are cut off, this flows on.

The Apostle is emphasizing, even as our Lord was, this element of spontaneity. And then there is the element of warmth. You can tell the difference between a genuine Christian and a man who is trying to persuade himself that he is in the Christian way. Is there not something different about the whole attitude, and the way in which they act? In the Christian there is spontaneity, warmth, movement, heart in everything he does. How different are correct mechanical prayers from the spontaneous warmth that characterizes the prayers of the true Christian!

Such, then, is something of the content of this word 'life'.

However small the amount of life may be in us, if it is there at all it is bound to show itself; and we cannot be Christians without it. 'To be spiritually minded is life'; it is there! And because it is there the Christian 'minds' the things of the Spirit; and as he goes on minding them the life grows, and he grows as the life grows. He was born a babe, he becomes a young man, he continues to mature and develop. The Christian does not remain static. There are various stages in the Christian life; it is an increasing growth; we 'grow in grace, and in the knowledge of the Lord.' There is this inevitable element of development, for life is never static.

This truth is also important in that it helps us to understand the position of what is called a backslider. The backslider is not dead; he is still alive. He is behaving very badly as a child of God, but he is still a child of God. In the last analysis a decision as to whether a man is a Christian or not is not reached only by what he does. The backslider does things he should not do. On the surface he may appear to be much worse than many a good, moral man who does not believe in Christ at all. But that shows the fallacy of judging only by what you see on the surface. The backslider, however grievously he may be sinning, is still a child of God, the seed of life is in him. How do we know that? The final proof is that the backslider always returns, the backslider inevitably repents with a godly repentance. He is miserable in his sin; he cannot revert totally to the ways of the world. All he does is done 'under condemnation'; he is miserable in it. He is trying to persuade himself that he is enjoying it but he is condemned the whole time. He feels he is a cad, he knows that he is going contrary to his new nature. That is why he touches depths of misery that no one else can know in this life. But it is all because he has life in him. It is there, covered over, held down. Say what you will about it, it is there; and because it is there it will reassert itself, it will manifest itself. It is bound to do so, it always does so. But – to return to a more positive view of it – the man who has this mind of the Spirit, the man who has this life, can say with Horatius Bonar:

> *I heard the voice of Jesus say,*
> *'Behold, I freely give*
> *The living water – thirsty one,*
> *Stoop down, and drink, and live'.*

[38]

Romans 8: 5–8

I came to Jesus, and I drank
Of that life-giving stream;
My thirst was quenched, my soul revived,
And now I live in Him.

You cannot have this life without knowing it. You may have your difficulties and your doubts, but if this life is in you, you will know that there is a difference, and that in spite of yourself there is a power within you, a presence, something other than yourself which is there, and do what you will you cannot get away from it. Sometimes the Christian may even get so far in a condition of backsliding that he even wishes he had never heard of Christian truth; but that is a proof that he has life, and that it is more powerful than he himself. It is 'the life of God in the soul of man'. We have already seen how our Lord states it in the 17th chapter of John's Gospel, verse 3: 'This is life eternal, that they might know thee, the only true God, and Jesus Christ whom thou hast sent.' In other words, where this life is found, there is always in some measure the knowledge of God. The Christian, at his worst, has some degree of a knowledge of God. God is not an abstract conception to the Christian; he knows that 'God is'; he has within him this sense of God, this realization, however dim and vague, that he is in fellowship with God. God is real to the Christian. There are endless degrees and variations in that knowledge; but basically a Christian is a man who does not rest on the proofs of the being of God; he knows not only that there is a God, but he knows God. He longs for a greater knowledge, he thirsts for a deeper knowledge; but though he cannot put it into coherent terms, and very often cannot explain it or express it, he knows that he belongs to God and that, whatever may happen to him, he is in the hands of God, and that 'neither death, nor life, nor angels, nor principalities, nor powers, nor things present, nor things to come, nor height, nor depth, nor any other creature shall be able to separate us from the love of God which is in Christ Jesus our Lord' (Romans 8: 38, 39). To have the mind of the Spirit is to have life. As you read your Scriptures look for this great theme, meditate upon it, concentrate upon it. It is, I say, ultimately the highest and the most glorious aspect of the Christian life. 'I am come that they might have life, and that they might have it more abundantly.'

[39]

Have we got this life, and are we enjoying this life? Do we know that we are alive from the dead, that we are alive unto God? Are we aware of this affinity with God, this thirst, this hunger, this desire for God, and all the manifestations of minding the things of the Spirit? They are all indications of life, and of the fact that we are alive unto God in Christ Jesus. Is our religious life a mechanical effort, or is there within us something that is holding us and mastering us? That is how we should think about the matter. The man who is trying to be a Christian is trying to hold on to something. The man who is a Christian feels that he is being held by something. It has been put into him, it is there; it may even seem to be in spite of him, but it is there. It is not what he is doing that matters to him; it is what has been done to him, it is what he has become, it is the awareness of this power within him – 'life'. To have the mind of the Spirit is to have life, life which is life indeed, 'life more abundant'; we are 'partakers of the divine nature', and have eternal life. In this sense, we are sharers of the life of God Himself, and in eternity we shall be ever drinking of it and living on it. Even here and now, as our Lord says, we should be 'living on him'. He says, 'As the living Father has sent me, and I live by the Father: so he that eateth me shall live by me' (John 6: 57). And again, 'Except ye eat the flesh of the Son of man, and drink his blood, ye have no life in you' (John 6: 53). Not in a mechanical or material sense, as the Jews foolishly thought, but spiritually. He is our life, He is 'the bread of life'; and we live on Him. We do not live on the world and its things, or on what it does for us, and what it provides for us. We live on Christ, and He is the mainspring of our life. We live on Him, we partake of and are sharers of His life. 'To be spiritually minded is life.' Thank God!

Four

*

For they that are after the flesh do mind the things of the flesh; but they that are after the Spirit the things of the Spirit.

For to be carnally minded is death; but to be spiritually minded is life and peace.

Because the carnal mind is enmity against God; for it is not subject to the law of God, neither indeed can be.

So then they that are in the flesh cannot please God.

Romans 8 : 5–8

We are still looking positively at the Christian. We have seen that he 'minds' the things of the Spirit, and that he does so because he is alive. 'To be carnally minded is death; but to be spiritually minded is life.' The Christian is alive spiritually, he has new life in him; he is a new creature, a new creation; he is alive from the dead, and he has powers and abilities which he did not possess before. The dead can do nothing; but the Christian is alive in a spiritual sense.

That is the point at which we have arrived. But here, at once, we notice that the Apostle does not merely say that the contrast between the non-Christian and the Christian is that the former is dead while the latter is alive; he adds another word. 'To be carnally minded is death, but to be spiritually minded is life and *peace*.' He adds this further word which we must now consider. Life seems to be the complete contrast to death; but the Apostle says 'life *and* peace'. Why the addition? Why did he select 'peace' in particular when he could have used other words? He is talking about the Christian as a man who is in the realm of the Spirit, and we know from Galatians 5 that the fruit of the Spirit is 'love, joy, (and then) *peace*'. Why did he not say then that 'to be carnally minded is death, but to be spiritually minded is life and love and joy?' Why does he speak of 'peace' instead of 'love and joy'?

[41]

It seems to me that there is only one adequate answer to the question. The Apostle is anxious to show how the righteousness of the law can be fulfilled in us, 'who walk not after the flesh, but after the Spirit'. There are certain obstacles to this fulfilling of the righteousness of the law, and he has been telling us what they are in his description of the man who walks 'after the flesh'. He 'minds' the things of the flesh, he is 'dead' spiritually, he is at 'enmity against God', 'he is not subject to the law of God, neither indeed can be', hence he cannot please God. So it is quite impossible that the righteousness of the law should be fulfilled in him. But now, on the other hand, he says this 'righteousness of the law' can be fulfilled in us. How and why? As we examine this word 'peace' we find the answer to that particular question.

Do you notice one peculiar thing here? In verse 5 the Apostle gives the two sides, the negative and the positive: 'They that are after the flesh do mind the things of the flesh; but they that are after the Spirit the things of the Spirit'. In verse 6: 'To be carnally minded is death' (negative); 'but to be spiritually minded is life and peace' (positive). But in verses 7 and 8 he only gives the negative and drops the positive. In verse 7: 'The carnal mind is enmity against God, for it is not subject to the law of God, neither indeed can be', and you expect him to add, 'but the spiritual mind can be subject to God'; but he does not do so. Then in verse 8 he says: 'So then they that are after the flesh cannot please God'. Then you expect him to add: 'but they that are in the Spirit can and do please God'; but he does not say it. Why not? My suggestion is that it has all been said in the word 'peace'; that he put in the word 'peace' here because it is the word that provides us with the complete contrast; it supplies the positives that are not actually stated in verses 7 and 8. So as we examine the content of the word 'peace' we shall incidentally be completing our exposition not only of verse 6 but also of verses 7 and 8. It was unnecessary to write out the positive in verses 7 and 8 because that has already been said.

And there is a further reason, surely, why he chooses this particular word *peace*. Whenever the Apostle thinks at all in terms of justification by faith, the first thing that comes to his mind is *peace*. We have already met with that at the beginning of chapter 5: 'Therefore being justified by faith we have peace with God'. And we shall find again in chapter 14 that he says exactly

the same thing in verse 17: 'For the kingdom of God is not meat
and drink; but righteousness, and peace, and joy in the Holy
Ghost.' 'Righteousness and peace' go together. Peace is the first
thing we experience as the result of this righteousness from God
which is in the Lord Jesus Christ. Clearly, therefore, it is a key
word in the New Testament, and in our understanding of the
Apostle's teaching, particularly at this point. But let us also
remember that what we discover about 'peace' provides us, once
again, with a thorough means of examining ourselves and our
state and condition as Christian people.

'To be spiritually minded is life and peace.' What is the content
of the term 'peace with God'? The righteousness of the law can
never be fulfilled in any man who is not at peace with God. The
Apostle has already told us that fact about the unbeliever. We
find it in verse 7. The unbeliever is not only spiritually dead, but
at the same time he is 'at enmity against God', his whole understanding of God is quite wrong. He regards God as an enemy;
God is someone whom he hates. He may say he believes in God,
but according to the Scripture he hates God; he feels that God is
against him, he wishes there were not a God. Obviously such a
man cannot possibly please God, neither can the righteousness
of the law of God be fulfilled in him. A second truth about the
unbeliever is that he is not subject to the law of God; he hates
the law of God. The world is demonstrating that today. It hates
even the very notion of law; it hates discipline, and what it
describes as freedom is nothing but licence. Man by nature, and
in sin, wants to be a law unto himself, he wants to do what he
likes to do, what pleases him, what takes his fancy at the moment;
and he objects to every suggestion of law and discipline and
government and order. The natural man is a spiritual anarchist
at all times; and nothing is becoming so increasingly evident in
our modern world, as it falls away from God and from religion,
as this element of anarchy and lawlessness and disorder that is
coming in, in every realm of life, and leading to terrible confusion
and chaos. The unbeliever is not subject to the law of God.
Indeed we are told more about him; he is not even capable of
being subject to it – 'neither indeed can be'. Because he is what
he is, because of the evil that is in him, and because of the perversion, the power of sin in him, he cannot even desire to be
subject to the law of God.

On the other hand, the Christian has 'life and peace', and primarily, 'peace with God'. Here the Apostle portrays a man who really has come to a knowledge of God. The first thing that is true about the Christian is that he is the only man who has a true conception of God. The first call in preaching always should be a call to repentance. That was John the Baptist's message, and also our Lord's first call. It had been central in the prophets' preaching. Repentance means to think again about God and yourself and the relationship between you; but the first call is to think again about God. The worst sin of all is the false thinking about God of which the natural man is so terribly guilty. But the Christian is one who has come to see and to know God – God as He is, God as He has revealed Himself – and the result is that he loves God. No man can be a Christian without realizing that in spite of his having been a rebel against his Creator, in spite of all that was so true of him in sin – the perversion and the foulness and the pollution – in spite of the fact that he deserves nothing but hell, God has so loved him as to send His only begotten Son into the world to save him. 'Herein is love, not that we loved God, but that he loved us, and sent his Son to be the propitiation for our sins' (1 John 4: 10). The Christian is one who has this knowledge, and the moment he realizes that, he has this new conception of God. God is no longer one whom he hates; rather is he overwhelmed by the love of God, the God who has done this for him. He 'did not spare even his own Son', He 'sent him in the likeness of sinful flesh and as an offering for sin'. 'Ah,' says this man, 'how wrong I have been to be at enmity against such a God. I see now the character of God; how wrong I was!' The enmity is banished, he sees God as He is, and he loves Him; the hatred has vanished completely. I quote John again in his First Epistle chapter 4, verse 16: 'We know the love that God hath to us.' That is what we have discovered. So we are at peace with God; the old enmity has gone. We realize that He has put our sins away; the barrier between us has been removed; the veil has been taken away, and we have entered into this knowledge of God which gives us life and peace.

Then, secondly, because of that, we are in no trouble any longer with regard to the law of God. 'The carnal mind is enmity against God', and therefore 'it is not subject to the law of God'. The natural man does not believe in the God who makes laws, nor in the God who, as a foolish preacher whose sermon I read recently put it, 'sat on top of Mount Sinai giving out His commandments'. No, he believes in a god whom he has conjured up in his own sentimental heart. But the Christian has a true view of law. It is no longer true to say of him that he is 'not subject to the law of God'; we must put it positively and say that 'he delights in the law of God'. 'His commandments are not grievous' says John of the Christian (1 John 5 : 3). They are grievous to the non-Christian; but they are not grievous to the Christian. A man who objects to the commandments is not a Christian. A man who objects to the demands of the Sermon on the Mount is not a Christian. The Christian feels that that sermon is exactly what he would expect from God, that that is how all men should live, and that if the whole world but lived in that way we should have Paradise once more. The commandments are an expression of God's character; they were designed for the good of man; and so the Christian says: 'O how I love thy law!' Even the Psalmist had been able to say that; and the Christian does so still more certainly; he delights in the law of God. He sees its glory, and its excellence, and he desires to keep it. That is an expression of this peace. Before we become Christians we are fighting against the law of God; the moment we become Christians that fight ends, and there is peace.

So this word 'peace' answers verse 7 step by step. The natural mind, the carnal mind, is 'enmity against God, is not subject to the law of God, neither indeed can be'. But of the Christian, you say at once: 'He can be subject to it, he is subject to it, he desires to be subject to it, and he goes out of his way to subject himself to it.' He 'hungers and thirsts after righteousness', he desires to keep the commandments which God has given. So in these various ways this man is at peace with God; and because he is at peace with God there is this wonderful possibility of the righteousness of the law being fulfilled in him. But in him only – which is exactly what Paul has said in verse 4: 'That the righteousness of the law might be fulfilled in us, who walk not after the flesh, but after the Spirit.'

But let us look at it also from the standpoint of the Christian man having peace within himself. Not only peace between him and God, who is outside him, but peace within himself! This can be divided into negative and positive aspects. Negatively, it means the end of the old restlessness. The first thing that happens to a man when he becomes a Christian is that he gets rid of the restlessness which characterized his old life. Restlessness is always a main characteristic of the life of sin. We find a perfect description of the matter in Isaiah chapter 57, verse 20: 'The wicked are like the troubled sea, when it cannot rest, whose waters throw up mire and dirt.' Such is man in sin. The 'sea' in the Bible generally means the ethnic nations, the unbelievers, the world at large. It invariably refers to non-Christians, and it is a very wonderful description of them. The Book of Revelation tells us that, when the final restoration takes place, the grand regeneration of all things, there will be 'no sea'. The sea's constant movement, the utter uselessness and waste of energy, and the churning up of mud and mire and wreckage, is a perfect representation of the life of sin. But that comes to an end when one becomes a Christian. Who does not remember that great and moving statement of St Augustine, 'Thou hast made us for Thyself, and our hearts are restless until they find their rest in Thee.' How obvious is this restlessness in the world today, amid all the uncertainty, the unhappiness, and the insecurity that characterizes life!

Then, secondly, the life of sin is a life of dissatisfaction. The extraordinary thing about the life of sin of which people boast so much, is that it never satisfies them. Over it all can be written, 'Vanity of vanities; all is vanity'. The life that people live outside Christ never gives them satisfaction; they spend large sums of money on it, but all in vain. That is because it is a life that stimulates, and draws out of us instead of giving to us. So it always leaves us tired, weary, exhausted, and in pain, suffering endless remorse. 'Vanity of vanities; all is vanity'. The wise man who wrote the book of Ecclesiastes had tried it all. He tried learning, he tried pleasure, he tried erecting great buildings, and much else. In that book you see a very able, intelligent man avidly trying to find satisfaction in life without God. He laboured at the task with great thoroughness, but he could not find it. 'Vanity of vanities; all is vanity' is his conclusion. But when you become a Christian that tragic situation ends.

The third great thing about the Christian is that he comes to the end of his futile seeking and searching for that which he cannot find. The non-Christian, as I have said, is always trying to find satisfaction – peace, joy truth – but he cannot find them. The

[46]

tragedy is that he boasts about his efforts, he boasts even of the search and the seeking. A popular criticism of Christianity is that it is dogmatic, that it claims to have 'arrived'. To the unbeliever the great thing is 'the thrill of the quest'. But what a sad condition – ever seeking and never finding, ever hoping but never really arriving, travelling with never an end to the journey!

But let us now turn to the positive aspect of our theme. The Christian is absolutely different – he has 'life and peace'. He rests in the truth. That is one of the most glorious aspects of the Christian position. The Christian is a man who has 'arrived.' The true preacher does not seek for truth in the pulpit; he is there because he has found it. 'Can the blind lead the blind?' Of course not, our Lord says; they will 'both fall into the ditch'. The Christian is not a man who is seeking for truth; he is one who has found it, or he has been found by it. I do not care which way the matter is phrased; the fact is that he has found it. A great statement to this effect is found in 1 Corinthians 2: 'But God hath revealed them unto us by his Spirit; for the Spirit searcheth all things, yea, the deep things of God. What man knoweth the things of a man, save the spirit of man which is in him? even so the things of God knoweth no man, but the Spirit of God. The natural man receiveth not these things, because they are foolishness unto him: neither can he know them, because they are spiritually discerned. But he that is spiritual judgeth all things' – he has an understanding – 'yet he himself is judged of no man. For who hath known the mind of the Lord, that he may instruct him? But we have the mind of Christ' (verses 10–16). Christ is 'the light of the world' and He has opened our eyes to see 'the light'. His statement recorded at the end of the eleventh chapter of Matthew's Gospel tells us so: 'I thank thee, O Father, Lord of heaven and earth, because thou hast hid these things from the wise and prudent' – the seekers after truth, the men who believe they can attain to it by philosophy – 'and hast revealed them unto babes. Even so, Father; for so it seemed good in thy sight.' The Father has 'revealed' the truth unto them; and the Son says: 'He that followeth me shall not walk in darkness, but shall have the light of life.'

This is true of every Christian. The Christian is the only man who understands life. The people who are living for pleasure, and the philosophers also, do not understand life; they are even prepared to admit it. The pleasure-seekers do not even think, the others try to do so, but without success. They cannot understand themselves, they do not understand man, they do not understand life, they do not understand death, and they try not to think about it for the reason that they do not know what lies beyond death. But the Christian is different; he is a man who has found peace in these respects, he has a philosophy of life, he has found it in the Bible. He says with Horatius Bonar:

> *I heard the voice of Jesus say,*
> *'I am this dark world's Light.*
> *Look unto Me; thy morn shall rise,*
> *And all thy day be bright.'*
> *I looked to Jesus, and I found*
> *In Him my Star, my Sun;*
> *And in that Light of life I'll walk,*
> *Till travelling days are done.*

The Christian is a man who understands the meaning of life in this world. He knows that believers are 'pilgrims and sojourners' here, we are children of God in an alien land, we are travelling home to God. Are you troubled about the state of the world, and perplexed that it should be as it is? You should not be, if you are a Christian. You should reason with yourself, 'Because the world is governed by sin and evil and the devil, it must of necessity be like this'. Christians are not surprised when international conferences fail, they are not surprised that the situation should go from bad to worse, because the Bible has taught them to expect such developments. The Christian has found the secret to an understanding of his own life, the life of the community at large, and the life of the world. He is not appalled by the thought of death; he knows he is ever moving towards it, but he also knows that he has something to look forward to beyond death. He has found rest in the truth; he has 'arrived'; he has a knowledge of the truth which has been revealed to him.

We must also emphasize that the Christian has an inner tranquillity; he has 'life and peace'. He is a man who is, as it were, living at the centre of a hurricane. It is said that at the centre of a hurricane there is a point of complete rest. Everything is turning violently and convulsively round and round, but not at the centre; that is fixed. So it is with the Christian. Thus the Apostle

Paul is able to say, 'In nothing be anxious'. 'Nothing!' It is a comprehensive, all-inclusive term. Throw into it anything that occurs to you, all the troubles and the difficulties and the problems and the trials that the world and the flesh and the devil can produce. 'In nothing be anxious, but in all things, by prayer and supplication with thanksgiving, let your requests be made known unto God: and the peace of God that passeth all understanding shall keep your hearts and minds through Christ Jesus' (Philippians 4: 6–7). Tranquillity, a centre of rest, inner peace! 'To be carnally minded is death, but to be spiritually minded is life.' But, thank God, it is also 'peace'; not only in the sense that you arrive at a philosophy, but that you are protected and guarded by the love of God and Jesus Christ, and by this knowledge of the truth.

Lastly, there is an inner harmony in the personality of the Christian. The restlessness of the unbeliever is ultimately due to the fact that there is a kind of duality in his very nature; there is a dichotomy in the very heart of his being; he is suffering from a central division in his personality. On the one hand he has a sense of right and wrong; on the other hand there is the influence of evil and sin. So he is divided at the very centre of his personality, and confusion reigns within him. But that is no longer true of the Christian. Does this mean that the Christian is perfect? By no means! But I assert – and I have been seeking to establish this ever since we began considering the 5th chapter of this Epistle – that this split personality no longer exists in the Christian. To state the matter otherwise – the Christian is no longer in the position of Romans 7: 24: 'O wretched man that I am! who shall deliver me?' That denotes central division, as the Apostle has pointed out. 'With the mind I serve the law of God, but with the flesh the law of sin. I delight in the law of God after the inward man: but I see another law in my members.' That, as we saw, describes a man under conviction of sin. But when a man becomes a Christian, that is no longer the case, for the Christian, as we have been noting at great length – and particularly in chapter 6 – knows that he himself is already saved. 'But,' you say, 'he still has a fight against sin.' Of course he has! Sin remains in his 'mortal body', in his 'flesh'. The struggle in the Christian is not a central problem, a struggle within the personality; he is now fighting against the relics of sin that remain in his mortal body, in his flesh – which is

[49]

a very different thing! The struggle is not central, at the heart of his personality. There he has found peace and rest; he knows that he is saved, and eternally saved, and that nothing can ever cancel out that work of God. He is already 'seated in the heavenly places with Christ Jesus'; and his problem, his struggle, is in his body, this body that is dying, this 'mortal body'. He also knows that there is shortly to be an end to that struggle. But there is no longer this mental struggle. So we can adopt the words of Philip Doddridge, and say:

Now rest, my long-divided heart;
Fixed on this blissful centre, rest.

'My long-divided heart!' We all know about that! But if you are a Christian your heart is no longer 'divided'; if you are a Christian, your heart is whole, it has been won by Christ. And even if you fall into sin it does not mean that your heart has become divided. That is due to the remnant of the old nature that remains in the body; it is not in the heart. 'Now rest, my long-divided heart.' It is no longer divided. The Christian's heart is fixed. That is the position of the Christian. He has found this place of rest and of peace in respect of his essential personality; there is no longer any division there.

But the Christian also has peace with others. I do not linger over this now but would mention that the whole of the fourteenth chapter of Romans is a commentary on this matter. In the church in Rome there was disputing over days, and observations of feasts, and food to be eaten or not eaten, and so on, and the Apostle reprimands them and upbraids them, and says: 'The kingdom of God is not meat and drink, but righteousness and peace, and joy in the Holy Ghost.' They must learn to understand one another. When there is a weaker brother who is in some confusion about these things, he must not be despised or set aside; instead, his fellow-Christians should feel sorry for him and help him. 'Bear ye one another's burdens, and so fulfil the law of Christ.' They were to receive one another, but 'not to doubtful disputations'. He that is strong ought to bear the infirmities of the weak. Such is the argument. The Christian has peace in that sense also.

This, then, is the Apostle's general statement in verses 5 to 7 of this chapter. But in order to complete his statement I must add a word about verse 8, where Paul phrases it negatively about the unbeliever, the man who walks after the flesh and who is in the flesh. He says: 'They that are in the flesh cannot please God.' But the opposite is true about the Christian; he is a man who can please God, and who does please God. In other words, Paul is just repeating what he said in the first half of verse 4, 'That the righteousness of the law might be fulfilled in us'. People in whom the righteousness of the law is fulfilled are people who please God. And that means not only that God looks down upon us as He sees us clothed with the righteousness of Jesus Christ, and that we are pleasing in His sight, but it also means that we are able to serve Him, and to keep His commandments; we are now capable of pleasing Him in a positive sense, capable of glorifying Him. The other man cannot please God, but Christians can please God.

Let me produce evidence to support this assertion. We are told in Genesis 5: 24: 'And Enoch walked with God: and he was not, for God took him.' Why did God take this man to Himself without his passing through death? The 11th chapter of the Epistle to the Hebrews gives us the answer. It runs: 'For before his translation he had this testimony, that he pleased God.' Enoch pleased God by keeping His commandments. Similarly Abel's offering had pleased God in a way that Cain's had not done. The people of God please God.

Our Lord Jesus Christ states the same truth in this way: 'Let your light so shine before men that they may see your good works, and glorify your Father which is in heaven' (Matt. 5: 16). Peter in his First Epistle, chapter 2 verse 9, puts it thus: 'Ye are a chosen generation, a royal priesthood, an holy nation, a peculiar people, that ye should show forth the praises of him who hath called you out of darkness into his marvellous light.' The Christian is not only a man who is declared just, he is a man who is meant to show forth the praises of God, to manifest them, to demonstrate them in his life. Peter tells us how he does so in verses 11 and 12 of the same chapter: 'Dearly beloved, I beseech you as strangers and pilgrims, abstain from fleshly lusts which war against the soul; having your conversation honest among the Gentiles; that whereas they speak against you as evil-doers, they may by your good works, which they shall behold, glorify God in the day of visitation.' God delights in people who live in that way. Consider also the 16th verse of the 11th chapter of the

Epistle to the Hebrews. The author is describing Abraham, and the other heroes of the faith, who at the command of God left their country and comrades and family and all, and went out, like Abraham, 'who went out, not knowing whither he went'. And he says about these men who gave such remarkable obedience to God's commandments and exhortations: 'Wherefore God is not ashamed to be called their God, for he hath prepared for them a city.' God is not ashamed to be called the God of such people, because they keep His commandments, because the righteousness of the law is being fulfilled in them. They are showing the results of His powerful working within them, the evidences of being under the reign of grace. God looks upon them and says, 'These are my people.'

Therefore I conclude by saying that while they that are in the flesh cannot please God, they that are in the Spirit, they that are in Christ, they that are governed by the law of the Spirit of life in Christ Jesus, and have been set free from 'the law of sin and death', can do so, and are doing so, and must do so. What the law could not enable them to do, namely, to show that the righteousness of the law was being fulfilled in them, 'the law of the Spirit of life in Christ Jesus' is doing. The Christian is a man who is justified and is in process of being sanctified. He is already sanctified in Christ Jesus in an ultimate sense, but he is progressively and increasingly being sanctified in experience. He will finally be entirely sanctified; he will be 'faultless and blameless'; he will be 'without spot, or wrinkle, or any such thing'; he will be 'holy and without blame', standing in the presence of God. The righteousness of the law is being fulfilled in all 'who walk not after the flesh, but after the Spirit'.

Five

*

But ye are not in the flesh, but in the Spirit, if so be that the Spirit of God dwell in you. Now if any man have not the Spirit of Christ, he is none of his.

And if Christ be in you, the body is dead because of sin; but the Spirit is life because of righteousness.

But if the Spirit of him that raised up Jesus from the dead dwell in you, he that raised up Christ from the dead shall also quicken your mortal bodies by his Spirit that dwelleth in you.

Roman 8: 9–11

In these three remarkable and most important verses, the Apostle sums up and applies what he has just been saying to these Christian people in Rome and also takes his theme a little further. As we have seen, his object, fundamentally, is to give these people assurance of their final and complete salvation. He grounds this upon what has happened to them, namely, that 'the law of the Spirit of life in Christ Jesus has made them free from the law of sin and death', and he has reminded them as to how that happened, and how the object of it all is 'that the righteousness of the law might be fulfilled in them'. He reminds them also that this is only true of those 'who walk not after the flesh, but after the Spirit'.

Next he comes to the application and, in a sense, in verse 9 he says it all again, as is his custom. Then in verses 10 and 11 he gives, as it were, a picture and a portrayal of the actual position of the Christian man. We shall see, later, how, in verses 12 and 13, on the basis of verses 9 to 11, he addresses an appeal and an exhortation to them.

As we approach these three verses, 9–11, we cannot but be impressed by the fact that, clearly, to the Apostle this is a most important matter. He is obviously very anxious that they should be clear about the point that all this is only true of those 'who walk not after the flesh, but after the Spirit'. This is obviously basic to our whole understanding of ourselves as Christian people. When the Apostle takes all this trouble, and repeats and repeats, it is clear that it is a point that can easily be misunderstood; but it is so vital that nothing can be taken for granted.

The first thing that strikes us in verse 9 is that Paul establishes beyond any doubt that all he has been saying so far applies to all Christians. As I have indicated repeatedly there is an exposition of the earlier verses which would have us believe that they are only descriptive of certain Christians, that is to say, of those Christians who have 'gone over' from chapter 7 to chapter 8. So we have been emphasizing that everything the Apostle tells us here is true of all Christians. This ninth verse puts the matter beyond any doubt at all. In verse 8 we read, 'So then they that are in the flesh cannot please God.' And in verse 9, 'But ye are not in the flesh', and in the Greek the 'ye' comes first. So we can translate thus: 'You, (being Christians), that is not true of you. You are not in the flesh, but in the Spirit'. And then, to make it doubly certain, he adds this striking statement at the end of verse 9: 'If any man have not the Spirit of Christ, he is none of his' – he is not a Christian at all. If a man has not the Spirit of Christ he is just not a Christian. Many are in trouble over the expression '*If so be* that the Spirit of God dwell in you'. But it is merely another way of saying 'assuming that'; and so it strengthens the whole case. 'But ye are not in the flesh, but in the Spirit, assuming that the Spirit of God dwell in you. Now if any man have not the Spirit of Christ, he is none of his.' It is a very powerful way of emphasizing the truth that without the Spirit of God in him a man is not a Christian at all. Or conversely, if a man is a Christian, the Spirit is of necessity in him. That is the contrast here presented to our view. The contrast is between those who are 'in the flesh', or 'after the flesh', or 'walk after the flesh', and those who 'walk after the Spirit' and who are 'in the Spirit'.

The Apostle works out a logical case in this way: the Christian is not 'in the flesh', and that is so because the Spirit is in him. If the Spirit is not in him he is not a Christian at all; therefore to be a Christian at all means that we are not in the flesh, but in the Spirit. So we establish beyond any doubt that the Apostle has all along been describing every Christian, any Christian, and not merely some special group of people who have had some additional blessing. In other words, what the Apostle is doing here is to remind Christian people of what is true of them. He began to do this away back in chapter 5 and then worked it out in detail in the first thirteen verses of chapter 6, and again very clearly in the first six verses of chapter 7. To 'have the Spirit of Christ' means that you are a Christian; to be a Christian means that you 'have the Spirit of Christ'.

There is another matter here with which we must deal because it has often caused much discussion. Notice the terminology the Apostle uses here with regard to the Spirit. 'But ye are not in the flesh, but in the Spirit, if so be that the Spirit of God dwell in you. Now if any man have not the Spirit of Christ, he is none of his. We have 'the Spirit', 'the Spirit of God' and 'the Spirit of Christ'. What is the significance of the variation? There is only one conclusion to draw, namely, that these terms are interchangeable; they all convey exactly the same meaning. In each instance the Apostle is referring to the Holy Spirit, the third Person in the blessed Holy Trinity. He refers to Him as 'the Spirit', he refers to Him as 'the Spirit of God' and 'the Spirit of Christ'. He follows the same course in other places also, so there should be no confusion. Yet some persist in asking, 'But why does he use these different terms?' Some have said that to 'have the Spirit of Christ' simply means to have the outlook and the mind of Christ, and that it does not mean that we have the Holy Spirit in us. But it most certainly means the Holy Spirit. By using one term at one moment, and another term at another moment, the Apostle is clearly indicating that the three terms are equal and synonymous and that in each case he refers to the Holy Spirit.

Why then does he draw this distinction? This is a difficult matter, and it has been greatly discussed. What it teaches surely is the doctrine of the Trinity, that in the Godhead there are three Persons – God the Father, God the Son, God the Holy Spirit. But it also emphasizes the aspect of the unity in the Trinity, the three Persons in the one great unity, for there is only one God. So the terms can be used interchangeably. It also establishes, surely, the equality of the three Persons in the blessed Holy Trinity. But, very particularly, it directs our attention to the way in which the Holy Spirit comes to us; and it is there, perhaps, that the different terms, 'Spirit of God' and 'Spirit of Christ', are seen to have significance and importance.

[55]

Sometimes in the Scripture the Holy Spirit is referred to as 'the promise of the Father'. In Ephesians 1:13 we read of 'the Holy Spirit of promise'. In the Old Testament God promised that He would send His Spirit upon His people; so, looking at it from that aspect, we can say that the Holy Spirit is sent by God. We can therefore speak of Him as 'the Spirit of God', the Spirit that is sent by God the Father. But then there are other clear statements to the effect that the Spirit is sent by the Lord Jesus Christ. Take, for instance, the 16th verse in the 14th chapter of John's Gospel: 'And I will pray the Father, and he shall give you another Comforter, that he may abide with you for ever'. What an interesting statement! 'I will request the Father', says our Lord, 'and he [the Father] will give you this other Comforter to help you after I am gone.' But then in the 15th chapter of John's Gospel, verse 26, we read: 'But when the Comforter is come, whom I will send unto you from the Father, even the Spirit of truth, which proceedeth from the Father, he shall testify of me.' And again in the 16th chapter of John's Gospel in verse 7: 'Nevertheless I tell you the truth; it is expedient for you that I go away; for if I go not away, the Comforter will not come unto you; but if I depart, I will send him unto you.'

There is, then, a sense in which God the Father sends the Spirit, there is another sense in which God the Son sends the Spirit, and in all cases it is clear that the Spirit is a Person. Hence we must never think of the Holy Spirit as but a force or a power or an influence; He is a Person – 'another Comforter'. The teaching is, that because of the work of redemption that the Son accomplished when He was here in this world, when He returned to the glory the Father gave Him the Spirit to give to the Church. Therefore we can say that the Spirit is given by both the Father and the Son, and so we can describe Him as 'the Spirit of God' and the 'Spirit of Christ'. The same Person, the Holy Spirit, given by the Father, given by the Son.

In one of the verses I have quoted there is the term 'proceedeth'. We must not elaborate this, but those who are particularly interested in theology will know that that term was the cause of the first major division in the universal Church. The Church was originally one, but she divided into two sections, the Eastern Church and the Western Church. There is much in the newspapers in these days about conversations between the Church of Rome and the Eastern Orthodox Church (the Greek Orthodox Church and the Russian Orthodox Church). These two great institutions, the Roman Catholic or the Western Church, and the Orthodox or Eastern Church separated the one from the other over this very matter. The Eastern Church claimed that the Holy Spirit proceeds only from the Father, the Western Church insisted that He proceeds also from the Son. So the Western Church says, 'proceedeth from the Father and from the Son also'. Protestantism followed the Church of Rome in saying that the Holy Spirit proceeds from the Son as well as from the Father. But the important matter for us is that we see the purpose of His being described as 'the Spirit of God' one moment, and 'the Spirit of Christ' at another moment.

We now turn to another matter. What truth concerning the Christian does this verse bring before us? The first thing we are told is that the Christian is 'not in the flesh'. Though he has already said it many times before, the Apostle thinks it is necessary to repeat it again. The Christian is not 'in the flesh', he is no longer governed by fallen human nature. 'The flesh' means man and his nature as the result of the Fall, as the result of sin, man without any of the influence of the Holy Spirit upon him. But the Christian is no longer 'in the flesh'. The Apostle has told us this very plainly in chapter 7, verse 5: 'For when we were in the flesh, the motions of sins, which were by the law, did work in our members to bring forth fruit unto death.' But why is that fact important again at this particular point? Let us turn again to John's Gospel, chapter 14, which is the best commentary on these verses, and, in particular, to verse 17. Our Lord was promising the disciples that He would give them 'another Comforter', and He says: 'Even the Spirit of truth; whom the world cannot receive, because it seeth him not, neither knoweth him: but ye know him, for he dwelleth with you, and shall be in you.' The significant thing there is that 'the world cannot receive him'. While we are 'in the flesh' we cannot receive the Spirit of God. In verse 19 he repeats the statement: 'Yet a little while, and the world seeth me no more. But ye see me; because I live, ye shall live also'. Indeed, it continues in verse 21: 'He that hath my commandments, and keepeth them, he it is that loveth me: and he that loveth me shall be loved of my Father, and I will love him, and will manifest myself to him'. That does not mean a physical manifestation; it means a spiritual manifestation through the Spirit. That can only happen to those who do not belong 'to the world', because 'the world' is entirely antithetical to this. It does not understand, does not see, does not know. So the Apostle is very careful to remind us that we are not 'in the flesh', because if we are 'in the flesh' the Spirit cannot be in us. We are in another realm.

So from the negative – 'ye are not in the flesh' – let us go on to the positive – 'but ye are in the Spirit'. Does the Apostle simply mean that believers are in a certain mood? We often talk rather loosely in that way. In the Book of Revelation we read that John on a particular day, 'the Lord's day', was 'in the Spirit'. But that is not the meaning that we have here. We say that a man can be preaching badly, or he may be preaching 'in the Spirit', 'in demonstration of the Spirit and of power'. But again, that is not the meaning here. Being 'in the Spirit', as used here, describes our state or condition; it is the exact opposite of being 'in the flesh'. We can state it thus. When we say that a man is 'in the flesh' we are not referring to a Christian who has fallen into sin. However much a Christian may sin he never goes back to being 'in the flesh'. 'In the flesh' is a state or condition. The Christian is no longer in that state; whatever his case he does not go back to it. 'In the Spirit' also denotes a condition. It means that the Christian is in a new realm. He was living before in the realm of 'the flesh', he is now living in the realm of 'the Spirit'. The Spirit is controlling him and leading him; he is 'walking in the Spirit', he is 'walking after the Spirit'. This is the great and profound change that takes place at conversion. It is not that a man just changes his beliefs and no more. No, he was in the realm of the flesh, and he is now in the realm of the Spirit. He was dominated by the flesh before, and governed by it; as Paul puts it in Ephesians 2: 2: 'We walked after the course of this world.' But the Christian, though he is in the world, does not walk 'after the course of this world'; he is now in a realm which is governed and controlled and dominated by the Spirit, he is 'in the Spirit'. Or, to go back to chapter 5, verse 21, he comes under the 'reign of grace'. 'The reign of grace' is the reign of the Spirit, it is 'the law of the Spirit of life in Christ Jesus'. That is the realm to which Christians belong. I am no longer 'under the law of sin and death', but I am under this new law, 'the law of the Spirit of life in Christ Jesus'. So the Apostle says that the Christian is one who is not in the flesh; but, positively, he is 'in the Spirit'.

But he goes on to say something yet more marvellous and wonderful. Not only is the Christian 'in the Spirit' but the Spirit is 'in him'. 'But ye are not in the flesh, but in the Spirit, if so be that the Spirit of God dwell in you.' And then – another term which is synonymous with 'dwelling' – 'If any man have not the Spirit of Christ, he is none of his'. 'To dwell' means to live in a certain place, such as a house, so the Apostle is saying that the Spirit of God dwells in the Christian as a man lives or dwells in a certain place, home or house. That is true of every Christian. Consider another statement of the same truth by the Apostle. He says in 1 Corinthians 6: 19: 'What? know ye not that your body is the temple of the Holy Ghost which is in you, which you have of God, and ye are not your own?' The thought of 'dwelling' occurs here again. Similarly it is found at the end of the second chapter of the Epistle to the Ephesians: 'In whom all the building fitly framed together growth unto an holy temple in the Lord; in whom ye also are builded together for an *habitation* of God through the Spirit.' And again in 2 Timothy 1: 14: 'That good thing which was committed unto thee keep by the Holy Ghost which dwelleth in us.' Then notice that in verse 10 of this 8th chapter of Romans, the Apostle says, 'If Christ be in you'. The truth is still more explicit in John 14 verse 23: 'Jesus answered and said . . . , lf a man love me, he will keep my words: and my Father will love him, and we will come unto him, and make our abode with him.' 'Make our abode' means 'make our home' with him. This is one of the most amazing statements that we can ever encounter. What it means is that, because the Holy Spirit dwells in us, it is also true to say that the Lord Jesus Christ dwells in us, and it is also true to say that the Father dwells in us. That is what Ephesians 2: 22 means by 'an habitation of God through the Spirit', and that obviously has reference to all who are in the Church. Here, the Apostle puts it in the singular, and it is therefore true of all who are Christians.

This is the ultimate doctrine, it is the highest peak of the Christian doctrine of salvation. Can we understand it? The nearest I can get to an understanding of it is this. The key is provided in Ephesians 3, verses 16 and 17. The Apostle says that he is praying to God 'that he would grant you, according to the riches of his glory, to be strengthened with might by his Spirit in the inner man; that [in order that] Christ may dwell in your hearts by faith'. The Holy Spirit comes into us and there works this operation in our inner man, which is called 'strengthening'. For what purpose? In order that the Lord Jesus Christ may come and make His home in our hearts! As we are by nature we could not receive Him; we need to be prepared, we need to be strengthened. There is an analogy in what we sometimes see happening to old buildings; they are under-girded, pins are put into them to strengthen the corners or the walls. So we can paraphrase: 'That you may be strengthened by the might of the Spirit in the inner man, in order that you may be a residence into which Christ can come and live.' But Christ is 'in the Father', so when He comes, the Father comes – 'I in them, and thou in me'. This is the way to understand this most exalted teaching. The Spirit of God dwells in the believer, and because of the unity in the blessed Holy Trinity, the Father and the Son are also involved and dwell in us through the Spirit.

This baffles the mind, and even the imagination; but I am concerned to emphasize by constant repetition that this is what we are told is true of all who are Christians. Oh, the privilege of being a Christian! Can you imagine anything higher or greater! We are not only in Christ, Christ is in us. 'I live; yet not I, but Christ liveth in me, and the life which I now live in the flesh I live by the faith of the Son of God, who loved me, and gave himself for me' (Galatians 2: 20). There is nothing in God's universe comparable to being a Christian. The world may despise you, and may laugh at you. 'Look at what you are giving up, look what you are losing, look at what you are missing of life,' they say. But our Lord has told us that the world cannot receive the Spirit, that it does not know Him, that it does not see or understand these things; hence it thinks we are fools. It did not know Him; it rejected Him, it crucified Him. And the real tragedy about the case of the non-Christian is that he does not know anything about the privileges we enjoy. If you are a Christian, then the Spirit of God and of Christ, the blessed Holy Spirit, dwells, takes up His home in you; and because He is there, the Father and the Son dwell in you also. So we begin to understand the meaning of Revelation 3: 20. Christ is in you, but in another sense He may be standing at the door and knocking and saying in effect, 'Why do you not enjoy my society? I want to sup with you, and to have fellowship with you.' It is because He is already there that He speaks in that way. This is His way of appealing to us to realize that which is true of us, and possible for us.

Do we normally think of ourselves as Christians in this way? When the devil attacks you, and comes to you to depress you, when you are weary and tired, and when you are persecuted and everyone seems against you, and you begin to wonder whether there is much point in being a Christian, this is the answer. Just remember who is dwelling and residing within you; just remember who has made His home in you. When you are tempted to sin, remember that your body is 'the temple of the Holy Ghost'. We approach these matters so negatively, and for that reason we fail so frequently. People come to me and say, 'I am praying God to deliver me from this sin . . . ' But what they really need is to realize that the Holy Ghost is dwelling in their hearts. That is the way to meet the devil. We must not be negative, we must not merely pray to be delivered. Realize who is dwelling in your body, then you will find it difficult to abuse or misuse that body. Let us meditate more upon these things, let us contemplate them, let us spend time with them, let us remind ourselves of them daily. It is the real secret of assurance and of enjoying the Christian life, of being 'more than conquerors', and of being such that God can use us to attract others to a like knowledge and to a like privilege.

The next thing we are told about the Christian is that he belongs to Christ. 'If any man have not the Spirit of Christ, he is none of his.' If any man has not the Spirit of Christ, he does not belong to Christ. 'None of His'! it is the genitive of possession. If a man has not the Spirit of Christ, Christ does not own that man. Putting it positively, it means that if the Spirit of Christ is in a man, Christ owns him, he belongs to Him. The Apostle says that elsewhere. We have already seen it in 1 Corinthians 6: 19, where, having reminded them that their bodies are the temples of the Holy Ghost which is in them, Paul goes on to say: 'And you are not your own, you have been bought with a price.' The Apostle John also describes the Christian in this way. Christians, he tells us, are those who belong to Christ, the people whom God the Father has given Him. 'Thine they were, and thou gavest them me' (John 17: 6). He is their Advocate with the Father, He is pleading their cause, He is their Intercessor, He is their great High Priest before the Father, interceding on their behalf. All the benefits and the blessings we enjoy come to us because we belong to Him. The figure which we met in chapter 7 verse 4 of being married to Him, is really the same. The husband owns the wife in that sense. We are His people, we are His flock. All these terms and notions convey the same idea; and there is nothing more wonderful than the realization that we belong to the Lord Jesus Christ.

And because we belong to Him, nothing can ever 'pluck us out of His hand'. For the same reason the Apostle will be able to say at the end of this great chapter, 'I am persuaded, that neither death, nor life, nor angels, nor principalities, nor powers, nor things present, nor things to come, nor height, nor depth, nor any other creature, shall be able to separate us from the love of God, which is in Christ Jesus our Lord'. We belong to Him, and because we belong to Him, what He has begun to do in us He will go on doing, and it will never cease, it will never fail.

Let me apply all this in a practical manner. All we have been considering becomes a test which we can apply to ourselves. How am I to know whether the Spirit of Christ, the Spirit of God, is in me, and dwells in me? The ultimate test, that by which I know whether I am a Christian or not, lies here: 'If any man have not the Spirit of Christ, he is none of his.' If any man has the Spirit of Christ, he is His. Do I have the Spirit of Christ? Does the Spirit of Christ dwell in me? How can I know? This is a much deeper test than the test of profession. Of course, we have to make our profession, we have to say what we believe. And we know that there is such a thing as intellectual assent only. But, here, we have a much more thorough test. A man can say 'I have always believed'. But the question is, Is the Spirit of Christ in him? The test is not membership of a church, not that you have been born in a given country, not your profession of belief, not your intellectual assent to propositions, not your works and deeds. Is the Spirit of Christ in you?

But what does the Apostle actually mean? Here, unfortunately, it is essential once more that we should emphasize the negative. What is it to have the Spirit of Christ? Some say that to have the Spirit of Christ is to be a Christ-like person. 'Catching the Spirit of Christ' is a phrase often used. People say that we need to 'catch' the Spirit of Christ. In other words you read the New Testament and what it says about Him, and so you 'catch' His

Spirit. They tell us that as we read the biography of a great man we should always try to catch his spirit. Children are told about great men, heroes in their day, and the hope is that they will 'catch the spirit' of such men. The notion is that you somehow take hold of it or imbibe it, as it were. That means that you lay hold of a hero's views, you hold to his teaching, and then you proceed to imitate his example, and you try to live like him. And when Christ is the hero, if you do that, they say, then you have got the Spirit of Christ in you.

The notion of 'having the Spirit of Christ' leads to some very strange and curious results. I am increasingly convinced that this is one of the greatest battles we have to fight for the Christian faith at this present time, for we are living in an age when people are being lauded and praised as Christians who themselves deny that they are Christians. I am sorry to mention names, but as they are mentioned so frequently in the newspapers and in religious papers and journals, I must do so. I have often heard people using this very phrase, 'having the Spirit of Christ', to prove that Gandhi, the Indian leader was a Christian. They say, 'Look at the man's life. He lived a life of poverty, he forsook the world and pleasure, he gave himself to helping poor people, he mixed with them, he ate with them, he dressed like them, and he denounced force and war. He was a pacifist, he believed in passive resistance. They say 'That is the Spirit of Christ, Gandhi lived a most Christ-like life', and some would even claim that he was the finest Christian of the twentieth century. But Mr Gandhi, as an honest man, openly rejected Christianity. He said that he was not a Christian but that he followed the Hindu religion. Yet foolish people, calling themselves Christians, take up this phrase 'having the Spirit of Christ', and maintain that Gandhi was an exceptionally fine Christian. 'What does it matter,' they say, 'that he did not believe your doctrine? Look at his life.'

But Gandhi is not the only one about whom that is said. I read recently in a religious newspaper a reference to the late Professor Gilbert Murray of Oxford. The heading to the article was 'Saint Gilbert'! The writer said that he had no doubt but that Professor Gilbert Murray was a Christian. Murray was a Professor of Classics, a great humanist, and a very good man, a noble type of man. You can use all such adjectives and I would yield assent to them all until you begin to call him 'Saint' and to describe him as a

Christian. I must add that the foolish man who wrote the article to which I refer, while saying that Gilbert Murray lived a life which approximated to the desiderata of sainthood or saintliness, also felt compelled to say, 'Actually, of course, I know that Gilbert Murray was a Rationalistic Agnostic'. Even so, he called him a saint on the ground that though he was such a great man he was a humble man, a most kind, a self-abnegating man. Look also, he wrote, at the good works he did, how he gave himself to working for the League of Nations Union and other causes. 'Ah yes', such persons say, 'he was actually a Rationalistic Agnostic; he said openly and plainly that he did not believe in God, he did not believe in Christ as the Son of God, he did not believe in the miraculous and the supernatural, but don't you see the Spirit of Christ in his life?'

Such is the popular notion. But that is in no sense what the Apostle means here; indeed, it is almost the exact opposite of what he means. It does not mean that you 'catch' the Spirit of Christ. Certain other men who deny some of the central tenets of the Christian faith, for example, Dr Albert Schweitzer, are nevertheless described as 'the greatest Christians of this twentieth century'. Why? In Schweitzer's case, because he gave up a great career and went to live in a tropical forest and built a hospital, and did most noble and charitable works. What matters it that he denies the doctrine? Look at him, he is imitating Christ; it is the Spirit of Christ that has led him to do all! But that is sheer denial of the Apostle Paul's teaching.

The Apostle's teaching does not mean 'catching the Spirit of Christ'; it does not mean living what is called this 'Christ-like life'. It means that the Spirit of Christ dwells in you, and the Spirit of Christ only dwells in those who no longer belong to the flesh and the world, but who have been regenerated by the Spirit, and who, because of re-birth, believe in the Lord Jesus Christ as the Son of God, and in His atoning death and in the whole of the apostolic message. The Spirit who dwells in the Christian has been sent, according to the promise of the Lord Himself, to glorify the Lord Jesus Christ. 'He shall not speak of himself, he shall glorify me.' The first thing the Spirit does is to glorify the Son of God, in His Person and His work. Therefore if a man does not believe in the Person of the Son, and in His work of atonement, and in all His other work, he has not got the Spirit of Christ in him. He may be a very nice man, he may be a very good-natured man, he may be a very good man, he may do very many good works; but he has not got the Spirit of Christ in him. For if he has the Spirit of Christ in him he worships the Lord Jesus Christ as God; he realizes that what saves him is that Christ died, being made a 'propitiation' for his sins, as Paul has already said in chapter 3, verses 25 and 26 of this epistle.

May God deliver us from this snare of regarding good, noble, nice, tender-hearted men, as men who necessarily 'have the Spirit of Christ'. To have the Spirit of Christ means that the Holy Spirit is dwelling in you, that you are no longer 'in the flesh' but 'in the Spirit', that you are born again, a new man, a new creation. The ultimate test is your relationship to, your view of, your attitude toward the Son of God, the Lord Jesus Christ.

Six

*

And if Christ be in you, the body is dead because of sin; but the spirit is life because of righteousness.

But if the Spirit of him that raised up Jesus from the dead dwell in you, he that raised up Christ from the dead shall also quicken your mortal bodies by his Spirit that dwelleth in you.

Romans 8: 10, 11

A better reading of these two verses affects the first words in both. Instead of 'And if' in verse 10, it is better to read 'But if' – 'But if Christ be in you'. Then instead of 'But' at the beginning of verse 11 it is better to put 'And' – 'And if the Spirit of him'. That carries forward the movement of thought; and there is no disjunction.

These two verses amplify the definition of the Christian still further. The Apostle has already contrasted him with the unbeliever and given us his positive characteristics. In verses 10 and 11, he sums up all that he has said, and in the light of it he proceeds to give us a clear definition and description of the state and the condition of the Christian man. As I have said, the first words are antithetical to what he has said in verse 9: 'If any man have not the Spirit of Christ, he is none of his. *But* if the Spirit be in you . . .' If a man is a Christian, then Christ is in him. He is defined as a man in whom Christ dwells. I remind you once more that the Apostle is describing all Christians, every Christian. I agree that there are differences amongst Christians. You can be a young Christian, 'a babe in Christ'; you can be a young man in Christ; you can be an old man in Christ. You can be, as it were, a poor sort of Christian, you can be a better type of Christian, you can be a good Christian. But, here, the Apostle reminds us of what is basically true of all Christians.

[66]

What then is true of all of us as Christians? And here Paul makes a most extraordinary and crucial statement. It is, that 'the body is dead because of sin, but the Spirit is life because of righteousness'. The best way to approach this statement is to remind ourselves of the Apostle's ultimate object in the whole of the chapter, namely, to teach the doctrine of assurance. His aim is to show us that, because we are no longer under the reign of sin, but under the reign of grace, therefore our final salvation is certain, sure, and guaranteed; nothing can cancel it. 'There is therefore now no condemnation to them which are in Christ Jesus.' Paul is working out that proposition. He says the Spirit of God and of Christ is in the Christian. Because of that he 'minds' the 'things of the Spirit', not 'the things of the flesh'. In verses 10 and 11 he puts the truth in a different and a most striking way. In verse 10 he tells us what is true of us now, our present position, namely, that 'the body is dead because of sin, but the Spirit is life because of righteousness'. Our future, our ultimate position, is explained in verse 11: 'If the Spirit of him that raised up Jesus from the dead dwell in you' – which is just another way of saying, 'If Christ be in you' – 'then he that raised up Christ from the dead shall also quicken your mortal bodies by his Spirit that dwelleth in you'. That is the future, the ultimate, the grand consummation!

We must now address ourselves particularly to the 10th verse, in which Paul reminds us of what is true of us now in this world. 'If Christ be in you on the one hand' – the Authorized Version does not bring that out as it should; it just says, 'If Christ be in you, the body is dead because of sin'; but there are words in the Greek which are not represented there, and which mean 'on the one hand'. It is important that this phrase should be included. 'If Christ be in you on the one hand, the body is dead because of sin; on the other hand, the Spirit is life because of righteousness'. That is the true translation of this verse. The Apostle is drawing a contrast.

'On the one hand', the Apostle says, 'the body is dead because of sin'. This is a most important statement theologically and from the whole standpoint of doctrine. I approach the exposition of this verse with unusual pleasure because it seems to me that this is a verse that tests the exposition we have been giving from verse 1 in chapter 5 and especially from verse 12 of chapter 5 onwards. It is a crucial verse; it tests whether what we were saying about chapters 6 and 7 was right or wrong.

'The body', he says. What does 'the body' mean? The actual word the Apostle used is the word that is used for our physical body, our physical frame. It is not the word he uses when he is describing the 'flesh'. Up to this point he has been talking about the 'flesh', which, as I was careful to point out, means human nature in a fallen state apart from the influence of the Holy Spirit. But here he is not talking about the flesh, he is literally talking about our bodies, as you and I normally talk about our bodies, flesh and blood and bones, and all the working, the organization of the body. It includes our capacity to reason and to think, for that is a function of the brain. I emphasize this because some interpret the term as meaning 'flesh', in the interests of their particular doctrine of sanctification. But the Apostle, who has been using the word 'flesh', suddenly changes his word and uses the word 'body'. He is not referring to corrupt human nature, but to our actual physical frame; and he opposes this – to make it still more certain – to the spirit. Man is body, mind (or soul) and spirit. We cannot now look into the distinction between soul and spirit. The soul can be regarded from two aspects – the spiritual side which links it with God, and the earthly side which links it with man, and life in this world. Now the body is contrasted here with that spiritual side or aspect. I emphasize this because we really must not play with the words of the Scriptures in the interests of our theories. The whole argument here is about the physical body. Consider the next verse: 'But if the Spirit of him that raised up Jesus from the dead.' Paul is there talking about the raising of the body of Jesus from the dead. He then makes it still more certain by saying: 'He that raised up Christ from the dead shall also quicken your mortal bodies' (He does not say 'flesh'). 'Your mortal bodies'! We take this, as the vast majority of commentators have done, to mean the actual physical body.

The Apostle says that 'the body is dead'. Here, again, in the interests of a theory there are those who say that it means, 'The body has been put to death', or 'the body has been mortified'. But it is to do violence to language to speak in this way; for the Apostle does not say that the body has been mortified, but that 'the body dead', and the translators rightly supply the little word 'is' – 'the body is dead'. The Apostle is not saying that because a man has become a Christian he has mortified the deeds of the body. When we come to verse 13 we shall find that the Apostle exhorts us to do just that – 'If ye through the Spirit do mortify the deeds of the body' – but he is not saying in verse 10 that we have done so. Instead he is saying that something is true of your body as you are now, as it is now – 'the body is dead'.

In the same way we must clearly observe that the Apostle does not say 'If Christ be in you, then the body will die, or will become dead, or shall die'. He says 'the body is dead' now. He is talking about what is true of us now, not of something that is going to happen to us. We shall find the key to the problem if we go back again to chapter 6 where Paul has really been saying the same thing. My whole exposition of this statement is to the effect that what we have here is a summing up in one verse of what was said in many verses in chapter 6: In other words, I repeat that there is nothing new in this eighth chapter so far. Go back to the twelfth verse of chapter 6, 'Let not sin therefore reign in your mortal body'. It is a 'mortal body', a dying body, a corrupt body. He says in chapter 6, verse 11: 'Reckon ye yourselves also to be dead indeed unto sin, but alive unto God through Jesus Christ our Lord.' Then 'Let not sin therefore reign in your mortal body'. It is precisely the same idea here in chapter 8. It means that the seed of death is in our bodies. The body is, as it were, the seat of death; there is a principle of decay and of death in the bodies of all of us, and the process of decay is increasing and growing. Ever since the Fall, the moment we enter into this world and begin to live we also begin to die. Your first breath is one of the last you will ever take! Such is the position of man as the result of the Fall; the principle of decay, leading to death, is in every one of us. As the result of the Fall the body of man is in a state of humiliation, weakness and death. Man's body is not what it was when God created him at the beginning when it was full of life and vigour. Ever since the Fall we are born with the seeds of illness, weakness, decay and death in us. The moment we are born we are beginning to die! The process of decay becomes obvious after a certain age; by the age of twenty-five we have all developed as much as we ever shall develop, and from then on the elements of decay become more and more obvious.

And not only is all this true of us, but the body is dead also in a moral sense. The body is the instrument that sin most readily

[69]

uses; it is, as it were, the seat of sin. The body gives sin its chance and its opportunity, and it remains there in the body. As we have seen in chapter 7, it tends to work through the passions and the desires which are 'inflamed' by the law. In other words, the body is the battleground in our struggle against sin, it is the main cause of pain in the believer in every sense, physical, moral, and spiritual. 'The body is dead.' It is a kind of 'dead weight'; it has a veritable 'law of sin' in its members, as we also saw in chapter 7. A man's body constitutes his greatest problem in this world. The Apostle sums up that fact in the statement that 'the body is dead'.

'The body is dead because of sin.' Sin is the culprit. The Apostle has already told us in chapter 5, verse 12: 'Wherefore, as by one man sin entered into the world, and death by sin; and so death passed upon all men, for that all have sinned.' These words tell us how and when sin came in. And sin, as we have seen repeatedly, is something that affects the whole of man. Adam's sin brought in death. When he sinned the whole of him died; he experienced an immediate spiritual death; and the seed of physical death was also implanted in him at the same time. So it is because of sin that the body is dead. If man had not sinned the body would not be dead, and man would not have died; his body was made perfect and it would have continued to grow and to develop until it was glorified. There was no decay in man's original body; but when sin came in, this element of death and decay, corruption and putrefaction came in. In 1 Corinthians 15 the Apostle works this out at length. It is by that first man that death came in; and therefore these bodies of ours are corrupt – 'sown in corruption' and mortal.

But, thank God, we can now look at the other side; for the fact that the body is dead is not the whole truth about the Christian. In contrast with death, Paul tells us that 'the spirit is life because of righteousness'. In the Authorized Version the 'spirit' is given a capital S, indicating that it means the Holy Spirit. But with the great majority of commentators I believe that this is a mistake, for it seems to me to vitiate the contrast that the Apostle is drawing. He is describing a Christian man; and he says 'On the one hand the body of this man is dead, but on the other hand his spirit is life'. The contrast is between body and spirit. To talk about 'the body' on the one hand, and 'the Holy Spirit' on the other is not a contrast, for the Holy Spirit is not a part of man though He dwells in the man; but the Apostle is giving us an analysis of a man. He does not say that 'the Holy Spirit dwells in him', but he says, 'the spirit is life because of righteousness'. Not only so, but if the Apostle really means the Holy Spirit, then, it seems to me, there is no complete statement here about the Christian man. All he would be saying is that because a man is a Christian, though his body is still dead because of sin, the Holy Spirit is in him, and because the Holy Spirit is in him, as the next verse says, he is going to be resurrected and glorified. But that seems to leave man, as he is now, incompletely described. All Paul would be saying is, Well, the Holy Spirit is in him. But I want to know more about the man. What is his condition now? what is he like?

So I suggest that here the Apostle means, not the Holy Spirit, but 'the spirit of man', this other part of man. Man, as I have explained, is body and spirit, or body and soul. Having told us what is true of the body in the Christian, Paul now tells us about the other side; and he says that this is 'life'. Again we must be careful to observe that he does not say 'shall have life'. He is not referring to the future, he is describing the state of the Christian man as he is in this world. He means that the Christian is alive. As 'dead' means 'having the seed of death', 'life' means 'having the seed of life'. The seed of life is in the Christian man. In other words his spirit has been made alive by the Spirit of Christ; that is to say, the Christian man is regenerate. Hence we must reject the idea that the phrase 'the spirit is life' refers to the Holy Spirit, for the truth about the Christian is not simply that the Holy Spirit dwells in him. He has been 'born again', there is 'a seed of God' in him (1 John 3: 9); he is 'a partaker of the divine nature' (2 Peter 1: 4). He is a man who has received life anew. Christianity, as Henry Scougal reminds us in the title of his famous book, is 'The life of God in the soul of man'. But if we interpret 'the spirit is life' to mean the Holy Spirit all this has to be left out. The truth is that here and now the Christian is a man who has new life; he is born again, born from above, 'his seed remaineth in him', the seed of God that was put into him at his regeneration.

In other words, the Apostle is saying again what he has said many times before. Consider chapter 6, verse 2. He has just asked the question (verse 1) 'Shall we continue in sin, that grace may abound?' He answers, 'God forbid. How shall we that are dead to sin, live any longer therein?' We are 'dead to sin', but that means that we are alive. He says that explicitly in verse 4: 'Therefore we are buried with him by baptism into death: that like as Christ was raised up from the dead by the glory of the Father, even so we also should walk in newness of life.' Verse 6: 'Knowing this, that our old man is crucified with him.' The 'old man' is dead, he has been crucified. The Christian has a new man in him. If you take this word 'spirit' as the Holy Spirit there is no mention of the new man at all. But the Apostle is talking about the new man. His spirit is alive, whereas it was dead before. The spirit of man died as the result of the Fall; but in the Christian it has been made alive again. There is no vacuum in man's life. The 'old man' is dead, the 'new man' is alive. Then in verse 11 in chapter 6 Paul puts it in an exhortation: 'Likewise reckon ye also yourselves to be dead indeed unto sin.' What then? 'And remember that the Holy Spirit is in you'? No, he does not say that, but 'Likewise reckon ye also yourselves to be dead indeed unto sin, but alive unto God'. The same thing, exactly! The Christian is 'alive unto God'. Then take chapter 6 verse 13: 'Neither yield ye your members as instruments of unrighteousness unto sin: but yield yourselves unto God, as those that are alive from the dead'. It is not merely that the Spirit is in him, the man himself is alive from the dead. Then in verse 23 of that chapter: 'The wages of sin is death; but the gift of God' – which we have already received – 'is eternal life'. If you are a Christian you have it now; you are not waiting for it. Your comfort and consolation is not merely that the Spirit of God is in you, but that you have already received eternal life. 'I am come that they might have life, and that they might have it more abundantly.' And so in chapter 8 verse 2 Paul tells us: 'The law of the Spirit of life in Christ Jesus hath made me free from the law of sin and death.'

Surely the expression 'the spirit is life' means that it is the spirit of man himself which has been regenerated. Consider what the Apostle says in Ephesians 2:1: 'You hath he quickened, who were dead in trespasses and sins.' Quickening means the imparting of life. So 'the spirit is life' means that life has been put into the spirit of man; he was dead before, and being dead he did not 'mind' the things of the Spirit, but only the things of the flesh. That is why he was 'at enmity against God and not subject to the law of God'; he was spiritually dead. But he is alive now, 'quick-ened', new life has been put into him, a new principle of life and of vigour. In Colossians 3 : 1 it is still clearer, and the statement there is enough in itself, I would have thought, to dismiss the notion that the Apostle is referring here to the Holy Spirit: 'If ye then be risen with Christ' – and 'if' means 'because you are' – 'seek those things which are above, where Christ sitteth on the right hand of God. Set your affection on things above, not on things on the earth'. Why do that? For this reason, 'For ye are dead, and your life is hid with Christ in God'. 'Your life.' Not the life of the Spirit only, *your* life. We were dead, but we are now alive, our spirits are alive; and we must not allow anything to rob us of that glorious statement.

This is, of course, just another way of saying what our Lord Himself has said once and for ever in John 5 : 24: 'Verily, verily, I say unto you, he that heareth my word, and believeth on him that sent me, hath everlasting life.' He is not expecting to receive it at some future date; he has it. The man 'that heareth my word, and believeth on him that sent me' is not simply a man that has the Holy Spirit in him; that is true, but there is more, 'he hath everlasting life, and shall not come into condemnation; but is passed from death unto life'. Or take John 11 : 25 and 26: 'I am the resurrection, and the life: he that believeth in me, though he were dead, yet shall he live: and whosoever liveth and believeth in me shall never die.' The Christian is alive; 'the spirit is life', and because his spirit is alive the Christian 'shall never die'. His body will die, but he will never die. That is the distinction. The body is dead, and the body will die physically, because it has this death principle in it already; but not so the spirit. See the same truth again in Revelation 20: 6: 'Blessed and holy is he that hath part in the first resurrection: on such the second death hath no power'. The man who has part in the first resurrection is the man who has been raised from death to life spiritually, in his spirit; on him the second death shall not come. But it will come on all others. There is no second death for the man who has been regenerated. For all these reasons, therefore, we cannot accept this word 'spirit' in verse 10 as a reference to the Holy Spirit. It is a reference to the spirit of man.

A Christian's 'body is dead, because of sin', but 'his spirit is life because of righteousness', that is, 'on account of righteousness'.

In explanation of the term 'righteousness' as used here, only one answer is possible; it assuredly means, 'the righteousness of God in Jesus Christ' which has been given the man. At this point I regret to have to disagree with Charles Hodge who makes this 'righteousness' entirely subjective. His interpretation, it seems to me, makes the Apostle say that because of a man's subjective righteousness he is alive in his spirit, which means that his righteousness is the ground of his living, which is a denial of the doctrine of justification by faith only. The Apostle surely refers to 'the righteousness of God in Jesus Christ', 'Christ's righteousness' which is imputed to us, and not only 'imputed' but also 'imparted'. 'God sending his own Son in the likeness of sinful flesh, and for sin, hath condemned sin in the flesh.' Why? 'That the righteousness of the law might be fulfilled in us.' Our verse 10 therefore means the righteousness of Christ which is imputed to us, put to our account; but more, it is also put into us, imparted to us.

The Apostle has said this many times in chapter 5. In the 17th verse of that chapter he says: 'For if by one man's offence death reigned by one, much more they which receive abundance of grace and of the gift of righteousness shall reign in life by one, Jesus Christ.' And again in verse 18: 'Therefore as by the offence of one judgment came upon all men to condemnation; even so by the righteousness of one' – that is Jesus Christ – 'the free gift came upon all men unto justification of life'. In verse 19 also: 'For as by one man's disobedience many were made sinners, so by the obedience of one shall many be made righteous.' And at the end of verse 21: 'That as sin hath reigned unto death, even so might grace reign through righteousness unto eternal life by Jesus Christ our Lord.' The reference is not to our subjective righteousness, but to the righteousness of Christ imputed to us in justification, imparted to us in sanctification.

What does all this mean? Sin and the Fall led to the death of man in every respect; he died physically, in the body; death entered his body as well as his soul and spirit. It was a complete, a total death. Man is 'dead in trespasses and sins'; he is dead in every respect. That is what sin did; and that is what man has inherited from Adam. That is the whole argument of Romans 5, verses 12 to 21. That is what the first man did for us. But the 'Second Man' has come to bring salvation, and salvation likewise is complete and entire. Why did Christ come? 1 John 3: 8 tells us that He came to 'undo', to 'cancel' the works of the devil. We need to be delivered from the death that has affected spirit, soul and body; and Christ has come to give us that salvation.

Our present position, according to what Paul says here in Romans 8: 10, is that as yet our salvation is partial. As regards my spirit I am saved, as saved as I ever shall be. I have been 'quickened with Christ', I have been 'raised with him', I am 'seated in the heavenly places in Christ', my spirit at this moment is alive 'in Christ Jesus'. I have been delivered from sin, from death, and the law. That is what he argued at length in chapter 6: 'How shall we that are dead to sin live any longer therein?' 'Know ye not that your old man was crucified?' He is dead, he has gone, he will never come back. I am alive. I myself am alive as much as I ever will be. I am 'alive unto God', I am 'risen with Christ'. I have finished with the law, I have finished with death. That is true of me, speaking of myself as a spirit, the spiritual part of myself. But that is not true of my body. My body is still 'dead because of sin'; I have not finished with sin in my body. I am not teaching that the body is essentially sinful in and of itself as a false dualism does. That is not what our verse teaches. It means, as I have said, that the body is still the seat of sin, that sin remains in the body. As regards my spirit I myself have been delivered from it; I am 'dead to sin'. These are the Apostle's statements.

In other words what Paul is saying in this tenth verse is what we saw so clearly in expounding chapter 6 verses 1 to 14, and especially verses 11 to 14. He says: 'Reckon yourselves' – realize, grasp, understand. He does not say, Persuade yourselves of something that is not true in order to overcome sin. He says, Realize what is true about you yourself, that you are dead indeed unto sin, and that you, yourself, are alive unto God through Jesus Christ. And because of that he says: 'Let not sin therefore reign in your mortal body.' It cannot reign in you because of what is true of you; but it seeks to reign in your mortal body. It is there, lurking, and always looking for an opportunity for entering into you. Do not allow it to do so. Why? Because 'you are dead to sin, and alive unto God', because you have finished with it, because you are in this other realm. You are alive in spirit, so do not allow sin to reign in that body of yours. You are going to be in that body until you die, but do not allow sin to reign there. Keep it under, 'mortify' it, as he is going on to tell us in verses 12 and 13. Such, he says, is the position of the Christian man. 'Let not sin therefore reign in your mortal body, that ye should obey it in the lusts thereof. Neither yield ye your members as instruments of unrighteousness unto sin: but yield yourselves unto God, as those that are alive from the dead, and your members as instruments of righteousness unto God. For sin shall not have dominion over you.' Why? 'Because you are not under the law, but under grace.'

The Christian, in spirit, is saved absolutely; but not in body. Sin remains in the body and leads to the principle of decay and death. The result of this is what the Apostle will tell us very plainly when we proceed to consider verses 22 and 23 of this chapter. He says: 'The whole creation groaneth and travaileth in pain together until now. And not only they, but ourselves also, which have the firstfruits of the Spirit, even we ourselves groan within ourselves, waiting for the adoption, to wit, the redemption of our body'. The body is not redeemed yet; it will be, but not yet. At the moment the body is 'dead because of sin', but its deliverance is coming. This is the characteristic teaching of the Apostle.

The 4th chapter of the Second Epistle to the Corinthians verses 7–18 is in many ways the finest commentary we have on Romans 8: 10, and especially verse 11: 'We which live are alway delivered unto death for Jesus' sake, that the life also of Jesus might be made manifest in our mortal flesh.' And verse 16 surely refutes finally the idea that 'spirit' in this 10th verse means 'the Holy Spirit': 'For which cause we faint not; but though out outward man perish, yet the inward man is renewed day by day.' My outward man is perishing; I get older every day; I lose something of my energy and strength and power; sickness and illness and disease come. Yet 'the inward man . . .' But if you interpret the word 'spirit' in Romans 8: 10 as meaning the Holy Spirit, where is your 'inward man'? 'The inward man is renewed day by day'. 'The spirit is life' is synonymous with 'the inward man'. Then in the first verses of chapter 5 of 2 Corinthians, the Apostle says: 'We know that if our earthly house of this tabernacle were dissolved, we have a building of God, an house not made with hands, eternal in the heavens. For in this we groan, earnestly desiring to be clothed upon with our house which is from heaven: if so be that being clothed we shall not be found naked.' Here again he is referring to this inward man, the regenerate man, 'this spirit that is life'. We who are alive shall not be naked, we shall have another garment to clothe our spirits. He works out that in the following verses: 'For we that are in this tabernacle do groan, being burdened: not for that we would be unclothed' – not that we would be disembodied spirits – 'but clothed upon, that mortality might be swallowed up of life'. Therefore he says, 'We walk by faith, not by sight', 'knowing that, while we are at home in the body, we are absent from the Lord'. 'We are confident, and willing rather to be absent from the body, and to be present with the Lord.'

We can sum it up in this way: it is because this is true that the Christian still has to 'watch and pray', it is for this reason that he has to 'put on the whole armour of God'. He himself is saved, but sin is waiting for its opportunity in his body. Therefore he has to keep on fighting against it, he has to 'mortify' his flesh, he has to 'keep under' his body, as the Apostle says in 1 Corinthians 9: 27. Sin cannot get him back to the realm of death again; but it can cause him great trouble. It is because the 'body' is still dead, on account of sin, that the Christian has to go on doing these various things; yet not in a hopeless manner. He does them full of confidence and assurance because he knows that in his spirit he is alive. He is certain of this. He has received the gift of life eternal, his 'spirit is life because of righteousness'. He knows that, whereas he himself is saved, while he is still in this world in the flesh he will have this fight to wage, but he knows also, as Paul is going to tell us in verse 11, that the fight will come to an end. The day will come when either we shall be raised from the dead and our bodies glorified, or, if we are still on earth when Christ comes again, 'we shall be changed in a moment, in the twinkling of an eye', and our bodies will be glorified.

Such is the position of the Christian now. 'If Christ be in you, the body is dead because of sin', but, thank God, 'the spirit is life because of righteousness'. This surely substantiates our interpretation of Romans 7: 24. A man who knows that his 'spirit is life' will never say, 'O wretched man that I am, who shall deliver me?' The Christian knows that he has been delivered, he knows that sin is still there trying to get a foothold in his body again, and drag him down. He knows it can never finally defeat him, so he does not cry, 'O wretched man that I am'. He says, rather,

[77]

'The body is dead, it is frail, it is weak, it is decaying. I am subject to tiredness and weariness and accident and illness and all these things that make life a burden to me as I get older and older. The body is dead, and I have always to fight sin because it tries to find entrance at that point. That is where it tries to get a seat, a fulcrum, its opportunity. I have this constant war to wage against sin there, but I am not fighting in a spirit of despair, because I know that my "spirit is life because of righteousness".' Romans 7: 24 is not a description of the Christian at his best; it is a description of a man 'under the law' who is under conviction of sin as the result of the operation of the Holy Spirit, but who does not yet realize what Christ has done for him. The Christian position is, 'The body is dead because of sin, but the spirit is life because of righteousness'. Though still in the body which is 'dead because of sin', I am 'dead indeed unto sin, but alive unto God through Jesus Christ our Lord'.

Seven

*

But if the Spirit of him that raised up Jesus from the dead dwell in you, he that raised up Christ from the dead shall also quicken your mortal bodies by his Spirit that dwelleth in you. Romans 8: 11

As we come to consider this verse we should bear in mind the setting and the context, for the Apostle is pursuing an argument which he began earlier. The object of the entire chapter is to give us assurance and certainty about our final, complete salvation. 'There is therefore now no condemnation to them that are in Christ Jesus.' That is the opening statement and the last is, 'In all these things we are more than conquerors through him that loved us. For I am persuaded that neither death, nor life, nor angels, nor principalities, nor powers, nor things present, nor things to come, nor height, nor depth, nor any other creature, shall be able to separate us from the love of God which is in Christ Jesus our Lord.' That is the conclusion; but Paul has been moving on to it step by step, stage by stage, from the very beginning. We have seen that in verse 10 the Apostle gives a definition of the Christian, a picture of the Christian, as he now is in this world and in this life. But he does not leave it at that; he throws his mind into the future, and in verse 11 we have an account of what is going to happen to us, what we shall yet be. As Christians we should never be troubled about our salvation. The fact that we are conscious of sin within, the fact that we are conscious of the strength of temptation, should not make us query our salvation. We are saved; but there is this kind of 'rearguard action', that we have to go on fighting with the sin that is left in the body. The Christian is already saved in the spirit, but sin remains in the body. The body is not yet saved.

[79]

But that is not the whole story; so we go on to verse 11: 'But if the Spirit of him that raised up Jesus from the dead dwell in you, he that raised up Christ from the dead shall also quicken your mortal bodies by his Spirit that dwelleth in you.' As we search into the meaning of this verse we are again compelled to start with two negatives, because so many misinterpret it. There are those who say that the Apostle is teaching here a kind of 'moral resurrection unto a new life'. Even the mighty John Calvin said that! He said that we are being told here of 'The continued working of the Spirit by which He gradually mortifies the relics of the flesh and renews in us a heavenly life', a kind of moral resurrection. I reject that interpretation for the reason that, if such be the meaning, then the Apostle is repeating himself unnecessarily. He has already said what Calvin says in verses 5 to 8 of this chapter. Certainly there is a moral resurrection. That is also the meaning of the words, 'the spirit is life' in verse 10. So Paul would merely be saying it all over again, without adding to his statement. But obviously the way in which he introduces it shows clearly that it is an addition to what has already been stated.

Another and a stronger reason for rejecting Calvin's interpretation is that, if it means just that, there is no real relevance in the statement 'he that raised up Christ from the dead'. The Apostle's argument is that what God has done to Christ He is going to do to us. Now there was no 'moral resurrection' in the case of the Lord Jesus Christ, because there was never any moral death. But what Paul is here referring to is something that had happened to the Son of God. Therefore it cannot have reference to any kind of 'moral resurrection'. Not only so, but I reject the interpretation for this further reason also, that it seems to miss the whole point of what the Apostle was setting out to say just here. It misses the climax to which he is leading us after what he has been saying in verse 10. So I reject the notion that we have here a description of moral resurrection.

Then there is another negative. The friends who believe in 'faith healing' are very fond of this verse, because they feel that it is a perfect statement of their doctrine. 'If the Spirit of him that raised up Jesus from the dead dwell in you' – that is, if you are a Christian, and therefore saved – they say, it then follows that 'he that raised up Christ from the dead shall also quicken your mortal bodies' – in other words, heal your frail bodies and give you perfect health – 'by his Spirit that dwelleth in you'. But I reject this interpretation also, and for the following reasons: To start with, it is entirely foreign to the whole context. Paul is not here concerned in any way with the problem of ill-health, and to introduce it would nullify the connection between verse 10 and verse 11. There, categorically, in verse 10, he has said that 'the body is dead', and remains dead, 'because of sin'. So he cannot be saying in verse 11 that 'by the Spirit the body can be delivered from all sickness', for he tells us that it is not delivered from it. While we are in this world the body remains 'dead because of sin'; so this second interpretation breaks the connection between the two verses. And, further, what about the statement concerning our Lord – 'If he that raised up Christ from the dead'? This is a reference to what actually happened to our Lord in the resurrection, and has nothing to do with sickness or illness. But it does have reference to the fact that He had died and that His body was buried in a grave and was then raised.

Indeed, it seems clear that there is no ground for the 'bodily healing' interpretation of this verse, except the desire to clutch at any verse that seems superficially capable of being pressed into such a meaning. I would indeed argue that this verse really militates against such teaching, which includes the claim that 'healing is in the atonement'. The atonement of Christ, say the faith healers, covers all the evil effects and consequences of sin. Not only my guilt and the punishment I deserved; it goes beyond that, and urges that all that the body has suffered as the result of sin is dealt with in the atonement. So a Christian should never be sick, should never be in ill-health; he should always enjoy perfect health, he should never die from any disease whatsoever. But the argument is incomplete. If you argue that all the effects of sin are dealt with directly by the atonement, then you should also say that a Christian should never die, because physical death is one of the consequences of the Fall and of sin. To be logical therefore he must say that a Christian is exempt from physical death. In an ultimate sense, as I intend to show, everything is in the atonement; but what the Apostle is saying here is that, while we are in this world and in this life, its benefits are only partial. We are already given all in the realm of the spirit –

'the spirit is life, because of righteousness' – but in respect of the body there is no complete deliverance here, that is yet to come. So we are left not only with disease, but also with death; it is in a 'mortal' body we live.

So we reject both those suggestions with regard to the interpretation of this verse and come now to our positive exposition. I have already hinted at it. The Apostle at this point is teaching the resurrection and the glorification of our bodies. 'But if the Spirit of him that raised up Jesus from the dead dwell in you, he that raised up Christ from the dead shall also quicken your mortal bodies by his Spirit that dwelleth in you.' Why do I argue that it must mean this?

I argue for this as the true meaning, firstly, because the very phrase, I say again, about the Lord being raised from the dead demands it. We have here a clear and unmistakable and indisputable reference to the physical resurrection of the Lord Jesus Christ in the body from the grave. That is the key to it all. It is what the Apostle is talking about. Notice that he states the fact twice, as if to make sure that we could not misunderstand it. 'If the Spirit of him that raised up Jesus from the dead dwell in you, he that raised up Christ from the dead shall also . . .' Truly a two-fold statement of the same overwhelming fact!

But, secondly, let us note that the two phrases about the Spirit dwelling in us clearly and obviously point to our physical bodies. 'If the Spirit of him that raised up Jesus from the dead dwell in you.' Then again, 'and shall quicken your mortal bodies by his Spirit that dwelleth in you'. The Spirit dwells in our bodies, in our actual physical bodies. The Apostle says so quite explicitly in 1 Corinthians 6: 19: 'Know ye not that your body is the temple of the Holy Ghost which is in you?' The Holy Spirit dwells in our body as Paul says here twice over. So the reference is to something that is going to happen to our bodies.

Thirdly, resurrection is the only interpretation that shows that the Apostle is working up to a climax. In verse 10 he says in effect: This is the position, your spirit is life because of righteousness, but your body at the moment, and while you are in this world, is dead because of sin. But all is well, for there is a time coming when even your body is going to be raised. That is the climax; and this is the only interpretation that leads to a climax. The Apostle is aiming at giving us comfort and assurance. He

[82]

shows why we should be rejoicing. We are already saved in spirit, and we shall be saved also in the realm of the body.

Consider next the word 'quicken' – 'shall also quicken your mortal bodies'. It is a very strong word. It is not the same word as the Apostle uses when he says 'the Spirit of him that raised up Jesus', and 'he that raised up Christ'. This word which is translated by 'quicken' means 'to make alive'. Our bodies need to be made alive, and that is what is going to happen to them. We are not merely going to be resuscitated, our bodies are going to be 'made alive'. At the moment they are frail 'mortal bodies', full of weaknesses and infirmities; they have the seeds of death in them. But they shall be 'made alive'. My spirit is already made alive, in the coming day my body will be made alive also.

That is the essential statement. But there are certain particular matters to which we must call attention. We are compelled, once more, to notice the doctrine of the blessed Holy Trinity, for it is here. In the middle phrase we read: 'He that raised up Christ from the dead shall also quicken your mortal bodies by his Spirit that dwelleth in you.' Here we find a clear reference to the fact that it is God the Father who is going to do this. And yet in the last phrase Paul clearly tells us that the work is going to be done by the Spirit – 'by his Spirit that dwelleth in you'. In other words, you get the same work attributed at one point to the Father and at another to the Spirit. In John's Gospel chapter 6 verse 40 the Lord Jesus Christ Himself says about a believer, 'I will raise him up at the last day.' So the Father is going to raise us, the Son is going to raise us, the Holy Spirit is going to raise us.

An interesting theological question suggests itself. A similar thing is said about our Lord Himself. In John 10:17 and 18 our Lord says quite specifically that He is going to raise Himself. He says further: 'I have power to lay down my life, and I have power to take it up again'. And yet the general teaching of the Scriptures is that He was raised by the Father. How do we reconcile these statement? Only by means of the doctrine of the blessed Holy Trinity, the three Persons in the one Godhead, the Three in One and the One in Three. And this verse in Romans 8 helps us to understand that doctrine. 'If the Spirit of him that raised up Jesus from the dead dwell in you, he that raised up Christ from the dead shall also quicken your mortal

[83]

bodies by his Spirit that dwelleth in you.' The Father uses the agency of the Spirit to do this, the Father uses the agency of the Son. We have met this great mystery already in verse 9: 'Ye are not in the flesh, but in the Spirit, if so be that the Spirit of God dwell in you. Now if any man have not the Spirit of Christ, he is none of his.' Do not try to understand it: no one can do so; it baffles the understanding, we can but recognize it and adore in wonder. That is why as Christians we are Trinitarians, and not Jehovah's Witnesses, or Unitarians. It is the Scriptures that lead us to be Trinitarians. We should glory and rejoice in this, because what we deduce from it is that the three blessed Persons in the Holy Trinity are concerned about us and our salvation. The Father planned it all; the Son came to execute it; and the Spirit applies it. What a wonderful plan of salvation! So we can attribute different aspects of the work to the Father or the Son or the Spirit, because the undivided Three are involved; and 'all the glory for all the work must be given to the three blessed Persons.

We have seen how the great division in the Church as between the Eastern Church and the Western Church took place very largely over this kind of point; so you and I should know something about these things. Those people in past centuries took these doctrines most seriously; how keenly they studied their Scriptures! We should do the same in our day and generation.

But let us turn to something more practical. Has it ever occurred to you to ask, as you have read this verse, why the Apostle expressed himself in this extraordinary manner? It seems to be a somewhat involved statement: 'If the Spirit of him that raised up Jesus from the dead dwell in you, he that raised up Christ from the dead shall also quicken your mortal bodies by his Spirit that dwelleth in you.' If his basic concern is to tell us that for the present our body is dead because of sin, but our spirit is life because of righteousness, but that all is well because God purposes to raise our bodies in a day yet to come, why did he not say it in the simplest possible way? Of one thing we can be quite sure; the elaboration of his statement was done quite deliberately. It was not that the Apostle was tired, or that he suddenly had become entangled in his words. His plain intention was to give us a key to the true interpretation of this most significant statement. He is emphasizing that the Holy Spirit

[84]

dwells in us. He starts with that; he ends with it, in order the more to emphasize it. This 'dwelling' is what matters. 'If the Spirit of him that raised up Jesus from the dead dwell in you' at the beginning; then at the end, 'because he dwells in you'. Here is the key. Because this fact of 'dwelling' is true, says the Apostle in effect, the believer can deduce certain things from it which are also equally true. It is because the Holy Spirit dwells in me as a Christian that I can be absolutely certain of the resurrection and the ultimate glorification of this mortal body of mine. That is what I want to know. I am saved; but I am still aware of sin; and the devil can come and use this mortal body of mine and its members to trap me. I want to get rid of his snare. That is what every Christian longs for. The Gospel message tells me that I can be happy about this, I can be certain about it; I have a guarantee that my body will be delivered. But what is my guarantee? It rests upon the fact that the Spirit of God dwells within me.

Let us analyse this statement. The Holy Spirit dwelling in a Christian is a guarantee in itself of his final redemption. But that can be yet stronger as Ephesians 1, verses 13 and 14 reminds us: 'In whom ye also trusted, after that ye heard the word of truth, the gospel of your salvation: in whom also having believed ye were sealed with that Holy Spirit of promise, which is the earnest of our inheritance until the redemption of the purchased possession'. The Holy Spirit can be so given that we have a 'seal', an 'earnest', that is to say, an unmistakable assurance. He is the guarantee that God Himself has given us an interest in this great salvation and its ultimate consummation.

Secondly, we can be quite certain of this because, if God has actually gone to the extent of giving us His own Holy Spirit, who can be described actually as the Spirit of God Himself – if (I say) God has gone as far as that with respect to us He is not going to stop short. God never starts a project without completing it. His work is never imperfect. 'He who hath begun a good work in you will perform it until the day of Jesus Christ' (Philippians 1: 16). If God has put His Spirit in you He will go on with His work in you until it is finally complete. What a tremendous deduction! But we are fully entitled to draw it. If the Spirit is in you, you can be quite certain that the divine work will be completed.

Then thirdly, the Spirit actually dwells in our mortal bodies. 'Your body is the temple of the Holy Spirit', said Paul to the Corinthians. Well then, if God puts His Holy Spirit into this mortal body of mine I argue that He is not going to leave the matter there; He is going to make that body worthy of the divine Person who has come to dwell within it. That is what the Apostle argues here. He has sent the Spirit into your body and He is going to make that body fit and worthy to have the Spirit within it.

Fourthly, the Spirit who is in us is the same Spirit who was in the Son of God, the Lord Jesus Christ. Not only so, but as Paul has told us in the preceding verses, we are 'in Christ'. We are no longer 'in Adam', but 'in Christ'. We were under the law, but now we are dead to the law. And as we saw in chapter 6, because we are 'in Christ' everything that has happened to Him is going to happen to us. We were crucified with Him, we died with Him, and our bodies will rise with Him. This is a certain fact. He was literally raised from the dead in the body; and so shall we be raised. 'Christ the firstfruits; afterward they that are Christ's.' The Apostle assures us that, if we have the Spirit in us, it means that Christ is in us, and we are in Christ, and therefore we can be certain of our resurrection.

Fifthly, our deliverance from sin and the Fall and all their consequences, would not be complete apart from the resurrection of the body. In the Fall, and as the result of sin, the whole of man fell. It was not merely man's spirit that fell; man fell completely as an entity, spirit, soul and body. It was a total fall. Sin and evil have infected the whole of man, including his very body; our bodies are 'mortal' bodies because of the Fall. If man had not fallen, and had never sinned, his body would not have been 'mortal'. But it has become mortal; it is a humiliated, frail, weak body because of sin and the Fall. Christ has come to redeem, to deliver us from the Fall, from all the consequences of sin. I argue therefore that He must complete the work by raising my very body. I am not completely saved until my body is saved. As my body has participated in the effects of Adam's one sin, so my body must participate in the effects of the action of this Second Man, this last Adam.

It is essential that we should emphasize the resurrection of the body. People who do not believe in the literal physical resurrection

[86]

of the body of Christ, or of our bodies, are not only denying the Scriptures but also missing one of the most glorious aspects of the Christian salvation. If my body is not in the hereafter to be redeemed and glorified, then Christ has failed at that point. Our bodies are as they are, subject to diseases, subject to death, the place where sin dwells, and where the devil is constantly tempting us and trying us, all because of sin and the Fall; and if we are not going to reach a stage and a point at which these evils no longer pertain to the body, then I say that the work of the Saviour will prove incomplete. But, thank God, the Apostle reminds us here that it will not be incomplete. Though it is true to say of us now that 'the body is dead because of sin', there is a day coming when it will no longer be true, for 'He will also quicken your mortal bodies by his Spirit that dwelleth in you'.

What does all this mean? We shall see the answer more clearly and fully when we come to verse 23: 'Not only they, but ourselves also, which have the firstfruits of the Spirit, even we ourselves groan within ourselves, waiting for the adoption, to wit, the redemption of our body'. The adoption is coming, but meanwhile, 'We that are in this tabernacle do groan, being burdened'. 'The whole creation groaneth and travaileth in pain together until now.' But the redemption of the body is to come; and we are waiting for it. This body is yet to be raised. The same truth is to be found in Philippians 3: 20: 'Our citizenship is in heaven, from whence also we look for the Saviour: who shall change our vile body that it may be fashioned like unto his glorious body, according to the (mighty) working whereby he is able even to subdue all things unto himself'. This present body is the body of my humiliation; He will change it so that it will be like 'the body of his glorification'. The Apostle John says the same: 'Beloved, now are we the sons of God, and it doth not yet appear what we shall be: but we know that, when he shall appear, we shall be like him for we shall see him as he is (1 John 3: 2).

This means that the Christian man at last will be completely redeemed and delivered. This is already the case in regard to the spirit; the day will come when it will be equally true of the body. It will happen when Christ comes again. Those who are still left on earth when He comes will be changed; but whether we shall have died and our bodies buried in a grave, or rotting in the bottom of the sea, whether we shall have been blown into pieces by bombs, it will not matter; whatever be our case, there will be this glorification, this 'mighty working whereby he is able even to subdue all things unto himself'. Such is the Apostle's teaching.

My body will be raised; I shall still have my identity; my body will be recognizable. Peter and James and John could recognize Moses and Elias on the Mount of Transfiguration. All will not appear the same. My essential body is going to be raised, this particular configuration that is mine. It is not a matter of molecules, it is not a matter of flesh and blood. As the Apostle says in 1 Corinthians 15: 'Flesh and blood cannot inherit the kingdom of God.' That is the reply to those who ask, 'How can your body be raised if it is blown to atoms in an explosion?' My body is the particular configuration that the atoms take in my case; and that is what is going to be raised. If we are still on earth when Christ returns there will be a mighty miracle wrought in our flesh and blood so that it becomes a glorified body. Therefore I argue that there is on the one hand a sameness and continuity, while on the other hand there is a difference in the actual constitution. The same body, but then glorified. 'It is sown a natural body, it is raised a spiritual body.'

The marvellous truth is that our bodies shall be like the body of his glorification. 'From whence also we expect the Saviour, who shall change our vile body that it may be fashioned like unto his glorious body.' This is our heritage as Christians; this is what is going to happen to us. How can we be dejected? how can we be unhappy? how can we go through this world groaning as miserable Christians? our very bodies are to be glorified. His body was glorified. Saul of Tarsus had a glimpse of it on the road to Damascus. The glorified body was the body in which He suddenly came into the room, though the doors were shut, and appeared to His frightened disciples.

Our bodies will be fashioned like unto His body of glorification. This means that this old body of mine will then be free from sin. It is not so now. My spirit is free (Romans 6: 18), but my body is not free. But then the body also will be free from sin, free from weaknesses and diseases, no longer subject to decay and death. It will be glorious, worthy of the spirit, worthy of the divine life that is in it. Let us remind ourselves again of the words of the Apostle in 1 Corinthians 15: 'So also is the resurrection of the dead. It is sown in corruption, it is raised in incorruption: it is sown in dishonour' – that is its condition now – 'it is raised in glory'. 'It is sown in weakness.' How true that is now! How weak are our bodies! But there will be no weakness in them then; we shall be filled with vigour and power and strength. 'It is sown in weakness; it is raised in power. It is sown a natural body, it is raised a spiritual body. There is a natural body' – we have it now – 'and there is a spiritual body' – we shall have it in the day of resurrection. 'The first man Adam was made a living soul; the last Adam was made a quickening spirit'; He will quicken my very body, and it will be a glorious body. All this will happen 'in a moment, in the twinkling of an eye, at the last trump: for the trumpet shall sound, and the dead shall be raised incorruptible'. This applies only to the Christian dead; not to the others who will not be raised incorruptible. 'The dead shall be raised incorruptible, and we shall be changed. This corruptible must put on incorruption, and this mortal must put on immortality.' This is going to happen; nothing is more certain. I know all this because the Spirit of God who is in me now is the guarantee that He is going to do it. He has put the Spirit into this body, this mortal, corrupt, frail, weak body; and that assures me that I am to be raised and changed and renovated. No weakness, no disease, no sin, no frailty, no decay, no death – immortality! Complete salvation! Body, soul, spirit, entirely, utterly, absolutely delivered from sin and all its effects and all its vestiges!

Hold on to the doctrine of the resurrection of the body. We shall not spend our eternity as disembodied spirits. We shall be there with the same essential body, but glorified. Your identity will remain, and will be preserved; but it will all be glorious. The effects and evil results of sin and the Fall will have been entirely cancelled and removed. There will even be 'a new heaven and a new earth, wherein dwelleth righteousness'. This old world will have been renovated and glorified in similar fashion, and you and I, Christian people, will be walking on it and dwelling in it like our blessed Lord. Glorified, perfect, complete, entire in every respect – the whole man, spirit, soul, body! Even the 'vile' body entirely delivered! At the present moment 'my spirit is life, because of righteousness', but my body is 'dead, because of sin'. Am I therefore dejected and despondent? A thousand times, No! This is only a temporary condition, this is only transient. The Spirit is in us, and because the Spirit is in us we know that even the body is going to be delivered. Satan will be completely routed, finally defeated, ultimately destroyed; and all will be glory for those who are Christ's, in whom His Spirit now dwells as a seal and an earnest of that glory indescribable which is yet to come.

Do you normally think of yourself in that way? Lift up your heads, look ahead. Listen to the voice and the testimony of the 'earnest' that is within you; and long and wait for 'the adoption, to wit, the redemption of your body'.

Eight

*

Therefore, brethren, we are debtors, not to the flesh, to live after the flesh.

For if ye live after the flesh, ye shall die: but if ye through the Spirit do mortify the deeds of the body, ye shall live.

Romans 8: 12, 13

These two verses apply what the Apostle has been stating from verse 5 to verse 8, and then still more clearly in verses 9, 10 and 11. The word 'therefore' tells us so. It is one of the most characteristic words of this Apostle. He always lays down his doctrine first, and then he applies it, by using this word 'therefore'.

In other words, we have here an exhortation and an appeal on the basis of what has gone before. This statement is important for two main reasons. Firstly, for our understanding of the actual teaching of the Apostle. It enables us to follow his argument as he works it out in this whole section. It is not enough to note his doctrine; the Apostle always applies it. It is because many fail to follow him when he comes to the application that they become guilty of what is called antinomianism, that is, the failure to put into practice what you claim to believe; indeed, still worse, the danger of imagining that if you believe the doctrines nothing else matters. That is a complete denial of the Apostle's teaching, for he always applies the truth. There is nothing more dangerous than to have a merely intellectual or theoretical interest in Christian truth. This 'therefore' comes to us as a warning of that terrible danger. We must pay careful heed always to every 'therefore' used by this Apostle.

But secondly, the statement in these two verses is of crucial importance from the standpoint of the New Testament doctrine of sanctification, and especially in the light of the various theories that are current with respect to that doctrine. I maintain that in many ways these two verses are perhaps the most important statement with regard to the practical aspect of the New Testament doctrine of sanctification in the whole of Scripture. I have already quoted them many times in dealing with this doctrine in previous verses, but now I shall show how crucial they are in that context.

There are certain preliminary observations which I feel constrained to make. It is here for the first time, in this chapter, that we come to the realm of practical application. All we have had up to this point has been a general description of the Christian – his character, his position. But now the Apostle has really come explicitly to the doctrine of sanctification. Here we are told exactly how, in practice, the Christian becomes sanctified. Or, to state it differently, here we are told in detail and in practice how the Christian is to wage the battle against sin, and especially as it tends to come to him, and to defeat him through his body. This is one of the chief problems of the Christian life.

How is one to live this Christian life? Observe the Apostle's method of answering the question. It is only as we realize what we are that we can possibly face the practical problem of waging this battle against sin. This is an important statement because people generally assume that the Apostle has already been dealing with this practical aspect of sanctification right from the beginning of the chapter.

What then is the Apostle's teaching? How is the Christian to meet the problem of sin while he is still in this life in this world? It is best to approach the problem by considering two schools of teaching that are very popular at the present time. It is the business of a Christian teacher, as I understand it from the New Testament itself, not only to give a positive exposition but also to oppose wrong teaching. The New Testament itself does that, but this approach is not popular today. People say, 'Don't be negative, give us the positive truth; don't be controversial'. But if error is being taught it must be corrected. Paul does this constantly. He exposes the false, warns against it, urges Christians to avoid it; at the same time he gives the positive truth. So we must of necessity do the same. What we believe is of vital importance, because it is going to affect our whole life and conduct. Let us look then at the two most popular theories with regard to this whole question of sanctification.

The first is what we can describe as the 'Perfectionist' teaching. It tells us that, as the result of an experience which is open to all Christians who seek it, sin can be totally eradicated out of us, and out of the whole of our nature. The teaching is generally put in terms of 'the baptism of the Holy Spirit'. It states that if a Christian is 'baptized with the Spirit' sin can be entirely removed from him, body, soul and spirit, and he can become entirely free from sin. He can have that as an experience; he has but to seek it, and to 'receive it by faith'. Those who urge this upon us are fond of contrasting this eighth chapter of Romans with the seventh chapter. Chapter 7, they say, shows the defeated Christian; but we need not remain there for the 2nd verse of this chapter tells us that 'the law of the Spirit of life in Christ Jesus has made us free from the law of sin and death'. That is 'the second experience', 'the baptism with the Spirit', the total eradication of sin. Sin is taken right out of the man, and from there on he has no problem of sin within him in any way; sin only reaches him from the outside. The man is in himself perfect. They admit that he does not know everything, that there is imperfection in that respect; but there is no moral imperfection.

Such teachers frequently quote two other statements which, they argue, support their contention. The first is in the 15th chapter of the Acts of the Apostles, verses 8 and 9. Peter is addressing the Council in Jerusalem and he says: 'God, which knoweth the hearts, bare them witness, giving them the Holy Ghost, even as he did unto us: and put no difference between us and them, purifying their hearts by faith.' This, they argue, is a similar statement to that in Romans; they received this blessing by faith, 'their hearts were purified by faith', sin was taken right out of them. Their other favourite quotation is what appears to be a similar statement in the 26th chapter of the Acts, verse 18, where Paul, addressing Agrippa and Festus, says that he was given a commission which included, 'Delivering thee from the people and from the Gentiles, unto whom now I send thee, to open their eyes, and to turn them from darkness to light, and from the power of Satan unto God, that they may receive forgiveness of sins, and inheritance among them which are sanctified by faith that is in me'. Here, they say, is their

teaching – 'sanctified by faith' – and there is no more to be said.
I have already dealt with that in expounding the second verse
in our chapter. As regards these two statements in the Book of
the Acts, it seems to me that the use which the sinless Perfectionists make of them is altogether at fault. What the Apostle Peter
is saying in Acts 15 is that by faith certain people had become
Christian believers. 'Sanctified' means to set apart. They were
Gentiles, but, having believed, they have been set in the same
position as Jewish believers. The question under discussion was
not sanctification, but whether Gentiles could become Christians
at all. The primary meaning of 'sanctified' in the Bible is 'to set
apart', and often the very context tells you in which particular
instance it means that alone and has nothing to do with sanctification as a theological concept. Similarly, in the 26th chapter of
Acts, the Apostle Paul was telling the Gentiles that they could
belong to that company that had been already set apart from
among the Jews to receive the Christians' great inheritance.
All who have believed the Gospel by faith are set apart in this
way and separated from all others in the world. Paul is not
considering the question of sanctification; all he is showing is
that this is the way of salvation. What entitles anyone to a
share in the inheritance is not sanctification but justification.
The erroneous teaching really implies that only those who have
received some 'second blessing' will share 'the inheritance of
the saints' in glory. I repeat, the statement in Acts 26 is an
evangelistic statement and has nothing to do with the doctrine
of 'sanctification'. And the statement in the 15th chapter is on
precisely the same line. The question before the Jerusalem
Council was not the possibility of becoming totally sanctified
but whether the Gentiles could be justified by faith as well as the
Jews. Had they become Christians at all? Was it right to admit
them into the Church? Had Peter and Paul been right when they
baptized them? Peter's defence was that it was quite clear that
God had dealt with them by the Holy Spirit and had given them
this ability to believe the Gospel. That is the argument. The
question at issue was whether they were Christians at all, and
if so, what was to be their pattern of life, and what was to be
their relationship to Jewish customs and practices? We shall
find further arguments against the Perfectionist teaching as we
work out further what the Apostle says.

A second view with regard to sanctification is that which teaches what it calls 'the principle of counteraction'. This second view entirely rejects the Perfectionist view. It says that sin is not eradicated in the believer, that it still remains in him, and that the believer still has to fight against sin while he is in this world. But, they say, he need not be a defeated Christian; a way of victory is possible. The Lord Jesus Christ can keep us living the victorious life. All we have to do is to believe the correct message. In the first, sin is entirely taken out of us – eradication! No, says the second, it is not taken out of us but if we learn the right way of relying upon the Lord Jesus Christ and 'abiding' in Him, He will obtain the victory for us, and all we do is to receive His victory. We rest in Him, we abide in Him, we look to Him; He will do it for us.

Certain quotations will set out this second view very clearly. I quote first one of the best known and most popular teachers of this particular view of sanctification. He says, 'Out of Romans 3 to 7'. Notice that he does not start with Romans 7, he goes back to chapter 3 – 'Out of Romans 3 to 7, into the victory of Romans 8.' Most Christians, he says, are in the position of what he calls 'Romans 3 to 7.' I cannot understand why the Romans 3 comes in at all – it is generally Romans 7 – but this particular preacher goes back to Romans 3. He says, 'You find the defeated Christian in Romans 3 to 7.' 'But,' he says, 'you need not stay there; you can leave that and go over into the victory of Romans 8.' Then he adds, 'Not that when you get there' – that is to say, Romans 8 – 'you have arrived, and that is it! Romans 7 is the battlefield, we are always in that, but Romans 8 is the secret of victory.' He goes on, 'The Lord Jesus Christ speaks a word to you that is backed by the authority of His holy life, His atoning death, His resurrection from the tomb, His ascension into heaven, and the outpouring of His Spirit, and He says to us' – incidentally, this comes in a sermon on 'the woman who had the spirit of infirmity' (Luke chapter 13), who was doubled-up and had been like that for eighteen years – ' "Woman (man), thou art loosed from thine infirmity". Not by a gradual process, but by an instantaneous crisis in which the grip of sin is set free from the life of a professing Christian and he is delivered from it in a moment.' Such is the teaching! The professing Christian is said to be like the woman who had this spirit of infirmity. Here is a person who has believed on the Lord Jesus Christ unto salvation, knows his sins are forgiven, and so on; he is 'born again.' Yes, a Christian, but living a defeated life, kept down by this spirit of infirmity; but if he only believes this message and turns to the risen Christ he can be delivered from it immediately. Christ will say, 'Woman (man), thou art loosed from thine infirmity.' This is a critical experience, the grip of sin is loosed in a moment. And the same writer continues: 'I am not here to say that God makes it impossible for a Christian to sin; I am here to say to you that He always makes it possible for the Christian not to sin, and I say that crisis comes at the moment that a Christian gives up the struggle, comes out into the open, confesses that he is absolutely hopeless, and hands it all over to the risen Lord.' 'Not gradually,' he adds, 'but immediately'! "Woman, thou art loosed from thine infirmity," and instantaneously, immediately, she was made straight and glorified God.' The important point is that the crisis comes at the moment that 'a Christian gives up the struggle.' That is the vital point, he 'gives up the struggle, and comes out into the open.' The moment one comes to that crisis, the moment one is prepared to be honest with oneself, and does not try to conceal sin any longer, but confesses it, and confesses further his absolute hopelessness, and then 'hands it all over to the Lord' to do it for him – then, simply resting on what *He* is going to do, and *His* victory, one is delivered, and set free. That is the way of victory; you just go on doing that and abiding in that.

I should perhaps point out that the first of the two quotations is taken out of a sermon on Balaam; the second, as I have already indicated, is based on the miracle worked on the woman who had the 'spirit of infirmity'. This in itself is surely significant. You very rarely find such teaching put forward in terms of a detailed exposition of the Epistle to the Romans itself; it is either in terms of an Old Testament story, or a New Testament miracle which is spiritualized and turned into a parable. Statements are made about Romans 7 and Romans 8, but very rarely indeed is the teaching presented in terms of an exposition of this Epistle itself.

But I desire to show that both teachings are indeed almost an exact contradiction of what the Apostle says here. Notice that the Apostle does not in any way appeal to us to 'surrender'.

Instead, he says: 'Therefore, brethren, we are debtors, not to the flesh, to live after the flesh. For if ye live after the flesh, ye shall die: but if ye through the Spirit do mortify the deeds of the body, ye shall live.' There is no word here about 'coming out into the open' and making some 'confession' and 'surrendering'. Neither does he teach that there is a victory possible for us which we can obtain immediately in a crisis experience. The second of the erroneous teachings emphasized that it was not 'gradually, but immediately' – a crucial, critical experience, 'you can get it now'. Is there any suggestion of that here in Romans 8? The Apostle is not asking us to consider the possibility of any fresh experience; he is saying in effect, 'As for you Christians, "the body is dead because of sin, the spirit is life because of righteousness", that is your position'. We know that body as well as soul will ultimately be saved; but what are we to do in the meantime? Does Paul say that we are to 'come out into the open, confess that there is nothing in us at all, that we are completely and absolutely hopeless; and hand everything over to the Lord Jesus Christ?' There is no such suggestion here whatsoever – none at all! The Apostle teaches the exact opposite. He is not holding before us any new possible experience which we have to receive. He is simply saying once more what he has said before in chapter 6 in verses 11, 12, 13: 'Likewise reckon ye also yourselves to be dead indeed unto sin, but alive unto God through Jesus Christ our Lord.' And especially, 'Let not sin therefore reign in your mortal body, that ye should obey it in the lusts thereof. Neither yield ye your members as instruments of unrighteousness unto sin: but yield yourselves unto God, as those that are alive from the dead, and your members as instruments of righteousness unto God.' Romans 8 repeats Romans 6; and yet we are told that we should be moving from Romans 7 right into the victory of Romans 8. The Apostle has already said in chapter 6 what he says here in chapter 8. It is the same appeal, only that he puts it in a more practical manner in chapter 8 than he did in chapter 6.

The Apostle's method is, once more, an argument, a deduction. He is not introducing a new doctrine in order to give us liberty. He is deducing from the doctrine he has been laying down. Neither is what he says here addressed primarily to a man's will. The erroneous teaching always addresses man's will, and tries to persuade him to 'surrender'. 'Are you willing to surrender?' it says. 'Are you willing to be made willing to surrender?' It assumes that the obstruction is in the will. But here the Apostle addresses his argument to the understanding, to our reason, saying in effect: 'If you see this truth, put it into practice; having seen it, act upon it'. It is, once more, a '*Therefore*' – in the light of all this – 'brethren, we are debtors, not to the flesh, to live after the flesh. For if ye live after the flesh, ye shall die.' It is reason followed by deduction, and it is directed to our understanding. This is of vital importance to us if we are concerned to have a New Testament view of sanctification.

Then secondly, there is a call for action on our part on the basis of this understanding. 'But', Paul says, 'if ye through the Spirit do mortify the deeds of the body. . . ' He does not say that 'by the baptism of the Spirit it is all done for us' and 'taken out of our hands'; he is not telling us that if we 'hand it over to the risen Lord' He will do it for us. Instead, he is telling us to do something. In other words it is the exact opposite of that other teaching; that is what is so astonishing, not to say alarming!

Ultimately the whole question of our belief of the Scripture is involved here. Are we to be guided by Scripture, or by an idea or theory that came to someone? The Apostle does not say that sin can be suddenly taken out of us and completely eradicated. Neither does he say that the risen Lord will do it all for us if we but 'hand it over' to Him. He shows, rather, what we have to do, and to continue to do, in the light of his teaching. 'Therefore, brethren, we are debtors, not to the flesh, to live [go on living] after the flesh. For if ye live [go on living] after the flesh ye shall die: but if ye through the Spirit do mortify the deeds of the body, ye shall live.'

It is important to notice that Paul uses the present tense here, of which a well-known dictionary remarks: 'It denotes that which is now going on, and indicates a continuous, repeated, or habitual action.' We have to go on mortifying the deeds of the body. We have to do it, and we have to go on and on doing so. That other teaching emphasizes the element of crisis. It emphasizes, negatively, that it is 'not gradually, but immediately'. Did not our Lord say to the 'woman with the spirit of infirmity' that it would happen to her there and then? 'Woman, thou art loosed from thine infirmity', and the account emphasizes that 'immediately she was made straight, and glorified God'. And that, it teaches, 'can happen to *us* immediately'. Yet here the Apostle emphasizes that we have to continue doing a certain thing repeatedly, habitually. It is not something instant and dramatic, something that happens in a crisis experience, but something we have to keep on doing. We have to keep on 'mortifying the deeds of the body'. Far from teaching something crucial, critical and immediate, the Apostle lays down for the Christian man a programme which he has to follow and to carry out. Such is the teaching here in the very heart of Romans 8. It is not that I need not go on struggling any longer, that I have just 'to hand it over to the Lord', and He will do it for me. No, I have to keep on mortifying the deeds of the body.

What we have in these two statements is an argument, and an indication of the action I have to take on the basis of the argument. The pivotal word is 'Therefore'. In the light of all that Paul has said, we who are Christians are not 'debtors to the flesh, to live after the flesh. For if ye live after the flesh, ye shall die'. There is nothing new offered here; all I have to do is to realize what is true of me now because I am a Christian, namely, that my body remains 'dead because of sin', but my 'spirit is life because of righteousness'. Not only so, but I have to realize also that the Holy Spirit of God dwells in me. 'Ye are not in the flesh, but in the Spirit, if so be that the Spirit of God dwell in you. Now if any man have not the Spirit of Christ, he is none of his'. Then further, 'If the Spirit of him that raised up Jesus from the dead dwell in you, he that raised up Christ from the dead shall also quicken your mortal bodies by his Spirit that dwelleth [now dwells] in you'. 'Therefore'! I am not told to 'hand it all over to the Lord'. The trouble with us is that we fail to realize that we are 'alive' in the realm of the spirit, and that we are dead to sin, dead to the realm of law and the flesh; that we are not 'in the flesh' but in the Spirit, and that the Holy Spirit of God dwells in us. And it is imperative for us to realize it! This is Paul's way of teaching sanctification; and this is true, as I have been emphasizing repeatedly, not of some Christians only, but of every Christian.

The first of Paul's deductions from the position in which God's grace has placed us is found in the word 'debtor'. 'Therefore, brethren', he says, 'we Christians are debtors'. Negatively first, 'we are not debtors to the flesh, to live after the flesh'. He means that we are 'under no obligation' to the flesh, to live after the flesh. Because of all that is true of us, we are under no obligation whatsoever to the flesh. How true that is! 'The flesh' is the cause of all our troubles. What has our flesh done for us? It makes us sin, brings us into misery, and into the realm of death. That has been the result of Adam's original fall. That is why we are all born 'in the flesh'. But the Apostle urges upon us that we are under no obligation to that any longer. Realize, he says, what the flesh did for you; but now you do not owe it anything, you are not a debtor to it in any sense. Do not pay it any allegiance, he says; do not show any subservience to it; have nothing to do with it at all. It is entirely against you; and you do not belong to it now. Our obligation is to Someone else. A hymn written by Philip Doddridge helps us to see this truth positively –

> *My gracious Lord, I own Thy right*
> *To every service I can pay;*
> *And call it my supreme delight*
> *To hear Thy dictates and obey.*

I am not a debtor to the flesh, but there is One to whom I am a debtor. Toplady uses exactly the same argument –

> *A debtor to mercy alone,*
> *Of covenant mercy I sing.*

This is where I am a debtor. I am not a debtor to the flesh; I have finished with it. I am a debtor 'to mercy alone'. This is where my obligation lies. See the same truth in the words of Robert Robinson –

> *O to grace how great a debtor*
> *Daily I'm constrained to be!*
> *Let that grace, Lord, like a fetter*
> *Bind my wandering heart to Thee.*

Such is the manner in which the Apostle introduces his argument to us. Realize the truth about yourself, what you are as a Christian! Then say to yourself, 'I have nothing to do with the realm of the flesh and sin at all; I am no debtor there, I have no obligation there. It has no claim upon me and I am not interested in it. I have served it too long. My debt, my obligation, my duty lie elsewhere. And I am going to pay my debt, show my gratitude, and honour my obligation.'

We have been looking at the way in which the Apostle introduces in general this great doctrine of sanctification. The essential
point is that it is a deduction from what is already true of us. It is
not something new, it is not a fresh experience to be sought; it is
the outworking of a truth. 'Sanctify them through thy truth: thy
word is truth.' It is not an experience which I get in a moment,
but something I have to go on doing. It is gradual, and it should
be progressive, and increasing; it should be a 'growth in grace
and in the knowledge of the Lord'.

That is but the beginning of this vital and most practical
teaching, which the Apostle puts to us in this striking way in
these two most interesting verses.

Nine

*

Therefore, brethren, we are debtors, not to the flesh, to live after the flesh.

For if ye live after the flesh, ye shall die: but if ye through the Spirit do mortify the deeds of the body, ye shall live.

Romans 8 : 12, 13

We continue with our consideration of this statement which is in many ways the crucial statement of the New Testament doctrine of sanctification. Having dealt with two popular misinterpretations of the doctrine we have started on the positive exposition of the Apostle's teaching. It is, that we should realize what we are, and that therefore 'we are not debtors to the flesh', but 'debtors to mercy', and 'debtors to grace'. We must now work this out in detail.

Notice first the Apostle's statement. In the light, he says, of what is true of us, we are not debtors to the flesh, that is, we must not 'live after the flesh'. To do so, he says, is ridiculous, is illogical, is inconsistent. I emphasize this because the New Testament always teaches sanctification in this way. It does not offer a fresh experience; it reasons with us. It does not say, 'Realize you can do nothing, and hand it all over to the Lord'. It is a reasoned argument which says, 'Do not be a fool. If you are rejoicing in the fact that you are a Christian, why then do you go on living as if you were still not a Christian?' It ridicules such behaviour. I shall give later several quotations which will establish this most important point, that it is an argument, an appeal to reason, to logic and to understanding. The negative ridicules the Christian who goes on living 'in the flesh'.

But why is it ridiculous? One reason is that we are no longer 'in the flesh'. Well, if we are no longer 'in the flesh', or 'after the flesh', why do we go on living in the flesh, or after the flesh? He has told us in verse 9, 'But ye are not in the flesh, but in the Spirit'. If, then, as a Christian you are no longer where you used to be, living a life 'after the flesh' and outside the life of God, and apart from the Spirit, but are now 'in the Spirit', why then do you go on living as if you were still 'in the flesh'? It is in this way that Paul teaches sanctification. By definition the Christian is one who has been taken out of the realm of the flesh, and has been put into the realm of the Spirit. Well, if that is so, live accordingly. A man who is proud of the fact that he is a citizen of a certain country will surely live according to the customs of that country, and not as if he belonged to some other country. That is precisely the Apostle's argument.

A second reason is that the 'flesh' no longer has any right over us. There was a time when it had. It is not only that we are no longer 'in the flesh', we are no longer controlled by the flesh. As far back as chapter 5, verse 21, we read: 'That as sin hath reigned unto death, even so might grace reign through righteousness unto eternal life by Jesus Christ our Lord'. Again in chapter 6, verse 14: 'For sin shall not have dominion over you: for ye are not under the law, but under grace.' And again in chapter 7, verse 5, the Apostle had said, 'For when we were in the flesh, the motions of sins, which were by the law, did work in our members to bring forth fruit unto death'. These and other similar statements assure us that our new position introduces us to an entirely new jurisdiction. Every man born into this world is born under the power of sin, the flesh, and the law. 'Behold, I was shapen in iniquity and in sin did my mother conceive me' (Psalm 51: 5). We have never been free; we are born 'the slaves of sin'. That is why a child, when it first exercises its will, almost invariably does something it is told not to do. We are born sinners, we are under the power and the jurisdiction and the dominion of sin. This shows itself in the form of 'the flesh'; and the law comes in as an aggravating factor. But we have been moved out of that position, we are no longer 'under the law', we are not 'under sin', we are not 'in the flesh'. We are 'under grace', we are in the 'reign of grace'. And the Apostle, in writing to the Colossians, describes the radical change by saying: We have been 'translated from the kingdom of darkness, into the kingdom of his dear Son' (Colossians 1: 13). So the Apostle's argument amounts to this: 'Why do you go on living after the flesh? You do not belong to that jurisdiction any longer, you are not in that kingdom. Cannot you see that you are a fool, that you are living as if you were still there under that old power? But you are not; it has no right over you. You are in this other kingdom, this kingdom of grace'.

Such is Paul's way of teaching sanctification. Let me use an illustration. It is said that when, after the American Civil War, slavery was abolished, many of the slaves in the southern States did not realize that they were now at liberty and had freedom. They had lived for such a long time in the old way as slaves, with masters over them, that they were still in fear. But as a result of the war and the victory of the North, slavery was abolished, and they were free men. But as they did not realize that fact they went on living as if they were still slaves. In order to set matters right, you do not tell such people to seek some new experience; all that is necessary is to say to them, 'By law, by enactment of Congress, there is no longer such a thing as slavery; you are a free man; behave as a free man. Do not go on living as a slave now that you are free.' That is the argument the Apostle uses here. 'Therefore, brethren, we are debtors, not to the flesh to live after the flesh.' We are in the Spirit; the Spirit of Christ dwells in us.

My third argument is based on what Paul has just been saying in verse 11. He says in effect: 'I have just been telling you that this problem of sin in your life is now only a residual problem. There was a time when you were completely "under sin" in body, mind and spirit. That is no longer true, for if Christ be in you, "the body is dead because of sin; but the spirit is life because of righteousness". Realize, then, that this is your position. You have been set free; you are as free now as you will ever be; you are "in Christ". You died with Christ, you have risen with Christ, you are seated in the heavenly places with Christ Jesus. That is your position now; sin is still left only in your body, your "mortal body". Do not live for the relic, for the remnant; do not live for the body, for the flesh; live to "the Spirit" which is "life" and freedom. Do not be inconsistent with yourselves. Realize that the fight that remains against sin is only a temporary and a passing one while you are still in this world; therefore do not live for "the flesh"; live rather as the man you are "in Christ Jesus", the man who is in the realm of the Spirit.'

As a fourth argument the Apostle in effect says: 'To live "to the flesh" means that you are reverting again to the realm of death. "For if ye live after the flesh, ye shall die". The life of "the flesh" always leads to death. You must not pander to it, for you do not belong any longer to the realm of death. "The Spirit is life because of righteousness." You know that your body still belongs to the realm of death – "The body is dead because of sin". But that very body is going to be delivered. "If the Spirit of him that raised up Jesus from the dead dwell in you, he that raised up Christ from the dead shall also quicken your mortal bodies by his Spirit that dwelleth in you." The present position is only temporary. So do not give in to the body; it is a "mortal body", but it is going to be delivered, and a day is coming when the whole man, body, mind and spirit, shall be entirely free from sin, and perfectly glorified, even as the Lord Himself.'

Paul's last, his fifth, argument tells us that to live after the flesh is to grieve the Spirit, who dwells in us. 'Ye are not in the flesh, but in the Spirit, if so be that the Spirit of God dwell in you.' The Spirit of God is in us as Christians; so if we go on living 'after the flesh' we are grieving the Spirit. The Spirit and the flesh are opposed to each other. 'The flesh lusteth against the Spirit, and the Spirit against the flesh; and these are contrary the one to the other' (Galatians 5 : 17). They are great antagonists. If, therefore, you realize that the Spirit of God is in you, you must realize at once that to go on living 'after the flesh' is to grieve the Holy Spirit of God that dwells in you.

That is the Apostle's argument. 'Therefore, brethren . . . ' 'Therefore – in the light of all these things I have been saying to you – we are debtors, not to the flesh, to live after the flesh; for if ye live after the flesh, ye shall die. Realize this, reason it through, be logical, work it out, be consistent with yourselves'. There is not a word here about seeking for some new experience, not a word about 'handing it over to the Lord'. It is an argument addressed to my mind, to my reason, and an exhortation based upon that argument.

We turn now to the positive side of the truth. We must not only not live 'after the flesh' for the reasons given; positively, we must actively 'mortify the deeds of the body'. We must look first at the general principle involved here. We shall consider later in detail what to mortify the deeds of the body means.

Why are we to engage in this work? We meet with the same argument; the 'therefore' still obtains. We are to do this because of what is already true of us; it is the only consistent thing to do. The basic truth about a Christian is that he has come to a realization that he was a sinner. He may have thought that he was a 'good fellow', and that all was well. He was living a good, clean, moral life, doing good, and there was no trouble. But the first thing that happens to a man when he becomes a Christian is that he is convicted of sin, and realizes that he is in a desperate condition, that all he has been relying on is of no value in the sight of God. The Apostle devoted the first three chapters of this Epistle to proving that 'there is none righteous, no, not one', that 'all have sinned and come short of the glory of God'. The Apostle Paul himself as a Pharisee was a most religious man, a most moral man, a most dutiful man; and yet he says that he came to see that all his righteousness was 'but as dung and refuse'; it was of no value at all (Philippians 3 : 8). That was the first thing that he came to realize. The Christian realizes the truth about himself, that he is a sinner in the sight of God, that his whole nature is twisted and perverted, and that there is a principle of evil in him. He comes to see that he is 'under the dominion of sin'. He did not know that before; he was 'blinded by the god of this world'; he was the dupe of the devil. He probably did not believe he existed; that proved how the devil had duped him so completely. But his eyes have been opened, and he sees that he has been the slave of sin and that his whole nature is twisted and perverted. He sees that his very views of God were false when he said that he did not believe this and that about God. He was simply setting up his own opinions. But now he realizes the enormity of his sin; he is profoundly convicted of it, and realizes that he was in the terrible danger of going to hell if he died in that condition. He sees that he is outside the life of God, and that nothing awaits him but hell. The Christian believes and realizes these things; and a man cannot be a Christian without some knowledge of them.

But then, in moving over to the positive, the man realizes what God has done for him in spite of his sin. This is the Gospel: 'I am not ashamed of the Gospel of Christ, for it is the power of God unto salvation to every one that believeth.' The Christian believes what Paul has said in the first three chapters of Romans; that though man had sinned against God, though he had rebelled and deserved nothing but perdition, yet God, in His infinite love and grace and mercy and compassion, not only sent His only Son into this world in the likeness of man, but even sent Him to the Cross, and 'set Him forth as the propitiation for our sins'. The Christian believes, that God, in love, has taken his sins, put them on His own Son, and punished them in Him, so that he, the believer, may be freely forgiven. Not only so, but the Christian man has been born again, he has been given a new life and a new nature and has become a child of God; he has been adopted into God's family and transferred into a new kingdom. He is in the new realm of grace. He was in Adam, he is now in Christ. He knows all this, and he believes that when he dies he is going to be with God and with Christ in the glory. He has proof of this, because God has put His Spirit, His own Spirit, within him, the 'Spirit of Christ', the 'Spirit of God', the 'Holy Spirit'. He realizes that the Spirit has been given to him in order that he may be made ready for his eternal home in the presence of God. He knows that his body and everything else will be entirely purged and delivered from sin, and that he will stand holy and blameless, righteous and glorified, in the presence of God. That is what a Christian believes.

'Very well', says Paul in effect, 'if you believe these things, how can you possibly go on living after the flesh? It was living after the flesh that brought you into trouble, pain, loss and eternal danger; it was because Adam fell and became a man "in the flesh", and passed that on to all his progeny, that you were what you were; are you going to continue to live in that way? You say that you rejoice in Christ and in your salvation; you believe that the love of God was so great that He sent His Son to die in order to deliver you; and yet you deliberately go on living the old life which made all that necessary. You say that it was your sin, and the sin of mankind, that caused our Lord to endure such pain and agony and suffering in the Garden of Gethsemane and on the Cross; you say you believe that, and yet you continue to do the very things that led to that suffering. Surely this is an impossible position. "Therefore, brethren, we are debtors not to the flesh, to live after the flesh". If you are honest and really believe and mean what you say, you will certainly tell me, "I want to have nothing more to do with that old life, and therefore I will mortify the deeds of the body which still tend to lead me to live after the flesh. I am going to kill the sin that remains in me, I am going to throttle it, I am going to put it to death". That is inevitable if you really mean and believe what you say. Be consistent, then, be logical, be positive!'

That is what you are at the moment, he says, but then consider what you are going to be. I have just told you, he says, that 'If the Spirit of him that raised up Jesus from the dead dwell in you, he that raised up Christ from the dead shall also quicken your mortal bodies by his Spirit that dwelleth in you'. If that is going to happen to your body, are you willing to allow that element which is still left in your body to control your manner of life for the remaining few years that you are in this world? Of course you are not! You are going to say, rather, 'I will end this folly and contradiction. I know that finally I shall be perfectly delivered; but I am going to mortify the deeds of this body now; I am going to keep it down; I am not going to allow this old body, this "dead" body, to control me.'

Such is the Apostle's argument, introduced by this 'Therefore, brethren'. There is nothing at all here about a second, a further experience. It is a reasoned argument addressed to my under-standing, and it calls for action. *I* have 'through the Spirit' to 'mortify the deeds of the body' for the reasons given. That is the Apostle's teaching with regard to sanctification; that is how the Christian becomes sanctified.

Here I must deal with a difficulty which some find in the way in which the Apostle puts his argument. They say, what about that 'if'? '*If* ye live after the flesh, ye shall die; but *if* through the Spirit ye do mortify the deeds of the body ye shall live'. This *if*, they feel, surely implies that the Apostle is saying that my posses-sion of eternal life is ultimately contingent upon what I do. The answer, of course, is that he is not saying that at all, for at this point he is not thinking in terms of cause and effect, but of means and end, which is quite different. He is not saying, 'If you do this, then that will happen'. That would be cause and effect. What he says is, 'The means to that end is . . . '

I must explain why I stress this matter. If the Apostle is saying here that my possession of eternal life is dependent upon my mortifying the deeds of my body, he would then be contradicting what he teaches everywhere else, and what the whole of the New Testament teaches. He would be teaching 'justification by works', and that my work of mortifying the deeds of the body obtains and secures eternal life for me. The Apostle himself has put the matter quite clearly in the last verse of chapter 6: 'For the wages of sin is death; but *the gift of God* is eternal life through Jesus Christ our Lord'. Indeed the whole thrust of this Epistle, especially in the first five chapters, is to teach us that justification is by 'faith only', and not by the 'deeds of the law'. The glory of the Gospel is that salvation is 'by grace', that it is 'the free gift of God', that when man can do nothing God gives him salvation freely. Obviously, therefore, the Apostle cannot suddenly in these two verses contradict what he teaches everywhere else, not only in this Epistle but in every other Epistle, and what is taught by all the other Apostles also.

But, further, take the very term 'ye': 'If ye live after the flesh, ye shall die'. Who are the 'ye'? They are the people who have already been made alive by the Spirit as we are told in verse 2: 'The law of the Spirit of life in Christ Jesus hath made me free from the law of sin and death'. Clearly, Paul is talking about those who are Christians as the result of the operation of the Holy Spirit upon them in their regeneration and all that follows from it. But not only so. If this is to be interpreted as cause and effect, then there is no possibility whatsoever of any doctrine of assurance, because if my future and my eternal safety depend upon what I do, then I am certainly lost. No man can keep himself finally. The Apostle never teaches that he can. Our assurance, which is the main theme of this whole chapter, rests upon the fact that we are 'in Christ', under the influence and power and realm and government of grace; and that alone makes our position safe.

What then, asks someone, is the Apostle saying here? I answer: It is a general statement, comparable to the form of speech which we use when we say to a person, 'If you put your finger into that fire you will be burned.' You do not say to the child, 'A person who puts his finger into the fire is likely to get burnt', you put it more directly and say, 'If you put your finger into the fire you will be burnt'. That is the form of speech we commonly use; and it is the form the Apostle uses here. He says: You and I are not debtors to live after the flesh, because people who live after the flesh are people (as I have already been telling you) who belong to the realm of death. He has already spoken in this way in verse 6, for instance, where he says, 'To be carnally minded [to live 'after the flesh'] is death; but to be spiritually minded is life and peace'. He is but saying the same thing in a slightly different form here: 'If ye live after the flesh, ye shall die'. A man who is living a life 'after the flesh' is not a Christian, he is not 'alive', he belongs to the realm of death. Realize that that is not true of you, and therefore in no sense can you go on living that kind of life.

On the other hand we make certain positive statements – 'If you do the right thing, certain results will follow. For instance, take exercise, get plenty of fresh air, eat good food, and you will be a healthy man'. Or, 'If you do these things you will be a healthy man.'

Here, means and end are in view, not cause and effect. In a sense, the Apostle is saying in a different way what he said in chapter 6 in verses 20 to 22: 'When ye were the servants of sin, ye were free from righteousness. What fruit had ye then in those things whereof ye are now ashamed? for the end of those things is death. But now being made free from sin, and become servants to God, ye have your fruit unto holiness, and the end everlasting life.' And then immediately, lest anyone might think that he inherits or gains everlasting life as the result of holiness, he says, 'For the wages of sin is death; but the gift of God is eternal life through Jesus Christ our Lord.' In other words, God sees to it that those who are His people are brought to that ultimate end and object by the means which He himself uses through the Spirit.

We arrive, then, at this general conclusion, that the Apostle teaches quite clearly that the way of sanctification is the way of realizing the truth about ourselves as Christians, and then putting it into practice. It is an argument, it is a deduction leading to an action of the will on our part which must be continuous.

Finally, let me show that this is not only the Apostle's teaching here but throughout his writings; and not only his teaching, but the teaching of other Apostles also. This will reveal the unscriptural character of the teaching that talks about 'passing over from the bondage of Romans 7 into the liberty of Romans 8'. If those two other theories were true, then, I argue, the Apostle would never have written the second half of every epistle to the churches that he ever wrote. In the second half of his church epistles he follows the pattern that we find here. He usually starts with the word 'Therefore', and then goes on to reason with, and to appeal to, and to exhort those early Christians to work out in practice what he has been saying in the first part of his Epistle. He does it again later in this very Epistle, in chapter 12: 1 and 2: 'I beseech you therefore, brethren, by the mercies of God, that ye present your bodies a living sacrifice . . . And be not conformed to this world: but be ye transformed by the renewing of your mind.' Then he goes on in detail to tell them how to live – the things that they must do, and the things that they must not do. In the First Epistle to the Corinthians, in chapter 6, beginning at verse 13 we find, 'Meats for the belly, and the belly for meats; but God shall destroy both it and them. Now the body is not for fornication, but for the Lord; and the Lord for the body. And God hath both raised up the Lord, and will also raise up us by his own power.' These words are an echo of Romans 8: 11. Again: 'Know ye not that your bodies are members of Christ?' Paul is reasoning, 'Shall I then take the members of Christ, and make them the members of an harlot? God forbid. What? know ye not that he which is joined to an harlot is one body? for two, saith he, shall be one flesh. But he that is joined unto the Lord is one spirit. Flee fornication.' This is not an exhortation to 'hand it over to the Lord', but to 'flee fornication'. You have to take to your heels and get away from it. To flee is something you have to do. 'What?' he continues, 'know ye not that your body is the temple of the Holy Ghost which is in you, which ye have of God, and ye are not your own? For ye are bought with a price: therefore glorify God in your body, and your spirit, which are God's.'

You find the same teaching at the end of the ninth chapter of that same First Epistle to the Corinthians: 'They which run in a race run all, but one receiveth the prize. So run, that ye may obtain' (v. 24). You have to run in such a way that you may obtain. You do not 'hand it over', you have to run. And Paul continues: 'And every man that striveth for the mastery is temperate in all things.' If a man competes in the races he abstains from too much food, from alcoholic drinks, and so on. A man who strives for the mastery in games is temperate; he controls himself, he disciplines himself. He takes himself in hand. He is not to say, 'I can do nothing'; he has to be temperate. 'Now they do it to obtain a corruptible crown; but we an incorruptible.' Next he says, 'I therefore so run, not as uncertainly; so fight I' – he is talking about boxing at this point – 'not as one that beateth the air'. What does he do? 'But I keep under my body'. This is the Apostle Paul's teaching. He says, 'I keep under my body, and bring it into subjection' – he is mortifying his body – 'lest by any means, when I have preached to others, I myself should be a castaway'.

Turn further to the Second Epistle to the Corinthians, chapter 6 verse 14: 'Be ye not unequally yoked together with unbelievers, for what fellowship hath righteousness with unrighteousness?' He is reasoning and using arguments. He is not telling the Corinthians to 'hand it over'; he is telling them why they must not do certain things and explaining the prohibition. He winds up that particular argument in chapter 7, verse 1: 'Having therefore these promises, dearly beloved'. Notice the 'therefore' once again. 'Having therefore these promises' – What next? 'Let us cleanse ourselves from all filthiness of the flesh and spirit, perfecting holiness in the fear of God.' Not only does he not tell us to 'hand it over to the Lord' who will do it for us, but he deliberately tells us to 'cleanse ourselves from all filthiness of the flesh and spirit, perfecting holiness in the fear of God'.

Once again, turn to the Epistle to the Galatians, chapter 5, verse 16: 'This I say then, Walk in the Spirit, and ye shall not fulfil the lust of the flesh.' Then in verse 24: 'They that are Christ's have crucified the flesh with the affections and lusts.' They have done it; they have crucified the flesh with the affections and lusts. 'If we live in the Spirit, let us also walk in the Spirit.' We have to 'walk in the Spirit'.

In the Epistle to the Ephesians Paul makes the transition from doctrine to practice in chapter 4, verse 1: 'I, therefore, the prisoner of the Lord' – 'therefore' again! – 'beseech you that ye walk worthy of the vocation wherewith ye are called, with all lowliness and meekness, with longsuffering, forbearing one another in love; endeavouring to keep the unity of the Spirit in the bond of peace'. Then, particularly from verse 17: 'This I say, therefore, and testify in the Lord, that ye henceforth walk not as other Gentiles walk' – not 'after the flesh' – 'in the vanity of their mind, having their understanding darkened'. What then am I to do? 'Put off concerning the former conversation the old man, and be renewed in the spirit of your mind; put on the new man.' Then he comes down to details: 'putting away lying, speak every man truth with his neighbour.' To the man who complains, 'I am tempted to lie constantly, what am I to do?', he does not say, 'Ah, do not struggle about that, hand it over to the Lord, ask Him to deliver you, ask Him to keep you from lying.' No, says Paul, 'Put away lying'. Because you are a Christian and a new-born man, 'put away lying; speak every man truth with his neighbour. Be ye angry, and sin not. Let him that stole' – is he to ask the Lord to deliver him from stealing? – 'Let him that stole steal no more; but rather let him labour, working with his hands the thing which is good, that he may have to give to him that needeth. Let no corrupt communication proceed out of your mouth.' You Ephesians, he says, are to do all this. And he goes on in the same strain to the end of that Epistle. The order is unchanged – first, doctrine; then deducing practical conduct from the doctrine.

Again, turn to Philippians 2 : 12, 13: 'Work out your own salvation with fear and trembling; for it is God that worketh in you both to will and to do of his good pleasure.' It is because God has worked in us that we can work it out, and we are called upon to do just that. Philippians 3 : 16 to 20: 'Nevertheless, whereto we have already attained, let us walk by the same rule, let us mind the same thing. Brethren, be followers together of me.' Not, 'Hand it over to the Lord', but 'Follow me,' he says; and then, 'Mark them which walk so that ye have us for an ensample (for many walk, of whom I have told you often, and now tell you even weeping, that they are the enemies of the cross of Christ: whose end is destruction, whose God is their belly, and whose glory is in their shame, who mind earthly things). For our conversation is in heaven; from whence also we look for the Saviour, the Lord Jesus Christ, who shall change our vile body . . .' Invariably it is the same style of argument.

Look at the matter in the Epistle to the Colossians chapter 3, the first ten verses: 'If ye then be risen with Christ, seek those things which are above, where Christ sitteth on the right hand of God. Set your affections' – you yourself have to do this – 'on things above, not on things on the earth. For ye are dead, and your life is hid with Christ in God. Mortify therefore your members which are on the earth.' It is the same in all the Epistles; it is something we have to do.

In the First Epistle to the Thessalonians, chapter 4 the first 5 verses, we read: 'Furthermore then we beseech you, brethren, and exhort you by the Lord Jesus, that as ye have received of us how ye ought to walk and to please God, so ye would abound more and more. For ye know what commandments we gave you by the Lord Jesus' – 'commandments'! – 'For this is the will of God, even your sanctification, that ye should abstain from fornication: that every one of you should know how to possess his vessel in sanctification and honour; not in the lust of concupiscence, even as the Gentiles which know not God.' It is still the same kind of argument addressed to believers.

In the First Epistle to Timothy, chapter 6, verses 11 to 16 we find: 'But thou, O man of God. . . . ' What is 'the man of God' to do? Is he to confess, to 'come out into the open' and admit that he is a complete failure, and then 'hand it all over to the Lord?' No, Paul speaks in a different way: 'But thou, O man of God, flee these things, and follow after righteousness, godliness, faith, love, patience, meekness'. 'Fight the good fight of faith, lay hold on eternal life, whereunto thou art also called, and hast professed a good profession before many witnesses', and so on. Still it is something we have to do.

Then in the Second Epistle of Timothy, chapter 2, beginning at verse 19: 'Nevertheless the foundation of God standeth sure, having this seal, The Lord knoweth them that are his. And, Let every one that nameth the name of Christ depart from iniquity. But in a great house there are not only vessels of gold and silver, but also of wood and of earth; and some to honour, and some to dishonour. If a man therefore purge himself from these' – purge himself; he does not 'hand it over' to be done for him – 'he shall be a vessel unto honour, sanctified, and meet for the Master's use, and prepared unto every good work. Flee also youthful lusts: but follow righteousness, faith, charity, peace, with them that call on the Lord out of a pure heart. But foolish and unlearned questions avoid. . . . '

Then in Titus 2:11: 'For the grace of God that bringeth salvation hath appeared to all men, teaching us' – What? – 'that, denying ungodliness and worldly lusts, we should live soberly, righteously, and godly in this present world, looking for that blessed hope . . . '

In the Epistle to the Hebrews we find the same teaching. Take the beginning of chapter 12. It is an exhortation to ' . . . lay aside every weight, and the sin which doth so easily beset us, looking unto Jesus'. What for? To 'do it for me'? No, but to follow His example, to do what He did. That is the argument. I am not to 'look unto Jesus' in the sense of doing nothing and asking Him to do it all for me. I see what He did, and I must live in the same way. And the same applies to all the warnings and the threatenings in that great Epistle. If it is just a question of 'handing it over', why the threatenings in chapter 6 and in chapter 10? The false teaching I am exposing renders them quite meaningless; but the Apostles never wrote such statements.

The same is found in the Epistle of James chapter 1, verses 22 to 27. We read: 'Be ye doers of the word, and not hearers only, deceiving your own selves', and similarly right on to the end of that first chapter. Again, take James 4, verses 7 and 8: 'Submit yourselves therefore to God' – Then, 'Resist the devil'. You and I have to do so. I have known many Christians people who have spent their lives in trying to 'surrender', trying to 'hand it all over'; and they were unhappy failures. Why? Because they did not 'resist the devil'. 'Submit yourselves therefore unto God. Resist the devil, and he will flee from you', says James. James does not bid us pray about this. 'Resist the devil and he will flee from you'. 'Draw nigh to God, and He will draw nigh to you.' Then, 'Cleanse your hands, ye sinners; and purify your hearts, ye double minded'. You have to do it; you have to wash your hands, and you have to purify your own hearts.

In the First Epistle of Peter, chapter 1, verse 13 we read: 'Gird up the loins of your mind, be sober, and hope to the end for the grace that is to be brought unto you at the revelation of Jesus Christ; as obedient children, not fashioning yourselves according to the former lusts in your ignorance: but as he which hath called you is holy, so be ye holy in all manner of conversation.' Peter then proceeds to give his readers reasons for doing what he bids them. In chapter 2, verse 11 he says: 'Dearly beloved, I beseech you as strangers and pilgrims' – not to 'hand it all over to the Lord' and to 'stop struggling against sin' – 'abstain from fleshly lusts, which war against the soul; having your conversation honest among the Gentiles: that whereas they speak against you as evil-doers, they may by your good works, which they shall behold, glorify God in the day of visitation.' Note especially the terms 'strangers and pilgrims' and 'the day of visitation'. And read further from verse 21 to the end of the chapter. In the third chapter Peter says much the same thing in verses 10 and 11: 'He that will love life, and see good days, let him refrain his tongue from evil, and his lips that they speak no guile. Let him eschew evil' – let him 'shy' from evil as a frightened horse shies, which is what 'eschew' means – 'Let him eschew evil and do good; let him seek peace, and ensue it.' Then in chapter 4 he is even more explicit in verse 1: 'Forasmuch then as Christ hath suffered for us in the flesh, arm yourselves likewise with the same mind: for he that hath suffered in the flesh hath ceased from sin; that he no longer should live the rest of his time in the flesh to the lusts of men, but to the will of God.' Then this argument follows: 'For the time past of our life may suffice us to have wrought the will of the Gentiles, when we walked in lasciviousness, lusts, excess of wine, revellings, banquetings, and abominable idolatries: wherein they think it strange that ye run not with them to the same excess of riot, speaking evil of you: who shall give account to him that is ready to judge the quick and the dead.' The Apostle Peter does not tell us to 'hand it over'. He says in effect, 'Do not be a fool. You have spent sufficient of your time in this world doing those things when you were a Gentile, and when you were living "in the flesh". Indeed, more than enough! Do not go on doing so; live to God who has loved you, and to Christ who has died for you.' And thus Peter builds up his argument, showing that it is primarily a matter of understanding, and then of putting it into practice by their own will, and by their own effort, because the Spirit is in them enabling them to do the will of God. Again, in the 5th chapter, Peter writes in verses 8 and 9: 'Be sober, be vigilant' – again, action by us – 'because your adversary the devil, as a roaring lion, walketh about, seeking whom he may devour: whom resist steadfast in the faith, knowing that the same afflictions are accomplished in your brethren that are in the world'.

Finally, in the First Epistle of John, chapter 2, verses 3 to 6, we find ourselves exhorted to 'keep his [the Lord's] commandments'. And in the third chapter and the 3rd verse: 'Every man that hath this hope in him purifieth himself, even as he is pure'. And in the last chapter of the Bible, the 22nd chapter of the Book of Revelation, verses 12–15: 'Behold, I come quickly; and my reward is with me, to give every man according as his work shall be. I am Alpha and Omega, the beginning and the end, the first and the last. Blessed are they that do his commandments, that they may have right to the tree of life, and may enter in through the gates into the city. For without are dogs, and sorcerers, and whore-mongers, and murderers, and idolaters, and whosoever loveth and maketh a lie'.

Thus we have seen that what the Apostle teaches about sanctification in Romans 8, 12 and 13 is the teaching of the whole of the New Testament Scripture.

Ten

*

Therefore, brethren, we are debtors, not to the flesh, to live after the flesh.

For if ye live after the flesh, ye shall die: but if ye through the Spirit do mortify the deeds of the body, ye shall live.

Romans 8: 12, 13

These two verses, as I have been emphasizing, are vital and crucial to a true understanding of the New Testament doctrine of sanctification and we are continuing to consider their message against the background of two well-known theories with regard to sanctification that were once very popular, and are still held by many. We have seen that, far from being an isolated statement, this is typical and characteristic of the New Testament as a whole. It does not stand alone. It is what the Apostles Peter, Paul, John, and James and the writer to the Hebrews teach unanimously.

But there are further proofs of the correctness of our interpretation. If either of the other interpretations is true then there is no need for any argument or deduction whatsoever. There would be no room left for any such procedure. Certainly there would be no variety in the argument. If the other teachings are true, then all that Paul, and the other Apostles, would need to have said when they wrote to Christians in the early churches who were confronted by the problem of having to fight against the world, the flesh and the devil, would be this: they would have written the first half of their epistles reminding the Christians of the great doctrines of the faith, and in the second half they would have said in effect, 'There is something further which we have to say to you. You must realize that you must not go on fighting and struggling against sin any longer. You must realize that you are helpless and hopeless, and that all you need to do is to hand

[118]

yourself and all your problems over to the Lord, and He will give you victory. As long as you abide in Him He will keep you in this position of victory, and all will be well.' That is all they would have said; there would have been no need to say anything further, no need of any argument, no need of any exhortation, no need to draw these great deductions out of the doctrines.

That, of course, is the precise content of these other teachings which we are criticizing and rejecting. All they say is that it is necessary to have this 'second experience', this 'crisis leading to a process'. And they are quite consistent in that respect. On their view that is all there is to say. But we have seen in our quotations, as we see here, that the New Testament writers have a great deal to say. Consider again the message of the Epistle to the Ephesians, from chapter 4: 17 to chapter 5: 8. Notice the progressive movement in the argument. Paul appeals to the Ephesians to show Christian conduct and behaviour because they have been born again. Then, in the second place, because God's Spirit is in them they must not 'grieve the Spirit, by whom they are sealed unto the day of redemption'. He then says, 'Ye are children of God; well, as children of God be followers of God'. Next he reminds them that Christ has died for them, and he deduces an argument from that great fact. Then he reminds them of the judgment which is to come.

Such is the New Testament method. It is not confined to just one message which is 'quite simple'. The erroneous teachings have only one message. All you need is this second experience in which you realize that everything is done for you. But, here, the great doctrines of the Christian faith are brought forward, and arguments are deduced from them. The doctrine of sanctification as found in the New Testament is not just harping on one theme illustrated by stories from the Old Testament and by New Testament miracles turned into parables. Instead, the total doctrine comes in: deductions are drawn from it and arguments are based upon it and worked out, leading to a final exhortation to put the total doctrine into practice. The erroneous theories concerning sanctification render the New Testament method unnecessary, otiose, and there is no room left for an appeal such as we have in the two verses – Romans 8: 12 and 13.

I have often discussed this matter with a friend, a very able man, who holds the first of the two theories, the Perfectionist theory, and I have often put before him the exhortation in this 13th verse, 'If ye through the Spirit do mortify the deeds of the body, ye shall live'. I have said to him, 'If it is possible for a man by an act of surrender, and of faith, to receive the baptism of the Holy Spirit and to have sin taken right out of him, then why did the Apostle ever write this particular verse?' He has to admit that he cannot answer. He admits that on his theory there was no purpose in doing so. If the sin is all taken out of us – eradicated – why are we exhorted to 'mortify the deeds of the body?' There is no answer from the standpoint of either of those theories. This one verse alone is sufficient to disprove them, quite apart from the other numerous statements we previously quoted.

Furthermore, these other theories, and particularly the second – that of counteraction – are quite inconsistent with the New Testament view of the Christian man. This again is of crucial importance. The counteraction theory states, 'The crisis comes in the moment that a Christian gives up the struggle, comes out into the open, and confesses that he is absolutely hopeless'. But that, surely, is a denial of the New Testament teaching. If the Christian man is 'absolutely hopeless', and can do nothing, then why are these appeals and exhortations addressed to him? Is it right, is it fair to address an appeal, an exhortation, a command, to a Christian man who is 'absolutely hopeless' and can 'do nothing'? Surely the very appeals, in and of themselves, presume an ability in the Christians to whom they are addressed. If a man is 'absolutely hopeless', all you need tell him is, 'Well, you can do nothing, so hand it over to the Lord and He will do it for you.' But these appeals and exhortations which tell us to do something, presume our capacity to do them.

But still more serious, it seems to me, is the fact that these erroneous theories, especially the second, are quite inconsistent with the New Testament teaching concerning regeneration and what we have already been told about the Christian man by the Apostle in this very Epistle to the Romans. I assert that according to the New Testament the Christian is not 'absolutely hopeless'; to say that he is so is to deny what the Apostle has already told us about him. First, consider the case negatively. The Apostle has already told us that the Christian man is 'no longer a slave to sin'. 'God be thanked', he says, 'that ye were the servants [the slaves] of sin, but ye have obeyed from the heart that form of doctrine which was delivered to you' (6: 17). Then he goes on to say, 'Being then made free from sin, and become the slaves of righteousness'. We must not say therefore that the Christian man is absolutely hopeless. Man is absolutely hopeless before his regeneration, because he is 'dead in trespasses and sins'; he is a 'slave' of sin, and is 'under the dominion' of sin. But in chapter 6: 14 the Apostle says, 'Sin shall not have dominion over you, for ye are not under the law, but under grace'. Indeed he has already told us at the beginning of chapter 6, 'What shall we say then? Shall we continue in sin, that grace may abound? God forbid. How shall we that are dead to sin, live any longer therein?' The Christian man absolutely hopeless? Of course he is not! It is a lie to speak of him thus. 'How shall we that are dead to sin live any longer therein?' I am no longer 'dead in sin', I am no longer hopeless; that is what the Apostle teaches. He has taken the trouble to tell us all these things, and he arrives at this exhortation in verse 13 chapter 8 in the light of all these things he has told us about ourselves.

Take another example. Paul has already told us that we are no longer in the flesh. In chapter 7: 5 he says, 'When we were in the flesh, the motions of sins, which were by the law, did work in our members to bring forth fruit unto death'. Of course – when we were 'in the flesh'! It was then that the motions of sin defeated us completely; but we are no longer 'in the flesh'. That is the marvel of our new position, says the Apostle. 'But now we are delivered from the law, that being dead wherein we were held; that we should serve in newness of spirit, and not in the oldness of the letter.' And as we have already seen in this 8th chapter, verse 9, he expresses it like this: 'But ye are not in the flesh, but in the Spirit, if so be that the Spirit of God dwell in you. Now if any man have not the Spirit of Christ, he is none of his.' So we must never say that the Christian is 'absolutely hopeless'. He was hopeless when he was in the flesh; but no longer so because 'ye are not in the flesh, but in the Spirit'.

Then follows the tremendous point that we are no longer 'under the law'. We go back again to chapter 6, verse 14, 'Sin shall not have dominion over you'. Why? 'Because ye are not under the law, but under grace.' And again in chapter 7: 5, 'When we were in the flesh, the motions of sins' – which were stimulated, energized by the law – 'did work in our members to bring forth

fruit unto death'. Then the whole of chapter 7 from verse 7 to the
end of the chapter, verse 25. I was at pains to point out that the
man described in Romans 7: 7 to 25 is not the fully regenerate
man. He is a man who is 'under the law', he has been awakened to
the truth about the law; he is under terrible conviction. The law
is convicting him, but he knows no more. And, as the Apostle
tells us, the more he knows about the law the more his passions
are inflamed within him. He says, 'I was alive without the law
once: but when the commandment came, sin revived and I died.
And the commandment, which was ordained to life, I found to
be unto death. For sin, taking occasion by the commandment,
deceived me, and by it slew me.' 'The law is spiritual; but I am
carnal, sold under sin. For that which I do I allow not; for what
I would, that do I not; but what I hate, that do I', and so on. It
comes to this, 'I see another law in my members, warring against
the law of my mind, and bringing me into captivity to the law of
sin which is in my members. O wretched man that I am!' That is
a description of man 'under the law'. But now – and this is the
glory of the Christian man's position – he is no longer 'under the
law'. That which happens when a man is 'under the law', namely,
that the law inflames his passions and aggravates his problem, is
no longer true concerning him, because he is not now 'under the
law but under grace'. And so, coming to the beginning of the
eighth chapter we have, 'There is therefore now no condemnation to them that are in Christ Jesus . . . For the law of the
Spirit of life in Christ Jesus hath made me free from the law of
sin and death' – free from all that Paul has been describing in
chapter 7.

Thus far I have stated the matter negatively. We must not say
the Christian is 'absolutely hopeless'. But look next at the case
positively. What is the positive truth concerning the Christian?
He was 'in Adam', he is now 'in Christ'. What Adam did was
imputed to him, what Christ has done is imputed to him. He
inherited much pollution from Adam; he inherits the exact
opposite from Christ. He has been taken out of Adam, and
'engrafted' into Christ. That was the great theme of the early part
of chapter 6. We must not say of a man who is 'in Christ' that he is
'absolutely hopeless'. The wrong teaching says that the Christian
gets his victory by passing over from Romans 7 into Romans 8:
'The crisis comes in the moment that the Christian gives up the

struggle, comes out into the open and confesses that he is absolutely hopeless.' A man who is 'in Christ' confessing that he is
'absolutely hopeless'! That is a travesty of, a denial of the plain
teaching of the Scripture. The Christian man is 'in Christ'. Not
only so, he is 'alive unto God'. 'Likewise reckon ye yourselves to
be dead indeed unto sin, but alive unto God through Jesus Christ
our Lord' (6: 11). Is such a man 'absolutely hopeless'? The thought
is ridiculous. He is a man who is now 'alive' and open to all the
gracious operations of the grace of God – 'alive' unto God, 'alive'
from the dead.

Furthermore the Christian man, though formerly 'under law',
is now 'under grace'. At the end of chapter 5 we are told, 'Moreover the law entered, that the offence might abound. But where
sin abounded, grace did much more abound.' And yet we are
told that the Christian man who is born again is 'absolutely
hopeless'! No, 'Where sin abounded, grace did much more
abound: that as sin hath reigned unto death, even so might grace
reign through righteousness unto eternal life by Jesus Christ our
Lord'. A man who is under 'the reign of grace' can never be
described as 'absolutely hopeless'.

And again, the Christian has a new principle of life in him.
'The law of the Spirit of life in Christ Jesus hath made me free
from the law of sin and death' (8: 2). Of whom is that written?
Of every Christian! That is the simple truth about any man who is
a Christian. He is no longer under 'the law of sin and death';
there is new life in him. Or take the Apostle Peter's way of putting
it: 'We are made partakers of the divine nature' (2 Peter 1: 4).
And yet I am told that such a man has to admit that he is 'absolutely hopeless', that he can do nothing, that he has to hand it all
over! The Apostle John states it thus: 'His seed remaineth in him,
and he cannot sin'. What seed? The seed of divine life, the seed of
the new nature, this new principle that has been put into him. It is
in him, and it will remain in him. Is such a man 'absolutely
hopeless'?

Or consider the way in which the Apostle Paul puts it in Ephesians 4 verse 16, where he reminds us that as Christians we are all
'members of the body of Christ'. 'From whom the whole body
fitly joined together and compacted by that which every joint
supplieth, according to the effectual working in the measure of
every part, maketh increase of the body unto the edifying of

itself in love.' Christ is the Head, and His life comes down through every member and part and portion of His body. We are parts of the body of Christ, and joined to Him who is the Head. And yet I am told that I have to confess that I am 'absolutely hopeless' and can do nothing, and have 'to hand it all over'. It is almost incredible. The Christian has a new nature, and therefore he has new motives, new desires – 'old things are passed away, behold, all things are become new' (2 Corinthians 5 : 17). The Christian is a man who says that the commandments of God are 'no longer grievous to him' (1 John 5 : 3) .They are very grievous to the unregenerate, but not to the regenerate. This man has a new life, a new outlook, new desires, new everything – he is a 'new creation'.

Then remember what the Apostle has been telling us about the Christian man in this very chapter. The Holy Spirit of God 'dwells' in him. 'But ye are not in the flesh, but in the Spirit, if so be that the Spirit of God dwell in you.' Then, 'If the Spirit of him that raised up Jesus from the dead dwell in you, he that raised up Christ from the dead shall also quicken your mortal bodies by his Spirit that dwelleth in you'. 'Know ye not', says Paul in I Corinthians 6; 'that your body is the temple of the Holy Ghost which is in you?' That is true of all Christians; the Holy Spirit is in us; He is working in us, and empowering us, giving us the ability; He is resident in us. So that John can say again, 'Greater is he that is in you, than he that is in the world' (1 John 4 : 4). He is in us. 'This is the victory that overcometh the world; even our faith.'

How does all this work out? asks someone. This is the New Testament teaching – 'Work out your own salvation with fear and trembling'. We have to do so. But note the accompaniment – 'Because it is God that worketh in you, both to will and to do of his good pleasure.' The Holy Spirit is working in us 'both to will and to do'. It is because I am not left to myself, it is because I am not 'absolutely hopeless' since the Spirit is in me, that I am exhorted to work out my 'own salvation with fear and trembling'. The Spirit is working in me to do that – 'both to will and to do'. Or look at the matter as it is put so plainly in the Epistle to the Ephesians in the second chapter, where the Apostle contrasts the position of the unregenerate with that of the regenerate. Salvation is 'not of works', he says, 'lest any man should boast. For we are his workmanship, created in Christ Jesus unto good works, which

God hath before ordained that we should walk in them' (verses 9 and 10). The unregenerate man can do no works that are of any value. He has to realize that salvation is all 'by grace through faith'. 'By grace are ye saved through faith; and that not of yourselves: it is the gift of God; not of works, lest any man should boast'. That is justification; that is the way in which you become a Christian! We are 'God's workmanship' in this matter, 'created in Christ Jesus'. What for? 'Unto good works, which God hath before ordained that we should walk in them.' He made us anew, gave us a new life, and a new nature, when we could do nothing, when we were dead and could do no works of any value. He has made us anew, and He has done so in order that we may put into practice these 'good works, which He hath before ordained'. That is the way it works; having been 'created in Christ Jesus' we now have the ability to 'walk' in these 'good works'. In the same way, the exhortation in Ephesians 4: 24, 'That ye put on the new man, which after God is created in righteousness and true holiness', is based on the same argument. The Christian is not 'absolutely hopeless'; quite the reverse. So he must realize who he is, and what he is. 'Be ye therefore followers of God, as dear children'. We are not 'hopeless', we are 'children of God'. And further, we have to realize that because we are children of God, and joined to the Lord Jesus Christ who is the Head of the body, there is a mighty power working in us to which nothing is impossible. The Apostle prays for the Ephesians, 'That the eyes of your understanding may be enlightened; that ye may know what is the hope of his calling, and what the riches of the glory of his inheritance in the saints, and what is the exceeding greatness of his mighty power, which he wrought in Christ when he raised him from the dead' (Ephesians 1: 18-20). Similarly at the end of Ephesians 3: 'Now unto him that is able to do exceeding abundantly above all that we ask or think, according to the power that worketh in us'. This power of God whereby He raised Christ from the grave, is already working in us as Christians, and it is 'exceeding abundant above all that we ask or think'. Realize this, says the Apostle, and because it is true, continue with your work!

Surely in the light of all this it is entirely wrong, and completely unscriptural, to try to get Christian people to say that they are 'absolutely hopeless', and that they can do nothing. What the Scripture says is: Realize who you are and what you are; realize that you have been raised from the dead, realize that you have been 'quickened', that you are 'born again', that you are 'in Christ'. Realize that God's power is in you; and that the Holy Spirit is resident in you, empowering you 'both to will and to do'. Realize what you are, and get on with the work of sanctification. You are not 'absolutely hopeless', the power is in you. 'Reckon yourselves to be dead indeed unto sin, and alive unto God through Jesus Christ our Lord'. The false teaching, it is clear, does not do justice to the New Testament doctrine of regeneration. A man who is born again is not 'absolutely hopeless', rather he is filled with hope because he is 'under grace'.

But look at the matter in yet another way. The teachings I am opposing are inconsistent with the principle of growth that is plainly taught in the New Testament Scriptures. They say that the Christian is absolutely static, that he never grows, never develops at all. Take the famous illustration that was used by one of its leading proponents to illustrate the teaching of 'counter-action'. 'Think of a poker,' said the illustration. 'What is true of a poker is that it is cold, rigid, and black. But put that poker into a fire. Watch a blacksmith doing so. He blows the bellows. What happens? The poker that was black and hard and rigid becomes red and soft and malleable, and can be bent. Ah yes, but only as long as it is still in the fire! If you take it out of the fire it will again become cold, black, and rigid.' In other words, there is no permanent change in the thing itself; it is only changed while it is held in the fire. There is no actual change in its constitution, it is the 'abiding' in the fire that makes the difference. The spiritual application was that as long as the Christian 'abides' in Christ he experiences victory.

The other illustration was about a man using a swimming-belt or a life-belt. The man in question cannot swim; but if he puts on a swimming-belt or a life-belt, though he cannot swim, he will not sink because he is held up by the life-belt. If he somehow wriggles out of the life-belt he will sink to the bottom, but if he gets hold of the life-belt again he will be kept afloat.

Those were the illustrations used to teach us the way of sanctification. As long as I 'abide' in Christ I shall have victory. The moment I cease to do so I revert to where I was before. All depends upon my abiding in Christ. That surely leaves no room for growth; whereas the New Testament teaching is full of the principle of growth. We start as 'babes in Christ'. John writes about 'little children', 'young men', 'old men' – terms which suggest growth, development and maturity. Is it conceivable that a man can spend years in communion with God and with Christ, and have the Spirit working in him and enlightening him with respect to the teaching of the Bible, and yet be exactly the same at the end as he was at the beginning? It is impossible. The truth is that the Christian must grow and develop and mature. He is exhorted to 'grow in grace and in the knowledge of the Lord'.

These illustrations are not only unscriptural, they are misleading. Contrast them with the scriptural illustration. The Christian is not compared to a poker put into the fire, but rather to a branch engrafted into a tree, with life and sap and vitality coming through the trunk and entering into it, and enabling it to bear fruit. Or he is compared to a living organism such as the body, not to something dead and inert kept in a fire. The illustrations are wrong. They leave out the element of life and power and growth, development and maturity, an increasing in fruitfulness as time goes on. But this is the New Testament doctrine, and it is the exact opposite of what we find in these other teachings.

When a Christian falls into sin, he does not go back to the beginning, thank God. So many think that he does! 'Ah,' they say, 'I have sinned, I have gone right back to the beginning'. But that is not true. An appropriate illustration at this point would be something like this. Think of a man climbing a mountain. At the very beginning of the ascent he falls. Well, he has fallen at the foot of the mountain. But he gets up and he goes on climbing ever higher until he has arrived at a point about half way to the summit. Suddenly he falls again. Does that mean that he falls all the way to the bottom of the mountain? Not at all! He has fallen, certainly, but he has not fallen back to the foot of the mountain; he has fallen half way to the summit, and he has not cancelled all that he has climbed. Thank God he has not! The same is true of the Christian when he falls into sin. It is wrong to say that he reverts again into the old condition of 'cold, black, rigid and inert'. It denies the element of new birth and life, and of growth and of development. He falls halfway up the mountain, and he he gets up and goes on again.

My illustration serves to clarify the Christian position. The Christian process of sanctification is vital, it is living; and it must never be thought of in terms of a life-belt or something mechanical, something external. The poker and life-belt analogies are completely false. The Christian is not an 'absolutely hopeless' man who is holding on to Christ. He is 'in Christ' and the life of Christ is working in him through the Holy Spirit. The false teaching constitutes a denial of the glorious doctrine of the union of the believer with Christ. He is not in or out of Christ according to whether he abides and holds on or lets go; he is 'in Christ', and he is always 'in Christ'. He does abide in Christ, and the divine 'seed' remains in him.

But let us proceed to another argument. We are told that the doctrine of the Apostle which urges us to 'mortify the deeds of the body' is discouraging 'because it leaves it all to us', whereas the other teaching is encouraging because it takes the problem out of our hands, and leaves it to the risen Lord, who will then keep us. Naturally that sounds most attractive, but when you examine it carefully you will very soon discover that in actual fact it is really discouraging, whereas the scriptural teaching is full of hope. This is so because the theory that seems so attractive at first, in the last analysis leaves the work all to you. 'How so?' says someone. Because of its purely conditional character! As long as you 'abide' in Christ He will keep you! As long as you keep the poker in the fire it will be 'red and hot and malleable', but if you do not keep it in the fire it will become 'cold and black and rigid' again. So you are kept in the victorious position as long as you keep on abiding in Christ! But how am I to do that? With the world and the flesh and the devil round and about me, and sin still in my body, how can I 'abide' in Christ? It is easy enough to say 'Christ will keep you' but that is only on condition that I hold on to Christ. It leaves it all to my holding on to Christ; it leaves it all to me; it is my abiding in Christ that really matters. It hands it all back to me, though it seemed to be taking it all from me.

But the teaching of the Apostle is quite different. It stresses everywhere that what matters is not our holding on to Him, but His holding on to us. He who took hold of us when we were 'dead in trespasses and sins' and who has 'quickened' us, has also 'begun a good work in us and will perform it until the day of Jesus Christ'. I am in His hands. It is not my holding on that matters, it is that He has laid hold on me, He has apprehended me,

He has arrested me, He has chosen me to be one of His own. He has taken hold of me and He is working in me powerfully. The Apostle says: 'This is the will of God, even your sanctification' (1 Thess. 4: 3). And if it is His will, He will carry it out. The author of the Epistle to the Hebrews puts it very strongly: 'Whom the Lord loveth he chasteneth, and scourgeth every son whom he receiveth'. 'If you are not enduring chastisement you are not sons, you are bastards' (Hebrews 12: 5–11). That means that if you are a child of God, He intends to sanctify you. The passage continues: 'We have had fathers of our flesh, which corrected us, and we gave them reverence: shall we not much rather be in subjection unto the Father of spirits, and live? For they verily for a few days chastened us after their own pleasure; but he for our profit, that we might be partakers of his holiness.' God's purpose is our sanctification, that we may be holy as His children, and if we do not listen to His appeals, He will chasten us; if we do not listen to the exhortations of His word and 'mortify the deeds of the body' and our 'members that are on the earth', He will scourge us. He may send an illness, He may ruin our circumstances, He may take some dear one from us by death. 'He scourgeth every son whom he receiveth.' 'Whom the Lord loveth he chasteneth.' This teaching tells me that I am in God's hands, that He is my Father, and that He intends to bring me to perfection. It is not dependent upon my holding on; it is He who has laid hold upon me, and has put His Spirit in me. And the Spirit works powerfully in me in order that I may both will and do of His good pleasure. So this, far from being discouraging, is the only encouraging teaching.

During my ministerial life, many have come to me saying, 'I do not seem to be able to surrender, I do not seem to be able to abide in Christ; I have been trying to surrender, and to abide'. They ask me to tell them what to do. The scriptural answer is, Realize the truth about yourself, cease to say that you are 'absolutely hopeless', because that is not true of you; you are born again, the life of God is in you, the Holy Spirit of God dwells in you, and He is almighty. Go on doing your work. 'But how can I?' they say. That is what the man with the withered arm might well have said to the Lord Jesus Christ when He said to the man, 'Stretch forth thine hand' (Mark 3: 1–5). But what is the use of saying that to a man whose trouble is that his arm is withered and helpless ? Yet that is what our Lord said: 'Stretch forth thine hand'. And the man did so, finding that he now had the power to do so because he was healed. Here, we are told, 'Mortify the deeds of the body'. 'How can I?' you say. The answer is that He is telling you to do so, and if you try you will find that you can do it – 'Stretch forth thine hand'. The power is given with the command; it comes to us through the Spirit. Never say that a Christian is 'absolutely hopeless'. A man who is 'born again', 'born of the Spirit' of God is not in that condition; he has life, he has power, he has ability.

Another argument that is often brought forward is the so-called argument based on results. Look at what it has done in practice, they say; look at the stories that people tell of the release they have had, and the happiness they have found, and so on – it must surely be right! But that is a most dangerous line of argument. Along that line you can prove almost anything. Go to a Christian Science meeting, and there you will find dozens of people who say that very thing. 'My life was miserable', they say; 'I was always in a state of failure, always suffering from nerves, could not do anything. I was taken to a Christian Science meeting, and there I heard about this way of healing and deliverance, that there was no such thing as evil, no such thing as matter, no such thing as pain, no such thing as disease. As a result 1 was entirely transformed; my whole outlook has been changed; I no longer worry; I no longer have those old troubles and problems that got me down'. Such is their testimony. Does that mean that Christian Science is true? Then go to the theosophists and they will tell you the same thing. Then, if you want to be still more intellectual and philosophical, go to people who teach what they call Anthroposophy and they will tell you much the same thing. Then try the Science of Thought teaching. Then, when you have finished with them, go to those who teach 'Positive thinking' and you will find that they also produce this identical argument. The Yogi treatment and philosophy, similarly, always claims to cure all your troubles. They all make the same claims, and then bring forward their witnesses to testify to the truth of what they are teaching.

But Christian people should not use such arguments. There is only one ultimate test for any teaching or theory; it is the test of the Word of God. What saith the Scriptures? We must not be guided by mere testimonies, but by the plain, clear teaching of the Word of God. And such we have in this Epistle to the Romans. The Spirit of God 'dwells in us' and 'we are debtors, not to the flesh, to live after the flesh'. Out upon the suggestion! 'For if ye live after the flesh, ye shall die: but if ye through the Spirit do mortify the deeds of the body, ye shall live.' As I said when we were considering the teaching of chapter 6, what Christian people need is not a casualty clearing station, or a hospital. The Church is not a hospital primarily, it is a barracks, and in the eighth chapter of Romans we are in this barracks once more, and Sergeant-major Paul is speaking to us. There we stand, a regiment of Christian people who have been failing and complaining that things are going wrong, and that we are not doing well! What does he say to us? Does he say, 'You are absolutely hopeless, there is nothing you can do, you must be brought into hospital; you have to admit that you cannot do anything; you must hand it all over, you must take hold of the electric current that is provided, and as long as you do so you will be filled with power?' Surely he says the exact opposite. I hear him saying. 'Attention! Realize who you are, man, stand up. Why are you slouching in that manner on this heavenly parade ground? Do you not realize that you are "children of the heavenly King"? Why are you groaning and moaning and apologizing? Do you not know that the Spirit of God dwells in you? do you not know that you are "partakers of the divine nature"? Why are you whimpering and crying? why are you talking so much about the world and the flesh and the devil? Do you not know that "He that is in you is greater than he that is in the world?" Stand up! Attention! March! "Quit yourselves like men." No more of this lethargy! No more of this weakness! No more of this moaning and groaning! Realize what God has done to you, realize what you are, and what He has made of you, and march with your heads erect as those who were once "in the flesh"; who once belonged to darkness but now are lights in the world.'

> *Children of the Heavenly King,*
> *As ye journey, sweetly sing.*

We are marching to Zion; so let us march as men worthy of our Commander, worthy of our God, worthy of our heavenly Father. 'Let your light so shine before men that they may see your good works and glorify your Father which is in heaven' (Matt. 5 : 16).

Eleven

*

Therefore, brethren, we are debtors, not to the flesh, to live after the flesh.

For if ye live after the flesh, ye shall die: but if ye through the Spirit do mortify the deeds of the body, ye shall live.

Romans 8: 12, 13

Having given a general exposition of these two verses, and especially in terms of the contrast their teaching presents to two popular theories of sanctification, we now approach their practical application. We have seen that sanctification is a process in which a man himself plays a part, in which he is called upon to do something 'through the Spirit' who is in him. We now proceed to consider what it is exactly that he has to do. The exhortation, the injunction, is: 'If ye through the Spirit do mortify the deeds of the body . . . ' The Christian is called upon to mortify the deeds of the body.

We must deal first with the word 'body', which means our physical body, our physical frame, as it did also in the tenth verse. It does not mean 'flesh'. Even the great Dr John Owen goes astray at this point and deals with it as the 'flesh' and not as the 'body'. But the Apostle who has talked so much about the 'flesh' earlier quite deliberately talks about the 'body'. He has done so in verses 10 and 11, and he did so also in the twelfth verse of the sixth chapter. He is referring to this physical body in which sin still remains, but which is one day going to be raised 'incorruptible' and glorified, to become like the glorified body of our blessed Lord and Saviour Himself. I emphasize again that we must be clear about this matter, because it is so liable to be misunderstood. The teaching is not that the human body is inherently sinful, or that matter is inherently sinful. There have been heretics who have taught that error, known as dualism. The New Testament, on the contrary, teaches that man was made perfect in body, soul and spirit. It does not teach that matter has always been evil, and that therefore the body has always been evil. There was a time when the body was perfect and entirely free from sin; but when man fell, when man sinned, the whole of him fell, and he became sinful in body, mind and spirit. But we have seen that in the new birth man's spirit is already delivered. He receives new life; 'The spirit is life, because of righteousness'. But still 'the body is dead, because of sin'. Such is New Testament teaching! In other words, though the Christian is regenerated, sin still remains in his mortal dying body. Hence the problem of living the Christian life, hence the fight and the struggle against sin as long as we are left in this world; for the body is still the seat and the instrument of sin and corruption. Our bodies are not yet delivered. They shall be delivered, but so far sin remains in them.

The Apostle, as we have seen, makes this quite clear. In 1 Corinthians 9: 27 he says: 'I keep under my body', for the body prompts us to evil deeds. It is not that the instincts of the body are in and of themselves sinful. The instincts are natural, and normal, and they are not inherently sinful. But the residual sin within us is always trying to turn the natural instincts in evil directions. It tries to turn them into 'inordinate affections', to exaggerate them, tries to make us eat too much, to drink too much, tries to make us indulge all our instincts too much; so that they become 'inordinate'. Or, to look at the matter from the opposite angle, this sinful principle tries to hinder us from giving attention to the process of discipline and self-control to which we are so constantly called in the pages of Scripture. Sin remaining in the body tends to act in this way. Hence the Apostle speaks of 'the deeds of the body'. It tries to turn the natural and the normal into something sinful and evil.

The term 'mortify' really explains itself. 'To mortify' is to deaden, to put to death, to render inoperative, to make extinct. And so the exhortation is that we must 'deaden', put an end to the 'deeds of the body'. This is the great New Testament exhortation in connection with sanctification from the practical standpoint, and it is addressed to all Christian people.

How is this work to be done? First, there are false ways of

attempting the mortification of the deeds of the body. We can sum them up under two main headings. Firstly, there is the Roman Catholic method, which is essentially the way of monasticism. It argues that while you are going about your business in this world you are in conflict with the world and the flesh and the devil, and they are certain to get you down. Therefore, if you desire to be what they call 'spiritual' – they divide Christians into the 'spiritual' and the 'ordinary' (the 'laity') – if you want to become a 'spiritual', you must go out of the world and enter a monastery, take certain vows, renounce the world. There you will be able to devote yourself entirely to the living of the Christian life. You must give up comforts and money, and live an abstemious life as regards food and drink, with frequent fasting, and in this way, says the Roman Church, you will be able to mortify the body. That was the fallacy which Martin Luther discovered, and its exposure was one of the prominent features of the Protestant Reformation. Luther and others found that a man can follow that rigorous programme most faithfully but still find that the fight is as hot and strong as ever. He does not escape from the problem of sin by going 'out of the world'.

But the Roman Catholic idea of mortification does not stop at that; they advocate also the putting on of camel-hair shirts, the wearing of articles of clothing that will hurt and annoy and irritate the body. The monk must do everything he can to despise and abuse the body. They used to indulge, at one time, in what were called 'flagellations'; they used literally to strike and hurt themselves, indeed almost mutilate the body; anything to keep it down and to crush it. In the journals and biographies of George Whitefield you find that before his eyes were opened, and while he was still trying to save himself, he practised this mode of 'mortification' and nearly killed himself. There is no doubt but that he undermined his health for the rest of his life by excessive fasting. The entire school of early Methodists tended to do the same. Whitefield, being a particularly honest man, attempted the work with an unusual thoroughness; but he found that it was all quite useless. The idea behind the practice is that if you starve the body, and do all you can to take 'the life' and energy out of it, it will not trouble you so much in this matter of sin. The answer to that is, as I have already suggested, that the people who have tried it most thoroughly are the very ones who are most eloquent in saying that it does not work, it does not succeed. It is not at all what the Apostle means by 'mortifying' the deeds of the body.

The second fallacy we can describe as 'legalism'. What we have just been describing is, in a sense, legalism also, but as legalism is found also in people who are not Roman Catholics we must put it under a separate heading. It can also be described as a 'false Puritanism'. I say 'false' Puritanism because it is in fact a denial of the teachings of Puritanism. Some of us have experienced this in our own lives. I personally was brought up in that kind of atmosphere. Our mentors did not teach us the great Puritan doctrines; but they did teach a kind of Puritan practice, without giving us the doctrine, without giving us the reason, without giving us the truth. It was a manner of life that was imposed upon us with great rigour, and was the chief characteristic of the Nonconformity of the end of the last century and the early part of this present century. It was the kind of life in which you 'scorned delights and lived laborious days'. It was a joyless religion, a form of legalism, a tyranny in which there was no happiness, no joy, no spirit of exultation. It was 'a religion of fear', a religion which led to morbidity and introspection, and very often despair. It was nothing but sheer legalism, a system of living, a code of ethics, a moral code imposed upon people in the wrong way.

These are the false ways of attempting to 'mortify the deeds of the body', and it was largely as a reaction against them that the theories with which we have been dealing came into existence. In spite of all that I have said about the Perfectionists and those who believe in the principle of 'counteraction', it can at least be said in their favour that they could see that the Roman Catholic way was wrong, and that this false Puritanism was equally wrong. They saw that they alike led to a miserable Christianity, a mere counterfeit of the true. In that, of course, they were quite right. It was in reacting against the counterfeit that they adopted their theories which, I am suggesting, are more psychological than spiritual. Their dislike of the wrong teaching was right; but unfortunately it drove them to other equally wrong teachings. They failed to understand the way in which the Apostle tells us to mortify the deeds of the body.

What, then, is the true way? The Apostle makes it plain. 'If ye through the Spirit do mortify the deeds of the body' – 'through the Spirit'! The Spirit is mentioned particularly, of course, because His presence and His work are the particular and peculiar mark of true Christianity. This is what differentiates Christianity from morality, from 'legalism' and false Puritanism – 'through the Spirit'! The Holy Spirit, as we have seen, is in us as Christians. You cannot be a Christian without Him. If you are a Christian the Holy Spirit of God is in you, and He is working in you. He enables us, He gives us strength, He gives us power. He 'mediates' to us the great salvation the Lord Jesus Christ has worked out for us, and enables us to work it out. The Christian must therefore never complain of want of ability and power. For a Christian to say 'I cannot do it' is to deny the Scripture. A man who has the Holy Spirit residing in him must never utter such an expression; it is a denial of the truth concerning himself.

A Christian, as the Apostle John says in the 16th verse of the 1st chapter of his Gospel, is one who can say, 'Of his fulness have we received'; and later on in chapter 15 believers are described as branches in the true Vine; so we must never say that we have no power. Certainly the devil is active in the world, and he is mighty in power; but 'greater is he that is in you, than he that is in the world'. Or take again that important statement in the First Epistle of John, chapter 5 vv. 18 and 19: 'We know that whosoever is born of God doth not keep on committing sin.' Such is the meaning of the 'sinneth not' of the Authorized Version. It is the present-continuous tense: 'We know that whosoever is born of God does not keep on sinning'. Why not? 'But he that is begotten of God, – that is the Lord Jesus Christ – 'keepeth him, and that wicked one toucheth him not'. This, says John, is the truth about every Christian. The Christian does not go on living in sin, because Christ is living in him, and that evil one cannot touch him. Not only does he not control him, he cannot even touch him. The believer does not come under the power of the evil one. And then to press it right home, John says in verse 19, 'We know that we are of God', but as for the world, 'the whole world lieth in wickedness'. The world is in the arms and in the bosom of the evil one, who controls it absolutely; he has the world and the men who belong to the world entirely in his grip and under his control, and such men are his utterly helpless victims. There is no purpose in telling such people to 'mortify the deeds of the body'; they cannot do so because they are in the grip of the devil. But the Christian's case is far different; the Christians is 'of God', and the evil one cannot even touch him. He can shout at him, he may frighten him occasionally; but he cannot touch him, still less control him.

These are typical New Testament statements about the Christian; and as we realize that the Spirit is in us we shall experience their power. We are called upon, then, to use and to exercise the power that is in us through the indwelling of the Holy Spirit. 'Therefore, brethren, we are debtors, not to the flesh, to live after the flesh. For if ye live after the flesh, ye shall die: but if ye through the Spirit' – who is resident in you – 'do mortify the deeds of the body, ye shall live'. The exhortation is to exercise the power that is in us 'through the Spirit'. The Spirit is power, and He is dwelling in us; and so we are urged to exercise the power that is in us.

But how does this work out in practice? We shall consider the matter in terms of the general and the particular. Let us see how this works out in general. To begin, we have to understand our position spiritually, for many of our troubles are due to the fact that we do not realize, and do not remember, who we are and what we are as Christians. People complain that they have no power, and that they cannot do this or that. What they really need to be told is not that they are absolutely hopeless, and that they must 'hand it over', but, rather, what all Christians are told in the 1st chapter of the Second Epistle of Peter in verses 2 to 4: 'Grace and peace be multiplied unto you through the knowledge of God, and of Jesus our Lord; according as his divine power hath given unto us all things that pertain unto life and godliness'. Everything that 'pertains unto life and godliness' has been given us 'through the knowledge of him that hath called us to glory and virtue'. And again: 'Whereby are given unto us exceeding great and precious promises; that [by means of these exceeding great and precious promises] ye might be partakers of the divine nature, having escaped the corruption that is in the world through lust'. Yet Christian people moan and complain that they have no strength. The answer to such people is: 'All things that pertain unto life and godliness have been given you. Stop moaning and grumbling and complaining. Get up and use what is in you. If you are a Christian the power is in you by the Holy Spirit; you are not hopeless.' But the Apostle Peter does not leave it at that; in the ninth verse of that same chapter of his Second Epistle he says: 'He that lacketh these things' – in other words, the man who does not do the things he has been exhorting him to do – 'is blind and cannot see afar off'. He is short-sighted, 'and has forgotten that he was purged from his old sins'. He has not got a true view of the Christian life. He is talking and living as if he were still unregenerate. He says, 'I cannot continue as a Christian; it is too much for me'. Peter urges such a man to realize the truth about himself. He needs to be awakened, he needs to have his eyes opened and his memory refreshed. He needs to be up and doing, instead of moaning over his deficiencies.

Furthermore, we have to realize that if we are guilty of sin we are 'grieving the Holy Spirit of God' who is in us. Every time we sin it is not so much that we sin and become miserable that chiefly matters, but that we are grieving the Holy Spirit of God who is dwelling in our body. How often do we think of that? I find that when people come to me about this matter they always talk about themselves – 'my failure'. 'I am constantly falling into this sin'. 'This sin is getting me down'. They talk entirely about themselves. They do not talk about their relationship to the Holy Spirit, and for this reason, that the man who realizes that the main trouble about his sinful life is that he is grieving the Holy Spirit, stops doing so at once. The moment a man sees that that is his real problem he deals with it. He is no longer chiefly concerned about his own feelings; when he realizes that he is grieving the Holy Spirit of God he takes immediate action.

Another most important consideration under this general heading is that we must always keep the ultimate goal in sight. Peter emphasizes this in that same first chapter: 'If ye do these things', he says, 'ye shall never fall: for so an entrance shall be ministered unto you abundantly into the everlasting kingdom of our Lord and Saviour Jesus Christ.' If you do these things which I am exhorting you to do, he says, your death, when it comes, will be wonderful; you will not just somehow enter into the kingdom of God, you will have an 'abundant entrance'; it will be a triumphant procession, the gates will be opened and there will be great rejoicing. He is not referring to our present salvation, but to our final glorification, our entry 'into the everlasting habitations'. So we must keep our eye on that goal. Our main trouble is that we are always looking at ourselves and at the world. If we thought of ourselves more and more as pilgrims of eternity (which is what we are) our whole outlook would be transformed. Paul has stated that here in the eleventh verse: Keep your eye on that, he says in effect; keep your eye on the goal. John says the same thing in his first Epistle: 'Beloved, now are we the sons of God; and it doth not yet appear what we shall be, but we know that, when he shall appear, we shall be like him, for we shall see him as he is. And every man that hath this hope in him purifieth himself, even as he is pure' (1 John 3: 2-3). The cause of most of our troubles as Christians is that we live too much to this world and in time; we persist in forgetting that we are only 'pilgrims and strangers' here. We belong to heaven: 'our citizenship is in heaven', and we are going there. If we but kept that in the forefront of our minds, this problem of our fight against sin would take on a different aspect. Human analogies show this clearly. Family loyalty is a great help in life. You are tempted to do something, but you suddenly remember who you are, and you say, 'I cannot let down my family, I cannot disgrace the family name'; so you don't do it. If you did not belong to the family you would have done it. Multiply that by infinity and remember that you belong to the family of heaven, and that you belong there.

My fourth point under this general heading can be put in terms of another statement by the Apostle Peter in the first chapter of the Second Epistle, verse 10: 'Wherefore the rather, brethren, give diligence to make your calling and election sure: for if ye do these things, ye shall never fall'. What you desire, (is it not?) is to live a life in which you do not fall. Very well, says Peter, 'If ye do these things, ye shall never fall'. He has already told his readers what 'these things' are. So if you do not wish to fall, he says, keep on doing these things. Or as Paul puts it in his Epistle to the Galatians, chapter 5, verse 16: 'Walk in the Spirit, and ye shall not fulfil the lust of the flesh.'

But we move on now from the general to the particular, reminding ourselves as we do so that all is done 'through the Spirit', and with a Spirit-enlightened mind. What have we to do in particular? The Apostle's teaching can best be considered under two main headings – direct or negative, and indirect or positive. Under the direct or negative heading the first thing is that the Christian must 'abstain from sin'. It is as simple and direct as that!

'Dearly beloved', says Peter in his First Epistle chapter 2; verse 11, 'I beseech you as strangers and pilgrims, abstain from fleshly lusts, which war against the soul'. That is as plain as a thing can be. There is no suggestion there of our being 'absolutely hopeless' and that we must give up the struggle and 'hand it all over' to the risen Lord. 'Dearly beloved, I beseech you as strangers and pilgrims, abstain from . . . ' – stop doing it, stop it at once, never do it again! You have to be a total abstainer from these sins, these 'fleshly lusts, which war against the soul'. You have no right to say, 'I am weak, I cannot, and temptation is powerful'. The answer of the New Testament is, 'Stop doing it'. You do not need a hospital and treatment, you need to pull yourself together and to realize who you are as 'strangers and pilgrims'. 'Abstain from . . . ' You have no business to touch such things. Recall again the teaching of the Epistle to the Ephesians, chapter 4: 'Let him that stole steal no more.' 'Let no filthy communication proceed out of your mouth'. None of this foolish talking or jesting! Don't do it! Abstain! It is as simple as that, and as practical as that. Stop it!

Secondly, and particularly, to quote the Apostle again in Ephesians 5:11, 12: 'Have no fellowship with the unfruitful works of darkness, but rather reprove them. For it is a shame even to speak of those things which are done of them in secret.' Notice what he says: 'Have no fellowship with them.' You must not only abstain from such things, you must have no fellowship with people who do such things or with that mode of life. 'Have no fellowship with them, but rather reprove them.' Your ruling principle should be not to associate with people of that type; to do so is bad for you, and will do you harm. The Apostle Peter in his First Epistle, chapter 3, verses 10 and 11, states it thus: 'He that will love life and see good days . . . ' – What has he to do? What must a man do who wants to live a full and a happy life, who loves life and would see good days? Is he to admit that he is 'absolutely hopeless' and to 'hand it all over to the risen Lord'? No! – 'He that will love life and see good days, let him refrain his tongue from evil, and his lips that they speak no guile: Let him eschew evil' – shy away from it like a frightened horse. You may not know anything about horses, but if you have ever ridden a horse you will know that it may suddenly shy away from a piece of white paper that is being blown about by the wind. He suddenly jumps to one side. That is what you have to do with sin, says the Apostle. If you love life and want to see good days, 'Refrain from evil, and see that your lips speak no guile; eschew evil and do good; seek peace, and ensue it'. We are to have no fellowship with evil, but to shy away from it, and to keep as far away from it as we can.

Another term is, 'Keep under' (1 Corinthians 9 : 27). 'I keep under my body', says the Apostle. 'Every man who strives for the mastery' – that is, who runs in races – disciplines himself. People who go into training for great athletic contests are very careful about their diet, they stop smoking and do not drink alcoholic beverages. How careful they are! And all because they want to win the prize! If they do that, says Paul, for those perishable crowns, how much more should we discipline ourselves! And he says that he kept under his body; he pummelled it, he hit it. The Apostle uses a boxing metaphor, as we have seen earlier.

The body must be 'kept under'. There is a hint as to how this is to be done in our Lord's words in Luke 21 : 34. He says: 'And take heed to yourselves' – He is talking to His followers – 'lest at any time your hearts be over-charged with surfeiting, and drunkenness, and cares of this life, and so that day come upon you unawares'. Do not eat or drink too much, do not be over-preoccupied with this world's affairs. Take sufficient food, take the right food; but do not be guilty of 'surfeiting'. If a man over-indulges his body in food or drink or anything else he will find it more and more difficult to live the sanctified Christian life, and to mortify the deeds of the body. Avoid all such hindrances therefore, and lead a regular, disciplined ordered life in every respect; otherwise your body will become lethargic and heavy and dull and listless; and there is such an intimate connection between the body and the mind and the spirit that you will find great trouble in your spiritual warfare. 'Keep the body under'.

Another maxim used by the Apostle in this Epistle to the Romans is found in chapter 13 at the 14th verse: 'Put ye on the Lord Jesus Christ, and make no provision for the flesh, to fulfil the lusts thereof.' If you want to mortify the deeds of the body, 'do not make any provision for the flesh'. What does that mean? We find very clear light as to the Apostle's meaning in the first of the Psalms. Here is the prescription; 'Blessed is the man that walketh not in the counsel of the ungodly, nor standeth in the way of sinners'. If you want to live this godly life, and mortify the deeds of the body, do not spend your time standing at street corners, because if you do so you are likely to fall into sin. If you stand where sin is likely to be passing by, do not be surprised if you go home miserable and unhappy because you have fallen again. Do not 'stand in the way of sinners'. Still less must you 'sit in the seat of the scornful'. If you go to such places it will not be surprising if you fall. If you know that certain people have a bad influence over you, avoid them, keep clear of them. You may say, 'But I mix with them in order that I may help them; and yet I find, every time, that they lead me to sin'. If that is so, you are not in a position to help them; avoid them altogether until you are strong enough to mix with them without falling.

The wise man says in the Book of Job: 'I made a covenant with my eyes'. Look straight ahead, he says, do not look to the right or to the left; watch your wandering eyes, those eyes that seem to move almost automatically, and that look for things that entice and incite to sin. Make a covenant with your eyes, says this man; agree not to look at anything that tends to lead you into sin. If it was important in ancient days, how much more so today, when we have newspapers, cinemas, hoardings, television sets, and so on! If ever men needed to make covenants with their eyes it is now. Be careful what you read. Certain newspapers, books, and journals, if you read them, will harm you. Anything that you find does harm to you and lowers your resistance you must avoid. Do not look in their direction; have nothing to do with them. 'Ah, but', you say, 'I thought Christianity delivered me from all that kind of thing.' It is because they have such ideas that people go rushing after the cults. And many seem to think that Christianity means that you book your ticket, and take your seat in some kind of celestial railway, and thereafter you are wafted passively to heaven without any further troubles. But that is not Christianity! It is a fairy-tale; it is the teaching of the cults. In God's Word you are told to 'mortify the deeds of the body', to 'make no provision for the flesh'. Thank God for a virile gospel; thank God for a gospel that tells us that we are now responsible beings in Christ, and which calls upon us to act in a way that glorifies the Saviour. So 'make no provision for the flesh'.

My next point is of high importance. Deal with the first motions and movements of sin and temptation within you; deal with them the moment they appear. If you do not, you are undone; you will go down, as we are taught in the Epistle of James: 'Let no man say when he is tempted, I am tempted of God; for God cannot be tempted with evil, neither tempteth he any man. But every man is tempted when he is drawn away of his own lust and enticed. Then, when lust hath conceived, it bringeth forth sin; and sin when it is finished, bringeth forth death' (1: 13, 14, 15). The first movement is enticement, a slight stirring of lust and enticement. That is the point at which to deal with it. If you fail to deal with it at that stage, it will overcome you. Nip it in the bud, deal with it at once; never let it get even a moment's foothold. Do not accept it at all. Perhaps you feel inclined to say, 'Ah well, I am not going to do the thing'. Ah, but if you accept it in your mind, and begin to fondle it there, and entertain it in your imagination, you are already defeated. According to our Lord you have sinned already. You need not actually commit the deed; to entertain it in your mind is enough, to allow it in your heart is sin in the sight of God, who knows all about us and reads even what happens in the heart and the imagination. Nip it in the bud therefore, have no dealings with it, stop it at once, at the first movement, before this wretched process that is described by James begins to take place.

But remember this – and this can be our next point – that that does not mean repression. If you merely repress a temptation or this first motion of sin within you, it will probably come up again still more strongly. To that extent I agree with the modern psychology. Repression is always bad. 'Well, what do you do?' asks someone. I answer: When you feel that first motion of sin, just pull yourself up and say, 'Of course I am not having any dealings with this at all'. Expose the thing and say, 'This is evil, this is vileness, this is the thing that drove the first man out of Paradise.' Pull it out, look at it, denounce it, hate it for what it is; then you have really dealt with it. You must not merely push it back in a spirit of fear, and in a timorous manner. Bring it out, expose it, and analyse it; and then denounce it for what it is until you hate it.

My last point under this heading is that if, nevertheless, you should fall into sin (and who does not?), do not heal yourself too easily, too quickly. Turn to 2 Corinthians 7 and read what Paul says about 'godly sorrow that worketh repentance'. Once more bring out the thing you have done, look at it, analyse it, expose it, denounce it, hate it, and denounce yourself. But not in such a way as to plunge yourself into the depth of depression and despair! We always tend to go to extremes; we are either too superficial or too deep. We must not 'heal the hurt of the daughter of my people slightly' (Jeremiah 6: 14) but neither must we cast ourselves down into despair and gloom, and say that it is all hopeless, and that we cannot be Christians at all, and go back again under condemnation. That is equally wrong. We must avoid both extremes. Undertake an honest examination of yourself and what you have done, and utterly condemn yourself and your deed; but then realize that as you confess it to God, without any excuse whatsoever, 'He is faithful and just to forgive us our sins, and to cleanse us from all unrighteousness' (1 John 1: 9). If you do such a work 'slightly' you will fall into sin again; and if you set yourself down in a pit of depression you will feel so hopeless that you will fall into more and more sin. An atmosphere of gloom and of failure leads to yet more failure. Do not fall into either of these errors, but attend to the work in the way in which the Spirit always instructs us to do it.

We turn now to the indirect or positive approach to the problem of mortification. We start with what Paul says in his First Epistle to the Corinthians, chapter 16, verse 13. Does he say 'Come into the open, confess that you are an absolute failure, that you can do nothing, give up the struggle, hand it all over to the risen Lord?' Far from it; but instead, 'Watch ye, stand fast in the faith, quit you like men, be strong'. What a thrilling, manly appeal, and what miserable specimens we many of us are! I am not surprised that the masses of the people are outside the Church. It is because they see us! But true Christianity says – 'Watch', 'Stand fast in the faith'. Know what the faith is and stand fast in it. 'Quit you like men, be strong'. Do not be a miserable weakling, moaning and grumbling and complaining that you cannot do this and that, and suffering, as Charles Lamb said, from the 'mumps and measles of the soul'. Be a man! Be strong!

Then secondly, 'Walk in the Spirit, and ye shall not fulfil the lust of the flesh' (Galatians 5: 16). These two things, Paul says, are opposite to one another; as the one goes up the other goes down. A good illustration of this is provided by those little weather instruments that people used to have, with a little wooden man and a little wooden woman attached to a little wooden house. The man came out when the weather was wet and cold, and the woman when it was fine. They could not be both out at the same time. So it is in the Christian life. 'The flesh lusteth against the Spirit, and the Spirit against the flesh.' So, 'Walk in the Spirit, and ye shall not fulfil the lust of the flesh'. Build up the spiritual man that is in you – walk, live your life 'in the Spirit'.

Then turn once more to Peter's words in his Second Epistle, chapter 1, verses 5–7: 'And beside this', he says, 'giving all diligence' – not 'handing it over' – 'add to your faith' – the faith you have. What are we to add to it? – 'Virtue', which means 'strength' – 'and to virtue, knowledge'. You should always be adding to your knowledge. You must shake yourself, you must read, you must study your Bible, you must read books which help you to understand the Bible, you must apply your mind. You will never make much progress if you lack knowledge. Then 'add to your knowledge temperance'. This means that discipline and self-control must be exercised. 'And to temperance patience.' How we need that with ourselves and with others! 'And to patience godliness.' That means living as Christ lived when He was in this world. 'And to godliness brotherly kindness; and to brotherly kindness charity,' that is, 'love'. *We* have got to engage in these activities; *we* have to add them to our faith, to add them one by one, and to keep on doing so. 'Giving all diligence' – set yourself to the task, and keep on at it. Then the Apostle gives us reasons for doing so. 'For if these things be in you, and abound, they make you that you shall neither be barren nor unfruitful in the knowledge of our Lord Jesus Christ.' 'But he that lacketh these things is blind, and cannot see afar off, and hath forgotten that he was purged from his old sins. Wherefore the rather, brethren, give diligence to make your calling and election sure; for if ye do these things, ye shall never fall: for so an entrance shall be ministered unto you abundantly into the everlasting kingdom of our Lord and Saviour Jesus Christ.'

We must be positive! I find this to be one of the most valuable points of all. Thank God, in my own experience, and in my experience in helping others, I have found this, I suppose – if I were to choose one thing as being the most valuable of all – to be the greatest of all helps in this matter of avoiding sin and living the Christian life. When people come to me and talk about their failures, and especially when they talk about one particular sin, I invariably say to them: You are looking at your life in the wrong way, you are too negative. Your ambition and desire should be very much more than to get rid of this particular thing that is worrying you, and getting you down. What you should really desire is to be a Christian worthy of the name, the sort of Christian of whom the Lord Jesus Christ is proud, and who will attract others to our Lord. Be positive; desire to be big and great, and to follow the saints who have 'adorned the gospel' in past ages.

We should look at ourselves, and our lives in this world, in the way indicated by the Apostle Peter in the First Epistle, chapter 2, verses 9 and 10. He does not tell believers that they are 'a miserable failure', and 'absolutely hopeless'. Instead he says: 'Ye are a chosen generation, a kingdom of priests, an holy nation, a people for God's own peculiar possession.' Why should we be careful always to remember this? It is, Peter continues, in order that 'ye should show forth the praises of him who hath called you out of darkness into his marvellous light'. Then he adds, 'Which in time past were not a people' – you were once only a rabble, a crowd – 'but are now the people of God: which had not obtained mercy, but now have obtained mercy'. If we but thought of ourselves in that way, if we only realized what we have been made by God in Christ Jesus, through the Holy Spirit, if we realized that we are this 'chosen generation', this 'royal priesthood', this 'holy nation', this 'peculiar people', and that God has made us to be these things, how different would our lives be! We are in this world to show the praises, the excellences of God. The world does not believe in God; it does not believe in the Lord Jesus Christ.

What is a Christian? According to Peter's Epistle – and it is the teaching of the New Testament everywhere – a Christian is a man whose main ambition, while he is in this life and this world, is to show forth the glories and the praises of God and of Jesus Christ. How does he do that? By being different, of course. So Peter goes on to say: 'Dearly beloved, I beseech you as strangers and pilgrims, abstain from fleshly lusts, which war against the soul; having your conversation honest among the Gentiles: that whereas they speak against you as evil-doers, they may by your good works, which they shall behold, glorify God in the day of visitation.' And it is to the extent that we realize this truth about ourselves, and that our calling and our main business in life is to testify to the grace and the glory and the love and the majesty of God, and that we are to be unlike everyone else in the world – it is, I say, to the extent that we realize this that we shall 'mortify the deeds of the body' and refuse to allow anything to mar this marvellous work which God has done in us.

The most terrible aspect of falling into sin is not so much that I have failed, or that I have fallen, or that I am miserable, or that I need release, but that I have failed God and misrepresented Him, and that men and women in the world will know nothing about His praise, His glory, His virtues, His excellences. They will say that to be a Christian makes no difference, that Christians are like themselves after all. They will ask, Where is the difference? So they dismiss Christianity and Christ. It is as we realize that we are His representatives, that we are the channels that He has chosen by means of which He will show forth His own glory, His own excellency, His own power and the wonders of His ways, that we shall proceed to deal with the problem of sin. He has put the Spirit within us, Christ 'dwells' within us, so we have the power. Therefore, in the name of God, and for the glory of God, and the honour of God, just as men and women are ready to die for 'King and Country', so should we be ready to live for the glory of God and His kingdom, and to the praise of His dear Son. This is the New Testament way of sanctification and of holiness. Let us, then, 'through the Spirit' and in these various ways, 'mortify the deeds of the body', make our 'calling and election sure', and thereby have 'an abundant entrance into the everlasting kingdom of God' when we die. And in the meantime let us 'show forth the praises of him who called us out of darkness into his marvellous light'.

Twelve

*

With this verse we come to a new sub-section of this 8th chapter. As we do so it is essential that we should be clear as to its setting, or its context. Nothing is more important in the interpretation of Scripture than to bear in mind the context. Nothing is worse than just to select a verse at random, or to extract a verse out of its context. That is always important in interpreting any Scripture; but it is unusually important here, because, as we have already seen, in this chapter the Apostle works out and develops a very sustained and closely knit and developing argument. It is therefore impossible to understand the real import of any one sub-section if we have not got an idea of the whole, and the relationship of any particular sub-section to the other sub-sections and to the entire massive argument. Our first business therefore is to be quite clear as to how exactly this particular statement which starts in the fourteenth verse and runs on to the end of verse 17 comes in at this particular point in the main argument.

Indeed, the Apostle himself insists upon our doing this, for he introduces the matter with the word 'For'. That is another of his characteristic words – 'For' – and it reminds us that though this is a new sub-section it is not independent of the previous one, but, rather, connected with it. My contention is that the great theme of this entire chapter is that of the security of the Christian believer. The message of the chapter is assurance of salvation, or, as I would prefer to put it, the absolute certainty of the 'final perseverance' of all who are truly justified in Christ Jesus by faith. Or, to put it in yet a different way, the theme is the absolute certainty of the final, complete, and entire salvation of the believer, even including, as we have seen, his body. That theme began, in a sense, back at the 1st verse of chapter 5. 'Therefore being justified by faith we have peace with God through our Lord Jesus Christ.' But not only that, 'By whom also we have access by faith into this grace wherein we stand, and' – here is the theme – 'rejoice in the hope of the glory of God'. His concern from there on is to show the basis on which we have the right to 'rejoice in hope of the glory of God'. He produces argument after argument, and especially in the crucial passage in chapter 5 verses 12–21, where he introduces the cardinal doctrine of the union of the believer with Christ. As he was 'in Adam' he is now 'in Christ'. That is the ultimate source and ground of assurance and of certainty.

He then had to turn aside to the digression of chapters 6 and 7 to deal with difficulties. Having done so he returns to his great theme in chapter 8, 'There is therefore now no condemnation to them that are in Christ Jesus'. The man who is in Christ Jesus has finished with condemnation, he is out of that realm altogether. 'The law of the Spirit of life in Christ Jesus hath made me free from the law of sin and death.' The Christian has finished with the law in that sense of condemnation. He is no longer 'under law', he is 'under grace'. In verses 2–4 the Apostle works out the theme of certainty and assurance in terms of our being entirely delivered from the law and joined to Christ by the Spirit. Then in verses 5–11 he puts the same matter of assurance and certainty in terms of the indwelling of the Holy Spirit within us, and His working in us for our sanctification, and our ultimate glorification, including the body itself. 'If the Spirit of him that raised up Jesus from the dead dwell in you, he that raised up Christ from the dead shall also quicken your mortal bodies by his Spirit that dwelleth in you.'

Our ultimate, complete and entire deliverance from sin is guaranteed by the indwelling of the Spirit. If the Spirit of Christ is not in us we are 'none of his'; but if He is in us, then we are His, and the Spirit, as he has been showing us in detail, proceeds with our sanctification. The whole object of salvation is 'that the righteousness of the law might be fulfilled in us, who walk not after the flesh, but after the Spirit'. The ground of assurance is that the Spirit is dwelling in us. Then comes the practical exhortation of verses 12 and 13: 'In the light of all this' he says, 'you are not debtors to the flesh, to live after the flesh. That would be utterly inconsistent with your whole position. We are to mortify through the Spirit the deeds of the body'.

There then is the argument as it has been developed up to the end of verse 13. We have the original statement in verse 1, and the two sub-sections (verses 1–4 and 5–13) show different aspects of our assurance and certainty.

We now come to a further argument which is introduced in this fourteenth verse. Observe that the Apostle does not introduce it abruptly. He never does so; each step always arises out of the last; each one leads to the next. We shall find exactly the same method at the end of this section and at the beginning of the following section at verse 18. To me it is a means of grace, and a source of great enjoyment, to watch the Apostolic method. It is always a thrill and a privilege to watch any great mind working; but when you have a colossus like the Apostle Paul, a man filled with the Spirit, nothing can be more entrancing than to watch him unfolding the truth and developing his argument step by step.

How does this section follow from the previous one? Paul has said in verse 13, 'If ye through the Spirit do mortify the deeds of the body, ye shall live'. He seems to say, If we are mortifying the deeds of the body by the Spirit in that way, it means that we are obviously being led by the Spirit to do so. And if we are thus being led by the Spirit, that is, in and of itself, a proof that we are 'the sons of God'. It is in this way that Paul arrives at this statement. He has told us to mortify the deeds of the body by the Spirit. No one but a Christian mortifies the deeds of the body, no one else submits to the leading of the Spirit. Hence the fact that you are doing so is proof positive that you are not only led by the Spirit, but are therefore, of necessity, sons of God.

So the Apostle has introduced his new theme – the assurance and absolute certainty of our final salvation in terms of our divine sonship. The theme runs on to the end of verse 17. It is one of the most glorious themes, not only of this chapter, and of this Epistle, but of the whole of Scripture. There is nothing more wonderful than that we should come to the realization that we are 'sons of God'.

Let us notice incidentally that the way in which the Apostle handles the doctrine of sonship in this paragraph supplies clear proof that the main theme of this chapter is certainty and assurance, not sanctification. There is a popular teaching which says that the first four chapters – indeed, some say the first five chapters – deal with justification. Then, they say, in chapter 6 the Apostle comes on to sanctification. But then there is all that argument in chapter 7 about the incomplete Christian. The man in chapter 7, they say, is justified but not sanctified. But then you turn over to chapter 8 and you find sanctification set forth again in a fuller sense. I have tried to demonstrate that that is a completely false reading and understanding of what the Apostle teaches. It is wrong to say that the fundamental theme of chapter 8 is sanctification. Sanctification comes in, of course, but only as a subsidiary theme. I say 'subsidiary' for the reason that sanctification is always subsidiary. It is real error to regard sanctification as an end in and of itself. But it is often regarded as such. That is so because so many approach the whole of the Christian life in a purely subjective manner – they start and end with themselves and their problems. They say: 'Here am I, a Christian man, but I am being defeated, and the greatest of all questions is, How can I be delivered from my life of defeat as a Christian? how can I have victory and live the victorious life?' That is the approach. So sanctification becomes the greatest and the most important question of all. But the Apostle's greatest concern is that we should know and realize that we are 'sons of God', that we should be rejoicing and praising God and crying 'Abba, Father', that we should be delivered from the 'spirit of bondage'. His desire is for us to be so sure of this that, no matter what may come to us from the outside, we shall remain fully confident that we are 'heirs of God and joint-heirs with Christ'; and if so be that we suffer with Him, we shall also be glorified with Him.

How often do you think of your coming glorification? How often have you heard sermons on glorification? The whole emphasis is on sanctification. We have 'movements' to teach and promote sanctification; but sanctification is only a part of the process that leads to 'glorification'. The Apostle's interest is always in glorification. As we have seen, he introduced it in chapter 5 in verse 2, and we shall find it elaborated later on in this very chapter, for instance in verse 30: 'Moreover whom he did predestinate, them he also called, and whom he called, them he also justified, and whom he justified' (then the leap!) 'them he also glorified'. There is actually no mention of sanctification there.

But, and especially during the last hundred years, interest has settled on sanctification. That has been so because we are so miserably subjective, because we fail to think of salvation in terms of what God has ultimately planned and purposed for us. His end is our glorification. Sanctification is designed to prepare us for glory that awaits us. What the Apostle is chiefly interested in in this chapter, from beginning to end, is our ultimate glorification, which includes the body itself – every part and portion of us. His argument is that, because this is God's plan and purpose for us, nothing will be allowed to prevent its accomplishment. The argument in the last sub-section was that He has put His Spirit in us, and the Spirit works in us to promote our sanctification, and enables us to mortify the deeds of the body in which sin still resides. 'But that is sanctification' says someone. I agree, but what it has ultimately in view is glorification. And here in this section he is still interested in our glorification, and shows how one of the guarantees of that is the fact that we are the 'sons of God'.

Negatively, he tells us that every man is not a son of God. Then he reminds us that only Christians are sons of God. Thirdly he explains what this sonship means. Next he shows how we may be sure of our sonship; and in the fifth and last place, he points to the consequences and the results of our sonship, or at least to some of them.

The first proposition is that not all are sons of God. 'For as many as are led by the Spirit of God, they', (which means, 'they, and they alone' – it is emphatic) 'are the sons of God'. This is an essential point in connection with our argument concerning assurance; but it is also important in that it denies, and gives the lie direct, to a popular present-day teaching which talks much about the 'universal Fatherhood of God', and the 'universal brotherhood of man'. Another form of that same teaching speaks of a universal salvation, that is, that everyone will be saved finally. We must not divide mankind, they say, into 'saved' and 'lost', because God is the Father of all; all are His children and therefore all are brothers. Salvation, they maintain, will ultimately be universal; the whole of mankind will be saved; also the fallen angels; and even the devil himself – if they believe in such a being.

It is important that we should be clear about this matter because it affects, profoundly and ultimately, our whole doctrine of salvation. And not only so, but it also means that if we adopt such notions we are no longer being guided by the Scriptures. It means that we have become philosophers and are arguing in a purely philosophical manner that, because God is a God of love, it follows of necessity that finally all will be saved. The philosophers argue that if God is love, and if God is holy and perfect, He cannot possibly allow any human being He has created to be consigned to everlasting damnation and perdition. That, they aver, does not fit in either with the idea of love or of justice. Because they do not understand such a possibility as damnation they reject it. They try, of course, to produce some scriptural evidence in favour of their contention, and they are fond of quoting what the Apostle Paul said in his address at Athens as recorded in the 17th chapter of the Acts of the Apostles, verse 28: 'For in him we live, and move, and have our being; as certain also of your own poets have said, For we are also his offspring'. The argument is that therefore we are all the children of God.

Let me give some brief indications of why we reject such teaching *in toto*. Had we nothing but John 8 : 44 it would be sufficient. Our Lord, turning to the Jews, said, 'Ye are of your father the devil, and the lusts of your father ye will do'. Similarly in the first chapter of John's Gospel in verse 12 we read, 'But as many as received him, to them he gave power (authority) to become the sons of God, even to them that believe on his name'. Not to all, but only to those who believe. Then in John 17, verse 9: 'I pray for them: I pray not for the world.' Note the division. This is part and parcel of the whole of the biblical teaching. The Bible divides all mankind into one or the other of these two groups; we are either God's people or else we are not God's people. We are either 'saved' or 'lost'; we are either 'alive' or 'perishing'. 'God so loved the world, that he gave his only be-gotten Son, that whosoever believeth in him should not perish but have everlasting life' (John 3 : 16). Of the man who does not believe we read that 'he is condemned already, because he hath not believed in the name of the only begotten Son of God' (verse 18). The Scripture everywhere emphasizes this great division. – 'You were' – 'You are'. The Bible teaches that we are either the children of God or else we are the children of wrath, the children of the devil. We are either children of God who are looking forward to the glory, or else 'the wrath of God abideth on us'. In this life and in this world our eternal destiny is decided. We are confronted always by these two possibilities. This is the major theme of the whole of the Bible. We are called upon to 'escape', to 'separate' ourselves from a condemned world, to 'flee from the wrath to come', to come out, to be separated, as God's people. We must be clear in our minds, therefore, that not all are the children of God. It is only those, and those alone, who are led by the Spirit of God who are the sons of God, says the Apostle. And, as we shall see, the whole idea of adoption makes this absolutely essential. There is no meaning in the doctrine of adoption unless it is our basic and fundamental postulate that every man by nature is a 'child of wrath', as Paul puts it in Ephesians 2: 3.

But what the Apostle is really emphasizing is that Christians are 'sons of God'. I am varying the emphasis. They, and they alone are 'sons of God'. Once more, unfortunately, I have to turn for a moment to a matter which is of great importance to some people. They say: 'In verse 14 you have the term "sons of God" but in verse 16 you have "children of God", and they are two different words'. What is the significance of this? There are those who would have us believe that this is of very great significance indeed. They go so far as to say that whereas all Christians are 'children of God', all Christians are not 'sons of God'. They teach that that not only affects our experience and our life while we are in this world, but that it will even affect us in eternity. They state that the *sons* of God will be in a more privileged position than those who are only the *children* of God. Some even go so far as to say that there is a type of teaching which you cannot give to the 'children' because they could not receive it and would not understand it. It can only be given to, and received by the 'sons'. So in a mixed congregation you must never give teaching that is for the 'sons' only. When the 'children' give evidence that they have become 'sons' as the result of some further experience you can then let them into the secret of this higher truth which the 'sons' alone are capable of receiving.

What have we to say concerning such teaching? We simply turn, of course, to the Scripture itself. In regard to this particular passage, any unbiassed and unprejudiced person must surely agree that the terms, 'sons', 'children', are interchangeable. A 'son' is a 'child' of course, but no emphasis is placed upon any distinction or difference between the two. The only reason for paying attention at all to this matter is that we are told in the Epistle to the Galatians in chapter 4: 'Now I say, that the heir, as long as he is a child, differeth nothing from a servant, though he be lord of all; but is under tutors and governors until the time appointed of the father. Even so we, when we were children, were in bondage under the elements of the world. But when the fulness of the time was come, God sent forth his Son, made of a woman, made under the law, to redeem them that were under the law, that we might receive the adoption of sons. And because ye are sons, God hath sent forth the Spirit of his Son into your hearts crying, Abba, Father' (verses 1–7). As this passage is very similar to the one with which we are dealing, we are compelled to pay some attention to it.

There is no question but that in this Galatians passage the Apostle shows that there is a difference between being a child and being a son. The difference is not one in relationship, but in our appreciation of our position. A little child, an infant – and that incidentally is the word that is used – is as much a child of the father as a grown-up adult person. But he is not as aware of it; he does not understand it as thoroughly; and that is what the Apostle is demonstrating there. He is showing that we as Christians, in contradistinction to the saints of the Old Testament, are in a position where we should have a larger and a fuller understanding and appreciation of what is true of us. We are no more 'children of God' than Abraham, the patriarchs, and all the saints, were; but we should have a deeper and a better understanding of that relationship. We enjoy a larger and a fuller sense of it, which leads to the cry of 'Abba, Father'. There are obviously variations and differences in understanding and appreciation among Christian people. But we must never press that point so far as to make of it an absolute division, and even one which will continue in glory. That surely is an utter denial of the Scripture, which teaches that all Christians, as sons, are being brought to glory, and that every one of us will arrive there. The two terms 'children' and 'sons' are certainly synonyms in this particular passage, for what the Apostle is emphasizing here is our relationship to God, and that as Christians we are 'sons of God'. A Christian is not merely a man who is forgiven. He *is* forgiven, thank God, he is justified and reconciled – all gloriously true, but we must not stop at that! What the Apostle wants us to realize is that we are 'sons' of God. A master can forgive his slave but he does not change the slave's status in doing so. That is the contrast the Apostle has in his mind. If we regard salvation merely as a matter of forgiveness or of reconciliation or of justification, and stop at that, we should probably still have a more or less slavish spirit. But, as Paul goes on to say, we must not have such a spirit. So we are to start on our Christian career with the realization that we are 'sons of God'.

The third point for our consideration is the meaning of this sonship. Once again we must lay down the proposition that none of us, by nature, is a child or a son of God. We are children of Adam. That is our parentage, that is where we belong by nature; the consequence being that we are 'the children of wrath'. We are all born with a fallen nature – 'In sin did my mother conceive me'. The Lord Jesus Christ is the 'only begotten' Son of God. He stands alone; He is unique, the only begotten Son of the Father, the only begotten Son of God. It is utterly unscriptural to say that all human beings are sons of God or children of God. We are all by nature as far removed from that as is possible. How, then, does anyone become a son of God? A term is used in this very section which gives us a preliminary understanding of the matter; it is the term 'adoption' – 'Spirit of adoption'. This is another great biblical doctrine, and we must consider its meaning. We are familiar with the fact that some husbands and wives may decide to adopt a child, and that that has to be done in a fully legal manner. It is an act whereby a person who is not by nature related to the married pair is now taken into the family, and is regarded as a son. He is given the privilege and the position of a son and behaves as a son. Such is adoption. And it becomes a picture of this great doctrine which we find in the Bible. Adoption is an act of God in which He takes us into His family.

Adoption is a legal action. It is not identical with justification; but it is very closely associated with it. When God legally, forensically, declares that he regards a man as just in Christ, he also adopts that person into his family. We must think of adoption therefore primarily and essentially as a great legal action on the part of God. I emphasize the matter because our fundamental theme, let us not forget, is assurance and certainty; and what adoption means is that because it is God Himself Who has adopted us in this legal manner, the action is an irreversible one. A particularly clear statement to this effect is found in the Epistle to the Ephesians: 'Blessed be the God and Father of our Lord Jesus Christ, who hath blessed us with all spiritual blessings in heavenly places in Christ: according as he hath chosen us in him before the foundation of the world, that we should be holy and without blame before him in love: having predestinated us unto the adoption of children by Jesus Christ to himself, according to the good pleasure of his will, to the praise of the glory of his grace' (1 : 3–6). Here we have a statement of the basis of our assurance in terms of sonship. It is the immutable, eternal God, 'the Father of lights with whom is no variableness, neither shadow of turning,' who has done this, who has taken this legal action, who has adopted us into His family, and put us into this position. *He* has done it, and because that is so, it is an irreversible action. The Christian who grasps this teaching will be certain of his glorification, and he will be able to face persecutions and trials and all else that is against him in this world.

But we can go still further. The Christian is not only one who has been adopted into God's family; something has happened to him; there has been a change of nature in him; he has undergone rebirth. He has been 'born again', he has been 'born of the Spirit'. Indeed John in his First Epistle says that we have been 'born of God'. 'Whosoever is born of God doth not commit sin'. Or, as Peter states it in his Second Epistle: 'We have been made partakers of the divine nature' (1 : 4). We shall go on to analyse something of the meaning and the content of all these terms and expressions; but what we have to lay hold on immediately is that not only is it true that we have been adopted, but also that we are 'in Christ', we are joined to Him. He took our nature, and we are in Him in that nature, and so in this extraordinary manner we are 'partakers of the divine nature' through the manhood of Christ and our union with Him. We are members of His body. So we do not stop short at adoption; we rejoice in the fact that as the result of the rebirth we are 'born of God', we are 'partakers of the divine nature'. In other words, we once more define the Christian in terms of the title of the book of Henry Scougal of 300 years ago: What is Christianity? It is, says Scougsl, *The Life of God in the Soul of Man*, and nothing less than that.

It is not surprising that the Apostle should emphasize the truth that 'as many as are led by the Spirit of God, they are the sons of God'. That is what we are now, nothing less; and we should always think of ourselves, therefore, in these terms. It matters not what may be happening without or within, this is the basic truth, this is the real ground of assurance. I am not merely forgiven; I am a son of God; I belong to the family of God. I was not a son of God by natural birth; but now I am.

We shall have to work out, as far as we can, the meaning and the content of this great term, and then go on to see how we can be quite sure that this is true of us; we shall also look at some of the glorious results to which it leads. But have we got hold of this glorious truth? Is this going to ring in our hearts and in our minds throughout the days that are coming, and for ever and for ever? The humblest Christian in the world is a 'son of God'. Lift up your head, and as you look around and see the world as it is, remember to look at it as a child of God, as one who belongs to the family of God. Then you will never know despair, you will never know panic, or terror, or alarm. You will be able to look at it all and see through it all and say, 'This is the victory that overcometh the world', in every sense, 'even our faith'. And it is this faith which brings us to this knowledge that we are 'sons of God'.

Thirteen

*

*For as many as are led by the Spirit of God, they are the sons of
God.*   Romans 8 : 14

The Apostle here, as a part of his teaching concerning full
assurance of salvation, reminds us of the glorious truth that,
though we are still left on this earth, and in spite of many things
that are true of us, we are nevertheless the sons, or the children
of God. We have begun to look at this term 'sonship' and have
seen that it means that we have been 'adopted' by God into His
family. We were all by nature the children of wrath, the children
of Adam, but now we have been adopted into the family of God.
More than that, we have been born again, we have been given a
new life, a new nature, we are 'partakers of the divine nature'.

But that is not all. Adoption and rebirth really tell only how
we become sons; we must look, therefore, more closely at what
the term itself implies concerning us. The first thing we notice is
that it involves the notion of similarity, or likeness. This is something that is true, of course, on the natural level. A son and a
father have similarities; they are alike, their kinship in the matter
of blood leads to certain likenesses. They have certain things in
common, a likeness of nature. This is also one of the amazing
aspects of our relationship to God as His sons. It means that
there is a likeness and a similarity of mind and of outlook. We
but note it at this point. As sons of God we now look at everything from God's standpoint, from the aspect of eternity. It was
not so before; but now we do so. This same apostle states the
fact in a very striking manner at the end of the second chapter of
the First Epistle to the Corinthians. He says: 'He that is spiritual
judgeth all things, yet he himself is judged of no man. For who
hath known the mind of the Lord, that he may instruct him?'

– and then this extraordinary statement – 'But we have the mind of Christ' (vv. 15, 16). In other words, as sons of God we have this 'mind', this 'outlook' of Christ. The mind of Christ, the Son of God, becomes our mind.

But then the expression includes also a similarity and a likeness in the matter of behaviour. This is taught in many places in Scripture. Our Lord teaches it, for instance, in the Sermon on the Mount, at the end of the 5th chapter of Matthew's Gospel where, in reference to loving our enemies and blessing them that curse us, he says: 'I say unto you, Love your enemies, bless them that curse you, do good to them that hate you, and pray for them which despitefully use you, and persecute you; that [in order that] ye may be the children of your Father which is in heaven: for he maketh his sun to rise on the evil and on the good, and sendeth rain on the just and on the unjust. For if ye love them which love you, what reward have ye? do not even the publicans the same? And if ye salute your brethren only, what do ye more than others? do not even the publicans so? Be ye therefore perfect, even as your Father which is in heaven is perfect' (vv. 44–48). Our Lord's exhortation is, that as our Father has dealt thus with us, and similarly with others, we are to do likewise. So sonship involves a likeness, a similarity in the whole outlook, and in conduct and behaviour.

This can be worked out endlessly; and this is the grand motive for sanctified living. This is the basis of the New Testament appeal for holy living. The motive should not be that we may be happier or that we may have victory over some particular sin. That is a very low motive, though the thing in itself is desirable. The way to put it is this, that we are to behave as children of our Father. 'Let your light so shine before men, that they may see your good works, and glorify your Father which is in heaven.' Our 'walk', our 'conversation', our life is to be of a kind that is reminiscent of God Himself. The same thought appears in the fifth chapter of Paul's Epistle to the Ephesians: 'Be ye therefore followers of God, as dear children; and walk in love, as Christ also hath loved us' (vv. 1, 2). The similarity and the likeness are to cover the whole of our existence and being and activity – outlook, understanding, conduct, and behaviour.

But in addition to involving the notion of similarity, the term sonship clearly carries certain other implications; and I know of nothing that is more comforting and consoling than to work them out. Consider, for instance, what it involves and implies concerning God's relationship to us. Is there anything more important for us than to know this? It is because this is a way of saying, as nothing else can say it, that God loves us, and loves us in a peculiar and a special manner. We know that God 'causeth his sun to rise on the evil and the good, and sendeth rain on the just and on the unjust', but God does not love the whole of humanity in the same way as He loves those who are His sons. He may manifest His benignity to all, and He does so in His kindly providence. But the vital distinction is the distinction between God's general attitude towards the whole of mankind and His peculiar, special attitude towards His own children, towards His sons.

Once more the human analogy conveys the idea to us at once. Whereas it is our business and our duty to be kindly disposed towards everyone, and to be ready to help everyone, it is right that there should be something special and additional in the case of those who belong to us, who are our own family. Paul expresses this in his Epistle to the Galatians: 'Let us do good unto all men, especially unto them who are of the household of faith' (6: 10). You do not expect a parent to treat all children in the same way as he treats his own children. He is to be kind and good to all, but because of the relationship there is something additional, something special and peculiar in his attitude to his own. In other words, what we are reminded of here is that, as God's children, His love to us is something which is special and peculiar.

How does this love show itself? It means that He takes a special interest in us, and has a special concern about us. It is God who in His grace and kindness and infinite condescension has chosen these terms. 'Sons' is one of the so-called anthropomorphisms. It is God coming down to our level and speaking of Himself, as it were, in human terms, in order that we may grasp a certain amount of the truth. And what He says is that, like the human, natural father, He as our Father takes a very special interest in us, in our well-being, in our welfare, in our good. The term necessarily carries that meaning, and we have to realize that God thus takes this special interest in us. A phrase used by our Lord puts it perfectly. He says that 'the very hairs of your head are all numbered'. That is the measure of the loving interest, and special concern, which God as our Father takes in us.

Then, at the same time, as a Father He plans for us. It is not merely that He is passive, that He is someone whom we approach when we desire something, and who gives us that something, and we thank him. That is true, but it does not stop there. The father plans for the child; the child is not capable of doing so until he attains maturity, so the father, with the child's interests and future in mind, has to do it for him. The child would like to spend all his time at play, but the father knows better; so he plans that the child should go to school and receive certain instruction, and do this and that. The father plans all. And God does that for us! The whole of our salvation is the result of God's great and glorious plan, His plan to bring us to glory. This is the great theme which runs through the whole of the Scriptures. Take, for instance, the statement of it which we find in the second chapter of the Epistle to the Hebrews, verse 10: 'For it became him, for whom are all things, and by whom are all things, in bringing many sons unto glory, to make the captain of their salvation perfect through sufferings'. God's plan is to bring His sons, His many sons, to glory, to that ultimate glory to which the Apostle has referred at the beginning of chapter 5 in this Epistle, and which he will deal with later in this very chapter.

How does God bring us to that goal? He does so by leading us, by directing us. 'As many as are *led* by the Spirit of God, they are the sons of God'. But, further, we are reminded in Hebrews 12, verses 6–10, that God as our Father, and in the light of His ultimate plan and purpose of bringing us to glory, also chastises us, as we have earlier. God takes this personal interest in us; and as His children we are not allowed to misbehave ourselves with impunity. He rebukes us, He chastises us, He punishes us, and at times we have to suffer; not because God delights in punishing us, but 'for our profit' and benefit, for our sanctification, that we may be holy. We do not welcome chastisement, but it is essential to the fulfilment of God's plan for us and His ultimate goal. God looks at us one by one, each one of us is His child, and He is interested in every one of us individually. So we begin to look at what is happening to us in a different way, and we thank God even for chastisement. 'Whom the Lord loveth', we read, 'he chasteneth, and scourgeth every son whom he receiveth'. Thus we see, even in moments and days, perhaps years of chastisement, the loving hand of God upon us. It is a difficult lesson to learn, but it is a most glorious one. And so we turn our very chastisements and moments of pain into something which gives us a glorious assurance of our relationship to our Father.

In addition, God provides for us, cares for us, and protects us. There is a restraining grace, and there is a grace that goes before us, a prevenient grace. We are surrounded by the grace of God. He protects us in various ways which we only come to realize, perhaps, afterwards. Looking back across your life in the light of certain incidents you see in the lives of others, you can say quite honestly, 'There but for the grace of God. . . . ' This is true, not only in the matter of our salvation, but in every aspect of our Christian life. We can see how we would have gone, as others have gone, into error or some apostasy, were it not for the restraining hand of God upon us. And He can restrain our enemies in order to protect us. This is something of the richness of this concept of our being 'the sons of God'. It is seen in that beautiful phrase, 'Underneath are the everlasting arms'. God foresees our every circumstance and need; and He is ever present, surrounding us with His love and His protecting arms.

Then look at sonship from another aspect; He is always ready to receive us, and to listen to us, and to grant us His blessing. He is more ready to give, than we are to receive. Our Lord says, 'Your heavenly Father knoweth the things that you desire of him before you even ask him.' All this is a manifestation of the great Father-heart and love of God towards His children, those who are His sons.

How practical these points are! How valuable it is to realize something of this when we pray to God, and when we go into His presence! We do not pray truly if we are doubtful and un-certain. We should go into the presence of God as a child goes to his father. We do it with 'reverence and godly fear', of course, realizing that our heavenly Father is who and what He is; but we should go with a childlike confidence and simplicity. If that is not true of us we are not praying truly. There are Christians who think that they must so safeguard the holiness and majesty and greatness of God that they virtually deny this doctrine of sonship; but it is God's own doctrine. We ought to go as children to our Father with confidence in our acceptance, and with full assurance. A formal, cold prayer is not a sign of great spirituality or of understanding. Let us be careful that we do not underestimate any aspect of the doctrine. Some of us are in danger of reacting overmuch against the glib, false familiarity that is displayed by some superficial Christians. I am not advocating such a course. We never like a child who is too familiar with a parent or who does not show respect to the parent. But do not react so violently against over-familiarity as to deny the doctrine of sonship. The doctrine of sonship is here for our help and encouragement; it is to teach us how to come into God's presence. When we as Christian people go to God, we are not going to the Judge Eternal, we are going to 'our Father which is in heaven'. Let us not forget that aspect of the matter. Or again, to use the language of the author of the Epistle to the Hebrews, 'Let us come boldly' – with confidence and assurance – 'unto the throne of grace'. We must emphasize 'the throne'; but we must emphasize the grace equally. We have passed from judgment unto life. We are the children of God.

The Apostle wants us to enjoy great assurance when we pray, and to realize that God is ready to listen to us. Think of the analogy of an earthly parent who may be very busy on some occasion. He may be a man of great affairs – the head of a great business, or a great professional man, whose programme is unusually full. Someone wants to see him; but he sends out a message to say that he cannot see anyone, however important. Suddenly he hears a little tap at his door, and he knows that it is his little child or grandchild who is there; immediately he stops working and opens the door. God is like that! God is our Father, and He is ready to listen to us, and to bear with us. 'He knoweth our frame.' We are, as Paul says, 'His dear children'. If we could but lay hold of this truth it would revolutionize our Christian experience.

In these ways we learn something of the content and the meaning of the term 'sons of God' as we think of it in terms of God's attitude toward us. Expand it for yourselves in terms of what you find taught here and there in the Scriptures. 'When my father and mother forsake me', says the Psalmist, 'then the Lord will take me up.' 'As a father pitieth his children, so the Lord pitieth them that fear him.' These are the terms in which the Scripture shows us God condescending to our low estate, in order that we may know the relationship, and rejoice in it, and act upon it as we come into His presence.

But we must also look at what this term tells us about our relationship to God from another aspect. It means that we no longer go to God with a 'craven fear'. Certainly we go to Him with 'reverence and godly fear', but 'craven fear' must be cast away. 'With boldness', 'with confidence', 'access with confidence' are Scripture phrases denoting the right approach. We come to the Father, says Paul, 'by one Spirit', 'We both [Jews and Gentiles] have access in one body unto the Father' (Ephesians 2 : 18). It is always thus, and Paul is concerned that we should rejoice in this freedom. We shall work this out in greater detail when we come to verses 15 and 16. But meanwhile let me ask: Is this the way in which we approach God when we go to Him in prayer? God deliver us from stereotyped formal prayers! Let us come to Him in this way. Some of us are critical of liturgies because they do not bring out this aspect as they should. There is a lack of this warmth, this intimacy, this assurance, this confidence; and to that extent they are not true to the New Testament teaching. Let us be guided by what God in His infinite kindness has chosen to tell us about ourselves.

Let us turn to the next question. I have suggested that there are some five main sub-divisions in this little section from verse 14 to verse 17. The first is that not everyone is a son; secondly, that all true Christians are sons; thirdly, that there are certain characteristic features of sonship. Now we come to the fourth sub-division, to inquire how we may be sure of our sonship. This is a most practical question. At this point the Apostle supplies a number of answers to this question. It is what is uppermost in his mind in the verses we are considering. He develops the idea of sonship mainly in terms of our assurance of sonship. The first thing he tells us is that we can be quite sure that we are sons of God if we are led by the Spirit of God. He has already referred to the Spirit as 'the Spirit of God' in verse 9, and as 'the Spirit of Christ', and in verse 13 he has said: 'If ye through the Spirit' – the Holy Spirit – 'do mortify the deeds of the body . . . ' So the reference here again to 'the Spirit of God' is not to some vague, general spirit that may be in us; it is specifically to the Holy Spirit Himself.

The Apostle's asseveration is that to be led by the Spirit is true, not of some Christians only, but of all Christians. There is an analogy in the Old Testament. The children of Israel were the children of God, they were His own peculiar people, and they were 'led' from the captivity of Egypt into the land of Canaan, the land flowing with milk and honey. How were they led? It was by a 'pillar of fire' by night, and a cloud by day. And there were detailed instructions about this. We are told that the cloud settled on the tabernacle; and while the cloud was on the tabernacle they did not move, they dare not move. But when the cloud was raised and moved, they moved; they followed the cloud. Similarly with the pillar of fire by night. In this way they were led through the Red Sea, and guided during their journeyings in the wilderness. Their entire life was governed by the movement of the cloud and pillar of fire. The Apostle teaches here that we are in a like condition. The leading is in a more spiritual form now; not so material as it was then. But we, as the children of God, are being led by the Holy Spirit from the Egypt, the bondage, the sin of this evil world to our heavenly Canaan, the Jerusalem that is above.

To the Christian this is life. The Christian is one who realizes that he is on a pilgrimage; that he is being led. There were enemies round and about the children of Israel. Problems arose – no food, no water, and many another problem. But unceasingly God was leading them by the cloud and the fiery pillar. The Apostle says that our Lord was there; He was the 'Rock' that followed them (1 Corinthians 10: 4). These are figures that show us the leading of God. And is there anything more comforting and encouraging than to think of our lives as Christian people in this way? To us this world is a wilderness. Is it not becoming more and more obvious that that is so? Do we not see it in the things that are happening – the pollution, the privations, the quarrelling, the fighting, the ugliness? This world is 'a howling wilderness'. But we are being led through it all to the Canaan of our desire, and we are being led by the Holy Spirit of God.

How does this take place? The term the Apostle uses is in the passive voice – 'as many as are led'. A better translation would bring out the continuous aspect; 'as many as are being led'. This must not be pressed to a ridiculous extreme. He does not say that we are put into an armchair and carried. 'Led' is the term he uses. But though we are being led, we are actually using our own feet and our own limbs. The passive element is emphasized by the fact that the directing is done by the Spirit of God, but in Christianity there is no 'lying on a bed of roses'. Any teaching which says 'It is quite easy, you have nothing to do but to hand it over' is always wrong and unscriptural. You are not a child carried in arms, you are a man, and are being led. You need the guidance and the direction, but you do the walking! So it is the passive voice and present continuous tense – 'As many as are being led by the Spirit of God', they can be quite certain that 'they are the sons of God'.

Again, when the Apostle says 'as many as are led' he does not mean that we are being 'forced' or 'driven'. That is an important distinction. Paul uses here the same word as we find in the first verse of the fourth chapter of Luke's Gospel: 'And Jesus being full of the Holy Ghost returned from Jordan, and was led by the Spirit into the wilderness.' I once heard a man say that that should read, 'and was driven by the Spirit'. That is quite wrong, as I shall explain later. The Holy Spirit had no need to 'drive' our Lord; and He never did. And the Spirit does not drive the children of God. What He does is to persuade them. He leads us by persuasion; not by brute force, not against our will. He persuades the will, which is a very different thing. There is no violence in Christianity. We are not saved violently even though the circumstances may be dramatic; it is always persuasion. A man is never saved against his will. To say that is to be ridiculous. What the Spirit does it to enlighten and persuade; so that we desire the things of God. He puts a new principle, a new disposition into us, and then we desire these things. Salvation must never be thought of as dragooning a man against his will, or forcing him. That is quite false. It is a matter of powerful persuasion. In 1 John 5 : 3, for instance, the Apostle says that the man who loves is the man who keeps the commandments: 'This is the love of God, that we keep his commandments.' And then he adds, 'And his commandments are not grievous'. They are not grievous to the Christian; but they are very grievous to the non-Christian. The non-Christian says, 'I do not want your Christianity, it is too narrow, with its commandments and prohibitions'. They are grievous to him, they annoy him, he hates them and detests them. But the Christian says, 'His commandments are not grievous'. He has been persuaded; he has a new understanding. Or, as our Lord states the matter in the Sermon on the Mount: 'Blessed are they that do hunger and thirst after righteousness, for they shall be filled' (Matthew 5 : 6). That is the position.

The Sons of God

The divine leading is stated in the form of a contrast in verses 8 and 9 of Psalm 32. God says: 'I will instruct thee and teach thee in the way which thou shalt go: I will guide thee with mine eye.' Then the negative: 'Be ye not as the horse, or as the mule, which have no understanding: whose mouth must be held in with bit and bridle, lest they come near unto thee.' Notice the contrast. We are not to be like the horse, still less like the mule, where a bit and bridle and force are needed. We are to be guided by God's 'eye'. All we do is to keep our eye on Him, and then we follow. That is how He leads and guides. The picture is not to be one of breaking in an obstinate mule or a wild colt. Or consider the matter as found in Isaiah 30, verse 21: 'Thine ears shall hear a word behind thee, saying, This is the way, walk ye in it, when ye turn to the right hand, and when ye turn to the left.' We hear this blessed voice speaking and whispering behind us; we hear and we respond. That is how God guides – by word, by persuasion!

In general, to be 'led by the Spirit' means that our life is guided and determined and directed by the Holy Spirit. That is what makes a man behave as a Christian. But it is never true of the natural man, who, at his very best, is neither guided by the Spirit nor led by the Spirit. At the lowest level he is guided by nothing but his own desires; he feels an urge to do something, and he does it. He feels a thirst, or hunger, or some other impulse; and he responds. He is like an animal. He is guided by his impulses, instincts, lusts, passions, desires, by all that is in his physical frame and his perverted mind. The natural man on a somewhat higher level may be guided by the mind of the world, as are the vast majority of people, for they do not think for themselves. They do what everyone else does. The goods they buy are what they see advertised. Their main reason for buying them is that they are told that everyone else is buying them. Such is their philosophy of life. They take their views, even their politics from their newspaper. They are led and guided by the powers that control the media – newspapers, radio, television, and so on. On a higher level again, some of them are led by their 'reason'. It is good that a man should be led by his reason; but natural human reason is not enough. Man's understanding is defective, he does not see the real subtleties of the situation. And the natural man at his best is guided by reason and common sense; never anything higher than that. He is not led by the Spirit; he uses his own understanding, his will-power and his own determination.

The Christian is in an entirely different position and category. He is not led by his natural powers but, ultimately, by the Spirit of God. The Spirit of God may lead him partly through his reason and in other ways, as I shall explain; but what is central about him is that he and his life are governed by the leading, the direction, of the Holy Spirit of God. That does not mean for a moment that he is perfect. He is not perfect. But it can rightly be said of him, that the main and obvious tendency and direction of his life is that which is dictated by the Holy Spirit. We shall go on to consider in detail how the Holy Spirit does this in actual practice, but at this point it may be good for us to pause and to meditate on that general statement.

Can you say that your life, taken as a whole – your thought life, your feelings, your actions, your will, your everything is under the direction of the Spirit of God? I am not asking whether you are perfect. I know you are not perfect, any more than I am perfect. But can you say this: 'With all my faults and failures, and all that is true of me, I can say that the directing force and principle in my life is the Spirit of God?' The Apostle Paul states that if you can say that, you are a son of God. That, then, is the question for you to face. Can you say this, are you sure of this? Is the main direction of your life being determined by the Holy Spirit of God? Is it your greatest desire that it should be? If it is, whatever else may be true about you, whatever your faults or failures, I say to you, on the authority of God Himself, you are a 'son of God'.

Fourteen

*

*For as many as are led by the Spirit of God, they are the sons of
God.*   Romans 8 : 14

We continue our study of the grounds on which we can be sure of
our sonship of God. The first reason, as we have seen, is that we
are 'led by the Spirit of God'. We have emphasized the fact that
though this is stated in the passive form we must not introduce
into the word the idea of 'force' or compulsion; we must not read
it as saying that 'as many as are *driven* by the Spirit of God, they
are the sons of God'. We dealt with this in terms of the statement
in Luke 4, verse 1, where we read, 'And Jesus being full of the
Holy Ghost returned from Jordan, and was led by the Spirit into
the wilderness.'

But someone may ask how we can reconcile that with the statement made in the 12th verse of the 1st chapter of Mark, 'And
immediately the Spirit *driveth* him into the wilderness'. It is quite
correct to say that the Greek word used in Mark 1 : 12 is not the
word used in Luke 4 : 1; neither is it the word used here in
Romans 8 : 14. It is also true to say that the word used in Mark
1 : 12 is a much stronger word than the word translated here as
'led', or the word translated 'led' in Luke 4 : 1. We can see therefore how the translators of the Authorized Version used the word
'driveth', and why some of the modern translations use the same
strong expression. Nevertheless, I suggest that in doing so they
are quite wrong, and that the translation 'driveth' is not justified.

It is generally agreed that the best available Greek–English
Lexicon at the present time is that of Arndt-Gingrich. In this
Lexicon – and the Grimm-Thayer Lexicon virtually says the
same – the word which is used in Romans 8 : 14, which is translated 'led', and which is the weaker of the two words we are

[170]

considering, is sometimes used in a legal sense. It is used, for instance, of someone who is being arrested or led away into custody by some person in authority. There are examples of this in the New Testament. Take for instance Mark 13 : 11, where our Lord says, 'But when they shall lead you and deliver you up' There is obviously a sense of force there. Our Lord is warning the disciples that the day may come when men will lay hands on them and lead them to the authorities and deliver them up to them. Another example of it is found in Luke 22 : 54: 'Then took they him and led him, and brought him into the high priest's house.' Obviously it carries the idea of force again. Then take Luke 23 : 32: 'And there were also two other, malefactors, led with him to be put to death.' Our Lord and the two malefactors were obviously led forcibly, to be put to death. This, I repeat, is the same word that is translated 'led' in Romans 8 : 14, and it is the milder of the two words. It occurs again in John 7 : 45 : 'Then came the officers to the chief priests and Pharisees; and they said unto them, Why have ye not brought him?' Again it is the same milder word. In Acts 21 : 34 it is still this milder word, 'And some cried one thing, some another, among the multitude: and when he' – the captain of the troops – 'could not know the certainty for the tumult, he commanded him to be carried into the castle', but clearly there it has the stronger meaning.

Obviously the same word can be used in different senses. But look now at the other (Greek) word in Mark 1 : 12, which is translated, 'The Spirit *driveth* him into the wilderness to be tempted'. According to this excellent Lexicon the first meaning is to 'drive out', to 'expel', to 'throw out more or less forcibly'. But then it goes on to say that it can also be used 'without the connotation of force'. Though this is the strong word it can have this second meaning which has no connotation of force, and means 'to send out'. There is an interesting example of this in Matthew's Gospel, chapter 9: 37–38: 'The harvest truly is plenteous, but the labourers are few; pray ye therefore the Lord of the harvest, that he will send forth labourers into his harvest.' If the translators of the Authorized Version had been consistent they would have translated thus: 'Pray ye therefore the Lord of the harvest, that he will "drive out" ("drive forth") labourers into his harvest.' But they did not do so, they very rightly used the milder expression 'send forth'. But I have heard Bible teachers who have argued that the Greek insists upon the translation 'Pray ye therefore the Lord of the harvest, that he will thrust forth. . . .' But, according to Arndt-Gingrich, they have no right to say that, because the Greek word has many meanings, and can be used in all these differing senses. 'Send forth' – the milder expression – is undoubtedly the right one in the context. Then there is the parallel in Luke 10: 2: 'Therefore said he unto them, The harvest truly is great, but the labourers are few; pray ye therefore the Lord of the harvest, that he would send forth . . . ' says the Authorized Version again; not 'driving', but 'sending forth'. They are not being 'driven' out to go and preach; they are 'sent forth'. The idea of force is quite out of place there, indeed the connotation of force is almost ridiculous at that point. Another example is found in Acts 16: 37, 'But Paul said unto them, They have beaten us openly uncondemned, being Romans, and have cast us into prison; and now do they thrust us out privily? nay verily; but let them come themselves and fetch us out'. There is no idea of force in the expression 'fetch us out'. They had been forcibly cast into prison, but now they want to be 'led out', to be let out in a different manner.

But perhaps the most conclusive argument is what is found in Matthew 7, verse 4. Here our Lord is dealing with the question of judging one another. He has said, 'Why beholdest thou the mote that is in thy brother's eye, but considerest not the beam that is in thine own eye?' Then he goes on to say, 'Or how wilt thou say to thy brother, Let me pull out the mote out of thine eye; and behold, a beam is in thine own eye?' Now the very word here translated 'pull out' is the word which the Authorized Version translates in Mark 1: 12 as 'driven'. Here is a man who is going to perform a very delicate eye operation; so if you insist that this word always means 'force', 'thrust', 'drive', let me express the hope that, if ever you have a foreign object in your eye, you may not be treated by such a violent oculist, or optician.

I have gone into this in detail deliberately in order to show the danger which confronts us as Bible students, and particularly when we begin to take an interest in New Testament Greek. There is the kind of man who is always ready to say dogmatically that any particular problem can be solved with ease by a knowledge of the Greek original. Nowhere is the adage about a little learning being dangerous more important than at this point. You do not thrust or force or drive 'motes' out of people's eyes. It is gentleness that is called for in the performance of such an operation!

That is the first part of my answer; and it really is enough in and of itself. Let us be sure, if we are looking at this word in the original, that we use an authoritative Lexicon, and that we consider all the possible meanings. And so you find that the two words – the one in Romans 8 : 14, and the one in Mark 1 : 12 – can be used either in a strong or a mild sense. But in addition to that, take one of the best commentaries on Mark's Gospel, that by J. A. Alexander. On Mark 1 : 12 he says: 'A strong expression for strong impulse urging Him in that direction.' A very good comment! In other words what we have to realize is that the only element of force which we can admit into this word at all is the force of persuasion. There is such a thing as the force of persuasion; but there is no violence involved there.

That is the distinction that I am concerned to emphasize. Let me use an illustration. There is, of course, a very strong element of force, a constraining element in love. Love is a sentiment that masters and governs; but you must never say that it is violent. The Apostle Paul says, 'The love of Christ constraineth us', but without any element of violence. It is powerful, but it is the influence of love. Or, to take another illustration, there is all the difference in the world between being persuaded by a reasoned argument, or a logical statement, or even by eloquence, and being compelled by force, or by the terrible use of what is called 'brain washing' which has been used so much by the various dictatorships of this century. People like Hitler do not persuade; they bombard the human mind in a violent manner. The only right way is the persuasion of reason, argument, demonstration, or even an eloquent statement of a case.

So the only force we can admit here in Romans 8 : 14 is the force of persuasion. The Christian man is not 'driven' by the Spirit. As we saw in Psalm 32, the nature of the mule must not be present in us. God's method is, 'I will guide thee with mine eye'. But perhaps the most convincing argument of all is that the New Testament teaching concerning the Holy Spirit everywhere suggests that the Spirit can be grieved by us. We can 'quench the Spirit', we can 'grieve the Spirit', terms which exclude any possibility that the Apostle teaches here that the Christian is being 'driven' by the Spirit. Let us not forget that the Holy Spirit is sensitive, that He is generally compared to a dove, and can be 'grieved', offended, and 'quenched'.

But, – to add yet another argument – whatever the translations may say, whatever words may mean in the Greek, we should be guided first and foremost by a clear theological understanding. This is to me the most important point of all. In other words, as I have already argued, it is inconceivable that there could have been any element of force or compulsion in the case of our blessed Lord Himself. It is inconceivable that the Holy Spirit would have to 'drive' Him in any respect. We must think in the terms which I have already quoted from J. A. Alexander, of 'A strong expression for strong impulse.' The impulse can be very strong, but there is no 'driving', there is no compulsion. There must never even be the suspicion of a suggestion that our Lord did anything against His most holy will.

The way in which we construe the word 'led' has a very important bearing on the doctrine of sanctification. The Holy Spirit never does violence to a man. There is no idea of 'thrusting' in the work of the Holy Spirit; He always persuades. The Holy Spirit never browbeats us; and if your interpretation of Scripture at any point gives the impression of browbeating or force or violence or thrusting, it is a contradiction of the teaching concerning the Spirit throughout the New Testament. In this matter of sanctification He leads, He persuades us. That is His method. So the correct translation is: 'As many as are led by the Spirit. . . . ' And this is not only important from the standpoint of sanctification. A similar point is made in the Second Epistle of Peter, chapter 1, verse 21: 'For the prophecy came not in old time by the will of man: but holy men of God spake as they were *moved* by the Holy Ghost'. Peter is not using the same word, incidentally, as is used by Paul; but it has the same idea. That is why I am using it as an illustration – 'as they were *moved* by the Holy Ghost'. There are those who say that it should be translated, 'holy men of God spake as they were *driven along*'. No, they were not in a gale, there was no storm; They were 'moved', or 'borne along'. If you introduce any element of violence, then you must say that the men who wrote the Scriptures were entirely passive, and that it was a matter of dictation. But it was not so. To believe in verbal inspiration, and in the inerrancy of the Scriptures, does not mean that we believe in a mechanical dictation, as would be implied by the word 'driven'. They were '*moved* by the Holy Ghost'. You can be moved by beauty; but there is no violence involved there. You can be moved by poetry, or by a hymn, and similarly you can be moved by the Holy Spirit. And that is His method with us at every stage, and in every aspect of our salvation and advance in the Christian life.

But let us proceed to consider the more practical matter as to how the Spirit leads us. There are two schools of thought on the subject of 'leading' and they differ diametrically from each other. One school thinks that this is a reference only to the matter of guidance. How am I to know what I am to do? Am I called to the ministry? Am I, or am I not, called to the foreign mission field? The other school would exclude such guidance altogether. They are so afraid of 'enthusiasm' and the excesses into which people who claim direct guidance by the Spirit tend to go that they say that the notion of guidance does not come into this verse at all, and that it must be rigidly excluded. In my view both schools are right and both are wrong! We have to consider both aspects here; but I do not hesitate to assert that the primary reference is obviously not to guidance as such but to the way in which we live in general; for we must not overlook the fact that verse 14 follows on verse 13, where we read, 'If ye through the Spirit do mortify the deeds of the body, ye shall live. For as many as are led by the Spirit . . . ' Clearly the primary reference is to 'the mortification of the deeds of the body' which has nothing to do with 'guidance', but has a great deal to do with practical daily life and living, and with what the New Testament calls 'our conversation' in this world. The first meaning, then, is that the Spirit leads us in general.

How does the Holy Spirit do so? He is the Spirit of truth: 'When the Spirit of truth shall come'. He is also the *Holy* Spirit. There we have the key to the understanding of this matter. Remember that this is not a theoretical question only. We are trying to discover for certain whether we are the sons of God or not; and the way to be sure of that, first of all, is to know whether we are being led by the Spirit. As He is the Spirit of truth it follows, therefore, that His leading of us is always in terms of, and in connection with, truth. To grasp this is of the utmost importance, for there are other spirits, evil spirits, false spirits.

The New Testament itself exhorts us to 'prove the spirits', to 'try the spirits', to 'test the spirits'. In other words I must realize that besides the Holy Spirit there are other spirits who are trying to lead me. How do I differentiate that which is true from that which is false? The answer is that the Holy Spirit always leads in terms of truth and along the line of truth. Here, therefore, I have a standard whereby I can test what I believe is the leading of the Holy Spirit in my life. We can lay it down as a proposition that the Holy Spirit normally leads us by means of the written Word, the Scriptures. They are His Word. It is He, as we have seen already, who moved certain holy men of old; it was He who gave them the message and guided them in the writing of the message. The same is true of the writers of the New Testament. So we can say that the truth which the Holy Spirit conveys to us is the truth which is written in what we call the Bible. Therefore, speaking generally, the Spirit leads us in this matter of sanctification, and in our Christian life and living as a whole, in and through the Bible.

I emphasize this for several reasons, first of all because it is at this point that we stand resolutely against the teaching of the Roman Catholic Church, which claims that she has received teaching beyond and additional to the Scriptures. You may go to a Roman Catholic and say, 'What grounds have you for worshipping, as you do, the Virgin Mary? What grounds have you for praying to the saints? What grounds have you for believing in what you call the assumption of the Virgin Mary – that she ascended to heaven literally in the body – or for the immaculate conception, for I do not find these things in the Scriptures?' 'Ah,' they say, 'these things have been revealed to us since then by the Spirit: they are part of the tradition received by and developed by the Church.' There is only one answer to such a claim; it is that the Spirit works in and through and with the Scriptures. It was the Spirit who guided the early Church to form and to delimit the canon of the New Testament, and there is nothing to be added to it, so that any claim for additional revelation must be rejected. In the Word itself is the whole of the truth that is necessary for us; and unless what purports to be something revealed by the Spirit tallies with what we read in it, we not only can, but we must, reject it as being false teaching.

But, unfortunately, the tendency to add to Scripture is not

confined to Roman Catholicism. There are types of teaching in evangelical circles which must be dealt with in exactly the same way. There is a popular teaching with regard to the Lord's Second Coming which is believed very commonly, and which is known as 'the preliminary rapture of the saints'. If you take the trouble to inquire as to the origin of this teaching – it dates from 1831 – you will find that it was given, so the claim runs, as a kind of vision to a certain man. It cannot be established from the Scripture, but it began to be taught then, and it has been taught more or less ever since. It all started as the result of a supposed vision which was received by one of the followers of the famous Edward Irving who founded what he called the Catholic Apostolic Church. It was accepted because this man said it had been 'revealed' to him.

There is another teaching which is not so popular, but which has gained a certain amount of currency in various evangelical circles, a teaching which is quite orthodox on the main matters of salvation but which adds many things to it. There are additions, for instance, with respect to the place of elders in the church, and their power over the ordinary church members. It teaches that the latter have to surrender themselves entirely to the government of the elders, to be ruled and governed by them as to their sphere of activity and other matters. Once more the claim is made that this was revealed to a particular man, who claimed to have had a certain experience in an hotel in America; and so he became the leader, not to say the dictator, of his particular movement.

The answer to such claims is that the Holy Spirit works in connection with the truth; and irrespective of what a man may say about a vision or an experience that he has had, if the teaching cannot be found in the Scripture, or be reconciled with the Scripture, it is to be rejected as false teaching. Even though the remainder of his teaching may be scriptural and accurate, he is in error and he must not be followed.

How, then, does the Spirit lead us in connection with truth? He does so by acting on our minds. The truth is a 'dead letter' to the natural man. As I Corinthians 2 reminds us, 'it is foolishness unto him'. Why do I believe it? How do I know that I am a Christian? The Spirit has come and has done something to me. As the Apostle puts it, 'God hath revealed them (the things of God) unto us by his Spirit; for the Spirit searcheth all things, yea, the deep things of God' (v. 10). 'For we have received, not the spirit that is of the world, but the Spirit that is of God, that we might know the things that are freely given to us of God' (v. 12). This is a description of the Spirit enlightening the mind. In connection with the work of the Holy Spirit, Paul prays for the Ephesians 'that the God of our Lord Jesus Christ, the Father of glory, may give unto you the spirit of wisdom and revelation in the knowledge of him: the eyes of your understanding being enlightened; that ye may know' (Ephesians 1:17, 18). John, in in his First Epistle chapter 2, verses 20 and 27, says: 'But ye have an unction from the Holy One'. He enables us to understand these things. 'The anointing', he says, 'which ye have received' will continue, and will guide you into the truth, and you will be able to differentiate between Christ and the antichrists. The 'anointing', the 'unction of the Holy One', the Holy Spirit, dispenses truth.

We can apply this most important test in practice. We must never forget that the Holy Spirit leads us to a knowledge and to an understanding of the truth. When we talk about being led by the Spirit the tendency of some is to begin to think of visions and ecstasies. But the vital question is, Has the Spirit been enlightening your mind? About what? About God Himself! It is the business of the Spirit to teach us, to lead us into the truth concerning God the Father as He has been revealed in and through the Son. This is the great theme of the Bible, and the Spirit leads us into and enlightens us concerning it. Similarly with regard to the soul and its needs. It is the Spirit who convicts us of sin. It is His special work to bring us to a conviction of sin, to enable us to realize our sinfulness, our alienation from God, and our lost estate, and to bring us to see that we deserve damnation and punishment. The natural man does not like such ideas; he hates them. But not so the man whose mind has been enlightened by the Spirit. He has seen what he is. He does not complain of condemnation; he condemns himself, he feels he is utterly unworthy. The Spirit leads us to this knowledge.

Similarly the Spirit leads us to a knowledge of the Lord Jesus Christ, His Person and His work. To have this knowledge is a proof that we are Christians. In 1 Corinthians 2 Paul says that 'the princes of this world did not know him, for had they known him they would not have crucified the Lord of glory' (verse 8).

And the princes of this world do not know Him today; they are utterly ignorant; the Spirit has not 'led' them to Him. But if He has led you, yo 1 can be sure that you are a 'son of God'. It is only the children who are led to this. The first Christian convert in Europe was a woman called Lydia, and of her we find it written, 'whose heart the Lord opened, that she attended unto the things which were spoken of Paul'. She knew nothing of these things before, but as she was listening to Paul, the Spirit opened her heart, so that she believed the truth concerning the Person of the Lord Jesus Christ and His work, and concerning the way of salvation. This is a part of the leading of the Spirit; and He leads us on and on into the truth more and more deeply, as we progress in the Christian life.

But more than that! The Spirit will lead us also into an understanding of the whole purpose of God with respect to this world. That needs to be emphasized at such a time as this. I know of no better test that you can apply to yourself to determine whether you are a child of God or not, than just this, What do you make of the world situation? Are you surprised at it? Are you amazed at it? Are you disappointed at it? Are you still looking to the statesmen and others to solve all problems and to put the world right? Do you still believe that some kind of Utopia is going to come? If you do, you can take it as certain that you are not being led by the Spirit, that you are not a child of God. But if, on the other hand, you are not surprised that things are as they are, if indeed you could almost have anticipated that it would be so, if you have never had confidence in such ideas because you believe the Bible when it says that there will be 'wars and rumours of wars' while there is sin and lust in the evil heart of man – then, I say, you are a 'son of God'. If, I repeat, you are not surprised at the state of the world, and you do not look for anything dramatic which will suddenly solve the world problems, and bring in a universal era of peace and plenty, happiness and friendship, then, I say, you have very good presumptive evidence that you are a child of God. It is the Holy Spirit alone who leads anyone to believe such truth. If you are looking to the return of Christ as your only hope, you can be certain that you are a child of God. The natural man ridicules such teaching and rejects it with scorn. He did not believe in our Lord when He came the first time; and he does not believe He is coming again. But the child of God does so, because it is taught so clearly in the Bible. As Paul says in writing to Titus: 'Teaching us that, denying ungodliness and worldly lusts, we should live soberly, righteously, and godly, in this present world; looking for that blessed hope, and the glorious appearing of the great God and our Saviour Jesus Christ' (Titus 2: 12, 13). That is our only hope. If that is your position, if you say that there is no other hope, then you are a 'son of God'. If you believe that God has a great plan and purpose for the ages, for the world, that it is all in God's eternal mind, and that it is all going to be brought to pass – if you believe that, you can be certain that you are a child, a son of God. The Spirit leads us by enlightening the mind.

He also leads us by working in our hearts and on our desires. 'Work out your own salvation with fear and trembling; for it is God that worketh in you both to will and to do. . . . ' 'Blessed are they that do hunger and thirst after righteousness.' It is the Spirit that causes them to do so. He governs and controls us in that way by His work of persuasion on our 'desires'. He does it positively by 'shedding the love of God abroad in our hearts' as the Apostle has already said of the Holy Spirit in verse 5 of chapter 5 of this Roman Epistle.

Lastly, the Spirit acts also upon the will, which needs to be persuaded. Paul prays for the Ephesians that they may be 'strengthened with all might by his Spirit in the inner man' (Ephesians 3: 16). The Spirit strengthens our wills and our determination in the inner man to live the Christian life.

So far, then, we have seen something of the mode or method of the Spirit's working as He 'leads' the children of God, although we shall have to proceed to consider the matter in detail. There is nothing more important than that we should be assured of our salvation, and know that we are the sons of God. And these tests which pertain to our general outlook and attitude as we walk and pass through this world of time show clearly whether we are sons or not. 'For as many as are led by the Spirit of God, they are the sons of God.'

Fifteen

*

For as many as are led by the Spirit of God, they are the sons of God.   Romans 8: 14

We return to the question, how may we know that we are sons of God? If the basis of my assurance is that I am a child, a son of God, then what I should want to know above everything else is whether I am truly a child or a son of God. We have seen that the Apostle gives us at least three reasons, if not four, whereby we may know with certainty that we are children of God. The first is that we are being 'led by the Spirit of God'.

There is one further point, more or less general, which we have to make before we can come to the particulars. There is an expression in the Epistle to the Galatians chapter 5, verse 17, which bears directly on this subject. 'The flesh lusteth against the Spirit, and the Spirit against the flesh; and these are contrary the one to the other'. Then, further: 'This I say then, Walk in the Spirit, and ye shall not fulfil the lust of the flesh' (v. 16). Also, 'If we live in the Spirit, let us also walk in the Spirit' (v. 25). Then again in verse 18: 'If ye be led of the Spirit, ye are not under the law'; in other words, if you are a child of God you are not 'under the law'. We have noted that truth many times as we have been studying this Epistle. But I call particular attention to verse 17 where the Apostle uses an interesting expression, saying that the Holy Spirit is 'lusting' within us 'against the flesh'. The flesh lusts against the Spirit; but the Spirit also lusts against the flesh. And the term 'lusts' means 'strongly desires', or 'exerts a very strong influence'. In other words, His desire on our behalf is that we should be saved from the influence of the flesh; and because of this He leads us and directs us.

Another extraordinary statement is found in the 4th chapter of

[181]

the Epistle of James. In the Authorized Version it reads: 'Do ye think that the Scripture saith in vain, The spirit that dwelleth in us lusteth to envy?' (v. 5). It is generally agreed that this is not a good translation. The Revised Version translation is, 'Doth the spirit which he made to dwell in us long unto envying?' That is better; but there is a still better translation in the margin of the Revised Version, and indeed in some copies of the Authorized Version also. It is, 'The spirit which he made to dwell in us he yearneth for even unto jealous envy'. But the best translation, surely, would be this, 'The Spirit which he [God] made to dwell in us, yearneth for us, even unto jealous envy'. It is generally agreed that that is the most accurate translation at this particular point.

That is a most encouraging and comforting statement. It says that the Holy Spirit whom God has caused to dwell in us who are Christians is yearning for our sanctification, yearning for our holiness, yearning that we may be worthy of our high calling, yearning that we may be truly children of God, and rejoicing in that fact. And the Spirit, we are told, not only yearns for us, but He does so even unto 'jealous envying'. Just as any parent worthy of the name is jealous for the well-being and the reputation of the child, or just as a lover is jealous for the well-being and the reputation of the object of his or her love, so the Holy Spirit is concerned about us, almost to the extent of having a kind of 'jealous envy' for us. We must not stumble at the word 'jealous'. We are told in the Ten Commandments that God says, 'I am a jealous God', and James uses the word in that sense; it is a strong expression to remind us of the greatness of the concern, and indeed the exclusive element in His concern for us. So we can think of ourselves in this way: As Christian people, we have been redeemed from sin, from the law, from death. God has also put His Spirit in us; but, as we have seen, it is still true to say of us that 'the body is dead because of sin'. And we have seen that this remaining sin that dwells in the 'mortal body' causes a conflict. 'The flesh lusteth against the Spirit'; this element of 'the flesh' that is still left in us, militates against our highest interests. But, thank God, the Holy Spirit militates on the other side. As it is true to say that 'the flesh' is trying to control us, and the devil uses the flesh to do so, it is equally true to say, and more so, that the Holy Spirit is on the other side with this 'jealous envy', rescuing and delivering us from the clutches of sin and the nefarious influences of the flesh as used by the devil.

This is clearly a most important aspect of our being 'led by the Spirit of God'. He is in us; and He is yearning for our full, final emancipation from sin in every shape and form, and our ultimate glorification. To that end He leads us on, yearning for us with a 'jealous envy'. He does so in every conceivable manner in order to bring us to this determined goal. So He operates upon the mind, the heart, and the will. We can therefore say that the Christian, as a son of God, is one who yields himself to this yearning of the Holy Spirit on his behalf, that he may arrive at the ultimate state of complete salvation and ultimate glorification.

To what, exactly, does this lead? That is to say, How may I know in practice whether I am a child, a son of God? The two passages we have examined will lead us directly to the practical answers to that question. If I am a child of God, the Spirit is yearning over me with a jealous envy, and because of that He is leading me and directing me, and working in me. How may I know whether that is happening in me? I want to suggest some practical tests before we come to the great test mentioned in verse 15, which is that I cry 'Abba, Father'.

First, if I am led by the Spirit, then He determines my general, my whole outlook upon life. That surely needs no demonstration. The Apostle says in 1 Corinthians 2 : 12: 'Now we have received, not the spirit of the world, but the Spirit which is of God; that we might know the things that are freely given to us of God'. If then we are led by the Spirit of God, we have an essentially spiritual outlook upon life. The first thing that differentiates the Christian from the non-Christian is this spiritual outlook. The other man has what Paul has already called 'the carnal mind', of which he has said, 'The carnal mind is enmity against God' (Romans 8 : 7). The Christian does not have a carnal outlook; he has a spiritual outlook. We must realize what that means in detail. He is a man who has a taste for spiritual things. Among other things, it means that he enjoys meetings in which Christian people meet together to study the Scriptures. The typical man of the worlds finds such meetings to be extremely dull, uninteresting and boring. He would not understand, he would not know, what it is all about. That is because the Spirit of God is not in him, and he cannot help himself. There is no point in asking a blind man to admire scenery; he cannot see it. In the same way the man who is not spiritual has no spiritual faculty, and therefore he cannot enjoy a meeting of a spiritual character. He is not interested in the exposition of the Scriptures, and has no desire to understand Scripture, because it means nothing at all to him. But if, on the other hand, we have an interest in these things, and really do enjoy that kind of meeting it is proof that we are spiritually minded. I know that there is a danger – perhaps not as great a danger now as fifty years ago – that a man may have a purely intellectual interest in these things. That is not at all common today; such people have almost disappeared, and they apply that kind of interest to other matters now. But one always has to bear that danger in mind; so this is not our only test.

I add another test – love of the brethren. That means that you delight in the company of spiritually minded people, that you like the society and the fellowship of Christian people, so that you delight in talking to them about these particular matters. A man who has the Spirit of God in him, and who is led by the Spirit, is a man who is concerned about the things of the Spirit. He is interested in his soul and in its destiny. In other words, he realizes that the most important things in this life are not the things which we see, but the things which we do not see. The Apostle states this truth in 2 Corinthians 4: 18: 'The things which are seen are temporal; but the things which are not seen are eternal.' The man who has the Spirit in him, the child of God, can say quite honestly that it is this hidden, unseen, part of himself and his life in this world which is to him the more important. There was a time when it was the other that interested him, the things that he could see and handle. They were the great things, and he could not abide spending an evening with himself and his own soul and spirit, examining himself and his spiritual state. That was terrible! But, now there is a great change; it is the 'inner' man that counts, not the outward man. So he can say that 'the inner man is renewed day by day', though the outward man is 'perishing' day by day.

In other words, if you can say that, more and more as you live, you look at your life in this world as but a pilgrimage, a journey, something temporary through which you are passing, and that you have an increasing consciousness within you that you belong to another realm, which is the real realm, then you need have no doubt about being a child of God. As Paul says to the Philippians in chapter 3, verses 20 and 21: 'Our citizenship is in heaven'. Or again in 2 Corinthians 5: 1: 'For we know that if our earthly house of this tabernacle were dissolved, we have a building of God, an house not made with hands, eternal in the heavens'. The true Christian thinks in this way. I am not asking whether you spend the whole of your time so thinking; but simply whether it is true to say of you that you regard yourself more and more in a spiritual manner, that you are becoming increasingly detached from this world, and that the realm to which you are going becomes increasingly important for you? If you can say that, you need have no doubt at all; you are a 'child of God'. No one else can speak in this way. It is one of the hallmarks of the true Christian.

Let me suggest a second test. The man who is led by the Spirit of God, is, by definition, a man who desires to live to God's glory. God made man for Himself; and as the answer to the first question in the Shorter Catechism of the Westminster Assembly reminds us, 'The chief end of man is to glorify God, and to enjoy Him for ever'. The natural man, the man who is still 'in sin', the man who is 'under the law,' does not live to glorify God. That is the meaning of what happened at the original Fall of man. After having lived to glorify God man began to live for his own glory. The devil tempted Eve along that line, saying, 'Hath God said, Ye shall not eat of every tree of the garden?' The devil suggested that God had spoken thus because He knew that the moment the first human pair ate of one fruit in particular they would 'become as gods'. They believed the lie, accepted the devil's suggestion, and began to live for their own glory. The moment, therefore, a man can say honestly that his supreme concern is to live to the glory of God he can be quite certain that he is a Christian, that he is a child of God. It is something that is only true of the man who has been regenerated. Our Lord Himself lived in this world entirely to glorify the Father. He says in His high-priestly prayer as recorded in John 17, 'Father, I have glorified Thy name'. To do so was His supreme desire. And as we are 'in Him' this will become progressively our supreme desire.

There are many tests which we can apply; and if any one of them is true it is enough in itself. But the greater the number that is true of us the more certain we can be, so we proceed to a third test. A man who is led by the Spirit of God always has a desire within him for a greater knowledge of God, and a greater knowledge of our Lord and Saviour Jesus Christ. That can be proved in this way. When our Lord promised the coming of the Spirit He said, 'He shall glorify me'; and He always does. So the way to know whether the Spirit is in you, and whether you are being led by the Spirit, is not to ask whether you have had some vision or known some ecstasy, or have 'spoken in tongues' or the like. Have you a great desire within you to know the Lord Jesus Christ? That is the supreme test. The Spirit always leads to Him. The Spirit is sent to glorify Him. And Christ, in turn, said that He was sent to glorify the Father. Hence when the Spirit is leading any person, that person desires to know the Lord Jesus Christ, and to know the Father, more and more. It is inevitable; and it is inevitable that it should be progressive.

How may I know whether all this is true? There are ways in which I can test it. Where do I find this knowledge? I find it in the Bible, in the Old Testament and in the New Testament. So anyone who is really searching for a knowledge of the Lord Jesus Christ, and of God, spends much time with the Bible, and does so in order to arrive at this knowledge. I emphasize the matter because, as we are all so prone to act mechanically, there is a danger that I may read my portion of Scripture day by day without realizing that my real motive is simply to keep to a rule that I have set myself. It may not be really to seek the Lord Himself; I may even be seeking a knowledge of the Scripture as such, in order that I may pass some examination on scriptural knowledge. But that is not seeking the Lord Jesus Christ, it is not seeking the Father. What the Spirit does is to make us seek for the Lord, to seek Him and the Father, that I may come into an intimacy of knowledge. 'This is life eternal, that they might know thee, the only true God, and Jesus Christ, whom thou hast sent' (John 17: 3). Have you this desire to know God? Can you really say that your greatest desire is to know God and the Lord Jesus Christ? If you can say so, you are a child of God.

This sonship not only shows itself in reading the Scripture, it shows itself also in prayer. Read the lives of the saints, and you will always find that they spent much time in prayer. And in praying, their supreme desire was that they might have this knowledge. Many hymns give expression to this –

Tell me Thou art mine, O Saviour,
Grant me an assurance clear.

*   *   *   *   *   *

O Love divine, how sweet Thou art!
When shall I find my willing heart
All taken up by Thee?

Such is the experience of the saints. If we know anything of this desire, the desire really to know, we shall be seeking Him, and seeking that knowledge by reading, studying, and meditating upon Scripture; and by prayer.

But consider a fourth test. Anyone who is 'led by the Spirit' is always concerned about his lack of love for God, and for our Lord, and says with the hymn-writer, 'Lord, it is my chief complaint that my love is weak and faint'. That is the concern of a man led by the Spirit. Nothing but the Spirit leads to that. But the Spirit invariably does so, because He is sent to glorify the Lord in salvation, the Father and the Son, and all They have done. So the question is, How great is our love to God? What is the measure of our love to the Lord Jesus Christ? We say we believe these great truths, but the proof that the Spirit is really leading and directing and guiding us, and that we not merely believe these things intellectually, is that we are concerned about this and troubled about it. We feel that our hearts should be aflame with love, that there should be a great and a burning and a holy passion within us, that with the whole of our being we should be loving God the Father, God the Son, and God the Spirit, and be filled with a desire to praise Him and to magnify Him as we ought. It is an absolute proof of the working of the Spirit that we should be concerned about the lack of this within us, that it troubles us, that it grieves us, and that we do everything we can in order to remedy it.

We can go on to yet more practical tests. Whoever is being led by the Spirit has an increasing awareness of sin within. There is no question about that. The Holy Spirit is the Spirit of light, and the Spirit of truth. He is the *Holy* Spirit. And as He leads and directs us it is always in this direction. And of course the moment He begins to do so we become aware of our real state within. This happens in conviction of sin before conversion, but it does not stop at that; it becomes still more intense afterwards, because the nearer you get to the light the more you are aware of the darkness. The greater the perfection and the purity, the more is every defect shown up. The hotter the contest or the competition, the more skilled the contestants in whatever branch it is, the more does any little blemish or defect appear by way of contrast. So as the Spirit increasingly leads us and guides us we have this increasing awareness of sin within us. And it leads to an increasing mourning because of sin within us, and because of finding that there are still these relics and remnants, and manifestations of that which belongs to the old life. This is again an invariable testimony on the part of all the saints of the centuries. They have had this awareness of what they call 'the blackness' or 'the plague of their own hearts'.

The reaction of the Christian to the committing of sin is similarly something quite new. When the natural man does that which is wrong he is annoyed with himself, he kicks himself metaphorically, but it stops at that. He is annoyed that he should be suffering because of what he has done. He may be annoyed because he has fallen short of his own standard, and failed to live up to his own code. It is but a manifestation of pride in some shape or form. But that is not the reaction of the Christian. When the Christian falls into sin he is aware of grief. And he is grieved because he knows that he has offended not so much against the law of God as against the love of God. This is a child's reaction. Any child worthy of the name is not so much afraid of punishment, is not merely conscious of having broken some rule, some law, when he becomes of an age to understand at all, but he realizes that he has hurt and grieved and offended against love. Nothing can lead to greater misery. This is what happens to the man who is led by the Spirit.

We can see these truths worked out in detail in the Second Epistle to the Corinthians chapter 7, where the Apostle shows the difference between what he calls 'the sorrow of the world' and a 'godly sorrow': 'Now I rejoice, not that ye were made sorry, but that ye sorrowed to repentance: for ye were made sorry after a godly manner, that ye might receive damage by us in nothing. For godly sorrow worketh repentance to salvation not to be repented of: but the sorrow of the world worketh death' (vv. 9, 10). Then he gives the proofs of a godly sorrow – 'For behold this selfsame thing, that ye sorrowed after a godly sort. What carefulness it wrought in you, yea, what clearing of yourselves, yea, what indignation, yea, what fear, yea, what vehement desire, yea, what zeal . . . In all things ye have approved yourselves to be clear in this matter' (v. 11). This is the reaction of a child. It indicates a relationship of love, not of law; and what the offender mourns most about is that he has sinned against love and grace, against mercy and compassion.

Let us go on to point number seven. The man who is led by the Spirit becomes increasingly sensitive to every approach of sin and evil, and to temptation. We are more on our guard; we have been heeding the warnings of the Scriptures and the exhortations – 'Watch', 'Take heed' – so, not surprisingly, we become very sensitive to the very approach of sin and evil; and we do not fall so directly, so immediately to temptation.

To put all this positively as an eighth point, we can say that the man who is led by the Spirit of God is aware in himself of desires and breathings after righteousness and holiness. 'Blessed are they that do hunger and thirst after righteousness, for they shall be filled.' Do you long to be holy, do you long to be righteous? Can you say honestly that you are aware within yourself of breathings after righteousness and holiness? If it is so, you stop committing the sins that dog your steps, or maybe one sin in particular. It is a bad sign when we are concerned over one sin only. That the concern is right in a sense, I grant – we should not fall to any one sin. But what should characterize us is a positive longing after holiness and righteousness? That is the real test. Those who are only interested in being delivered from one particular sin that gets them down are very immature Christians, mere babes in Christ. The man who is being led steadily onwards by the Spirit has positive desires and yearnings and breathings after holiness and righteousness.

The man who is really led by the Spirit will also translate such feelings into action; and we have already seen, partly in verse 13, what he does. 'If ye live after the flesh, ye shall die: but if ye through the Spirit do mortify the deeds of the body, ye shall live.' So the man who is led by the Spirit is actively engaged in mortifying the deeds of the body. We have already dealt with this matter. Being aware that sin remains in his 'mortal body', and being aware of the subtlety of the devil, and the devil's desire to trap him and to reign in his mortal body, this man does everything he can to rid himself of his sin. He is aware that certain things encourage sin, so he does his best to discourage them. He makes no 'provision for the flesh'. A practical test in this respect is our attitude to pornographic literature. If you desire that pornographic literature should be published freely you are without a doubt, making 'provision for the flesh'. Men may call it great literature but it is certain to do harm. It inflames the passions, the motions of sin in the flesh. Anyone who is anxious to mortify the deeds of the body obviously makes no provision for the flesh. Indeed, he goes beyond that, he deliberately discourages certain elements within himself, and goes out of his way to do so. He keeps a careful guard over his eyes, and his ears. He is careful about everything, the company he keeps, the people to whom he talks. If he knows that they are doing him harm he avoids them, it matters not who they are. That is the way to mortify the deeds of the body. You do everything you can to put an end to every influence that tends to make you worse than you were, or has a tarnishing and a polluting effect upon you. You deliberately avoid it and keep clear of it.

In these ways among others we mortify the deeds of the body. In other words it is a question of our whole relationship to what the New Testament calls 'the world'. James says 'The friendship of the world is enmity against God'. If you are led by the Spirit you will not be a friend of the world; you cannot be, because the world is enmity against God, and the Spirit always leads to God. The man who is led by the Spirit realizes that the world is always against him in its outlook, its ways and its ambitions, and so he avoids it and keeps clear of it. 'Love not the world, neither the things that are in the world,' says John: 'for all that is in the world, the lust of the flesh, and the lust of the eyes, and the pride of life, is not of the Father, but is of the world' (1 John 2: 15, 16). These are the things that do harm to the soul. Peter gives similar teaching: 'Dearly beloved, I beseech you as strangers and pilgrims, abstain from fleshly lusts, which war against the soul; having your conversation honest among the Gentiles' (1 Peter 2: 11, 12).

A tenth and last test as to whether or not we are being led by the Spirit is, Are we manifesting the fruit of the Spirit? In Galatians 5 the Apostle contrasts the 'works of the flesh' and the 'fruit of the Spirit'. It follows as the night the day that if we are being led by the Spirit we shall be manifesting, more and more, the 'fruit of the Spirit'. And the fruit of the Spirit is, 'Love, joy, peace, longsuffering, gentleness, goodness, faith, meekness, temperance'. Here we have nine particular tests which we can apply to ourselves. 'Love' to God and to man; 'joy', the Spirit always leads to joy. We find Paul saying later in this Epistle, that 'The kingdom of God is not meat and drink, but righteousness, peace, and joy in the Holy Ghost' (14 : 17). How much 'joy in the Holy Ghost' is present in our lives? Then 'peace'! Not only peace within, but peace with others because we are at peace with God. 'Longsuffering' is a never-absent fruit of the Spirit. As God is patient with us we become more and more patient with others as we are led by the Spirit. 'Gentleness' – that is equally true. Our Lord Himself was gentle. We read of Him, 'The bruised reed he will not break; the smoking flax he will not quench'. But this is not incompatible with 'righteous indignation'. He was angry with the Pharisees because of their hypocrisy, and He called them 'hypocrites' in very plain language. His gentleness is ever a characteristic of those who are led by the Spirit. 'Goodness' explains itself, as does 'Faith', which here means faithfulness. 'Meekness' is another invariable characteristic. The Holy Spirit always leads to humility and to meekness. If a man is aware of the truth about himself, and of what still remains in him, he will of necessity be humble and meek. I have known people who have claimed to be led by the Spirit to an unusual degree, but there was an absence of meekness and humility in them, indeed at times there was spiritual pride and self-satisfaction. That is never the characteristic of the man or woman who is being led by the Spirit. Then 'temperance', which means self-control, discipline. The Spirit is a spirit of order. The Apostle writes to Timothy, 'God hath not given us the spirit of fear; but of power, and of love, and of a sound mind' (2 Timothy 1 : 7). 'A sound mind' means discipline, temperance, continence, self-control. The disciplined person is not swayed by every whim, impulse and feeling that may come to him, nor is he at the mercy of anything that may happen to meet him; there is a steadiness, a control, a temperate element in all his actions, conduct and behaviour.

Such, then, are some of the tests suggested by the Scriptures themselves. What we have to do is to apply the tests to our own lives. In a sense, as I have already said, any one of them is enough, but we should be able to find something of each one of them in ourselves. Are we becoming increasingly spiritually minded?

Are we longing more and more for a knowledge of God? Are we really longing to know the Lord Jesus Christ and His love better? Is our love increasing as we go on? Every day, every year we live we should know Him better, and love Him more truly. Let me ask a still more practical question, and I would press it especially upon those who have passed middle-age. Can you say that you are thinking more and more of that 'land of pure delight' to which you are going? The New Testament holds us face to face with that challenge. Paul in the midst of his tribulations could say, 'Our light affliction, which is but for a moment, worketh for us a far more exceeding and eternal weight of glory; while we look not at the things which are seen, but at the things which are not seen: for the things which are seen are temporal; but the things which are not seen are eternal' (2 Corinthians 4: 17, 18). He says to the Colossians, 'Set your affection on things above, not on things on the earth' (3: 2). What is a Christian? Paul, in writing to Titus, says that he is a man who is 'looking for the appearing of the great God and our Saviour'. I have said that I am applying this test to people well advanced in age, but perhaps I should not have spoken in that way. In Whitefield's Journals you will find that in his twenties the great preacher often longed to be in 'that land'. This was not morbidity, it was true Christianity. The more we are led by the Spirit, the more we shall be weaned from this old sinful world, and the more we shall know something about the desire 'to depart and to be with Christ, which is far better' (Philippians 1: 23).

Are we testing ourselves as we ought? That is what being 'led by the Spirit' means. As He leads us He will always be leading us in the direction of the Father and the Lord Jesus Christ, that we might know Them, and love Them, and long to spend our eternity with Them, looking for the great day when Christ will come and destroy all evil in the world and all His enemies, and establish His glorious kingdom. This 'blessed hope' means much to the one who is led by the Spirit. 'Every man that hath this hope in him purifieth himself, even as he is pure' (1 John 3: 3). Take any one of these great New Testament statements, and again, take them all together: Are we being led by the Spirit? Are we spiritually minded people? Are these the things which matter to us above everything else? Are these the things in which we delight and glory? Let every man examine himself; and God grant that we may be able to say 'Yes'. I am not asking whether you are perfect with respect to any one of these questions. I am simply asking – and I do so to encourage you – Do you find in yourself any evidence of these things? If you do, you are a Christian. If there is but little, a mere trace, you are a very small infant and you have perhaps only just been born. That is a beginning! But do not stay at that point. You must 'grow in grace, and in the knowledge of the Lord'. We are not to remain infants, we must go on and become 'babes', boys, 'young men', middle-aged, 'old men' in Christ. Is there an increasing maturity about us? It should be so; and if we are led by the Spirit it will be so. No one should feel discouraged. If there are but glimmerings of life in you, it is sufficient. But the Spirit 'yearns' to lead you on, He is 'yearning' for you with a 'jealous envy'. His desire is that you should be someone in whom God, as it were, can take pride. The Epistle to the Hebrews says of Old Testament saints, 'God is not ashamed to be called their God' (Hebrews 11: 16). And the Holy Spirit's earnest desire is that we become such that God will be proud of us, and will be able to make known to 'the principalities and powers in heavenly places', through us, His 'manifold wisdom' (Ephesians 3: 10). May the Holy Spirit lead us on and on in these endless glories, that we may become more and more living 'epistles of Christ, known and read of all men'!

Sixteen

*

For as many as are led by the Spirit of God, they are the sons of God.

For ye have not received the spirit of bondage again to fear; but ye have received the Spirit of adoption, whereby we cry, Abba, Father.   Romans 8: 14, 15

We have been considering the tests which we must apply to ourselves in order to make sure that we are being led by the Spirit of God – tests of conduct and behaviour, tests of desire, and so on. But there are those who would interpret this phrase 'being led by the Spirit of God' as referring to the matter of guidance in our lives. We all need guidance as to what we are to do with our lives. The people to whom I refer teach that as Christians we should receive direct guidance concerning all the details of our lives, and they tell us that they themselves constantly enjoy such 'leading of the Spirit'.

I have already indicated that I do not regard this phrase as referring to guidance in that sense; indeed I would almost be prepared to go so far as to say that such guidance is really not referred to at all in verse 14. However, I hesitate to go quite as far as that. But it is certainly not the main emphasis, and for this very good reason, that it is much too subjective a test. It is, alas, but too easy to persuade yourself that you are being guided directly by the Spirit. Some of the greatest tragedies in the history of the Church have resulted from the actions of fanatical persons who were quite certain that they were being led by the Holy Spirit to do this or that. Oftentimes their actions were diametrically opposed to the plain teaching of the Scripture. They 'felt' that they were being led and guided by the Spirit. But 'feeling' is too subjective a test, and therefore I cannot believe that the Apostle has it in his mind as a practical test which we can apply to ourselves, for it exposes us to the vagaries of subjectivism. However, we cannot go so far as to say that it is altogether and entirely excluded, for there are notable examples and illustrations in the Acts of the Apostles where the Holy Spirit did lead and guide the Christian Church in a most explicit and direct manner.

Take, for instance, what is recorded in chapter 13, verse 2: 'As they ministered to the Lord, and fasted, the Holy Ghost said, Separate me Barnabas and Saul for the work whereunto I have called them.' We do not know the exact manner in which the Holy Ghost gave the Church at Antioch these instructions. He may have impressed it upon the mind of a number of the Christians together, so that they all felt an urge and a leading to do this to Barnabas and Saul. The Holy Spirit is able to impress His will upon the mind. He can keep something before us constantly, so that we cannot get away from it. We are conscious of a pressure on the mind and on the spirit; we feel something urging us in a given direction. That may be the leading of the Holy Spirit. There is another illustration of the same thing in Acts 15 : 28, in connection with the account of the council at Jerusalem. The message which was sent by the council at Jerusalem to the Christian churches was, 'For it seemed good to the Holy Ghost, and to us, to lay upon you no greater burden than these necessary things'. The Holy Ghost had made clear what His leading, His guidance, was in the particular matter under debate. They had been discussing it together, and they say in effect that what they had reasoned out corresponded with, tallied with, what the Holy Ghost Himself was indicating to them.

But perhaps the most striking examples are to be found in the 16th chapter of the Acts in verse 6 and 7: 'Now when they had gone through Phrygia and the region of Galatia, and were forbidden of the Holy Ghost to preach the word in Asia, after they were come to Mysia, they assayed to go into Bithynia' – and as the Revised Version puts it rightly – 'the Spirit of Jesus suffered them not.' Here are two striking statements. They were 'forbidden of the Holy Ghost to preach the word in Asia', and 'the Spirit of Jesus suffered them not' when they attempted to go into Bithynia. Again, we are not told how the Holy Spirit did this; but what is made plain is that He did prohibit them. Have we not all known something of this in personal experience? With your reason and understanding you may have examined the pros and cons of a certain proposal, and you may have arrived at your decision. Let us suppose, for example, that you have decided to do a certain thing; but then you begin to feel something that you cannot explain, but of which you are very conscious; you begin to feel a pressure in your spirit prohibiting you from doing the very thing you have decided to do with your mind and with your reason. That, I believe, is very often, if not always, the pressure of the Holy Spirit. I am talking, of course, about Christian people who have honestly told God that their one desire is to do His will. They have rightly used their mind, their understanding, and they may have consulted others before arriving at their decision. But in spite of that there seems to be some pressure on their spirit, a definite sense of restraint; a door seems to be closed in the spirit and they feel that they cannot proceed. I take it that Paul and his companions experienced something of this kind on those occasions referred to in Acts 16 verses 6 and 7.

There is no question but that the Holy Spirit does guide; but I repeat that I am convinced that that is not what was uppermost in the mind of the Apostle here, because in verse 13 he had been dealing with the question of sanctification, and especially in terms of 'mortifying the deeds of the body'. The leading by the Spirit clearly follows directly from that verse, and is associated directly with it.

We come now in verse 15 to another test we must apply to ourselves in order to make sure that we are indeed the sons or the children of God. To be assured of salvation is the highest privilege of the Christian believer in this world of time. I sometimes feel that it is true to say that a man's spirituality can be tested, perhaps, more thoroughly by this verse, and the verse that follows, than by almost any other statement in the whole of the Scripture. It is particularly interesting and fascinating to test commentators by their view of these two verse. Those who are mainly intellectual, it seems to me, have not even begun to understand these two verses, and they miss the point completely. The more spiritually minded the commentator the more he will find riches in verses 15 and 16. Verse 15 is a most important verse from the standpoint of assurance of salvation; it gives us something over and above what we have obtained from verse 14. Verse 14 was wonderful, it was enough, but 'the riches of God's grace' give yet more. As Christians, God is our Father, and His desire is that we shall be delivered from all doubt, so He multiplies the proofs. But further, this verse is most important from another aspect; it casts great light upon chapter 7 verses 7 to 25; and I shall show that it is one of the means of justifying the exposition we gave of those controversial verses.

The first question that engages our attention is the used of the word 'spirit' twice over. 'For ye have not received the spirit of bondage again to fear; but ye have received the Spirit of adoption, whereby we cry, Abba, Father.' There is a comparison and a contrast. There are two sides to the statement – negative and positive – but the same word, 'spirit', is used in both. Is the meaning the same in both cases? There are those who say that in both instances it means just a disposition, a feeling. They maintain that the Apostle is virtually saying, Now we as Christian people have not received a heavy spirit of bondage and of fear and of discouragement and of lassitude; we have received a cheerful spirit, a joyful spirit. In other words they say that on both sides the word 'spirit' here stands for disposition or feeling. Hence the Apostle is saying that when we were not Christians we had a spirit of bondage and of fear, but now that we have become Christians we have a cheerful spirit of adoption, whereby we cry, Abba, Father. It is true to say that we often use the word 'spirit' in this way. We read in the Bible of a man having a spirit of meekness, or a meek spirit. We also talk of a spirit of disobedience, and in the same way of a man being in 'good spirit' or 'bad spirit'. The contention is that the Apostle uses the words here in that sense.

On the other hand there are those who reject such an exposition; and it appears that the translators of the Authorized Version belong to this second group, because we find that in the first use of the word 'spirit' it is spelt with a small 's', whereas in the second use it is spelt with a capital 'S'. 'Ye have not received the spirit of bondage again to fear [small 's'] but ye have received the Spirit [capital 'S'] of adoption, whereby we cry, Abba, Father.' The idea is that it means in the first instance a disposition or feeling, but that in the second case it means the Holy Spirit. On what grounds do these interpreters base that teaching? Their argument is that it is the Holy Spirit who produces our adoption, so that when the Apostle talks about 'the Spirit of adoption' he means the Spirit who creates the adoption within us. That may, or may not, be true. I would prefer to say that it is the 'Father' rather than the 'Spirit' who does the adopting. The Spirit plays His part, of course; but it seems to me that adoption is primarily the work of the Father.

But there is another and more cogent reason for regarding this second use of 'Spirit' as a reference to the Holy Spirit. In Galatians 4: 6 we read: 'And because ye are sons, God hath sent forth the Spirit of his Son into your hearts, crying, Abba, Father'. This is obviously parallel with the statement in Romans 8: 15, and explicitly we are told in Galatians 4: 6 that it is the Holy Spirit, the Spirit of God's Son, who is sent into our hearts, and thereby leads us to cry out, 'Abba, Father'. I would argue that this is quite conclusive in and of itself. So this second view asserts that we must not say that the two uses of the word 'spirit' simply refer to disposition or feeling. It is quite clear that, at least in the second instance, it is the Holy Spirit Himself. I want to suggest, however, that we cannot leave the matter there, and that we must regard the reference to 'spirit' in both instances as being to the Holy Spirit, the first as well as the second.

The second school says that my suggestion cannot possibly be correct because the Holy Spirit cannot be described as a 'spirit of bondage'. Does not 2 Corinthians 3: 17 tell us, they say, that 'where the Spirit of the Lord is, there is liberty?' How then can the Spirit ever be a 'spirit of bondage'? And, surely, they maintain, it must never be said that the Holy Spirit of God could possibly produce a sense of bondage, for He produces adoption, whereby we cry, 'Abba, Father'. And so they argue that the contrast here is between the unbeliever on the one hand, and the believer on the other; the contrast between the pre-conversion and the conversion state.

My reply to that second school is along the following lines. First, the whole context here is that of the Holy Spirit Himself. That is, to me, the most important factor. The Apostle has been dealing with the Holy Spirit almost from the commencement of the chapter; but certainly in the immediate context he is dealing with the Spirit. 'For if ye live after the flesh, ye shall die: but if ye through the Spirit [capital 'S'] do mortify the deeds of the body, ye shall live. For as many as are led by the Spirit of God, they are the sons of God. For ye have not received the spirit of bondage...'

The entire context is the Holy Spirit. 'The Spirit itself', says verse 16, 'beareth witness with our spirit, that we are the children of God.' So that when Paul does come to deal with our 'spirit' he says so explicitly in this same verse 16.

A second answer is that it is surely most unlikely that the Apostle would change the meaning of the same word without giving us some indication that he is doing so. He could have done so easily. He is putting before us a contrast, and if the contrast is to be perfect – that is, if you are to preserve the balance of the two statements – then surely this crucial word 'spirit' must carry the same meaning on the one side as it does on the other. We should always be very careful, and hesitant, about accepting a change in the meaning of a word without having some very good reason for doing so.

My third answer is that it is quite unscriptural to say that the unconverted apart from the Spirit have a 'spirit of bondage' and of 'fear', for this is far from being the case. Indeed the main trouble with the unbeliever is that, though he is 'dead in trespasses and in sins', yet he feels quite secure. He is not troubled about himself and about his eternal future. The Apostle has already told us that about himself in chapter 7, verse 9, where he says, 'For I was alive without the law once'. He gloried in his security, and was highly pleased with himself. He tells us the same thing in that fascinating bit of autobiography in the third chapter of the Epistle to the Philippians, where he could boast that he was 'a Hebrew of the Hebrews, of the tribe of Benjamin', who, as far as keeping the law was involved, believed himself to be perfect, leaving nothing more to be desired. That is not 'the spirit of bondage', nor is it 'the spirit of fear', but the spirit of security and self-satisfaction. It is the picture of a man who is perfectly happy about himself. I argue therefore that it is impossible for the first part of this fifteenth verse to be a reference to the unconverted person, 'dead in trespasses and sins', utterly lifeless, not touched at all by the operations of the Holy Spirit.

That leads to my fourth answer, which is to emphasize the word 'received' and especially the word 'again'. 'For ye have not received again, but ye have received . . . ' On both sides of the statement we find this word 'received', which suggests that the persons to whom Paul is referring had at one time 'received' the 'spirit of bondage', even as they have now 'received' the 'Spirit of adoption'. It was not always so. They have 'received' the spirit of bondage to fear; and they have 'received' the Spirit of adoption. We lose the force of the parallelism if we do not say that. And this becomes more important still when the word 'again' is introduced. 'For ye have not received again the spirit of bondage to fear.' That means, You did once receive the spirit of bondage to fear, but you have not received it 'again'. So we take the two words together, the 'receiving' and the 'again', and it helps to develop the argument and to bring us to this position – that the Apostle is saying here that a Christian is a man who once received a 'spirit of bondage to fear'. How did he receive it? As the result of the operation of the Holy Spirit upon him! In other words, it is the Holy Spirit who produces 'the spirit of bondage to fear', He alone can do it. And He does it by means of, or through, the law of God.

Let me establish and prove my contention. The best exposition, I am suggesting, of the first half of this fifteenth verse is the seventh chapter of this same Epistle, verses 7 to 25. There we find that the Apostle says: 'I was alive without the law once: but when the commandment came, sin revived, and I died.' He thought that he understood the law, but he discovered that he was mistaken. It was the Holy Spirit who really 'brought' the law to him; then he was truly made to see the spirituality of the law. 'We know that the law is spiritual' – but he did not know that, until the Holy Spirit had brought him to see it. When he was 'alive without the law' he did not understand it. The Holy Spirit came and applied the law to him truly for the first time, and he was deeply convicted. The result was, as we have seen, that he found himself to be in a state of terrible bondage which made him say, 'We know that the law is spiritual: but I am carnal, sold under sin'. 'If then I do that which I would not, I consent unto the law that it is good. . . ' 'For that which I do I allow not: for what I would, that do I not; but what I hate, that do I' – and so on, throughout the rest of that seventh chapter. It was the Holy Spirit who did these things to him. This is a most important point. The law itself does not do so and cannot do so. The Jews were confronted daily with the law of God and they had a mechanical, intellectual knowledge of it. But they never came under its power; it never convicted them truly, as we see in the case of Paul himself when Saul of Tarsus. It is the Holy Spirit alone who can do that. There is no other power which can produce a 'spirit of bondage and of fear' except the Holy Spirit. But that is exactly what He does when He begins to work in us the work of conviction.

But not only can the law not do the work; it is equally true to say that circumstances cannot do so. They can frighten us, they can alarm us; they can stop people sinning for a while, and for a while cause them to try to live a good life. But that is not the 'spirit of bondage to fear', which means real conviction of sin. Take, as a notable example of true conviction, that found in the sixteenth chapter of the Acts of the Apostles – the case of the Philippian jailer. The earthquake took place and the man comes trembling and saying, 'Sirs, what must I do to be saved?' It was not the earthquake that produced that effect. That man had been in earthquakes before. Men can pass through earthquakes and many other calamities without ever being compelled to say 'Sirs, what must I do to be saved?" It was not the earthquake that convicted the jailer; it was the Holy Spirit. The Holy Spirit may have used the earthquake, in part; but the earthquake alone could not induce conviction. Men can go through wars and be brought face to face with death, and not be any better or brought to conviction of sin. The two world wars in this century have not led sinners to repentance – if anything, to the opposite. Nor do calamities work repentance; it is only the Spirit of God, the Holy Spirit, that can lead to 'the spirit of bondage to fear'.

As a further illustration, take that found in the second chapter of the Acts of the Apostles. The Apostle Peter is preaching to sinners on the Day of Pentecost, and suddenly, we are told, 'they were pricked in their hearts, and said unto Peter, and to the rest of the apostles, Men and brethren, what shall we do?' Why did they cry out in that way? There is only one answer; it was because they had been brought to a spirit of bondage and of fear. The Holy Ghost had been poured out upon Peter and the other apostles and He was using Peter as he was preaching and expounding the Scriptures. His Jewish listeners were simply animated by a spirit of curiosity and knew nothing about either 'bondage' or 'fear' when Peter began to preach. But as he went on, and applied his message, a tremendous power of conviction came upon them, and in a spirit of bondage and of fear they cried out, saying, 'Men and brethren, what shall we do?' That was the result of the work of the Spirit convicting them of sin.

[201]

We find frequent mention of such an experience as we read the biographies of the saints. They tell you how they passed through terrible periods of bondage and of fear. John Bunyan tells us in his 'Grace Abounding' that he was in this condition for eighteen months; so much so, he tells us, that on certain occasions he wished that he were not alive, or that he were an animal, even a dog or a horse, for he knew that they had no souls to perish in hell as (he says) 'mine was like to do'. On another occasion, he tells us, this spirit of bondage and of fear was so terrible that he could have sworn that he smelt brimstone in the air. That was a 'spirit of bondage', a 'spirit of fear'; and that was the work of the Holy Spirit convicting John Bunyan of sin. In earlier days he had felt very free, very careless and apparently happy.

But to see this on a big scale you have simply to read the history of any one of the great revivals of religion. When the Spirit of God comes down in revival His first work invariably is to humble people, to convict them profoundly of sin, to make them feel utterly and completely hopeless. This happens to people who had never felt such a thing before. A great spirit of conviction possesses them, they groan in agony, and may fall to the ground in torment. That is a 'spirit of bondage' and a 'spirit of fear'. They feel that nothing can be done for them, and this is the result of the outpouring of the Holy Spirit. How ridiculous it is, therefore, to say that the Holy Spirit could never do such a work! Our Lord had said that the Holy Spirit would reprove, or 'convict the world of sin, and of righteousness and of judgment' (John 16: 8). The Holy Spirit brings us down and shows us our need; and in this way He brings us into a spirit of bondage and of fear. How foolish it is, therefore, to take just one text out of its context and say, 'Ah, but Paul says, "Where the Spirit of the Lord is, there is liberty" '! That is the ultimate end of the process; but it is not the beginning. The Spirit who gives the liberty starts by producing a spirit of bondage and of fear. I argue that the Apostle, here in Romans 8: 15, uses the term 'Spirit' in the two parts of his assertion in the same sense, and in both instances he is speaking of the Holy Spirit Himself.

Take a further argument to clinch this matter. It is only as we interpret this verse in this way that we bring it into line with, and show that it is parallel with, the almost identical argument which the Apostle uses in the 4th chapter of the Epistle to the Galatians where he draws the same contrast. 'I say that the heir, as long as he is a child, differeth nothing from a servant, though he be lord of all; but he is under tutors and governors until the time appointed of the father. Even so we, when we were children, were in bondage under the elements of the world. But when the fulness of the time was come, God sent forth his Son, made of a woman, made under the law, to redeem them that were under the law, that we might receive the adoption of sons. And because ye are sons, God hath sent forth the Spirit of his Son into your hearts, crying, Abba, Father.' These statements are but an elaboration of the two halves of this fifteenth verse of the eighth chapter of the Epistle to the Romans. Furthermore, I would argue that we find exactly the same thing at the end of the 4th chapter of the Epistle to the Galatians, from verse 21 to verse 31, where again Paul draws this same contrast, putting it in terms of the child of the bondwoman and the child of the freewoman. So this interpretation not only suits its own immediate context, but also brings it into line with the analogous statements which the Apostle makes elsewhere.

I am happy to be able to add, as a final bit of evidence for this exposition, that I am not alone in suggesting it. It has become inevitable, as far as I am concerned, as the result of my exposition of chapter 7. I quoted this verse while expounding that chapter. But I have been very happy, since then, to discover that one of the greatest of the early Puritans, John Preston, who was chaplain to King James I and King Charles I for a while (but a true Puritan revered by the later great Puritans such as John Owen and Thomas Goodwin and others) expounds this verse in precisely this manner. I shall give some quotations from his works later. And the same is true of Thomas Horton, another of these great Puritans, and also Thomas Goodwin himself.

What then is our doctrine? It is that this 'spirit of bondage and of fear' is the peculiar work of the Holy Spirit Himself. It is one of the things the law cannot do, which partly explains why the law had not solved the problem. But it is the Spirit's first work. He generally does it, as I have been emphasizing, through the law. It was necessary in the case of Paul himself, as it is in the case of all others. He comes to us when we are careless and indifferent and feeling quite secure, with never a thought about the soul and about the judgment of God and eternal punishment; He applies the law to us, and as He does so He produces this 'spirit of bondage and of fear'.

What then are the manifestations of this spirit? The first, of course, is a sense of condemnation. That is what happened to the Apostle himself. Chapter 7 verse 10 again: 'And the commandment, which was ordained to life, I found to be unto death.' And in the next verse: 'For sin, taking occasion by the commandment, deceived me, and by it slew me. Was then that which is good made death unto me?' All along, it led to a sense of condemnation, which is the first evidence always of the 'spirit of bondage and of fear'. A man is awakened to the fact that he is a sinner, that he is in an utterly wrong relationship to God, that he is condemned by the law of God, that he is under the wrath of God, that his whole eternal destiny is to be one of torment if he should remain and die in that condition.

But not only so; at the same time he is given a sense of his inward depravity. In chapter 7 the Apostle keeps on telling us so. In verse 14, for instance: 'We know that the law is spiritual: but I am carnal, sold under sin.' The natural man never has such a feeling; he has no knowledge of such an experience. It is only a man who is under conviction of sin by the Holy Spirit, as He applies the law, who comes to realize that his very nature is carnal, and that he is 'sold under sin'. Paul says the same thing again in the 17th verse of chapter 7: 'Now it is no more I that do it, but sin that dwelleth in me.' Verse 18: 'I know that in me (that is, in my flesh), dwelleth no good thing.' Verse 20: 'If I do that I would not, it is no more I that do it, but sin that dwelleth in me. I find then a law, that when I would do good, evil is present with me.' Verse 23: 'I see another law in my members, warring against the law of my mind' – and so on. He has become aware of his inward depravity. He had never realized that before. He realizes now not only that he does things which are sinful, but that there is something much worse than that! Why does he ever desire to do such things? What is it that leads him to do so? And he is given to see that it is his nature which is utterly depraved, carnal, and 'sold under sin'. 'In me (that is, in my flesh) dwelleth no good thing'. He is a mass of corruption. It is the Spirit alone who can bring a man to see that; and when that happens the man is conscious of a terrible 'bondage' and a terrible 'fear'.

That in turn leads to the next step, namely, that he realizes his utter inability to rid himself of his sin. This again is the great theme of the 7th chapter. Look at it in verse 15: 'That which I do I allow not; for what I would, that do I not; but what I hate, that do I'. Verse 18: 'I know that in me (that is, in my flesh) dwelleth no good thing: for to will is present with me, but how to perform that which is good I know not.' He is in bonds, he cannot live as he would. He loves the law but he cannot keep it; he is helpless. He says the same thing again in verse 21: 'I find a law, that, when I would do good, evil is present with me.' And again verse 23: 'I see another law in my members, warring against the law of my mind, and bringing me into captivity to the law of sin which is in my members.' He is bound, he is helpless, he is incapable. He sees the nature of the law now, and its spirituality; he would like to keep it, but he cannot keep it. He is fettered, tied, in captivity, a serf. It is only the Spirit that brings a man to see that! And finally it leads to a sense of complete hopelessness and indeed of despair. It makes him say, 'O wretched man that I am! who shall deliver me from the body of this death?' He cannot deliver himself; he has tried, and has failed. The evil principle that is in him is too strong for him. These are manifestations of the 'spirit of bondage' and the 'spirit of fear'; and they are produced only by the Holy Spirit of God.

That 'spirit of bondage', which I have been describing, always precedes the 'Spirit of adoption'. The apostle is building up his case. There are grounds for assurance of salvation in the first half of this fifteenth verse, as well as in the second half. The 'spirit of bondage and of fear' is evidence of the working of the Holy Spirit. I trust also that we have seen again yet more clearly that the so-called 'man of Romans 7' is, as we have said, not the full-grown Christian at the height of his Christian experience. No, he is a man who is only in a state of conviction, 'under the law'. He is not undisturbed spiritually, but he is not regenerate; he is a man in this preliminary stage, under conviction of sin as the result of the Spirit's work. He has been awakened to the true nature of the law, and he realizes that he is not only in a state of bondage, but also in a state of the utmost danger. He is under condemnation; and he cannot deliver himself from the guilt of sin, nor from the power of sin. He would give anything if he could but do so; but he cannot. So he is left in a state of bondage and of fear. We 'receive' the spirit of bondage and of 'fear'; and when we 'receive' it that is how it shows itself.

Seventeen

*

For ye have not received the spirit of bondage again to fear; but ye have received the Spirit of adoption, whereby we cry, Abba, Father.

Romans 8: 15

We are still examining the first half of this verse – 'Ye have not received the spirit of bondage again to fear'. The Apostle's assertion is that the Holy Spirit is not giving 'again' a spirit of bondage, but rather a 'Spirit of adoption'. He also makes it clear that the spirit of bondage always precedes the Spirit of adoption. The word 'again' shows that clearly. We have also seen that there is real value from the standpoint of assurance even in the negative statement, because the spirit of bondage and of fear is a clear indication of the working of the Holy Spirit. It is the first preliminary work of the Spirit in bringing us to salvation and is therefore an indication of sonship.

But, someone asks, 'What of non-Christians who have often been frightened under the preaching of the Gospel?' My reply is that they still have not known 'the spirit of bondage again to fear'. They have known merely a temporary alarm. The same happens to such people when they look at certain types of play or drama. They are terrified by some powerful impulse. But every fear is not this 'spirit of bondage again to fear'. This, as we have seen, has certain definite and peculiar characteristics, among which is a very real sense of sin. It is not merely the fear of hell; it is a fear of the holiness of God; it is a fear produced by a sense of our own inward corruption. So I argue that the only people who have ever known truly the 'spirit of bondage again to fear' are those who have really been convicted by the Spirit and have seen the spirituality of the law and the consequences that follow.

But this negative statement is of great value also, in 'testing the spirits'. We are aware that we have an antagonist, an adversary, who often persuades people that they have the Spirit of adoption when that is not true of them. The devil is always ready to make us feel secure and happy if thereby he can lull us into a kind of carnal peace, which will mean that we are no longer troubled about our salvation. It is important therefore, as the New Testament frequently exhorts us, to 'test' and to 'prove the spirits', because every spirit is not of God. And the devil sometimes persuades people that they are saved people, Christians, and sons of God. It is important therefore that we should be able to differentiate between the true Spirit of adoption given by the Holy Spirit, and the counterfeit of the devil. It is just here that this 'spirit of bondage and of fear' becomes invaluable as a test. If we have never known the 'spirit of bondage and of fear' we had better examine very carefully what may appear at first sight to be the Spirit of adoption. I lay down this proposition, that 'the spirit of bondage and fear' always precedes the 'Spirit of adoption'. John Preston, one of the Puritans to whom I have referred, states the matter in this way: 'If thou never hadst the spirit of bondage, certainly thou hast not yet received the Spirit of the Son: for the Apostle speaks of it here as the common condition to all Christians, they do not receive the spirit of bondage again; you had it once, but now you have the Spirit of adoption. I say, every man must have this spirit of bondage, and the ground of it is this, because no man can come to Christ except the law be a schoolmaster to bring him to Christ. Then he says, 'And there is very great reason for it, because otherwise we should never know the love of Christ. He that hath not known what the spirit of bondage is, what these fears are, what the terrors of conscience are in some measure, knows not what Christ hath suffered for him, or what deliverance he hath had by Him; besides he will not be applyable to Christ.' His argument is this. Why does any man ever go to Christ? why does he ever apply to Christ? What reason has he for doing so except this one reason, that he has known this spirit of bondage, this fear, this unhappiness? Preston uses the argument of the word 'again' even as we have done. He says, you first receive that spirit, and then you receive this Spirit of adoption.

There are certain points we must note before we go further. The degree to which this spirit of bondage is experienced may vary considerably in intensity. I am not saying that all must have experienced this 'bondage and fear' with the same intensity, but that all Christians must have experienced it in some measure. Certainly the records of the saints make it clear that there has been considerable variation in the intensity of the feeling; and we must be very careful not to go wrong at that point. There are some who would standardize the experience of conversion. But they are not entitled to do so in terms of Scripture. There are some who would say that unless a man has known a particularly deep agony of repentance he is not a Christian. But all that the Scripture says is that one must know something about this spirit of bondage and fear which is produced by the Holy Spirit.

An objection is often put forward at this point. Someone says, 'Very well, I am prepared to accept that in general, but what about the case of people who have been brought up in Christian homes? Do you really postulate that they should know this "spirit of bondage and of fear?" We can well understand how a man who has been brought up in a pagan atmosphere, or who has lived a very dissolute and evil life, when suddenly confronted by the truth may pass through a great period of crisis and of agony, and may experience great bondage and condemnation. But', they continue, 'what of those who have always been brought up in a Christian atmosphere, who have been taught the truth from their early childhood, and who have almost unconsciously believed in the Lord Jesus Christ and the truth concerning Him which has always been presented to them? They have never committed gross sins, they have never been violent sinners; is it right therefore, is it reasonable to say that even they must have known this spirit of bondage and of fear?' That is a good and a very important question, because it deals with a very common position and it applies to large numbers of people who say, 'I cannot speak of any dramatic experience; I do not know exactly when I was converted'. There is no difficulty about that up to a point; for there is no necessity that conversion should be sudden or dramatic. But when they go on to say that for the same reason they have never known any 'spirit of bondage and of fear', then I believe I can convict them of error. I do so along the following lines.

First, it seems to me that they are guilty of false reasoning, for they are virtually putting a premium on sin. They are more or less saying that what determines the presence or the absence of this spirit of bondage and of fear is the amount of sin that has been committed. That is a very dangerous and a very grievous fallacy. Let me state it in the following way. There is a well-known statement at the end of the seventh chapter of Luke's Gospel which seems to me to deal with this matter finally; but it is often misinterpreted. Here it is, beginning at verse 36: 'And one of the Pharisees desired him that he would eat with him. And, behold, a woman of the city, which was a sinner, when she knew that Jesus sat at meat in the Pharisee's house, brought an alabaster box of ointment, and stood at his feet behind him weeping, and began to wash his feet with tears, and did wipe them with the hairs of her head, and kissed his feet, and anointed them with the ointment. Now when the Pharisee which had bidden him saw it, he spake within himself, saying, This man, if he were a prophet, would have known who and what manner of woman this is that toucheth him: for she is a sinner. And Jesus answering said unto him, Simon, I have somewhat to say unto thee. And he saith, Master, say on. There was a certain creditor which had two debtors: the one owed five hundred pence, and the other fifty. And when they had nothing to pay, he frankly forgave them both. Tell me, therefore, which of them will love him most? Simon answered and said, I suppose that he to whom he forgave most. And he said unto him, Thou hast rightly judged. And he turned to the woman, and said unto Simon, Seest thou this woman? I entered into thine house, thou gavest me no water for my feet: but she hath washed my feet with tears, and wiped them with the hairs of her head. Thou gavest me no kiss: but this woman since the time I came in hath not ceased to kiss my feet. My head with oil thou didst not anoint: but this woman hath anointed my feet with ointment. Wherefore I say unto thee, Her sins, which are many, are forgiven; for she loved much: but to whom little is forgiven, the same loveth little. And he said unto her, Thy sins are forgiven.'

That statement throws great light on the matter before us. Our Lord says, 'Her sins, which are many, are forgiven; for she loved much: but to whom little is forgiven, the same loveth little'. The false interpretation of that says, Here was a woman who had been living a very evil life; Simon, on the other hand was a Pharisee, and had lived a good life; therefore, they say, because she had sinned so much more and had been forgiven so much more, she loved more. But what a terrible thing to say! It would ultimately involve us in arguing that we had all better sin as much as we can, because the more we sin the more we shall be forgiven, and the more we are forgiven the more we shall love. That is obviously quite impossible as Christian teaching.

Our Lord is certainly not teaching any such thing. His teaching is, that what matters is not the amount of sin we have committed, but our realization of our sinfulness. What He is saying is that it is the one who realizes the extent of sinfulness, and therefore the extent of forgiveness, who loves much. He cannot mean anything else; because, as I have said, if you put any other interpretation on His statement, you put a premium on sin. It is the realization of sin that really matters; and this is something that is as possible to a person who has been brought up in a Christian home as it is to one who has been brought up in a pagan atmosphere. This is of crucial importance. I knew a lady who was greatly troubled by this very matter – indeed, I have known many such. She had observed that certain church members who had once been violent drunkards, and so on, seemed to have remarkable joy. They had experienced a dramatic conversion, a great change in their lives. And this good lady said that she almost wished at times she had been a terrible drunkard in order that she might have this won-derful experience of conversion leading to such great joy. The fallacy there is surely obvious. The Gospel is never an incitement to sin, and never leads us to say, 'Let us continue in sin, that grace may abound'. We have already seen in chapter 6 that that is entirely false teaching, and is indeed the very opposite of what the Apostle would have us believe.

My second answer is one which I must handle with particular care, because I am anxious not to discourage anyone. But, on the other hand, it is our business to apply the truth, and to be honest with it. There is such a thing as mere 'believism', or what the fathers used to call 'fideism'. It means simply *saying* that you believe that Jesus Christ is the Son of God and that He died for your sins. This is the peculiar danger facing all who have been brought up in Christian homes and in a Christian atmosphere. They hear this teaching; then there may be a call in a meeting for those who are prepared to say that they believe to come forward, and say so; and they do so. There may be a high emotional element in the meeting, and so they 'go forward' or give some other indication that they do believe that they are sinners and that they believe that Jesus Christ is the Son of God, and that He has died for their sins. They are then told that they are Christians, that they are children of God. That may be true; but it may not be true. It may be purely intellectual and notional. If this happens without any conviction of sin, or without any true understanding of salvation, then I would be most unhappy about it. Many have said that they believe when they have been desperately ill, or because they have suddenly had a sight of hell. They do not want to go to hell; and they do want to go to heaven; so they say they believe, and then they are assured that all is well. But, surely, that comes very far short of what the Bible means by conviction of sin. It certainly does not conform to what we have seen to be the characteristics of the 'spirit of bondage again to fear'. There is the very real danger that many who are assumed to be Christians, and who themselves assume that they are Christians, are not really Christians at all. That is why the Apostle urges the Corinthians and others to 'examine themselves, to prove their own selves, to make sure that they are in the faith' (2 Corinthians 13: 5). We are exhorted to do that by the New Testament, and if we cannot stand the testing and the examination of the New Testament, then there is something seriously wrong with us.

I remember once being in a conference where I had been asked to give some addresses on the Holy Spirit, His person and His work. I was informed during the conference that certain people present on one of the evenings had been somewhat alarmed, and that some of them were beginning to feel that they were not Christians at all. This was a conference of fairly young people, and the authorities responsible for the conference – at least some of them – came to me with deep concern. They were troubled at the fact that these young Christians were being upset and disturbed, that some of them were beginning to feel that they were not Christians at all, and that they had been mistaken. My reply to this, of course, was simply to say that if these young people's Christianity could not even stand up to the test of an exposition of the biblical teaching concerning the work and the Person of the Holy Spirit, what hope would they have on the day of judgment 'when the secrets of all hearts shall be disclosed?' If the faith we think we have cannot stand up to the test of an exposition of Scripture, what kind of faith is it? Are people who say that they believe to be put into some kind of spiritual glass-house, under special protection? Must they never be made to feel unhappy? That is the position into which we get, at times, when we are not scriptural. We are so anxious to have converts, and so much concerned that they should never be disturbed! On the other hand we should thank God for every time that we are disturbed. We should thank God when we are ever forced to examine ourselves, to make sure whether we are in the faith or not. There is no greater danger to our highest interests than this kind of 'easy believism' which is really not the work of the Holy Spirit at all.

My third answer is that the Holy Spirit, being the Spirit of truth, and the Spirit of holiness, always produces a sense of sin and conviction. He has been sent into the world for this very purpose, as we have seen. What the Holy Spirit does, in other words, is to reveal God to us; He reveals the character of God, the holiness of God. He reveals at the same time the law in all its spirituality; and thereby He reveals us to ourselves. So when the Holy Spirit does His work it is inevitable that, in some degree or other, it should make us say –

> *Just and holy is Thy name,*
> *I am all unrighteousness;*
> *Vile and full of sin I am,*
> *Thou art full of truth and grace.*

It is quite inevitable. The Holy Spirit always does that work. He also reveals the Lord Jesus Christ to us as Son of God, and Saviour. But why do we need a Saviour? Because of the holiness of God, the holiness revealed by His law, and our own sinfulness and imperfection. The Holy Spirit, in convicting us, of necessity reveals these things to us. And as He does so He produces this 'spirit of bondage', and this 'spirit of fear'. My argument is that the Holy Spirit cannot lead us to God in any sense without giving us some impression, some idea, of the holiness of God, and the glory of God, and the majesty and the righteousness and the justice of God. And such a revelation invariably produces this sense of bondage and fear.

But in the fourth place, let me add another argument to the foregoing. It is because of what I have just been saying, that we find that the experience of all the saints has always been that the more the Holy Spirit works in them, not only is their understanding of the being of God the greater, but so too is their knowledge of their own sinfulness and unworthiness. All the saints have testified to this, that as they have grown in grace and in the knowledge of the Lord they have seen the depth of sin within themselves in a manner and measure that they had never imagined before. The further they go on, the more they are aware of their utter dependence upon the Lord Jesus Christ. There is, surely, no need to prove this. 'God is light, and in him is no darkness at all.' God's being is one of absolute holiness. What does Christianity do? It brings us into a knowledge of God, and into communion with God. And the nearer you get to God, and the more you see His holiness, so much the more do you see your own imperfection, your own unworthiness and your own sinfulness. There is no need to argue about this, it follows as the night the day. Any deep knowledge of God implies a deep knowledge of holiness; and it is accompanied by an equally deep knowledge of sin within and of everything that is unworthy and unlike God. So as the saint grows he has an increasing awareness of his own sinfulness and unworthiness.

Let me add a fifth proof of my contention. Here I turn to the evidence provided by the great revivals of religion. It is common to all of them at all times, and in all countries. Revival comes to people who have been members of the Christian Church perhaps for fifty years, and there is no doubt about their belief in the Lord Jesus Christ. They have also realized something of their sinfulness. Suddenly the Spirit is outpoured upon them. Their testimony is that their first experience is one of terrible and awful sinfulness. They can scarcely believe it, they are horrified at the sight. For a while they begin to wonder whether they had ever been Christians at all; they had never realized the depth of sin within them. Then, on the other hand, they come to see more clearly than ever before the perfect work of the Lord Jesus Christ. Though they now see their sinfulness to be much deeper and greater than they had ever imagined, they see also that the efficacy of the blood of Christ is also much greater than they had ever realized before. But my argument is this, that in revival the Holy Spirit is doing His work in unusual, exceptional power, and whenever He does so, what happens is that Christian people become aware of the glory of God and the holiness of God in a much greater measure. Though this is not actually the spirit of fear and bondage, it illustrates the results of the Spirit's action.

[213]

That is, on a big scale, what we find in many individual experiences recorded in the Bible. Take the case of Isaiah as he describes it at the beginning of his sixth chapter. He was a man of God, a man who was called by God and trained by God. He is suddenly commissioned for his work as a prophet by means of a vision of the glory of God, and he tells us what happened to him. He felt a sense of his own utter unworthiness: 'Woe is me! for I am undone; because I am a man of unclean lips, and I dwell in the midst of a people of unclean lips . . . ' What produced such a feeling? Was it that he had suddenly committed some special sins? Not at all! What gives us conviction of sin is not the number of sins we have committed; it is the sight of the holiness of God. It is light that reveals darkness. It is the contrast to the light that exposes the darkness; it is purity that reveals impurity. So the entire argument about the spirit of bondage and fear not applying to those who have been brought up in a Christian atmosphere is based on a complete and utter fallacy; it is something of which we must be very wary.

My sixth and final argument derives from the fact that I have generally discovered that the people who say that they have never known this 'spirit of bondage and of fear' are also people who have to say honestly that they have not really known also the 'Spirit of adoption, whereby we cry, Abba, Father'. They say, 'I have never known that "spirit of bondage and of fear" because I was brought up in a Christian home, and there was never a time when I did not know these things; I took to them without knowing it, it was inevitable'. And at the same time they confess that they do not know 'the Spirit of adoption, whereby we cry, Abba, Father'. They are often doubtful and troubled about themselves, they lack a real assurance of salvation. It appears that the two things go together. As they lack the one they lack the other also. The Apostle's negative statement therefore is of very great importance. The Holy Spirit as the Spirit of truth, the Spirit of holiness, must of necessity produce this sense of condemnation and of sinfulness, this sense of bondage, of inability, of helplessness. He reveals the power of sin, that terrible power that finally makes a man cry out, 'O wretched man that I am! who shall deliver me from the body of this death?'

These then are my answers to the question about the case of those who have always been brought up in a Christian atmosphere. But let me emphasize certain important additional points, although the first of them I have already touched upon. I am not stressing the degree of intensity of the feelings I have been describing. I have mentioned the case of John Bunyan and how for eighteen months he passed through a terrible agony of this 'spirit of bondage and of fear'. There are people who foolishly assert that, if a man has not experienced such an agony, he has never been convicted of sin. That is sheer nonsense, of course, because it places too much emphasis on the degree of the intensity of the feeling. All I am asserting is that you must have known it in some degree. It can be strong, it can be weak, just as the Spirit of adoption can be strong or weak, and as there are degrees in intensity in natural human love. I am simply saying that at some point or other, in some degree or other, there must have been this spirit of bondage, this awareness that we are sinful and unworthy and helpless, that we cannot save ourselves, and that we need to be delivered. It is not sufficient merely to hear someone presenting the Lord Jesus Christ as Saviour and merely to say without feeling anything, 'I believe those words, I say that I believe them', and then to be told 'You are saved, you are a Christian, all is well'. That is not true conversion, because in true conversion there is always some degree of realization of the horror of sin within, and of the fact that we are bondslaves to sin, and there is also the desire, I say, to be delivered from it.

My second comment is that a concern about the lack of assurance, or a concern about a lack of love to God, is, in itself, an expression of the spirit of bondage and of fear. I not only say that for your comfort, I am compelled to say it by the teaching of the Scripture. The unregenerate man is never concerned and worried about his lack of love for God – never! It is impossible that he should be because of what the Apostle has already told us in the seventh verse of the 8th chapter: 'The carnal mind is enmity against God; for it is not subject to the law of God; neither indeed can be. So then they that are in the flesh cannot please God.' The natural man, the unregenerate man, is never concerned about his lack of love to God. Neither is he ever concerned about a lack of assurance of salvation. He cannot be because 'the natural man receiveth not the things of the Spirit of God, for they are foolishness unto him; neither can he know them, for they are spiritually discerned'. If, then, you really have a concern about your lack of assurance, or your lack of love for God and the Lord Jesus Christ, I suggest that it is a part of the spirit of bondage and of fear. That also can vary in degree and in intensity.

My third, and last remark at this point is to say that surely, therefore, nothing is more important for us than that we should examine ourselves in the light of this statement. Have I ever known in any degree this spirit of bondage to fear? If you really have this knowledge – it matters not to how small a degree – it will be one of the chief things in your life. It will not leave you alone. If you have not got an assurance of your salvation you will be so unhappy that you will do something about it; you will not be content just to allow the feeling to pass; you will give yourself no rest or peace until you have it. You will say to God, 'Search me, try me, reveal unto me my state, my condition'. You will ask God to deal with you in such a way that anything and everything that is standing between you and this knowledge may be removed. That is proof positive that the Holy Spirit is dealing with you. In other words, if we examine ourselves, and prove ourselves, and test ourselves, and give ourselves no rest or peace until we can say quite definitely 'I have known the spirit of bondage and fear; and further, I now know something about the Spirit of adoption also, whereby I cry, Abba, Father', your case is clear.

We have spent much time on this negative because, as I am trying to show, it is one of the most valuable proofs of our sonship. A man who has known this spirit of bondage and of fear can be quite certain that he is a son of God. If you have not known it in some degree, then it is my duty to tell you that you had better examine yourself, that you had better 'prove your own self', to see 'whether you are in the faith or not', as the Apostle expresses it in the last chapter of the Second Epistle to the Corinthians. If we have never known any spirit of danger and of fear we should begin to search and to examine ourselves most seriously and immediately. This is not to say that we are to try to be unhappy, or seek to make ourselves miserable or anything of the kind. It is just to face this obvious truth that the Holy Spirit, being who and what He is, and being sent to do His special work, invariably as He reveals God and the Lord Jesus Christ, must produce in us this sense of total unworthiness. If we have not known this sense of unworthiness, if we have not known some sense of desperation within ourselves, and concerning the sin that is within us, how can we claim to have a real knowledge of God?

There is all the difference in the world between this and simply recognizing that certain things are bad and wrong, and that we should not do them. This latter does not involve a sense of sin within, a sense of the corruption of our nature, a sense of the utter holiness of God.

This negative, I repeat, is of great importance. The Spirit produces the spirit of bondage and fear; it is His work, He does it, He always does it, He must do it. How then can we be happy about ourselves if we have to say, quite honestly, that we have never known anything of this spirit. The fact that you have been brought up in a Christian home does not make the slightest difference. Whatever your upbringing, whatever you have been, whatever you have done, as it was with the prophet Isaiah, whenever we get anywhere near to God our first instinct will be to go and hide ourselves. Read the accounts in the Bible of the men who have had visions of God, for example, John in the Book of Revelation. He says that when he had a glimpse of the glory of the Lord he 'fell down as one dead'. We have no conception of God in His glory, His greatness, His majesty, His holiness. Try to think of it – 'God is light, and in him is no darkness at all'. What produces the spirit of bondage and fear is not your upbringing, not the number of sins you have committed, not the sheltered life you may have lived; it is your relationship to God, your knowledge of God. Essentially, it is not negative, but positive. Thus it comes to pass that those who are most aware of their sinfulness, those who are most aware of the love of God in forgiveness, are not of necessity those who have been drunkards or murderers or adulterers; they are those who, positively, have the greatest knowledge of God. What determines the sense of sin and the sense of forgiveness is our knowledge of God. We must not look at this matter negatively. So seek God, seek the knowledge of God, and forget all else. It matters not what you may have been. To know something of God means to know something of the depth of sin within yourself and to see the absolute need of what has been done alone through God's dear Son, and especially by His death upon the Cross.

Eighteen

*

For ye have not received the spirit of bondage again to fear; but ye have received the Spirit of adoption, whereby we cry, Abba, Father.   Romans 8: 15

We have seen that this is a most important and helpful verse from the standpoint of assurance of salvation and of our sonship of God. I have tried to prove that the mere fact that one has ever had the spirit of bondage and of fear is in itself a very good test of sonship; and in any case, it is a very good test to apply to what may appear to be the Spirit of adoption; for the spirit of bondage always precedes the Spirit of adoption. I have argued that it is impossible to have the Spirit of adoption without having first had the spirit of bondage. I have emphasized that there are various degrees of the spirit of bondage; but that in some degree, in some shape or form, it must have been present. I have quoted one of the great Puritans, John Preston, in support of that contention.

Let me further add a quotation from George Whitefield, the great evangelist. He says, 'First we hear Moses' voice, we hear the voice of the law. There is no going to Mount Zion but by way of Mount Sinai; that is the right straight road. I know some say they do not know when they were converted; those are, I believe, very few: generally, nay, I may say almost always, God deals otherwise. Some are, indeed, called sooner by the Lord than others, but before they are made to see the glory of God, they must hear the voice of the law; so you must hear the voice of the law before ever you will be savingly called unto God.' That is the statement of the man who, it seems to me, is the greatest evangelist England has ever known, a man who delighted in preaching the gospel of salvation. 'First we hear Moses' voice, the voice of the law.' 'No going to Mount Zion but by way of Mount Sinai.'

Let us now leave the negative aspect of the statement and turn to the positive. It is, of course, the positive aspect that the Apostle was anxious to emphasize at this point. It is that those who are the 'sons of God' have been delivered from the spirit of bondage and of fear. 'Ye have not received the spirit of bondage again to fear.' You did receive it once; but that is not what you have received now. In other words one of the characteristics of the sons of God, at least of those who know of a surety that they are the sons of God, is that they no longer have the 'spirit of bondage again to fear'. That has gone, and has been replaced by the 'Spirit of adoption, whereby we cry, Abba, Father'. The Apostle is marshalling the evidence for assurance, and one of the most powerful bits of evidence is that you no longer have the spirit of fear and of bondage; it has disappeared. The negative is most important here, that old spirit has gone. The coming of the Spirit of adoption is an additional matter. For the moment the important point is that the Christian, the son, should have lost the spirit of bondage and of fear.

This is not a new thought suddenly introduced at this point in the Epistle; the Apostle has been saying it over several chapters. Indeed, I suggest, as I have suggested so many times, that he began saying it in chapter 5. Paul's whole argument, as I understand it, is that the man who realizes truly that he is 'justified by faith' is in a position to claim complete and full salvation in an ultimate sense. We find it at the beginning of chapter 5: 'Therefore being justified by faith we have peace with God through our Lord Jesus Christ.' And if you have 'peace with God' you cannot at the same time have the 'spirit of bondage and of fear'. But not only that: 'By whom also we have access by faith into this grace wherein we stand, and rejoice in hope of the glory of God.' A man who is 'rejoicing in hope of the glory of God' is no longer under a 'spirit of bondage' or a 'spirit of fear'. It is quite impossible, the two conditions are not compatible. Again we have it at the end of the fifth chapter: 'Where sin abounded, grace did much more abound: that as sin hath reigned unto death, even so might grace reign through righteousness unto eternal life by Jesus Christ our Lord'. Once more, there is the statement of the 14th verse of chapter 6: 'Sin shall not have dominion over you.' Why not? Because 'ye are not under the law, but under grace'. And in the 17th verse of chapter 6: 'But God be thanked, that ye were the

The Sons of God

servants of sin [the bondslaves of sin], but ye have obeyed from the heart that form of doctrine which was delivered you.' Still more strikingly in chapter 7 verse 4: 'Wherefore, my brethren, ye also have become dead to the law by the body of Christ; that ye should be married to another, even to him who is raised from the dead, that we should bring forth fruit unto God.' 'But now we are delivered from the law, that being dead wherein we were held; that we should serve in newness of spirit, and not in the oldness of the letter' (v. 6). Then in this 8th chapter the resounding statement in the first verses, the keynote of the whole chapter: 'There is therefore now no condemnation' – there never can be – 'to them which are in Christ Jesus'. Verse 2: 'The law of the Spirit of life in Christ Jesus hath made me free' – 'made', the aorist; it has happened – 'made me free from the law of sin and death'. The object of the entire chapter is to give us, in detail, evidence to support, and to maintain, these two contentions that confront us in the first two verses.

This teaching is by no means confined to the Epistle to the Romans. We find precisely the same teaching in Galatians chapter 4. There is the same contrast, beginning at verse 1: 'Now I say, That the heir, as long as he is a child, differeth nothing from a servant, though he be lord of all; but is under tutors and governors until the time appointed of the father. Even so we, when we were children, were in bondage under the elements of the world. 'But' – here is the turning point – 'when the fulness of the time was come, God sent forth his Son, made of a woman, made under the law, to redeem them that were under the law, that we might receive the adoption of sons. And because ye are sons, God hath sent forth the Spirit of his Son into your hearts, crying, Abba, Father.' And we have already quoted from the end of that chapter the contrast between the two sons, the one of the bondwoman the other of the freewoman. 'Now we, brethren, as Isaac was, are the children of promise' – that is our position as Christians! We do not correspond to the son of Hagar; we correspond to the son of Sarah, we are like Isaac. 'But as then he that was born after the flesh persecuted him that was born after the Spirit, even so it is now. So then, brethren, we are not children of the bondwoman, but of the free.' That is the same contrast as we have here in this 15th verse.

Look also at the 8th chapter of the Epistle to the Hebrews.

[220]

The Author is concerned to show the pre-eminence and the superiority of our Lord over all others, and he does so for this reason: 'But now hath he obtained a more excellent ministry, by how much also he is the mediator of a better covenant, which was established upon better promises' (v. 6). Then he goes on to compare and to contrast the first covenant with this new covenant; God says that he is going to lay aside the old one: 'Wherefore I will make a new covenant with the house of Israel; not according to the covenant that I made with their fathers.' Why? 'Because they continued not in my covenant, and I regarded them not, saith the Lord. For this is the covenant that I will make with the house of Israel after those days, saith the Lord; I will put my laws into their mind, and write them in their hearts', and so on. That new covenant, let us remember, is not for some Jews who are yet going to appear; it is for Christians now. This is Christianity, the new covenant with Christian people. The Author urges these Hebrew Christians to realize that they were under that new covenant; and therefore, instead of looking back to Judaism, they should be rejoicing in the new covenant, and in what God has done for them in and through His Son, our Lord and Saviour Jesus Christ. This is the same contrast as we have here in this 15th verse of the 8th chapter of the Epistle to the Romans. The same is found in the 12th chapter of the Epistle to the Hebrews, in verse 18: 'Ye are not come unto the mount' – you have not gone back to Sinai, you are not at the foot of Mount Sinai – 'the mount that might be touched, and that burned with fire, nor unto blackness and darkness, and tempest, and the sound of a trumpet, and the voice of words; which voice they that heard intreated that the word should not be spoken to them any more'. Even Moses had said, 'I exceedingly fear and quake'. We have not come unto that again. Well, where are we? 'Ye are come unto mount Sion, unto the city of the living God, the heavenly Jerusalem, and to an innumerable company of angels, to the general assembly and church of the firstborn', and so on. We have not gone back to Sinai with its threatenings, and to the spirit of bondage and of fear that it produces; we have come to the heavenly city, this mount Sion of God, the city of the living God, the heavenly Jerusalem.

The same emphasis is found in 1 John 4, beginning at verse 16: 'And we', Christians, sons of God, 'have known and believed the love that God hath to us.' 'God is love; and he that dwelleth in love dwelleth in God, and God in him. Herein is our love made perfect, that we may have boldness in the day of judgment: because as he is, so are we in this world. There is no fear in love; but perfect love casteth out fear; because fear hath torment. He that feareth is not made perfect in love. We love him, because he first loved us.'

Everywhere we find exactly the same contrast as we have here in this eighth chapter of the Epistle to the Romans. In other words it comes to this; the Holy Spirit, who in His first work upon us produces the 'spirit of bondage and of fear', in His further work delivers us from that spirit. 'We have not received the spirit of bondage again to fear'. It works in this way. Having brought us to that position of bondage and fear, He unfolds, He reveals and discloses to us the Lord Jesus Christ in all the glory of His Person, and in all the perfection of His offices, especially His work on our behalf. The moment we see His glory the spirit of fear and of bondage disappears. They cannot exist together. Really to know the truth about the Lord Jesus Christ, and to have it applied to us by the Holy Spirit, of necessity delivers us from the spirit of bondage and of fear. That is the Apostle's contention. You once had that old spirit but you must no longer have it; you have not received 'again' the spirit of bondage to fear, but have been delivered from it.

There are certain questions that arise at this point. People may say, 'Now that is very nice, that is very comforting, I like to hear it. But there are other Scriptures which trouble me. You seem to be selecting portions out of the Scriptures which prove your case; and by doing so, of course, you can prove anything. Heretics always flourish by picking out what suits them and ignoring all that is against them. Are you not guilty of that?' They then proceed to quote verses such as the following. In 2 Corinthians 5: 11 Paul says: 'Knowing therefore the terror of the Lord, we persuade men; but we are made manifest unto God; and I trust also are made manifest in your consciences.' In Philippians 2, verses 12–13 we find: 'Wherefore, my beloved, as ye have always obeyed, not as in my presence only, but now much more in my absence, work out your own salvation with fear and trembling, for it is God which worketh in you both to will and to do of his good pleasure.' Work out your salvation 'with fear and trembling'. How can it be

said that the Christian should no longer have the spirit of bondage
and of fear when he is told to work out his own salvation 'with
fear and trembling'? And what is to be said about the end of our
quotation from the twelfth chapter of the Epistle to the Hebrews,
'See that ye refuse not him that speaketh; for if they escaped not
who refused him that spake on earth, much more shall not we
escape, if we turn away from him that speaketh from heaven:
whose voice then shook the earth: but now he hath promised,
saying, Yet once more, I shake not the earth only, but also heaven.
Wherefore we receiving a kingdom which cannot be moved, let
us have grace whereby we may serve God acceptably with
reverence and godly fear: for our God is a consuming fire'? And
what about those terrifying minatory passages at the beginning
of the 6th chapter of the Epistle to the Hebrews, and again in the
10th chapter of that Epistle? How can they be reconciled with
the statement that we have not received the spirit of bondage
again to fear?

How do we answer these very searching questions? We start
by saying that Scripture never contradicts itself. With this fundamental postulate we invariably approach this or any other problem in interpretation. We are told to 'compare Scripture with
Scripture'. It can never contradict itself because it is all given by
the one Holy Spirit. So when we come across an apparent contradiction we start by laying down the principle or principles of
which we are certain, and then we seek for the explanation. In
this particular inquiry we must note that there is an essential
difference between a 'spirit of bondage and of fear' and 'reverence
and godly fear'. 'Reverence and godly fear' is not a 'fear that hath
torment'; but the other fear has torment in it. It is bondage, it is a
terrifying fear, it is that which makes a man cry out in despair
'O wretched man that I am! who shall deliver me?' He is in an
agony, he is beside himself. The Scriptures nowhere exhort us
to be in an agony of fear. The Epistle to the Hebrews tells us that
we must approach God 'with reverence and with godly fear'
because He is a 'consuming fire'. But the same writer, in the same
Epistle, says, 'Let us therefore come boldly unto the throne of
grace'. He appears to be contradicting himself, but he is not doing
so. How can we come with 'reverence and godly fear' and at the
same time 'come boldly' with confidence, with assurance – 'in
full assurance of faith'? The answer is to realize that he is exhort-

ing us to remember always who God is, and what God is. In other words we are not to rush into the presence of God; we are never to be glib in His presence. We are to remember always that God is a consuming fire, and we must therefore always approach Him with 'reverence and godly fear'. But that does not mean that we are to be in a craven condition or to feel the 'fear that hath torment', for, as John says, that would mean that we have no love. The reconciliation of the apparent contradiction lies in the difference between respect and fear. When you respect a person you do not fear that person. What you fear is that you may do something to displease him, and that, not because you fear that he may punish you, but sometimes even because you may feel that, because he is who and what he is, he will not punish you! Reverence is ultimately based upon love, it is the recognition of the greatness of the privilege of being allowed to approach God. There is nothing craven about that; there is no torment in it; there is no bondage in it.

We are always in danger of pressing these things to extremes. Some are so anxious to show that they have not got 'the spirit of bondage again to fear', that in their prayers they say 'Dear God'. You never find that expression in the Bible. You should never say 'Dear God'. Our Lord did not speak thus; He said 'Holy Father'. Others press the idea of 'reverence and godly fear' so far that it becomes a spirit of bondage and fear, and a craven spirit. These apparently contradictory statements are compatible with one another. While I must always be careful to realize who God is, I must not be uncertain about my relationship to Him; indeed, it is because I am certain of the relationship that I am reverential. My reverence is not based on ignorance, but on knowledge. It should be clear, then, that 'reverence and godly fear' is not the same thing as 'the spirit of bondage again to fear'.

But take a second question. 'Are you arguing', asks someone, 'that because the Christian, the son of God, has lost the spirit of bondage and of fear, it means that he will never again feel depressed, will never have a sense of desertion, feeling that God has turned His back upon him?' How many have argued like that! 'You are asserting dogmatically', they say, 'that the son of God no longer has the spirit of bondage again to fear; well then, if I ever feel depressed and uncertain, does not that prove automatically that I am not a Christian?' It does not mean that for a moment! To say that the Christian has been delivered from the spirit of bondage and of fear does not mean that he will never again know any sense of depression or of desertion. What then is the explanation? I reply in this way. Take a man who is suffering from a depressed spiritual condition. What is the cause of the depression? Sometimes it is a matter of temperament, or a matter of psychology. Whether we like it or not, we have to recognize the fact that we are not all the same. Some are born with a tendency to introspection and morbidity; others are obvious extroverts who never look inwards at all, and live on the surface. The first man is subject to various moods and states and feelings of which the second man knows nothing. We are born with our temperament and we cannot change it. We all belong by birth to one psychological category or another, and we have to recognize it. There are some people, then, in the Christian life who, merely in terms of their natural constitution, will be more subject to these moods and states of depression and of fear than others. But my argument is that the fact that they are subject to these moods and states has nothing to do with the statement that they have been delivered from the spirit of bondage again to fear. I demonstrate my assertion in this way. Take two persons who are subject to constitutional depression, one an unbeliever and the other a believer. Go to the unbeliever, and tell him about this great passage of Scripture; and you will not help him at all. He will remain exactly as he was before you began to speak. But then go and do exactly the same with the other depressed person, who is a Christian, and immediately he will respond. This is not theory only, it works in practice.

We must take a further step. If you go to a man who is in 'the spirit of bondage and of fear' – that preliminary work of the Spirit – and quote these consoling, comforting Scriptures to him, you will find that they do not help him. 'Ah', he says, 'I know that is not true of me.' You cannot help him at the moment. Go to this other person who is truly a Christian, but is depressed at the moment, and quote these Scriptures to him, and you will find that he will respond to them gladly and happily. Whenever people of this type hear these comforting Scriptures they jump at them, and they are delivered from their depression. That is, to me, an absolute proof that they are not back again under the spirit of bondage and of fear. They have come right out of that, but because of their natural temperament, they are a little depressed temporarily. The way to differentiate and to discover the true position is to apply the Scriptures to them. If they respond to the Scriptures they are not under 'a spirit of bondage and of fear', but in a state of temporary depression though they are children of God.

When a man becomes a Christian he is still essentially the same person as regards temperament. I am not saying that you should give in, or give way, to your temperament. You must not do so. As a Christian you must learn to control your temperament. But you have that particular temperament, and it will always remain with you. There were obvious differences among the Apostles. John and Peter were two very different men even after their conversion. Paul was yet different from both. The temperament is not done away in conversion; we are not all made identical the moment we become Christians. Some have a battle to fight that others know nothing of. But then they in turn have a battle of which the first mentioned know nothing. Undoubtedly there are some people whose peculiar battle is this tendency to a natural depression, but the way to prove that they are Christian, and that they are not under the spirit of bondage is to apply the Scripture to them; and as true Christians they will invariably respond to it. They leave Christian services in which this kind of problem is dealt with, always feeling happy and relieved. You talk to them after a few weeks and you may find that they are a little depressed again; but give them the same treatment, and they will be restored to assurance; and so they may go on.

That, I suggest, is a proof of two things. The first is that they are truly children of God. The second is that they have this peculiar temperament and psychological make-up to fight, and that they are not quite able to do so as they ought. They fail in their understanding of the situation; they mistake their natural temperament at times for an absence of true Christian faith. But here is the way to test it; while they respond to the statements and exhortations of the Scriptures it is a sign of life.

Sometimes Christian people are in a state of unhappiness about their souls because they have fallen into sin. 'You say', says someone, 'that once a man is a child of God he loses the spirit of bondage and of fear. But what if he falls into sin? what if he becomes a backslider? Will he not be miserable, and unhappy?

will not thoughts come to him as to whether he is a Christian or not?' My answer still is that, whatever may be the condition and the feelings of the backslider, even at his worst, he is still not back in or under the spirit of bondage and of fear. What is the difference? He is conscious that he has sinned; but he is conscious that he has not sinned against law, but against love. The sinning of the Christian is not the same as the sinning of the man 'under the law'. The unbeliever under conviction by the Spirit sins 'under the law'; hence this spirit of bondage and of fear. He knows he has sinned against law, and there is a 'fear which hath torment'. But the believer, however grievously he may sin, does not go back 'under the law'; he realizes that his sin is a sin against love. Though he has sinned, he does not have a sense of final condemnation; he still knows that he is not 'under condemnation'; neither has he a sense of utter hopelessness. The feeling of the Christian who backslides, who falls into sin, is that he finds it extremely difficult to forgive himself; but he knows that God forgives him. In a sense, what makes it difficult for him to forgive himself is the very fact that he knows that God is forgiving him.

We know something of this, even in a natural sense, when we have sinned against a parent or someone whom we love very much. You know that they forgive you before you ask them; but that is what makes it almost impossible for you to ask them; you feel you are a cad. You are not 'under the law', you are sinning against love; and the very fact that you know that they are willing to forgive you makes you hate yourself and reprobate yourself all the more.

When a child of God sins he does what David did in Psalm 51. When David had committed adultery, and then murder in addition, and was made by Nathan the prophet to face it all, he was in a terrible state. He felt he was a worm, and less; he could not forgive himself. So what did he do? He went to God! That is what the backslider always does; he goes back to God and says, 'Against thee, thee only, have I sinned and done this evil in thy sight'. He says further, 'That thou mightest be justified when thou speakest'. He goes back to the One he has offended. Why? Because he knows that he is still a child of God in spite of his sin. The believer knows this when he sins, and when he thus condemns himself he knows that it is still true to say: 'If we confess our sins, he is faithful and just to forgive us our sins, and to cleanse us from all unrighteousness' (1 John 1:9) He knows all this, so he is not back 'under' the spirit of bondage and of fear. He cannot go back to that! Even in the depth of his sin, and when he cannot forgive himself, he is still not in bondage, he still knows it is true to say, 'There is therefore now no condemnation to them which are in Christ Jesus'.

'You are surely inciting people to sin by speaking in this way', says someone. I am quite happy about such a charge, for it is the charge that was brought against Paul: 'Let us sin, that grace may abound'. True preaching of the gospel in its fulness always exposes itself to the charge of antinomianism. But there is no need to be afraid; for 'the child of God' cannot play fast and loose with these things; it is always the man who does not understand who falls into that trap. The child of God cannot speak in that way, because he is miserable even in his sin, and because he knows his relationship to God.

Let us turn now to a third problem. What about a Christian man suffering satanic attacks, the devil or some of his emissaries making a peculiar target of him? Such things sometimes happen in the Christian life. A satanic attack is a terrible experience, when the devil, as it were, tries to do with us as he did with our Lord in the temptation in the wilderness. He brings his great batteries to bear upon us and tries to prove to us that we are not the children of God. This can be dreadful, a terrifying experience, as some of the saints have testified. Does not such a happening put us back under the spirit of bondage again to fear? The answer is still the same, and for this reason – and this is where doctrine is so important – that it is only the Holy Spirit who can produce 'the spirit of bondage'; even the devil cannot do so. Thank God he cannot! He tries to produce it, but he fails. The Holy Spirit alone can produce 'the spirit of bondage and of fear'. This is demonstrated by the fact that, however grievous and hot the attack, the Christian is always enabled to repulse the devil; and the Apostle Peter exhorts us so to do. 'Your adversary the devil, as a roaring lion, walketh about seeking whom he may devour.' What are you to do? 'Whom resist steadfast in the faith!' (1 Peter 5:8). The moment you do that he disappears. 'Resist the devil, and he will flee from you' (James 4:7). But how am I to know whether I am suffering from a satanic attack, or am in 'the spirit of bondage again to fear'? The answer is to apply the Scriptures once more;

and if you can respond to the Scriptures you can be sure that it is a satanic attack.

Let me give one illustration of this matter from my own experience some twenty-five years ago. I was working in my study one morning when I was told that there was a man at the door who was very anxious to see me. On going to the door I found there a man in a state of great agitation, who said, 'My father is sitting in that car out there, and he is in a desperate state'. He said that his father had just come out of a mental nursing home where he had been for six weeks, and he pleaded with me to see him. The poor man was brought into my room. His hair was dishevelled, and he had not shaved for days. He was a big, tall, powerful man – indeed almost alarming in appearance. He was desperate, frantic and almost tearing his hair out. This was his story. He had been converted in a very dramatic manner in the Welsh Revival of 1904-5. His whole life had been changed; he had been delivered from drunkenness and had become a wonderful Christian man. But partly as the result of that change he began to prosper in business, and gradually the devil, seeing his opportunity, tempted him and he had been backsliding. The first sign of decline was worldliness, then he had taken to drink and had ceased to go to his place of worship. In other words, he had gone back in his practice and conduct to the life of the world, and he had been doing this for several years. Suddenly, without any apparent reason or explanation, he had awakened to the seriousness of his back-sliding, but at this point the devil came in and said to him, 'Ah well, your case now is hopeless. You were converted in 1904, but before that time you had been an unbeliever, you were ignorant, you knew nothing; now you have sinned against the light and against the Holy Ghost; there is no forgiveness for you'. He believed this, and soon he had become desperate. They called in his doctor who gave him sedatives, but without any effect; they called in other doctors who prescribed more sedatives, still with no effect. Then they called in a mental expert who immediately diagnosed, as such men always do, 'religious mania'. There are many people in mental institutions who should not be there at all. If you show any unusual concern about your soul you are standing in great risk of being put into a mental institution as a case of 'religious mania'. The man became a voluntary patient in a nursing home, and there they treated him with various drugs for six weeks. But far from getting better, he continued to get worse. Finally he insisted on going home, and now he was sitting in my study. Indeed he was not sitting, he was pacing up and down, tearing his hair – desperate, violent. I tried to pacify him a little, first of all, and got him to sit down.

Then after hearing his story I began quoting and expounding Scriptures to him. I asked him to give me a Scripture which proved that a Christian man who fell into sin could never be forgiven again. I explained to him that that was not '*the* sin against the Holy Ghost'. A man who has committed *the* sin against the Holy Ghost is not concerned about forgiveness; he ridicules the grace of God and the Gospel; so this man's very concern about forgiveness, and his grief because he has 'let down' his Saviour, was a proof that it did not apply to him. I kept on and on; and this continued for some forty minutes. I did nothing but quote the Scriptures. Eventually the man became quiet and peaceful. But I was not satisfied until I had got him to thank God and to praise God, and had seen him smile. Then I told him to be prepared for further onslaughts. I warned him that the devil would certainly not give him up at all easily; he would come back. But all he (the sufferer) had to do was to quote the Scriptures I had quoted to him. I knew, for certain, that I would see him again, and he returned in about a week, if I remember rightly. Once more he was desperate and violent; but it only took me some twenty minutes this time to pacify him and to make him praise God. Again I did nothing but quote Scripture. This process had to be repeated some two or three times and eventually he was entirely delivered and resumed an active Christian life.

The way in which you differentiate between the spirit of bondage and backsliding is by the application of Scripture. This man was delivered clinging to the Scriptures. He was delighted to hear them, although at first I had to persuade him, and to show him that he had nothing to say on the other side. So my visitor was not under 'the spirit of bondage again to fear'. It was a satanic attack that had followed a period of backsliding. Had he been truly 'under bondage' I might very well not have been able to help him at that time. The moment a man gives an immediate response to the Scriptures, you can be sure that it is not 'the spirit of bondage'. A Christian does not go back to that, even under a terrible satanic attack.

Let me mention one further problem. Take the question of desertion. Christian people feel at times that God seems to have turned His face away from them, and they say, 'I am dry, I am cold, I do not seem to be able to find God. I used to have liberty in prayer, but it is gone; God seems to have deserted me.' You may argue that a man who has such feelings must surely be in 'the spirit of bondage and of fear'. But I still contend that it is not so. God does sometimes appear to avert His face from us. If you fall into sin you will find, sometimes, that you do not immediately get back to where you were, even when you have confessed your sin. God, as it were, keeps you in a place of repentance for a while, and seems to turn His face away from you. Indeed this may well be one aspect of his 'chastisement' of us. 'Whom the Lord loveth he chasteneth'. He does this in different ways. Sometimes we seem to be left as was poor Job. That is a very definite experience through which Christians sometimes have to pass. But, you say, while they are in that condition, is not that the 'spirit of bondage'? It is not, for this reason, that a man in that state never cries out saying, 'Who shall deliver me from the body of this death?' But that is what the man who is in a 'spirit of bondage and of fear' does cry out. Job does not use any such words. He does not say, '*who* shall deliver me?' He says, 'O, that I knew where I might find him' – and there is a world of difference there! The first man can but cry 'Who shall deliver me?' 'Is there anyone anywhere?' That is not the case with the second man, the Christian who is deserted. He says, 'O that I knew where I might find him!' He knows He is there, somewhere. He is like the little child who has disobeyed his parent and wants the normal happy relations to be restored. But the parent, for his correction, will not look at him. And there is the little child clutching at the parent, and trying to get the parent's face to turn round and look at him! It is an entirely different situation. The Christian who is conscious of desertion does not cry out in despair; he cries out as William Cowper does in his hymn:

> *Return, O holy Dove return,*
> *Sweet messenger of rest;*
> *I hate the sins that made Thee mourn*
> *And drove Thee from my breast.*

He knows that all is still well ultimately; but he is not being smiled upon at the moment, so he cries, 'Return' – 'Come back'. He is talking to Someone whom he knows. So the two states are entirely different and should never be confused in the mind of the Christian.

There is a glorious statement of the matter in the Song of Solomon, in the fifth chapter, beginning at the first verse. 'I am come into my garden, my sister', says the bridegroom. He had come to call her; but she had gone to bed and did not want to rise. 'I have put off my coat', she says, 'how shall I put it on? I have washed my feet; how shall I defile them? My beloved put in his hand by the hole of the door, and my bowels were moved for him. I rose up to open to my beloved; and my hands dropped with myrrh, and my fingers with sweet-smelling myrrh, upon the handles of the lock. I opened to my beloved; but my beloved had withdrawn himself, and was gone: my soul failed when he spake. I sought him, but I could not find him; I called him, but he gave me no answer.' What does she do? She rushes out. 'The watchmen that went about the city found me, they smote me, they wounded me; the keepers of the walls took away my veil from me. I charge you, O daughters of Jerusalem, if ye find my beloved, that ye tell him, that I am sick of love.' Such is the reaction of one who feels deserted. That is not 'the spirit of bondage again to fear', it is a longing for the restoration of a broken communion; and the two states are entirely different. I close by quoting a comforting statement of a great French Christian. Pascal, dealing with such a case, tells the troubled one, 'God says, "Thou wouldest not be seeking me unless thou hadst already found me".' It is not a cry in the dark! The one who feels deserted seeks the One whom he knows, but whom he cannot find at the moment. That is not 'bondage', that is not 'fear'; in a sense it is quite the opposite. It is a longing for communion with the beloved One whom, in some way or another, we have offended, and have caused Him to turn away from us.

The Christian, I assert, has been delivered once and for ever from 'the spirit of bondage again to fear'. Praise God!

Nineteen

*

For ye have not received the spirit of bondage again to fear; but ye have received the Spirit of adoption, whereby we cry, Abba, Father.   Romans 8: 15

So far we have been concentrating on the first half of this statement, the negative half. We turn now to the second half which reminds us that we have been delivered from the spirit of bondage and of fear. This is also the third proof of the fact that we are sons of God. We no longer are under the spirit of bondage and of fear; we have been delivered from it. To be delivered from that bondage, and to be able to say that we are no longer in that condition is a very powerful proof indeed of the fact that we are the Sons of God.

But the second half of this verse tells us positively, that we have also 'received the Spirit of adoption, whereby we cry, Abba, Father'. It is no longer merely the absence of the old feeling. That is wonderful, and negative mercies and blessings must never be despised. But we are not left at that point; we are given this positive blessing of having the 'Spirit of adoption, whereby we cry, Abba, Father'. This, of course, is a much stronger proof of our sonship than anything we have considered hitherto. Because it is positive it is of necessity stronger. The Apostle has an ascending scale of values here; we go up and up as we consider his proofs of our sonship. The first thing we have to realize, he tells us, is that the Holy Spirit Himself produces this knowledge of our adoption, and the cry, Abba, Father. We have noted earlier that the Authorized Version indicates that clearly by putting a capital 'S' at this point. But let us again remind ourselves that, were there any doubt about this, the parallel passage in Galatians 4: 6, really puts the matter beyond any doubt. 'Because ye are sons, God hath sent forth the 'Spirit of his Son' – the Holy Spirit, capital 'S' again – 'into your hearts, crying, Abba, Father'. The Apostle says there quite clearly that it is the Holy Spirit Himself who cries 'Abba, Father'. But here he says that 'we have received the Spirit of adoption, whereby *we* cry Abba, Father'. The two statements are not contradictory. It is not that the Spirit cries for Himself unto God as Father, it is the Apostle's way of saying that the Spirit in us leads us to cry, 'Abba, Father'.

There is a perfect parallel to this in the 26th verse of this 8th chapter, where he says, 'Likewise the Spirit also helpeth our infirmities: for we know not what we should pray for as we ought: but the Spirit himself maketh intercession for us with groanings which cannot be uttered'. But this does not mean, as we shall see, that we at that point are doing nothing, and that the Holy Spirit is Himself groaning. The Holy Spirit never has any need to groan, and He never does groan. What the Apostle means is that the Holy Spirit within us is prompting us, and urging us, and causing us to groan. We do not know what we are saying, we are emitting groans only, but it is the Spirit within us that leads us to do that. And, in exactly the same way, when we take Galatians 4: 6 with Romans 8: 15, we see that what is being taught is that the Holy Spirit by His operation within us leads us to cry 'Abba, Father.' But it is very definitely and distinctly the operation of the Spirit that leads us to do it. It is not we ourselves; it is the Spirit prompting us, urging us, leading us, and giving us many reasons for doing so. That is our first point, and we have to emphasize it in order that we may preserve the parallel which we find in the two sections of our verse. It was the Spirit that produced the feeling of bondage and of fear. The Spirit Himself does not know that fear, but He produces it, His operation leads to it. And in exactly the same way, on this other side, it is He who leads us to this feeling and desire to cry 'Abba, Father'.

Secondly, let us look at the nature or the character of the proof that is provided by the Spirit, in this way, of our sonship. It is important that we should be clear about the nature and the character of this proof; and I am emphasizing this particular point because I find that many of the commentaries really miss it altogether. Many of them interpret this in terms of what we have already dealt with in verse 14, where we were told that, 'as many as are led by the Spirit of God, they are the sons of God'. They

teach that 'the Spirit of adoption' is but the result of our being
led by the Spirit, a kind of deduction we draw by applying the
tests to ourselves. But this would be mere tautology. There would
be no advance in the thought, and we should not be given a yet
stronger reason or proof for knowing our sonship. But as we
have seen, there is a definite gradation and progress here, leading
to a climax. So I am concerned about the nature and the character
of the proof we are dealing with; and therefore I first put the
matter negatively. This 'Spirit of adoption' which cries, 'Abba,
Father' is not something that you deduce from various tests. We
convinced ourselves that we are 'sons of God', led by the Spirit,
by applying some ten tests to ourselves. But what we have here is
not something that is deduced from the truth stated in verse 14,
not merely another way of saying that we are being led by the
Spirit; it goes well beyond that statement.

This is something subjective, something which essentially
belongs to the realm of feeling and subjectivity, and the emotions.
It is something within us at a deeper level than the level of the
intellect. That seems to me to be the vital point in this statement.
In other words this does not result from certain actions on our
part; it is the Spirit that produces it in us. It is not something of
which you persuade yourself. As we have seen, by applying
various tests you can persuade yourself whether you are, or are
not, being led by the Spirit, but that is not the position here. This
is not in the realm of intellectual argumentation or demonstration;
it is something of which one becomes conscious. This is – to use
the obvious and the simple analogy – comparable to what we know
in human love. You do not persuade yourself that you are in love;
at least, if you do, or have to do, you are not in love! This is not a
matter of persuasion; it is something you know; you become
conscious of it. It is on a deeper level than that of the intellect and
of reason and of argumentation. This is, in my view, a vital
principle. It not only demonstrates the advance in the thought, it
also shows us the graciousness of God in giving us these further
proofs, these yet more certain proofs. So the nature of this proof
is thoroughly subjective, and it is produced by the operation of
the Holy Spirit.

What exactly then is the Apostle telling us? The first thing he
tells us is that it is a 'Spirit of adoption', by which he means that
it is a consciousness of the fact that we have been adopted into

the family of God. A consciousness of it, and not merely a belief of the fact! We dealt with the matter as we were expounding verse 14. As sons of God we are not only regenerated; over and above that, we have been adopted into God's family. The whole notion of adoption, let me remind you, carries with it a legal element, it carries the connotation of a standing and of a position. It was a Roman term, something with which most people living in the Roman world were quite familiar. But it was not common amongst the Jews living in Palestine. If a person wished to adopt an 'outsider' into his family, he did so by means of a legal document. The transaction had to be carried out legally so that the person adopted might know that he had a true standing. So the Apostle's use of the term is certainly interesting. It teaches us that, first of all, we have to believe that we are not only given a new nature, but that we are in truth, and in fact, made members of the household of God by adoption. That is the doctrine taught here and elsewhere, as in Ephesians 1, verses 3 and 4. What the Apostle is emphasizing here is that not only must we believe this doctrine, and accept it with our minds, but we must also be conscious of it, and feel it; there must be the Spirit of adoption in us as the result of this work of the Holy Spirit.

Paul is really telling us that we are to feel – and I am emphasizing feeling – in this sense, what our Lord Himself felt. Go back again to Galatians 4: 6: 'Because ye are sons', says the Apostle, 'God hath sent forth' – note he does not say 'the Holy Spirit' – 'the Spirit of his Son into your hearts'. He expressed the truth in that way deliberately, in order to make us conscious of the fact that, as the result of this action of God in our adoption, we have, in one sense, a standing in the sight of God comparable to that of His own Son, our Lord and Saviour Jesus Christ. A number of other statements confirm this. In our Lord's high-priestly prayer recorded in John's Gospel chapter 17, verse 23, we read that our Lord greatly desires His Father so to deal with His disciples, 'that the world may know that thou hast loved them, as thou hast loved me'. In certain ways, this is one of the most astounding statements in the whole of the Bible. For God to love us as He loves His only begotten Son eclipses all else. But for this our Lord prayed. And I suggest that what we have here, in this 'Spirit of adoption', is that we should be aware of the fact that God, as it were, has put us alongside His Son.

There are many other Scriptures that confirm this suggestion. For example, in the 2nd chapter of the Epistle to the Hebrews the emphasis falls on this selfsame point. Concerning our Lord, whom the Author describes as 'the Captain of our salvation', he says: 'Both he that sanctifieth and they who are sanctified are all of one: for which cause he is not ashamed to call them brethren, saying, I will declare thy name unto my brethren, in the midst of the church will I sing praise unto thee. Behold I and the children which God hath given me.' And then, 'Forasmuch as the children are partakers of flesh and blood, he also himself likewise took part of the same'. He is our Brother! He has become, He has made Himself our Brother! He is, as we are told later on in this 8th chapter of this Epistle to the Romans, 'the firstborn among many brethren'.

It is almost impossible to grasp so great a fact, yet we are taught clearly that one of the marvellous things that happens to us in redemption is that we become 'children of God', members of His family, and, in this extraordinary sense, 'brethren' of the Lord Jesus Christ. So the Spirit we have within us, this Spirit of adoption, is 'the Spirit of God's own Son'. The feelings that the Son entertained, as our Mediator, to the Father, are to be the feelings that should move all believers. It is 'the Spirit of God's own Son' that is put into us, and that is 'the Spirit of adoption'. We feel, we know in the depth of our being, that we have been put alongside our blessed Lord Himself in this matter of sonship. I emphasize that it is our Lord's character as Mediator that is under consideration, and not His eternal Sonship. He is the only begotten Son; we are adopted. But as adopted we have this feeling of sonship that He had in His mediatorial capacity. As He addressed His Father, so too are we to address His Father and our Father.

Thirdly I would emphasize that this 'Spirit of adoption' is essentially a matter of our feelings towards God. It is not merely that we believe the teaching of the Scriptures about these things; much more is involved. We really know it, we feel it. We must remember, of course, that there are variations in the intensity of this feeling; but I am asserting that there must be a measure of this feeling if we really have 'the Spirit of adoption'. It is not merely that we are to be conscious of the fact that God is blessing us and is gracious to us. That is wonderful, and that is a part of the proof of our sonship. But Paul's statement goes further still; it involves our feelings with regard to God who is blessing us. It is a definition of our response to Him. You can be conscious of God's gracious dealings with you without being conscious of 'the Spirit of adoption' within you. You can say, 'I know that God is blessing me in this unusual manner', but so far you may only be looking at what God is doing for you. But what is emphasized here is the feelings that rise up within you towards God. John expresses this in his First Epistle: 'We love him, because he first loved us.' The first thing we become conscious of is the fact that God loves us. Now you can be conscious of God's love for you, and believe it, and know it, without at the same time being able to say that you also are aware of this love in yourself to Him. That is the kind of distinction I am drawing, and here the emphasis is upon our reciprocation, our response, to our realization of God's blessing upon us. It is in the realm of our feelings, our subjectivity.

But let us go on a further step, a fourth, by asking how this Spirit of adoption which is within us shows and expresses itself. First of all, it does so through the feelings we find rising within us as we read the statements of the Scriptures with respect to our relationship to God as His children. We all know from experience what it is to read these great and glorious statements, and to accept them with the mind, and indeed to feel that they are wonderful; but this statement goes beyond such an experience. The 'Spirit of adoption' means that they warm your heart as well as kindle your mind and imagination; they move you; and you are aware of being moved, as a child is moved when he is aware of expressions of affection on the part of the parent. So that is a very good way of testing whether you have the Spirit of adoption. You not only accept them and delight in them with your mind, you are also aware of a heart-warming effect.

It is very difficult to put these things into words. An analogy is found in connection with preaching. It is possible for the hearer to enjoy the preaching from the standpoint of the intellect alone. We can appreciate an analysis of a portion of Scripture, and the working out of the details. An exposition can be done well, or can be done badly. When it is done well, you sit and listen, and it gives you great satisfaction, perhaps even great pleasure. But it may remain something purely intellectual; a kind of display which you enjoy, and which you might wish to be repeated time after time, but it terminates there. How different it is when you feel that the truth which is thus being put before you somehow comes to you in a very personal way, and moves you, and thrills you. It may cause you to weep silently, and if not to weep, at least there is about it a melting, a moving quality. Why? Because you know that it is true of you. It is wonderful as a concept, that God, the infinite and eternal God should adopt people who have been 'born in sin, and shapen in iniquity', into His family. That is a very wonderful and thrilling thought; but as long as it is in the mind only, it lacks this most vital additional quality, namely, that you know that this is true of you. When that is present it humbles you and moves you and melts you. It is a response, a response in the depth of the person, to these glorious statements that are made concerning us in the Scriptures.

But it is also a general feeling which we have within us of our new relationship to God. We become aware that we have certain filial feelings within us with respect to God. In other words we no longer simply believe in God. That should be true of everyone, and is true of all who have been wrought upon by the Holy Spirit. The man who has 'the Spirit of adoption' is certainly orthodox, but he goes beyond orthodoxy; he has a feeling of love toward God; he delights in God; he knows something about enjoying God. 'The chief end of man is to glorify God and to *enjoy* him for ever' runs the answer to the first question in the Shorter Catechism of The Westminster Assembly. We not only believe in God, or believe about him; but we 'enjoy Him'. The Christian delights in the Lord, and in fellowship with his God; he longs for Him, and for an ever greater and deeper knowledge of Him. He may be conscious of this perhaps even when he is not reading the Scriptures at all, but just sitting and meditating. He may not even be meditating, but suddenly the consciousness of it all comes to him. It may be the result of something that happens, or a phrase or a verse comes into his mind, and he is reminded at once of his relationship to God. Immediately he has a sense of rest and of security, a feeling that he is in God's hands, that God is his Father, and that nothing can really harm him. He may have this experience when everything is going well; he gets it still more when things are going wrong; a feeling that 'underneath are the everlasting arms'. You cannot define it, you just know it is true.

You know that nothing will ever be allowed really to harm you because you are a child of God, because God is your Father. Previously we were looking at, and considering what is true of us, because God is our Father – what He does to us, and so on. Now we are looking at the whole matter from another angle. The Christian man knows all this in an experimental sense; he feels it, he is conscious of it. So he has a sense of rest, of peace and of quiet within, and a serene joy.

The peculiar character of this sense of rest and joy is emphasized particularly by the Apostle in the phrase we are examining. 'We have received', he says, 'the Spirit of adoption, whereby we cry, Abba, Father.' This defines the way in which we approach God, and in particular, of course, our prayer life. Let us therefore examine it and analyse it. Take, first of all, the term itself. This 'Spirit of adoption', he says, is something 'whereby', 'as the result of which', we 'cry Abba, Father'. 'Abba, Father'!

What do the words mean? Why the two words? There are those who have said that the explanation is quite obvious. The word 'Abba', they remind us, is an Aramaic word, a word in the language that was used freely in Palestine in the time of our Lord. The word translated 'Father' was in the original in Greek. So the Apostle uses the two words – Aramaic and Greek. What we have here, they argue, is the Apostle's way of saying that God is not only the Father of the Jews but now also Father of the Gentiles who believe in the Lord Jesus Christ. It is just a way of saying ultimately that it does not matter to what nationality you belong; if you believe in the Lord Jesus Christ God is your Father.

That, of course, is quite true; but it by no means exhausts the explanation of the use of the two words. Surely the Apostle is not concerned primarily, if at all, at this point to say that this great blessing is for all nations. What he is concerned to say, surely, is that 'Abba' was the word that was used familiarly by children talking to their fathers. It is like the word 'Papa', which children frequently use, or some such term. A little child does not always address his father as 'father'; he uses terms such as 'Papa', 'Dada', 'Dad'. That is the kind of meaning represented by this word 'Abba'. It was a child's word, a familiar word lisped by a little child. It was the instinctive word that the Apostle himself had probably used, and that was invariably used by all children belonging to the Jewish race.

But still more important is the fact that slaves amongst the Jews were never allowed to use this term with regard to a 'free' man. That distinction had been preserved. Whether that was right or wrong need not be considered here but it was a fact that only the children of a 'freeman' were allowed to use the term 'father'; the slave children were not allowed to use the term. So this term has a very interesting significance. By using it the Apostle reminds us that we are no longer slaves, we no longer have the 'spirit of bondage again to fear'. The 'spirit of bondage' is the spirit of a slave. He says that we have finished with slavery, so we are entitled to use this term 'Abba'. What a transformation! It cuts right across what used to be true, and is another way of emphasizing that we are no longer under the spirit of bondage and of fear.

A significant light is cast upon this expression, 'Abba, Father,' in the Gospel according to St. Mark, chapter 14, verse 36. Our blessed Lord in the Garden of Gethsemane said, 'Abba, Father, all things are possible unto thee'. These are the very words used by our Lord at the time of His great agony. He used them when He was sweating great drops of blood. This is the cry He uttered, 'Abba, Father'. And that is the very cry, the Apostle tells us, that comes out of the heart of the one who realizes that he has been adopted as a child of God.

But let us next notice the word 'cry'. 'We have received the Spirit of adoption, whereby we *cry* Abba, Father.' It is a very strong word, and clearly the Apostle has used it quite deliberately. It means 'a loud cry'. Some of the authorities tell us that it originates in the screeching of a certain kind of bird, and that it is a 'cry of vociferation.' In other words it expresses deep emotion. This is not special pleading on my part; I am just reporting what the Lexicographers say, the men who approach the meaning of words in a thoroughly scientific and cool and detached manner. 'Cry' they tells us, is a very profound word, 'a loud cry expressing deep emotion', it expresses 'fervency', 'earnestness', 'importunity'. So when we have the Spirit of adoption we *cry,* 'Abba, Father'.

What then does this imply? Obviously, in the light of all we have seen, it implies real knowledge of God. I mean that God is no longer to us a distant God. Each of these expressions – 'cry', 'Abba', 'Father' – conveys the idea that we are speaking to Someone whom we know. He is not merely a God in whom we believe intellectually, theologically, theoretically, doctrinally only. All this is possible to one who is not a child of God at all. I have repeatedly told you that there is such a thing as a mere intellectual assent to truth. There is a purely academic kind of belief. The Apostle does not mean that! He has chosen terms which preclude such a meaning, and he insists upon this further emphasis. To the Christian man God is no longer a distant God. That was so once; and while it was so the man had the spirit of bondage and of fear. But the Apostle rejoices in the fact that we are delivered from the spirit of bondage and of fear. And the first proof of that is that God is no longer Someone in the distance; He becomes Someone whom we know. He is a God to whom we have been 'brought nigh', as Paul puts it in Ephesians 2. He says to the Gentiles: 'Ye were afar off, but now have been made nigh.' To whom? To God, 'by the blood of Christ'. In other words he says that the relationship that subsists now is that between child and parent. God is no longer away in the distant heavens. He is there, but to the child He is not only there, He is near, and so he approaches Him as a child, and as His child –

Centre and soul of every sphere
Yet to each loving heart how near.

At the same time the Apostle tells us in these terms exactly how such a child speaks to God. He does not do so in a formal manner, nor in a mechanical or cold manner. This, as far as I am concerned, is the determining factor as regards liturgical services. There is nothing here about a 'beautiful', 'dignified' service. Rather we are looking at a child; there is no dignity in a child, still less pomposity. And there is nothing 'dignified' about the term 'Abba'. As I have been showing, it is familiar rather than dignified.

It is very interesting to notice that as men and women know less and less about a living spiritual experience, the more formal does their worship become. This has been most striking during the present century. Increasingly nonconformists have been introducing a liturgical element into their worship. This is because of the low level of spirituality. Conversely, when people come to a living experience of God they rely less and less upon forms, even if they are found in Roman Catholicism. You can read about this in the lives of some of their saints – for instance,

Archbishop Fénelon, Madame Guyon, and others who undoubtedly had an evangelical and living experience of grace and of salvation. The same is true of Pascal and the Jansenists. They paid less and less attention to forms, and got into trouble for that reason. The more formalized your religion, the more dead it becomes, and the less spiritual.

But here, the emphasis is on the opposite characteristic. The man who has the 'Spirit of adoption' does not pray in a formal mechanical, cold manner. His worship and praying are spontaneous; it is the spontaneity of the child who sees the father and says, 'Abba'. And not only spontaneity, but confidence also! The little child has confidence. He does not analyse it, he is incapable of doing so, but the child knows that 'Abba' is his father. Grown-up people may be standing back at a distance, and showing great deference, and being very formal; but the little child comes running in; he rushes, and holds on to his father's legs. He has a right that no-one else has. It is not a matter of argument or logic or understanding; it is instinctive, a confidence born of a knowledge that is deeper than words, deeper than understanding itself. 'The heart', says Pascal, 'has its reasons, that reason knows nothing of.' Thank God! And in addition to confidence there is warmth, affection, rejoicing, happiness. 'We have received the Spirit of adoption, whereby we cry, Abba, Father.' Do you not hear and feel the warmth, the affection, the exuberance, the rejoicing, the child in the presence of the Father, in the very words?

There is also another element that comes in, especially in times of crisis and difficulty, times when things are going wrong. A little child is in a street, and a bully comes along. The child gives a screech – 'father'! The same is true in illness, accident, or some such happening, and from the depths comes this cry. That is the content of the word 'cry' – it is a 'deep elemental cry'. Go to Gethsemane, look at it there. It was there in His agony, when He saw the cup, the drinking of which was essential to man's salvation, and which meant His separation temporarily from the face of His Father. It was that that produced that elemental cry from the depths of His being, 'Abba, Father'.

All this, and very much more, is the content of the words, 'We have received the Spirit of adoption, whereby we cry, Abba, Father'. This does not imply any diminution in the 'reverence and godly fear'. The adopted child of God always remembers

[243]

that his heavenly Father is the Almighty God. But there is no contradiction. To the cold theologian there may be contradiction, but there is none to the child. The two things are perfectly compatible, as we saw when we looked at these two elements in the Epistle to the Hebrews: 'Let us therefore come boldly unto the throne of grace,' and 'God is a consuming fire'. We have noted how the child feels with respect to God, and that is how he speaks to Him. That, says Paul, is the Spirit we have received.

The Apostle does not stop negatively at saying that we have been delivered from the spirit of bondage and of fear; positively we have this Spirit of adoption, which makes us cry 'Abba, Father'. It is only those who are sons of God, and know that they are sons of God, who can ever speak and feel like this in the presence of Almighty God. None other can. You cannot persuade yourself into doing this. You can never persuade yourself to say 'Abba, Father'. If you try, you will find that the words will freeze on your lips; they will not get any further. But you will suddenly find yourself doing it, and you will be amazed at yourself. Only the child cries 'Abba, Father.' Therefore, if you have ever known yourself crying 'Abba, Father', you can be certain that you are a child of God.

Again, this can only be done through our blessed Lord and Saviour Himself. You can believe in God apart from the Lord Jesus Christ, but you will never know Him as 'Father' without Him. He Himself said so: 'I am the way, the truth, and the life; no man cometh unto the Father but by me' (John 14: 6). You can come to the Creator and the Lord of history with your mind; you can come to the Dispenser of great gifts with your intellect and understanding; but you will never come to the 'Father' except in and through the Lord Jesus Christ, and except God sends His Spirit into your heart. And when He does so, the cry comes welling up out of the depths, 'Abba, Father'.

How much do we know of this? This is real Christianity. Is it not extraordinary that so little attention is given to it? The chief explanation is that we are so much interested in our own activities and problems. How can I be delivered from this sin? How can I have guidance? How can I have this and that? Such is the way in which we approach these things; and we miss the most glorious elements. The most glorious truth about us as Christians is our personal relationship to God. But we in our self-centredness – the curse of the century – have our movements to teach us how to get rid of particular sins, or to get rid of our problems, and how to obtain nice and pleasant feelings. We search and crave for 'The Christian's Secret of a Happy Life'. And that so often comes between us and the most wonderful experience of all. The ultimate object of salvation is not merely to keep us from hell, not merely to deliver us from certain sins; it is that we may enjoy 'adoption', and that we may become 'the children of God' and 'joint-heirs with Christ'. The 'summum bonum' is to 'see God', and while in this life, to know God intimately as our Father, and to cry 'Abba, Father'. Have you ever known it? This is what is offered us in the Gospel of our Lord and Saviour Jesus Christ. God forbid that any of us should stop at any point short of it!

We shall go on to consider how we come to this position, if we are not there already. Can we do anything about it? We can! We have already been doing much – to know about the possibility of it is a tremendous step in itself. There are many who do not know as much as that. They remain content with 'being saved.' They believe that all they have to do is just to maintain that knowledge, and to be delivered from certain besetting sins. Examine yourself. To cry 'Abba, Father' is one of the most glorious proofs of sonship, higher than anything we have considered before. And yet, blessed be the name of God, it is not the end. We have not finished, there is still more to come!

Twenty

*

*For ye have not received the spirit of bondage again to fear; but ye
have received the Spirit of adoption, whereby we cry, Abba,
Father.*   Romans 8: 15

We have really finished our exposition, as such, of this great and
important verse, which is, as we have seen, one of the proofs
with which the Apostle supplies us of the fact that as believers we
are the children, or the sons, of God. The Spirit we have received
is not a 'spirit of bondage', but is a 'Spirit of adoption, whereby
we cry, Abba, Father'.

But there seem to me to be two matters which call for urgent
consideration before we leave the Apostle's statement. Firstly, it is
most important that we should remind ourselves again that the
'Spirit of adoption' is not essential to salvation, for a person can
be a Christian and yet know little or nothing about this Spirit of
adoption. As I say this I am well aware that the majority of the
Protestant Reformers would not have agreed with my statement,
for they tended to teach – Luther and Calvin in particular, but
others also – that assurance of salvation was necessary to salvation. They failed to draw a distinction between salvation itself
and the assurance of salvation. So they tended to teach that a man
was not saved unless he knew he was saved, that is to say, unless
he had assurance. Some Christians still adhere to this teaching.
They say that it is inconceivable that a man who believes on the
Lord Jesus Christ, and is born again, has not some kind of
assurance of his salvation.

This is obviously a very important matter. If we say that everyone who is a child of God must have this Spirit of adoption, in the
sense we have been indicating, then it follows that a very large
number of people, whom we have always regarded as Christians,

are not Christians at all; and there are some who do not hesitate to say that. I was reading a modern American author recently, and found that he did not hesitate to assert that in his opinion at least two-thirds of the people who were members of churches, and who claim to be Christians, are not Christians at all. He based that opinion on the fact that they do not have an assurance of their salvation. They say that they believe on the Lord Jesus Christ, but if you ask, 'Do you know that your sins are forgiven?' they say, 'I would not like to say that'. You ask them, 'Do you know that you are a child of God?' and they reply, 'Well, I believe I am, but I am not prepared to say that I know I am'. Clearly, they have not got this 'Spirit of Adoption, whereby we cry, Abba, Father', and therefore this preacher does not hesitate to say that they are not Christians. Now if his premise is right, then his deduction is right; that is what makes this matter so important. If you insist that every Christian must know that he has this 'Spirit of adoption', then it is very certain that there are large numbers of people who call themselves Christians, and who have always regarded themselves as Christians, who are not really such at all.

As we examine this position let us remember that we have no right to water down the Apostle's statement in any way. We have emphasized that the word 'cry' is a very strong one, meaning an elemental cry coming from the depths. It is not just saying, 'Abba, Father', it is crying 'Abba, Father.' The author of the Epistle to the Hebrews tells us that our Lord Himself in the Garden of Gethsemane uttered His cry, 'Abba, Father,' in that way: 'In the days of his flesh, when he had offered up prayers and supplications with strong crying and tears' (5 : 7). It was not a mere 'speaking', it was a profound emotion; and the Apostle says that this Spirit of adoption leads to such an emotion.

But let me now demonstrate that the teaching which makes assurance essential to salvation is not tenable at all. The compilers of the famous Westminster Confession of Faith investigated this question, and saw that it was causing a number of truly Christian people to be in trouble. In the Confession (chapter XVIII) they draw a distinction between being saved, and knowing that you are saved. They say that a person can be saved and yet lack assurance, and that assurance is not essential to salvation. The very notion of justification by faith alone means that you are resting on that which you believe, whatever your feelings may happen to be. So there is an essential difference between believing on the Lord Jesus Christ and trusting Him for salvation, on the one hand, and having an inward assurance of that salvation, on the other.

A second reason for rejecting the claim that assurance is essential to salvation is based upon what we have already seen in verse 14. We came to the conclusion that a man who can say that he is being led by the Spirit of God is a Christian, and that that is a ground of assurance. But it is possible for a man to be able to say that he is convinced that he is being led by the Spirit of God, and still not have the 'Spirit of adoption, whereby we cry, Abba, Father'. There is a vital distinction between the two. These are steps to assurance but the one is higher than the other. We interpreted verse 14 in terms of some nine or ten questions; and I ventured to say that if a man could say 'Yes' to *one* of the questions he was undoubtedly a Christian, and if he could say 'Yes' to all of them, he could be quite certain that he was a Christian. But all those tests taken together come short of the 'Spirit of adoption'. So I repeat that this 'Spirit of adoption' is not absolutely essential to salvation.

But there is a still further question to be considered. There are people who say, 'Surely, as you read the New Testament, you are given the impression that everyone has this Spirit of adoption! The Apostle does not say "some of you have received. . . .", but he says, "Ye have not received the spirit of bondage again to fear, but ye have received the Spirit of adoption, whereby we cry, Abba Father". He seems to be stating that this was true of all the Roman Christians: and parallel statements elsewhere in the New Testament all seem to be saying the same.' The answer surely is that most of the early Christians, if not all, had full assurance of salvation, the reason being that in New Testament times the Holy Spirit had been poured forth in unusual profusion. This is very clear, of course, in the second chapter of Acts; and that seems to have been repeated. Wherever the Gospel went there was a mighty authentication of the truth; the Spirit 'fell upon them'. In other words it was what we may term a time of exceptional spiritual power, later repeated in times of 'revival'. During such times it is generally the case that the majority of Christians are in an unusually happy state and enjoying a great assurance of salvation.

Now as most of the New Testament Epistles were written to such
people, it is not surprising that they were written on the assumption that their recipients had all had the great experience which
leads to this 'Spirit of adoption', and indeed, even beyond that,
to what we shall be considering in the 16th verse, 'The Spirit
himself bearing witness with our spirit that we are the children
of God'. It is quite clear that the early Church was in this exalted
condition in respect of experience, a condition which has not
persisted, alas, in the subsequent history of the Christian Church,
but which, as I say, is repeated from time to time during an
awakening or a period of revival.

We turn now to a second question – How is this Spirit of
adoption received? We have drawn attention to the fact that the
Apostle uses the term 'received' both in the negative and the
positive sense; but the question remains, How is this received?
We have also emphasized that this is subjective; it is a feeling,
and not a question of a man persuading himself, or deducing it
from the Scriptures, but an elemental feeling within, something
that has been poured in by the Spirit, leading a man to cry 'Abba,
Father'. So we now ask ourselves, How is this Spirit of adoption
received? I sometimes think that there is perhaps greater confusion in evangelical circles concerning this particular point, than
concerning any other single matter. This is largely due to a popular
teaching which – misunderstanding our text and many others
like it – goes under the name of 'Take it by faith'. It says, 'As you
took your justification by faith, so take your sanctification by
faith in the same way. Take a further experience of the Holy
Spirit by faith in the same way. Take the "fulness of the Spirit" by
faith'. Many say the same with regard to physical healing. This
teaching speaks in this way: 'Don't be concerned about your feelings; take the Word of God, believe it, accept it, act on it, and then
go to God and thank Him that you have received the blessing
even though you may not have felt anything.' In other words,
when they come across this word 'receiving' they put the whole
of the emphasis on what we do, upon our taking, upon our
believing. It is all our voluntary action; by faith we lay hold upon
what is offered to us, and at once it becomes ours. Yet the fact is,
that nothing robs so many people of the experience described in
this 15th verse so much as this particular teaching; and the

tragedy is that it is offered to us to help us to get the experience. Let me put it before you in the form of a quotation. It actually refers to the baptism with the spirit but deals with our word 'receive'.

'How is this Baptism with the Holy Spirit received? God's Word says, "Received ye the Spirit by the works of the law, or by the hearing of faith?" (Gal. 3 : 2); and again, "He therefore that supplieth to you the Spirit, and worketh miracles among you, doeth he it by the works of the law, or by the hearing of faith?" (Gal. 3 : 5); "receive the promise of the Spirit through faith" ' (Gal. 3 : 14). The way of receiving this blessing is not by works, nor by law, nor by excitement or noisy demonstration. The only way to receive the Baptism with the Spirit is by faith.

'But why have so few received this gift? Because this gift is for the thirsty, and so few are thirsty. If one is living in sin, there is no thirst. Drinking of the world's cisterns never really satisfies, and will take away the keen edge of the real thirst (that causes one to come to Christ for this great gift).

'Another important fact that we need to understand is that it is Jesus Christ who gives this gift. From his own invitation in John 7 and also from the words of John the Baptist, we learn that Jesus Christ is the Baptizer'. . . . 'Peter also definitely designated Jesus Christ as the one who poured out the Spirit in that wonderful experience, for he said on the day of Pentecost, "Being therefore by the right hand of God exalted, and having received of the Father the promise of the Holy Spirit, He hath poured forth this, which ye see and hear". This verse clearly shows that after His exaltation, it was Jesus Christ Himself who received this wonderful gift, and who now pours it forth (gives it). Thus, from first to last, Jesus Christ remains the centre of our Christian experience. This is very important and absolutely essential, lest one be led off from the truth of the centrality of Jesus Christ.'

Then again:

' "If any man thirst, let him come unto me and drink", Jesus said. Thus Jesus compared this experience of receiving the Baptism with the Holy Spirit to a thirsty man drinking water. And how does one drink? Drinking is the easiest and most natural thing in the world for a person to do. One who is thirsty does not have to be taught how to drink, for he simply opens his

mouth and takes in. Drinking is as easy as that. The application
is clear. The Holy Spirit is a definite Person and though we cannot
see Him, He is all around us. Like the air, He is here and at the
same time in China and in Africa and in India. In receiving the
Baptism with the Spirit, it may help to tell the Lord, "I know
that the Spirit is here. I am thirsty for Him; I want Him. May He
come upon me now. May He fill me now. Just as I breathe in this
air, I receive Thy wonderful Holy Spirit." '

The writer then goes on:

'F. B. Meyer's experience of the Baptism with the Holy Spirit
may prove both interesting and helpful to those who are seeking the
Lord. In his book, *The Christ-Life for the Self-Life,* he writes, 'I had
been a minister of a large influential church, but I was unhappy;
for I was conscious that I had not received the power of the Holy
Ghost. Then I went up to that little village, Keswick, where a great
number of God's people had gathered to seek and receive the
power of the Holy Spirit. One night they had elected to have a
prayer-meeting from nine o'clock to eleven and onwards to pray
for the Holy Ghost. I joined them and found a great many people
were agonizing. But I was too tired to agonize, and somehow
felt that God did not want me to agonize hour after hour. I had
to learn to take what God wanted to give. I had only to take. That is
what little children do at meal time. For instance, tomorrow your
little girl will come down to breakfast very hungry. The bread
and milk, or the oatmeal is on the table. You do not say 'Little
girlie, run upstairs and agonize, roll on the floor for an hour, and
then come down'. You say, 'Little one, I am so glad you have a
good appetite. Now there is your chair; in you get; say your
prayer; and start away.' That is what God says to the soul. All
nights of prayer for the Holy Ghost are principally necessary to
get people who pray into a fit condition to receive the Holy
Ghost; for when people are ready, the Holy Ghost will come
without agonizing.

' "So I left that prayer-meeting at Keswick. It was eleven
o'clock or half past ten, and I crept out into the lane away from
the village. As I walked I said, Oh my God, if there is a man in
this village who needs the power of the Holy Ghost to rest upon
him, it is I; but I do not know how to receive Him. I was too
tired, too worn, too nervously down to agonize.

' "A voice said to me, 'As you took forgiveness from the hand of the dying Christ, take the Holy Ghost from the hand of the living Christ'.

' "I turned to Christ and said, 'Lord, as I breathe in this whiff of warm night air, so I breathe into every part of me Thy blessed Spirit'. I felt no hand laid upon my head; there was no lambent flame; there was no rushing sound from heaven. But by *faith,* without emotion, and without experience and without excitement, I took for the first time, and I have kept on taking ever since.

' "I turned to leave the mountain side, and as I went down, the tempter said, "You have got nothing. It is moonshine."

' "I said, 'I have'.

' "He said, 'Do you feel it?'

' "I said, 'I do not'.

' "Then if you not feel it, you have not got it.'

' "I said, 'I do not feel it, but I reckon that God is faithful, and He could not have brought a hungry soul to claim the Holy Spirit by faith, and then have given a stone for bread, and a scorpion for fish. I know I have Him because God led me to put in my claim." '

That is a typical and characteristic statement of this teaching both by the author of the book, and by the famous F. B. Meyer. The whole of the emphasis is placed upon our taking; receiving is interpreted in terms of our activity in taking. All depends upon whether we are ready to take, whether, like the little child, we sit down at the table and take of the food that is there before us, whether we breathe in the air that is round about. It is our taking by faith that matters. They actually say that you can 'take the Holy Ghost' in this great fulness and yet feel nothing at all. Indeed they stress repeatedly that you must pay no attention to your feelings; it is a pure act of faith. They claim that their case is based upon certain passages of Scripture such as Galatians 3, verses 2, 5 and 14, and also John 7, verse 39. It is important therefore that we should examine these passages, and as we do so we shall find that they misinterpret them.

The statements on which they rely in Galatians 3 are concerned to emphasize that one enters the Christian position not as the result of works but as the result of faith. But what they miss is that the Apostle is dealing there with nothing but justification, in the first instance. Then, when he goes on to the Spirit, he asks his question, 'Did you receive the Spirit by the works of the law, or by the hearing of faith?' They interpret Paul's dismissing of reliance upon works to mean that these people had received this gift of the Spirit in the same way as they had received their justification – by an act of faith only. But of course that is not what the Apostle is saying. What the Apostle says is that the whole position of the Christian is one of faith, that the Christian does not rely upon his works. Everything in the Christian life ultimately is based upon faith. And the Apostle actually says no more than that! He is not saying that the gift of the Holy Spirit came to the Galatians in this particular way, as our two authors suggest. All he is saying is that we receive the gift of the Holy Spirit because we are in the position of faith and no longer 'under the law'.

But let me adduce some further reasons for speaking as I do. Surely this other teaching, though it reminds us that the Holy Spirit is a Person, nevertheless seems to forget that fact at this point. It falls into the error of talking of the Spirit as if He were a liquid that could be poured out, or as if He were like the air which can be breathed in. But the Holy Spirit is a Person! He is God, the third Person in the blessed Holy Trinity; and we Christians cannot take Him just as we breathe in the air, whenever we like, and whenever we choose. What we are taught is that we have to be subject to the Spirit, we have to surrender to the Spirit, and we have to be very careful not to 'grieve' or to 'quench' the Spirit. But there is never any suggestion anywhere in Scripture that we can take Him in this simple and almost casual manner. This teaching seems to me to do violence to the very Person of the Holy Spirit Himself.

The real trouble, however, arises in connection with the word 'receive', for they interpret the word 'receiving' in terms of an activity, a taking, on our part. We must look into this, not only carefully but in a technical manner, for it is a matter of urgent importance in evangelical thinking at the present time.

When we consult our Greek New Testament we find that the word 'receive' is used in our translations to translate several different Greek words. All the Greek words translated as 'received', except the one that is used here in Romans 8 : 15, carry an active sense, not a passive sense. They are words which put the emphasis upon our activity, upon our taking. Take, for instance, Acts 2:41: 'Then they that gladly received his word were baptised: and the same day there were added unto them about three thousand souls'. It is obvious from the whole context that the word 'received' there has a very active sense. The Apostle Peter was preaching; some hearers believed what he said and some did not. What we are told is that 'they that received' – that is, believed and took – his word – were baptized. We find the same in Acts 18:27: 'And when he was disposed to pass into Achaia, the brethren wrote exhorting the disciples to *receive* him', again an obvious active sense. We have the same again in Acts 28:28: 'Be it known therefore unto you, brethren, that the salvation of God is sent unto the Gentiles, and that they will *hear* it.' Though the A.V. translation has 'hear' at this point, and it is a different word in the Greek, it might also very well be translated 'receive', obviously an active sense once more.

But we must look at another word which is also translated 'receive'. In Acts 22:18, Paul is describing his vision in the temple: 'And I saw him saying unto me, Make haste and get thee quickly out of Jerusalem: for they will not *receive* thy testimony concerning me.' In other words, they are going to reject it. Clearly the word is a very active word; it means 'to accept', 'to admit', or 'to delight in'. But take yet another word translated as 'receive'. It is found in this Epistle to the Romans in chapter 14 verse 1: 'Him that is weak in the faith *receive* ye, but not to doubtful disputations.' Again in the third verse of that chapter, 'Let not him that eateth despise him that eateth not; and let not him which eateth not judge him that eateth: for God hath *received* him'. Obviously it is used in an active sense. In Philemon, verses 12 and 17, the same word is used. Paul is writing to Philemon and asking him to *receive* Onesimus. He might not want to, but he is urging him to do so. It carries an active sense. We have another word in Philippians 2:29. The word there means 'to admit into intercourse'. And a somewhat similar word again in Matthew 18:5: 'Whoso shall *receive* one such little child in my name *receiveth* me': obviously an active sense. We find it again in Acts 8:14: 'Now when the Apostles which were at Jerusalem heard that Samaria had *received* the word of God' – that they had believed it, had taken it, had accepted it. We have the same in Acts 11:1 and in Acts 21:17. Another very interesting example is found in 1 Corinthians 2: 14: 'The natural man *receiveth* not the things of the Spirit of God: for they are foolishness unto him'. It is obviously used in a very active sense there. And the same meaning in Galatians 4: 14; in Colossians 4: 10, James 1: 21, and other places. The word means 'take', 'accept'. All these words obviously carry an active meaning and put their stress and emphasis upon our taking, and they are all translated by the word 'receive'.

What then of the word that is used in our text, Romans 8: 15? This is a different word in the Greek – not one of the words we have been examining. The two best lexicons, Grimm-Thayer and Arndt-Gingrich, agree in saying that this word is used in two main senses. One is a more active sense, and the other a more passive sense. They both give examples to illustrate this. In an active sense it is found in Matthew 26: 26. It is the word used in our text but it is used in an active sense: 'And as they were eating, Jesus *took* bread, and blessed it, and brake it, and gave it to the disciples, and said, *Take,* eat; this is my body'. 'Jesus took bread.' It is this same word, but it obviously has an active meaning there. There is another example of its use in Luke 20: 28–31. Here our Lord is dealing with the catch question put to Him by the Sadducees, about the woman who married seven brothers in turn: 'Master', they said, 'Moses wrote unto us, If any man's brother die, having a wife, and he die without children, that his brother should *take* his wife, and raise up seed unto his brother.' The narrative goes on to say that the second took her to wife, the third took her, and so on. The word translated there as *took* is the word that we have here twice in Romans 8: 15. Another important example of its use is found in John 1: 12 which reads, 'But as many as *received* him' – as many as believed on Him. It is the active sense. Those who actively, voluntarily and willingly believed on Him, received Him, 'to them gave he the power to become the sons of God'. This is a very important and significant example, as we shall see in a moment. Another is found in John 5: 43: 'I am come in my Father's name, and ye *receive* me not'. Obviously it is active. The Lord says, You are rejecting me, but He puts it, 'you *receive* me not'. It indicates an activity on their part. We find the same word in John 10: 18: 'No man taketh it from me' – talking about His life – 'but I lay it down of myself. I have power to lay it down, and I have power to take it again. This command-

The Sons of God

ment have I *received* of my Father.' Again in John 12: 48, and in John 17: 8: 'I have given unto them the words which thou gavest me; and they have *received* them.' He is referring to His disciples, and not to the world, so He obviously uses the word in the active sense. Another example is found in Acts 27: 35. These, then, are examples of the active sense of this word.

But then our authorities tell us that the same word is used in a more passive sense when it means 'to receive what is given', 'to gain', 'to get', 'to obtain'. In these instances it does not mean 'to take'. It means that I 'get' or 'gain' or 'obtain' something, that I 'receive' what is given. They give many illustrations of this. Take Matthew 7: 8: 'Every one that asketh *receiveth;* and he that seeketh findeth; and to him that knocketh it shall be opened.' That is a passive use. It does not mean that every one that asketh 'taketh'. No, to every one that asketh, it shall be 'given'. The emphasis is upon the giving here, not upon the taking! We have the same in Matthew 20: 9: 'And when they came' – that is, the labourers hired for work in the vineyard – 'that were hired about the eleventh hour, they *received* every man a penny'. Can it be suggested that that was active? The whole context tells us that it was not. They were very much annoyed because they were not given more. It was not that they 'took' the penny in an active manner; but that was all they 'received', that was all they were given. Far from being active it was very passive indeed. Next, let us contrast John 1: 16 with what we have met with in John 1: 12: 'As many as received him, to them gave he power to become the sons of God' (verse 12). 'And of his fulness have all we received, and grace for grace' (verse 16). Verse 12 tells us about people who believe on Him. Verse 16 tells us what the people who believe on Him are given, what they have received. We have been 'given' and we have 'gained' something of His fulness. It is entirely passive, and different from the activity of the twelfth verse.

Let me give further examples of this contrast. There is one in John 7: 39. In the Book of Acts there is a whole series of texts carrying this passive sense – 7: 53; 10: 43; 16: 24; 20: 24; 26: 10. Let us look at Acts 10: 43 because it is a very interesting and important case. The word occurs in the account of what happened in the household of Cornelius: 'To him give all the prophets witness, that through his name whosoever believeth in him shall *receive* remission of sins'. Believers do not 'take' remission of sins;

[256]

they 'receive', they are given remission of sins. How different the whole atmosphere and context is from the activity of the words we have been looking at previously! Turning again to 1 Corinthians 2, we have already looked at verse 14; but let us look also at verse 12: 'Now we have received, not the spirit of the world, but the Spirit which is of God.' What Paul is referring to is the spirit we 'have been given'. In talking about the 'natural man' in verse 14 he says: 'The natural man receiveth not' – there is an activity, an active rejection with contempt. But the context of verse 12 is: 'But God hath revealed them unto us by his Spirit, for the Spirit searcheth all things, yea, the deep things of God' (verse 10). He says that this is the Spirit we have *received,* not the spirit of the world, but the Spirit that is of God. God has given us this Spirit. There is no activity here, there is no talk about 'taking'; the emphasis falls on what we have received. We have the same in 1 Corinthians 3 : 8, where we read: 'Now he that planteth and he that watereth are one: and every man shall *receive* his own reward according to his own labour'. Obviously there is no emphasis on 'taking' there. Paul is saying that in the day of judgment every man is going to 'get' his own reward according to his own labour. There is no suspicion or suggestion there of our taking actively as if we are 'breathing in the air'; the reward will be 'meted out' to us. But the word is rightly translated 'receive'. We find the same thing in the fourteenth verse of the same chapter: 'If any man's work abide which he hath built thereupon, he shall *receive* a reward.' The emphasis there is not upon the man stepping forward and taking. Of course not! It is given to him in the graciousness and the goodness and kindness and love of God. The same usage is also found in 1 Corinthians 4 : 7; 9 : 24; and 14 : 5; in 2 Corinthians 11 : 24; and in Hebrews 2 : 2, which is particularly important.

The Hebrew Christians are being told why they must be very careful to hold on to the Gospel, why we Christians must 'pay the more earnest heed to the things which we have heard, lest at any time we should let them slip. For if the word spoken by angels was steadfast, and every transgression and disobedience *received* a just recompence of reward ...' Is there any suggestion of 'taking' in this 'receiving'? Of course not! The emphasis is upon the giving. It is the same in Hebrews 11 : 8 and 13; also in James 1 : 7, 12 and James 3 : 1 which reads: 'My brethren, be not many masters, knowing that we shall *receive* the greater condemnation'. Do we 'take' such condemnation in as we 'breathe the air?' Can we 'take in' condemnation as if we sat down and ate our breakfast? Certainly not! the meaning is entirely passive. James 4: 3, and 5: 7 read to the same effect. The latter reads: 'Be patient, therefore, brethren, unto the coming of the Lord. Behold, the husbandman waiteth for the precious fruit of the earth, and hath long patience for it, until he *receive* the early and latter rain.' Does the farmer 'take' the early and the latter rain? It is poured down upon him, and he 'receives' it, These senses of the word 'receive' are entirely passive. 1 Peter 4: 10 and 2 Peter 1: 17 bear the same interpretation. The latter refers to our Lord with Peter, James and John on the mount of transfiguration, and says: 'For he *received* from God the Father honour and glory, when there came such a voice to him from the excellent glory, This is my beloved Son, in whom I am well pleased.' 1 John 3: 22, shows a similar usage: 'And whatsoever we ask, we *receive* of him, because we keep his commandments, and do those things that are pleasing in his sight.' There are also a number of examples of the same thing in the Book of Revelation.

To complete my list of quotations, I must add that there is a whole series of the same passive meaning of this selfsame word in this very Epistle to the Romans. Here is the list. In chapter 1 verse 5, Paul talking about himself says, 'By whom [the Lord Jesus Christ] we have *received* grace and apostleship'. Paul did not 'take' his apostleship; it was 'given' to him and he never ceased to be amazed at the fact that Christ should ever have given it to him. Then in chapter 4: 11 we read: 'And he [Abraham] *received* the sign of circumcision.' He did not 'take' it, it was put upon him, 'a seal of the righteousness of the faith which he had being yet uncircumcised'. Again in chapter 5: 11: 'And not only so, but we also joy in God through our Lord Jesus Christ, by whom we have now *received* the atonement.' Entirely passive! It is not of our taking; it is what has been given to us through Him. The final example is in chapter 13: 2: 'Whosoever therefore resisteth the power' – he is talking about 'the powers that be, that are ordained of God' – 'resisteth the ordinance of God: and they that resist shall *receive* to themselves condemnation'. Obviously it is entirely passive there also.

We have gone through that technical list of words and meanings in order that we might be in a position to deduce from it a vital argument concerning the exact meaning of the word 'receive' – 'We have not *received* the spirit of bondage again to fear; but we have *received* the Spirit of adoption, whereby we cry, Abba, Father'. Is this 'Spirit of adoption' something that I can 'take' whenever I like? Do I just 'take' it, and though I may feel nothing, say that I have got it? Do I just 'take it by faith'? Work it out in terms of these technical matters I have put before you. Go through all the illustrations and examples; look up these words in their various contexts, and you will arrive at the inevitable deduction with regard to this matter that it cannot carry the meaning of 'taking'.

Twenty-one

*

For ye have not received the spirit of bondage again to fear; but ye have received the Spirit of adoption, whereby we cry, Abba, Father.   Romans 8: 15

We continue our study of how we are to 'receive the Spirit of adoption whereby we cry, Abba, Father'. We have been examining in detail the different words translated 'receive' in the New Testament. It is important that we should carry this in our minds as we resume. We have seen that quite a number of different words in the original are translated by the word 'receive', and also that practically all those words, apart from the one that is used in this verse carry a very definite active sense and meaning. As regards this word itself – the word in the original that is here translated 'receive' – we have found from the authorities that this is a word that is used in both an active and in a passive sense, and we have looked at examples and illustrations of both usages. All the illustrations I have given of the passive sense of this word were instances which had nothing directly to do with this question of receiving the Spirit. I deliberately kept that back in order that we might deal with that question as a whole. I was simply concerned to show that the word is used with regard to other matters in this passive sense, and where we find the passive sense, it means 'to receive something that is given', 'to gain', 'to get', 'to obtain'.

The question that arises then is this: Which of the two senses does it carry in Romans 8: 15 ? What is the verdict of the lexicons ? They supply large numbers of illustrations showing the active and the passive sense and usage of the word; but when you need them most of all they do not help you! Not one of them makes any reference to Romans 8: 15. Once more we are reminded that ultimately these matters cannot be decided in purely linguistic terms. These linguistic helps are of great value as far as they go; let us make full use of them. But here is one of those instances where they do not solve the problem for us; and we are left to other considerations in deciding. As I hope to show, there are sufficient reasons for coming to the conclusion that here we are dealing with the passive sense.

This verse alone, in and of itself, surely solves the problem; in its first half, the use of the word 'received' settles the matter. 'For ye have not received the spirit of bondage again to fear, but ye have received the Spirit of adoption, whereby we cry Abba, Father.' It is inconceivable that in this first usage it should have any active sense at all. Can we imagine anyone 'taking' or 'breathing in' a 'spirit of bondage and of fear?' Of course not! That is something that happens to us; and it is a very miserable and unhappy state to be in. No one has ever voluntarily 'taken' such a spirit. As we have already seen, it is something that the Holy Spirit brings to pass in us. And as the word is obviously entirely passive in that first half, so, by implication, it is in the second half also. The Apostle's statement is that what has been given to us is not 'the spirit of bondage again to fear'; but 'the Spirit of adoption, whereby we cry, Abba, Father'. As the active sense is an utter impossibility in the first half, so, to keep the parallel and maintain the balance of the verse, it must be clearly the same in the second half. So this one verse would have been sufficient in itself to establish the meaning, but owing to the popularity of the false teaching, I am anxious to give all the available evidence to show that there is nothing really to support it.

My second argument is as follows. All the statements which we shall find when we come to look at the teaching concerning the 'receiving' of the Holy Spirit in any sense teach invariably this same passive sense. Most of them actually refer to the baptism with or in the Spirit. The basic statement with regard to this whole matter is found in Luke 3 : 16, and in the parallels in the other Gospels, where we are told that John the Baptist, when he realized that some of the people to whom he was speaking had come to the conclusion that he was the Christ, said, 'I indeed baptize you with water; he shall baptize you with the Holy Ghost and with fire'. That is the basic statement, and there we are given the key to the whole doctrine. John was comparing and contrasting what he was saying and doing with what the Lord Jesus Christ was about to do. He was not thinking at all about people 'receiving' in the sense of 'taking' in an active manner. John's whole point is the contrast – 'I am baptizing with water'; 'He will baptize you with the Holy Ghost'. The activity is on the side of the one who does the baptizing, not on the one who is being baptized.

It is important to observe how frequently these words of John the Baptist are quoted in other places in the New Testament. Our Lord Himself, for instance, quotes them in the statement at the beginning of the Acts of the Apostles where He says: 'John truly baptized with water; but ye shall be baptized with the Holy Ghost not many days hence' (1: 5). But the important verse in that chapter is verse 8: 'But [He says] ye shall receive power, after that the Holy Ghost is come upon you: and ye shall be witnesses unto me both in Jerusalem, and in all Judaea, and in Samaria, and unto the uttermost part of the earth'. Our Lord is clearly not making a prophecy to the effect that the disciples were going to 'take' the Holy Spirit afterwards. He is telling them that the effect of His sending the Holy Ghost upon them not many days hence would be that they would receive a power that they lacked, but of which they would shortly be fully conscious. In both statements He emphasizes the 'giving'. He is going to send the Holy Ghost upon them, and with the Holy Ghost the gift of the power without which they could not witness. He is not referring to any action on their part in the sense of their 'taking' something that is being offered to them. He is going to 'give' them the Holy Ghost, and thereby He is going to give them the power.

When we come to the second chapter of the Acts of the Apostles we find the same emphasis running right through the chapter. The apostles and others are met together in the Upper Room and 'suddenly there came a sound from heaven as of a rushing mighty wind, and it filled all the house where they were sitting. And there appeared unto them cloven tongues like as of fire, and it sat upon each of them. And they were all filled with the Holy Ghost, and began to speak with other tongues as the Spirit gave them utterance'. Again the entire emphasis is upon what happened to them; it is all 'given'. They had been waiting ten days, and nothing had happened, but suddenly something is done to them. The Holy Ghost is sent upon them, and they become conscious of His coming. They 'were all filled'. They did not decide to 'breathe in' the Holy Spirit as one may breathe in the air; He was sent upon them, and they were filled. They were passive. There is no suggestion at all of any activity on their part. Next, Peter's sermon explains this great event which had created such a stir and commotion, causing the people to come crowding together to ask what it all signified. Some of them said 'These men are filled with new wine', but Peter stood up and explained the happening in terms of what had been promised in the Old Testament. He expounds, in particular, words found in the prophecy of Joel: 'It shall come to pass in the last days, saith God, that I will pour out of my Spirit upon all flesh', and so on. As Peter proceeds with his exposition he refers to our Lord and says that this event on the day of Pentecost is the final proof that He is the Son of God. He works out the doctrine concerning the Person of our Lord; and everywhere his point is that it is our Lord who had done this great thing that had happened to them as apostles. We find it specifically in verse 33: 'Therefore being by the right hand of God exalted, and having received of the Father the promise of the Holy Ghost, he hath shed forth this, which ye now see and hear.' This is a crucial verse, and it contains our word 'received' – exactly the same word in the original as we have in Romans 8 : 15. It tells us that our Lord and Saviour Jesus Christ had 'received' of the Father this promise. There is no suggestion of any activity on the part of our Lord, of His having taken it. What Peter is saying is that owing to His work and His obedience and all that our Lord had done, when He had completed the work of salvation on earth, He returned to heaven and God received Him by giving Him this gift to give to us. You cannot read into the word 'received' in this context the sense that our Lord here actively decided to take the Father's gift. He is rewarded – 'being by the right hand of God exalted, and having received of the Father the promise of the Holy Ghost'. The Spirit was given to Him that He might give the Spirit to us.

Exactly the same truth is taught in the fourth chapter of the Epistle to the Ephesians, verses 8 and following: 'When he ascended up on high, he led captivity captive, and received gifts for men'. He received them and He passes them on. There is no suggestion of His actively laying hold upon something and taking it to Himself. But to return to Acts chapter 2 – there is in verse 38 another statement which bears upon our inquiry. To the people under conviction who were crying out and saying, 'Men and brethren, what shall we do?', Peter said, 'Repent, and be baptized every one of you in the name of Jesus Christ for the remission of sins, and ye shall receive the gift of the Holy Ghost'. Was Peter here saying 'You will then be made willing to desire and to take the gift of the Spirit?' Surely he is saying that the Spirit will be given to them. He is not saying that at some later stage they are going to be made, as the phrase goes, 'willing to be willing' to receive it. There is no suggestion of that at all. But he is saying that if they repent and believe, then they will receive this gift. So the verb 'receive' cannot be active in this context; clearly it is in the passive.

Another example is found in Acts 5, verse 32. Peter and John are on trial, and Peter, having spoken about our Lord and what had happened to Him, says, 'We are his witnesses of these things; and so is also the Holy Ghost, whom God hath *given* to them that obey him'. The phrasing is significant. The Greek word used there is not the one we have in Romans 8: 15, but it reminds us that whenever we have this teaching concerning the coming of the Spirit in this way upon believers, the emphasis is always on the 'giving' by the Father or by the Lord Jesus Christ, and never on an active taking by us. 'Whom God hath given to them that obey him': they obey God, and He gives them this gift of the Holy Spirit.

In Acts, chapter 8, certain statements throw great light on this subject, for example, verse 15. Peter and John, having heard in Jerusalem what was happening in Samaria, went there, and upon their arrival they prayed for the disciples, that they might receive the Holy Ghost. Then there follows the explanation in verse 16: 'For as yet he was fallen upon none of them; only they were baptized in the name of the Lord Jesus.' All this was after Pentecost, though according to the popular teaching the Holy Ghost was given once and for all at Pentecost, and all we have to do now is to take Him 'as you breathe in the air', and so on. It is quite clear, however, that Philip the evangelist was not aware of such teaching, otherwise he would have told the believers in Samaria that the Holy Ghost had been given on the day of Pentecost and all they had to do was to 'take him by faith'. And there would have been no need for the apostles to go from Jerusalem to Samaria. But that was not the case. Philip had preached, and many people had believed and had been baptized in the name of the

Lord Jesus. But we are told that the Holy Spirit had not yet 'fallen' upon any of them. The receiving of the Holy Spirit is the result of His 'falling' upon us. We do not 'take' Him; He 'falls' upon us. But verse 15 emphasizes that Peter and John prayed for them – *prayed* for them – 'that they might receive the Holy Ghost'. Surely if this receiving is something that one does volitionally and actively there was no need for the Apostles to pray for them. Exhortation rather than prayer would have been called for. They would simply have exhorted them to receive Him 'just like breathing in the air'.

But further, in verse 17 we read, 'Then laid they their hands on them' and as the result of that action these people 'received' the Holy Ghost. In other words the apostles were praying that they might have the power to 'give' this gift to these Samaritans who 'received' it in the sense that the Spirit was 'given' to them and 'fell' upon them. Confirmation of this is found in verse 18: 'Simon saw that through the laying on of the apostles' hands the Holy Ghost was given'. He saw that it was in the power of these apostles to 'give' people the gift of the Holy Spirit. The whole emphasis is upon 'giving', not upon 'taking'. Next 'Simon offered them money, saying, Give me also this power, that on whomsoever I lay hands he may receive the Holy Ghost'. Here the word 'receive' in the Greek is the same as in our verse, Romans 8 : 15. Simon was really saying, 'Give me this power so that when I lay my hands on a man he will have the Holy Spirit'. It is the exact opposite of urging people to 'take' the Holy Spirit by faith. His reasoning was, 'I can see that this is something these men are able to give. I would like to have the power to be able to do the same thing, so that when I put my hands on people they may receive it from me'. The emphasis is entirely on the activity of the giver, not the activity of the one who receives. These are crucial statements.

In Acts 10 where we have the story of the conversion of Cornelius and his household, there is another important statement. Peter was invited to speak, and in verse 44 we read: 'While Peter yet spake these words, the Holy Ghost fell on them'. Even as Peter was speaking, obviously to his amazement and that of the hearers, the Holy Spirit fell upon them. Next we are told: 'They of the circumcision which believed were astonished, as many as came with Peter, because that on the Gentiles also was poured out the gift of the Holy Ghost. For they heard them speak with tongues, and magnify God. Then answered Peter, Can any man forbid water that these should not be baptized, which have *received* the Holy Ghost as well as we?' Again we have the word – the word used twice in the Greek in Romans 8: 15 – translated by 'received'. Peter was in a dilemma, and did not know what to do. He was in trouble over this whole question of the Gentiles becoming Christians. That is why God had given him the vision at Joppa. But now he sees quite clearly that the Holy Spirit had 'fallen' on these people as He did on himself and the other apostles on the day of Pentecost, and that they received the Holy Spirit. In the light of these events he has no hesitation in baptizing these people. But all this becomes meaningless if you put an active sense on the word 'received', and say that these people, while listening to Peter expounding the gospel, decided at that point that they were going to 'receive the Holy Spirit by faith', to 'take Him by faith' though they did not feel anything.

This is confirmed in chapter 11, verse 15: 'As I began to speak, the Holy Ghost fell on them, as on us at the beginning. Then I remembered the word of the Lord, how that he said, John indeed baptized with water; but ye shall be baptized with the Holy Ghost. Forasmuch then as God gave them the like gift as he did unto us, who believed on the Lord Jesus Christ; what was I, that I could withstand God?' Peter baptized them, not because they said that they had believed, or had taken this gift by faith; he baptized them for one reason only, because of what God had done to them. It was God sending the Spirit on them that finally convinced Peter and his party. So the whole emphasis is on the activity of God in the giving, and on the passivity of the groups of disciples in the 'receiving'. That is surely an irrefutable argument. Peter makes it patently clear. His problem concerning the baptizing of these Gentiles would not have been solved if the 'take it by faith' teaching were true, and these people had simply said that, though they felt nothing, they believed the Word and had decided to 'take' the gift that was offered them. That would never have satisfied Peter and his Jewish companions with their strong prejudices. But when God has given the gift in an obvious manner, and the people as passive recipients are proving that the Spirit has entered them, and that they are filled with the Spirit, Peter is absolutely convinced. There is no other conceivable interpretation of that incident.

[266]

That brings us to our last example in the Acts of the Apostles, in chapter 19, verse 2. Paul had arrived at Ephesus, 'and finding certain disciples he said unto them' – reading from the Authorized Version – 'Have ye received the Holy Ghost since ye believed?' It is generally agreed that the correct translation is; 'Did you receive the Holy Ghost when you believed?' 'They said unto him, We have not so much as heard whether there be any Holy Ghost'. Then Paul preaches the gospel to them and baptizes them. Here, then, are men who have now believed on the Lord Jesus Christ truly, knowing what they are doing, and Paul has baptized them – 'When they heard this, they were baptized in the name of the Lord Jesus'. But still they have not received the gift of the Holy Ghost. What happens? 'And when Paul had laid his hands upon them, the Holy Ghost came on them; and they spake with tongues, and prophesied' (v. 6). Again, this is a crucial statement. According to the popular but false teaching, what would have happened would have been something like the following. Paul would have said, 'Well now, you have been baptized in the name of the Lord Jesus Christ, but that is not all, you must also receive the gift of the Spirit. You have only to believe what I am telling you, and to take Him by faith. Do not worry about your feelings, just take Him by faith and He will fill you.' But that is not what happened. After the same manner as Peter and John had done in Samaria, Paul 'laid his hands upon them, the Holy Ghost came on them, and they spake with tongues, and prophesied.'

There, then, is the main evidence for our contention. In a sense we have already considered parallel evidence in the Epistle to the Romans in chapter 5, verse 5, where we read: 'And hope maketh not ashamed; because the love of God is shed abroad in our hearts by the Holy Ghost which is given unto us'. We do not take it; 'the Holy Ghost is given to us'. It is interesting to notice that the terms which are constantly used are 'poured forth', 'shed abroad', and 'fell upon'. None of them suggests that we actively, voluntarily, 'take in'. And as we have already seen we have precisely the same emphasis in Galatians 4: 6 where we read: 'And because ye are sons, God hath sent forth the Spirit of his Son into your hearts, crying, Abba, Father.' The Scripture goes out of its way, as it were, to tell us that it is God who 'sent him forth', and into our hearts. There is another relevant word in the

First Epistle of John, chapter 2, verse 27. John is writing about the antichrists and the confused teaching. 'But', he says, 'the anointing which ye have received of him abideth in you, and ye need not that any man teach you: but as the same anointing teacheth you of all things, and is truth, and no lie . . . .

What conclusions do we draw from all this? The first is that the meaning is surely quite clear in all these instances; the emphasis is always upon the 'giving' and not upon the 'taking'. It is clearly passive.

Secondly, there is not a single instance on the other side, of anyone deciding to 'take this by faith'. Not a single instance in the whole of the New Testament! Nowhere is there any teaching in the New Testament exhorting people to take this gift of the Spirit by faith. Always it is the Spirit 'coming upon' them, their 'receiving' in the passive sense. Is it not astonishing that a teaching could ever have become so popular without any evidence to support it in the Scriptures?

But consider a third argument. Take the question, which we have come across several times in these examples, of the laying-on of hands. It happened in Samaria, it happened again in Ephesus. It did not happen in the case of Cornelius and his household. Consider this in the light of 1 Timothy 4: 14: 'Neglect not the gift that is in thee, which was given thee by prophecy, with the laying-on of the hands of the presbytery.' I refer to it because it is in line with the examples we have found in the Acts of the Apostles. The very fact that there was this symbolism of laying-on of hands in and of itself suggests strongly that the important element in this experience is the 'giving' of the gift, not the 'taking'. If it were a question of taking you would not need this laying-on of hands; all that would be needed would be teaching and exhortation. But that is not what God has ordained. God ordained that this gift should come in this extraordinary way through men who had this power of giving by the laying their hands on others, clearly indicating that the gift is being transmitted by them. The recipients do nothing; hands are placed upon them and they passively receive. That is the meaning of the word 'receiving' as found in Romans 8: 15.

An illustration from everyday life may help at this point. It is not to be compared with illustrations from the Scriptures, but certain people seem to be helped in this way. Is not this question of 'receiving' comparable to the way in which we speak when we receive a parcel. Imagine that someone has sent you a parcel. He waits a few days or weeks to receive a letter from you thanking him for the parcel; but nothing arrives. What does he do, therefore? He writes a letter asking 'Have you received the parcel which I sent you?' What does he mean by 'receive'? Is he saying, 'Were you not willing to take that parcel I sent you? Did you decide not to take and accept the gift that I sent you?' He means nothing of the sort. What he means is, 'Has my parcel arrived?' He is not thinking of any active 'taking' on your part; he is thinking solely in terms of his having 'sent' it, and nothing else.

Or take it the other way round. A man has received a parcel. He writes, 'I write to acknowledge the receipt of your gift'. He is not saying, 'Having thought about it, I decided that I would take your parcel'. Of course not! 'I am writing to acknowledge the receipt of the parcel you were good and kind enough to send to me. I am not only letting you know that it has arrived safely, but that I am pleased with it.' The very word 'receipt' in and of itself tells us this. The activity is on the part of the man who sends the gift, not of the one who receives it. The latter is only passively acknowledging it. The whole emphasis in our common usage of this word corresponds to what we have seen so clearly in the Scriptures themselves.

Let me take up one other point. Why is all this so important, and why have we spent so much time on it? The first reason is that the teaching I have opposed does not acknowledge the sovereignty of the Holy Ghost as it should. You cannot 'take' the Holy Ghost in that way just when and as you please. He is a Person, He is a sovereign Lord. That is emphasized in 1 Corinthians 12 which deals with the question of the gifts of the Spirit. He dispenses as He decides and sees fit (verse 11). He is the third Person in the blessed Holy Trinity, and we must never speak of Him as if He were not a Person, as if He were just like the atmosphere which we can breathe in whenever we like. He is a sovereign Lord, even as the Father is and the Son is.

Secondly, I would remind you that even our justification is not 'taken' in that way. That other teaching, you remember, is generally put in this way, 'As you took your justification by faith, take this further blessing by faith'. But 'justification' cannot be taken whenever you like. No man can decide in an almost casual manner when he is going to be justified; it is the action of God, it is something that happens to us. Let us never forget that! Even our justification is given; it is something that comes to us through the instrumentality of faith. But faith is never anything more than the channel. It is not our faith that lays hold of it; it is, rather, that it comes to us 'through' faith. It is not our faith that justifies us; we are justified through faith.

There is no such thing as 'bare faith'. Faith is never bare. Faith is not just a matter of saying 'Yes, I believe, I accept that teaching'. There are many who misinterpret Romans 10: 8 and 9 in that way. 'What saith it? The word is nigh thee, even in thy mouth, and in thy heart: that is, the word of faith, which we preach; that if thou shalt confess with thy mouth the Lord Jesus, and shalt believe in thine heart that God hath raised him from the dead, thou shalt be saved'. Certain people misinterpret that to mean: If a man says 'Yes, I believe that the Lord Jesus Christ is the Son of God and that he died for my sins', he is saved thereby. They say to an enquirer, 'Are you prepared to say that?' 'Yes', says the other. 'Very well,' they say, 'you are saved'. But the Scripture does not say so. 'If thou shalt confess with thy mouth the Lord Jesus, and shalt believe in thine heart' – that is to say, with the totality of your being. The 'heart' is the centre of the personality. It is not feeling only, it is the centre, the whole man – 'if thou shalt believe in thine heart that God hath raised him from the dead'. If a man believes this truth in his heart his whole life will be governed by it. Then, and not till then, can it be said, 'thou shalt be saved'. Faith, I repeat, is never 'bare' in that sense. It is not true faith unless an element of feeling is involved. If there is no such element it may be nothing but intellectual assent, nothing but a kind of 'historical faith'. There is nothing to stop anyone saying, 'I believe that; I believe that evidence'. That does not make him a Christian. The devils believe that, they know that, but they 'tremble' at it. We must be very careful lest we substitute a mere intellectual assent to a number of propositions for real faith. Faith is deep, and a man does not really have true faith without experiencing rest in his soul. 'Being justified by faith' – as we saw in Romans 5: 1 – 'we have peace with God'. And a person must not say that he has faith until he knows something about the peace and rest. So we must be very careful about this 'bare faith'. True faith involves feeling and the will as well as the intellect. 'Faith without works is dead.

My third argument draws attention to the fact that in every single instance that is given in the New Testament of people 'receiving' this gift of the Holy Spirit, it is always accompanied by much and strong feeling, and by the knowledge that they have received it. Not only does the man himself know it, everyone else knows it. Consider the apostles on the day of Pentecost! Did they receive the Holy Spirit by faith without feeling anything at all? That, we are told by the wrong teaching, is what happens. The answer of the New Testament is that when the Holy Spirit came upon the early Christians they knew it. Peter was a transformed man; not only so, everyone in Jerusalem knew that something strange had happened. The strangers knew it, and asked, 'What is this?' Some thought that the Apostles and the others were 'filled with new wine'. The whole city was filled with wonderment. Everyone knew it in Samaria. Simon the sorcerer, looking on, could see that, as the result of Peter and John laying their hands on believers, they were changed. That something had happened to them was obvious to all. The people themselves knew it, everyone else knew it. The same was true in the household of Cornelius, as we have seen; and also in Ephesus. And yet a certain teaching tells us to 'take it by faith', and not to worry about feelings. 'You may feel nothing at all', it says, 'but if you believe this Word and its teaching you can take the Holy Spirit by faith irrespective of any feeling.' The whole of the New Testament teaches the opposite. So does the subsequent history of the Christian Church, both in general in times of revival, and also in the case of individuals. Take the famous example of Whitefield. He knew when it happened to him and soon everyone else knew it! When it happened to John Wesley in Aldersgate Street on May 24th, 1738, he knew that his 'heart was strangely warmed', and everyone else soon knew it. You cannot be 'baptized' or 'filled' with the Spirit without knowing it. It is the greatest experience one can ever know. The teaching that assures us that we may feel nothing at all runs entirely contrary not only to the teaching of the Scripture but to the recorded experiences of countless Christians throughout the centuries. We have worked out this argument concerning the word 'received' in terms of the baptism with the Spirit, but all that is equally true of receiving the Spirit in conviction and adoption as used in this 15th verse.

Twenty-two

*

For ye have not received the spirit of bondage again to fear, but ye have received the Spirit of adoption, whereby we cry, Abba, Father.
                                                        Romans 8: 15

As we continue our exposition of this verse I would remind you that I am not attempting to deal in these sermons with the whole of the work of the Holy Spirit. We are concerned in particular about the exact way in which we 'receive' 'the Spirit of adoption whereby we cry Abba, Father', which is one of the grounds of our assurance of salvation. As we have seen, a person can be a Christian without this assurance; but he cannot be a Christian without having the Holy Spirit. No one can ever be convicted of sin without the Holy Spirit, or truly believe without the Holy Spirit. The Spirit is an absolute essential. But we are not here dealing with that matter, but with 'assurance' of salvation.

The receiving of 'the Spirit of adoption' is a very special form or type of assurance. I venture to call it the second type of assurance. The first we found in verse 14: 'As many as are led by the Spirit of God, they are the sons of God.' If a person is satisfied, having tested himself, that he is being led by the Spirit, he can be assured that he is a son of God. That is the first type of assurance. But in this fifteenth verse there is another, and what I would describe as a higher type of assurance. It is the assurance that a Christian has who is aware within himself of the Spirit of adoption that makes him cry 'Abba, Father'. Furthermore, I am suggesting that this is one of the manifestations of 'the baptism with the Holy Spirit'. A further manifestation is the one we shall find in verse 16: 'The Spirit itself [or Himself] beareth witness with our spirits that we are the children of God'. My contention is that these are the two main manifestations of 'the baptism with the Holy Spirit' – that which happened to the Apostles and others on the day of Pentecost, and to the believers in Samaria, and to Cornelius and his household, and to those disciples at Ephesus when Paul laid his hands upon them. These are the two phases, two aspects, of the baptism with the Holy Ghost. You can be a Christian without this baptism as the Apostles were before the day of Pentecost. This is the special assurance that is given to Christians. It is something we should all enjoy, but it is not essential to salvation. But the fact that it is not essential does not mean that we should not have it, or that we should not seek to have it. I am not giving a complete account of the various operations of the Holy Spirit, but dealing only with this particular activity.

The point we have been emphasizing is that the 'receiving' of the 'Spirit of adoption' is passive, and not active. It is not something which we are to 'take', still less are we to 'claim' it. Instead, we 'receive' it. The New Testament evidence is quite overwhelming on this matter. 'But what of Ephesians 5 : 18,' asks someone, 'where we have the injunction "Be filled with the Spirit"?' There is no difficulty about that, because the context presupposes that we have already received the Spirit. Ephesians 5 : 18 should be translated thus: 'Go on being filled with the Spirit.' You have received Him; well, do not grieve Him but go on being filled with Him. In any case Ephesians 5 : 18 refers to sanctification and not to the subject of assurance with which the Apostle is dealing here. The entire section which includes Ephesians 5 : 18 is part of the practical section of that Epistle; and it is concerned with holy living, with sanctification. It is not surprising that there should be confusion, because the very word 'filled' tends to cause confusion in and of itself. Here we are face to face with the whole problem of language. When you are baptized with the Spirit you are 'filled' with the Spirit; but you can be 'filled with the Spirit' in the sense of Ephesians 5 : 18 without being baptized by the Spirit. We ourselves are responsible for being filled with the Spirit, and the Apostle tells us in the passage in Ephesians how to do that. But we are not responsible for the baptism with the Spirit which is something that we receive in a passive manner; it is given to us.[1]

At this point I must mention the danger of introducing

[1] For a further exposition of this see my *Life in the Spirit* (Banner of Truth Trust 1974).

unconsciously into our minds an element of psychology, and in particular, that which goes by the name of Couéism. Coué introduced a way of helping people who suffer from some kind of neurosis or slight depression. Such people are not suffering from any organic disease, but they do not feel well. Couéism is a psychological system for curing such people. It just teaches them to say to themselves, 'Every day and in every way I am feeling (or getting) better and better'. Keep on saying that to yourselves, he told them, and you will soon begin to feel better. And it works! At any rate in certain cases. Such people do not really change their condition at all, but they persuade themselves that they are better, and they begin to feel better. I am suggesting that the teaching which comes to us and says, 'Take this promise because it is there in the Word of God; believe it; accept it; it doesn't matter whether you feel anything or not; just say, It must be so; I must have received it, because it is offered and I have "taken" it. I do not feel anything, I do not feel any different, but I must be different because it is promised.' 'Take it by faith'; say to yourself 'I have got it', thank God for it and go on your way rejoicing because you have it. I can see no difference between that teaching and Couéism. It appears to me to be nothing but sheer psychology; you are deliberately persuading yourself that you have something. You have no evidence that you have it; but you just go on telling yourself that you have it.

But this applies not only to Couéism, Cnristian Science does precisely the same thing. A man is suffering from an illness and they come to him and say: This is quite wrong, there is no such thing as matter, and therefore there can be no such thing as disease, and because there is no such thing as disease there can be no such thing as pain. If you only realize that, you will find yourself in perfect health. That, again, can be highly successful when people have nothing very much wrong with themselves. The principle, again, is self-suggestion; you are addressing yourself and bombarding yourself with an idea. And I can see no difference in principle between this and the teaching which says, 'Take it by faith; it doesn't matter whether you feel anything or not; just believe you have it and thank God for it'.

All this leads to the danger of giving us a false peace, a false sense of release, and a false sense of power. This is one of the most subtle forms in which the devil may work. In the name of

Christianity we may merely be persuading ourselves, and giving ourselves a kind of false peace. It is possible by sheer psychological means to have a kind of release which is entirely artificial, and also even a sense of power. Many businessmen – commercial travellers and others – who feel nervous and apprehensive go in for this treatment, this training, and they find that it gives them confidence and assurance. Hence we must examine this kind of teaching very carefully. Not only can I not fit it into the New Testament teaching, but it seems to me to belong to this other category.

But still worse, there is a real danger, that while you are persuading yourself that you 'have' the blessing of which Romans 8 : 15 speaks, in reality you have nothing at all. If this blessing is indeed given by God, nothing that we can do can ever give it to us; therefore, if we think that we have 'taken' it, we really have not taken anything, and are left with nothing but delusion. That is the most appalling danger of all.

Let me illustrate this matter by means of an analogy. The teaching that we take this blessing by faith belongs to the same category as that concerning physical healing, which is also popular at this present time. It claims that 'healing is in the atonement', and bases its claim on a statement in the Gospel according to St Matthew (8 : 17). We read that our Lord healed certain people, 'that it might be fulfilled which was spoken by the prophet Esaias, saying, Himself took our infirmities and bare our sicknesses'. It then goes on to argue that healing is in the atonement, and that if you believe in the atonement, if you believe that the Lord Jesus Christ died to save you from all your sin and weakness and sickness, and is your personal Saviour and Redeemer, then you should not suffer from any diseases. All you have to do is to take the promise by faith. He has promised to heal you, so go to Him. Take the promise, take the healing that He is offering you. But you may say, 'But I do not feel any different'. 'Of course not,' they reply, 'but that doesn't matter. What you feel is irrelevant. You must take this by faith; you have to believe His naked, His bare word that He will heal you. Do so, and thank Him for the healing which He has already given you, though you may feel no different; and soon you will begin to feel better.' This is an exact parallel with this other teaching about the fulness of the Spirit. But what happens? Tragic events sometimes!

I once knew a minister who was taken up with this teaching about faith-healing, as was his wife also. The poor woman developed a cancerous growth, and believing this teaching, they naturally would not even begin to consider the possibility of an operation. She was strongly advised to have one immediately, and told that there was a chance of a complete cure. But, in their view, to agree to an operation would be lack of faith. They went to a meeting held in St Martins in the Field and during the healing ceremony the woman went forward to be healed. There she accepted, she 'took this promise' of healing, and claimed that she had been healed. She immediately thanked God for it. She and her husband then went back to their church, made a public statement about what had happened, and repeated it in other places. But in less than three months the woman was dead.

I knew of another minister in a different part of the country in whose case exactly the same thing happened. Those concerned were so confident of the healing that they spoke about it in a meeting of ministers and deacons, and were chiding unbelievers for their lack of faith. In ten days' time the minister's wife was dead. She had 'taken her healing by faith'. She felt no different; she said so, she had taken it by faith. She had obeyed the injunction to believe, and to pay no attention to her feelings; and had been convinced that not to do so would be to dispute the Word of God. In a previous volume I have referred to a well-known instance of this same thing in the biography of the great Andrew Murray of South Africa.

I have given these illustrations because the teaching involved is based on precisely the same argument as is used in connection with 'receiving' the fulness of the Spirit. But there are those who say, 'I would not dream of saying these things in connection with healing, but I do say them about the fulness of the Spirit'. To them I reply that it is exactly the same principle in both cases. You 'take it by faith', you do not trouble yourself about your feelings; you thank God for it, believing that you must have it because you have believed. But the real truth may well be that you have nothing at all except some temporary psychological benefit. You cannot 'take' this blessing any more than you can 'take' physical healing, or than the Church can 'take' revival whenever she decides to do so. One of the great troubles in the Church today is due to the fact that there are so many people who have 'taken' so much 'by faith' that they know virtually nothing of the great spiritual experiences of the saints of past centuries.

This explains why there are so many unhappy people in our churches. For years they have been trying to persuade themselves that they have 'received' this blessing; and yet, when they really examine themselves in the light of the New Testament, they know that they have not got it. Hence whenever they hear a testimony or read a book about it they are in trouble again. They feel that they must have had it because they have 'taken' it; and yet they do not feel any different; and when they face the full content of the meaning of the words 'cry' and 'Abba, Father', they cannot honestly say that they have ever known that! Then they read books and biographies, such as we have already mentioned, and they realize that they have not 'received' what is proclaimed in them; so again they try to 'take it by faith' and, persuade themselves that they have it. Many spend a whole lifetime in that way; and they are unhappy and miserable. They go to meetings where this is 'offered'; they go forward to 'receive' it, and yet they never seem to have it. The 'take it' teaching is one of the most prolific causes of unhappiness in the Christian life, quite apart from the intellectual and spiritual confusion to which it leads.

But we must go yet further. I suggest very seriously that this teaching of 'take it by faith' is the greatest single hindrance to a true and deep experience of 'the Spirit of adoption whereby we cry, Abba, Father'. That is why I am so much concerned about it and have given it such attention in detail. It is a hindrance to a deep experience, of necessity, because it keeps Christians at a superficial level. It does so because it deliberately discourages self-examination. The moment you begin to ask yourself questions you are warned against doing so because thereby you are guilty of a lack of faith. You must not go back on the statement that you have 'taken it by faith'; you must not examine or question yourself. 'No', they say, 'do not do that; look to the Lord and abide in Him; hold on to your new position. It is the devil who is trying to tempt you, and to shake your faith'. The entire teaching forbids your examining yourself; you are strongly discouraged from looking into yourself at all. Thus you are insulated from ever receiving the real experience itself. Believing that you already have it, and believing that it is wrong even to question whether you have it, how can you possibly ever have it? That is why

I say it is the greatest single hindrance to a deep experience.

And, of course, having thus persuaded us that we have it, and that it is wrong even to raise a question about it, or to examine ourselves as to whether we have it or not, it then goes on to discourage us from ever seeking it. The man who has 'received' no longer seeks. But it is better to have nothing than to have a counterfeit. The publicans and the harlots went crowding into the kingdom of God before the Pharisees and scribes because the Pharisees and scribes thought they were already children of the Kingdom, (Matthew 21: 31, 32). They were the religious people, and they needed nothing! The Pharisee in the temple, depicted by our Lord in His parable, says: 'God, I thank thee, that I am not as other people are.' He has everything, so he does not ask for anything. There is nothing more dangerous than a counterfeit. False religion is the greatest danger of all. 'A half truth is a greater evil than a lie.' If there is an inadequate building on a site it must be knocked down and the rubble cleared away before the contractor can start building a new one. But if there is an empty site, a bare plot of ground, he is saved all that trouble and effort and expense. The task is much easier. I have already applied this analogy to the case before us.

Most serious thinkers will agree that the main trouble in the Church today – and I am speaking of evangelical churches in particular at this point – is the appalling superficiality. This is made very clear as we read the biographies of men who have lived in past centuries. Take, for example, the Journals of George Whitefield; read that man's experiences of the love of God and of Christ, and his love to them. How superficial most of us are by contrast! Why? Because we think we have 'taken it by faith'; and so do not examine ourselves. But what do we really have? Have we ever really cried 'Abba, Father' with a cry coming up from the depths of our being? That is what we should be saying; that is what the Spirit can enable us to say. Any teaching which prevents us from examining and searching ourselves, testing and proving ourselves, condemning our own superficiality, and from seeking for something bigger and deeper is of necessity condemned. And such is the invariable effect of the teaching which tells us to 'take it by faith and not to worry about our feelings', and to thank God for it, because we have taken it, and assume that all is well.

But let us now turn to the positive side of the truth. How is the blessing to be obtained which gives us 'the Spirit of adoption, whereby we cry, Abba, Father'? Recognition of the profound character of the experience must be our starting-point. We must recognize the full content of the important words used here. 'Cry', we must remember, is the word used of our Lord in the Garden of Gethsemane. With strong crying and tears he cried 'Abba, Father'. This, then, is a profound experience; it moves one to the very depths. As we have seen in the various chapters of the Acts of the Apostles which I have quoted, it is so profound and dynamic that all could see that it had happened to the people involved in it. There is nothing more profound. Let me quote some words spoken by Charles Haddon Spurgeon which will give us some impression of the depth of the experience. He said, 'May the Holy Spirit grant that we may not say a word which is not strictly verified by our experience'. He was preaching on this very theme which we are considering. He says, 'I do not want to say a word which has not been verified in my experience; but I hope we can say that we have had converse with the Divine Father. We have not seen Him at any time, nor have we beheld His shape. It has not been given to us like Moses to be put in the cleft of the rock and to see the back parts of the train of the invisible Jehovah. But yet we have spoken to Him, we have said to Him "Abba, Father"; we have saluted Him in that title which came from our very heart. "Our Father, who art in Heaven". We have had access to Him in such a way that we cannot have been deceived.' Spurgeon is not talking there about merely 'saying your prayers'; he is not talking about ordinary prayer, as we say. He says, 'I hope I am not exaggerating'. 'Yes', he continues, 'I can testify to this, I have spoken to Him in that particular manner. We have had access to Him in such a way that we cannot have been deceived about it, the thing really happened in this tremendous fashion. . . . We have found Him, and through the precious blood of Christ we have come even to His feet; we have ordered our cause before Him, and we have filled our mouth with arguments. Nor has the speaking been all on our side, for He has been pleased to shed abroad by His Spirit His love in our hearts. While we have felt the Spirit of adoption He on the other hand has shown to us the loving kindness of a tender Father. We have felt – though no sound was heard – we have known – though no angelic messenger gave us witness – that His Spirit did bear witness with our spirit that we were born of God. We were embraced of Him, no more at a distance.' Let me repeat that: 'We were embraced of Him, no more at a distance.' He had known what it was to be at a distance, and he had prayed and worshipped at a distance. No more at a distance now! 'We were embraced of Him, we were brought nigh by the blood of Jesus.' What a wonderful statement! That is how Spurgeon puts it.

Let me remind you of how Thomas Goodwin, one of the great Puritans of three hundred years ago, states the matter. He used a remarkable illustration. He pictures a man walking along a road with his little boy, holding hands – father and son, son and father. The little boy knows that this man is his father, and that his father loves him. But suddenly the father stops, picks up the boy, lifts him up into his arms, embraces him and kisses him and fondles him. Then he puts him down again, and they continue walking. The boy is no more a son when he is being embraced than he was before. The father's action has not changed the relationship; it has not changed the status of the boy; but oh, the difference in the enjoyment! It is a wonderful thing to be walking along holding your father's hand; but it is an incomparably greater thing to have his arms enfolded around you. 'He has embraced us', says Spurgeon, and He pours His love upon us and He 'fondles' us. That is what is described in Romans 8: 15; it is an extra, a plus. You can have assurance apart from this; this is the extra assurance. This is God making it certain; and it produces in us the response of our 'crying Abba, Father'. Let us realize, then the profound character of the experience. This is not light and superficial and ordinary; it is not something of which you can say, 'Don't worry about your feelings'. Worry about your feelings? You will have such a depth of feeling that for a moment you may well imagine that you have never 'felt' anything in your life before. It is the profoundest experience that a man can ever know. You cannot 'take this by faith'. If you know anything about it, you will realize that at once.

Secondly, we must realize that it is something which is 'given' and that we can neither 'take it' nor 'claim it'. It is God who gives this; and He gives it in His own time and in His own way. We receive it, that is all. He gives. And He decides when and how and where. Leave it all to Him. We must not talk about 'claiming' or 'taking'; it cannot be done. It is given, and ours is but a response to what He gives.

'Is there nothing for us to do?' asks someone. We must be very practical about this; so we begin by emphasizing what we are not to do. We are not to agonize for it. I have already mentioned how F. B. Meyer made light of the idea of agonizing. He referred to certain people in Keswick who had decided to have a long meeting to wait for the coming of the Spirit. He said, 'I could not wait and agonize; I went out for a walk on to the mountain and there I took it by faith. I felt nothing at all, but I just took it and thanked God for it.' He then ridiculed the other teaching by asking us to think of a man saying to his little girl who comes down to breakfast, 'Now little girlie, go upstairs and agonize and roll on the floor asking for food'. 'How nonsensical!' he says; 'she just comes down and sits at the table and takes it.' I am very happy at this point, but not for the same reason, to agree with F. B. Meyer that you do not have to agonize for this blessing. The New Testament does not tell us to do so.

Again, I do not believe in 'tarrying meetings'. They are not held very often today, but a hundred and fifty years ago they were very common indeed, and especially in Methodism. In 'tarrying meetings' people who desired this blessing met together and decided they would stay until they had it. They might stay for hours, they might stay through the night; sometimes they stayed a number of days. I do not accept that idea because I do not find it in the Scriptures. Not only so, I see there, again, the danger of the psychological element coming in. If you go to such a meeting saying that you are going to stay there until you get the experience, the probability is that something will happen to you, but you will not necessarily get this blessing. You may get a psychological experience which will be partly produced by your fatigue and tiredness and excitement, and by what other people are saying round and about you, and by all the singing and the shouting. Because this is 'received' passively you have no right to go to a 'tarrying meeting', and set a time limit, or postulate that it is going to happen at a given time. As it is the sovereign gift of God He determines the time as well as everything else.

My third negative is that you do not receive this by someone laying hands on you. There are many who teach that all you have to do is to go to certain people who, by laying their hands on you, can give you this gift. Now it is quite clear that the Apostles had that gift, and that, in New Testament times, it was confined to them. It was a part of their calling, their authority, and their uniqueness. In any case it did not happen in that way in the case of Cornelius and his house. While Peter was still preaching the Holy Spirit fell upon them. Not only so, but the whole subsequent history of the Christian Church shows that the laying on of hands is not the usual way. Take the notable cases of men who have suddenly received this extraordinary gift of God which has led to their crying 'Abba, Father'. Rarely, if ever, has it happened as the result of the laying on of hands. The case of Whitefield is doubtful, but in the case of the Wesleys and some of the great Puritans whom I have quoted, and others, in no instance is there any suggestion of the laying on of hands. Here again the psychological element tends to come in.

But we turn now to the positive aspect. What are we to do? If you really desire the blessing, prove that you do so by living a life of obedience. If a child wants a particular gift or object he immediately puts on his best behaviour. If he still believes in Santa Claus he is told by his parents that if he is not a good boy he will not be visited by him. If he is older and looks to his parents for gifts he does his utmost to please them. Of course! And it is exactly the same in our relationship to God. Do you really want to know God and Christ? Go out of your way to please Them. Do not expect to have the 'Spirit of adoption' while you are obeying and pleasing the devil. 'He that saith, I know Him, and keepeth not his commandments, is a liar, and the truth is not in him' (1 John 2: 4). If you desire this Spirit, show it in your life. Give every evidence you can. We always desire to please those whom we love.

Secondly we must pray for the blessing and seek it, expressing a longing for it. Surely that is what our Lord means in Luke 11: 13 and the parallel in Matthew 7: 7: 'Ask, and ye shall receive; seek, and ye shall find; knock, and it shall be opened unto you.' He is talking about the Holy Spirit. He encourages us by saying, 'If ye, being evil, know how to give good gifts unto your children, how much more shall your Father, which is in heaven, give the Holy Spirit to them that ask him?' So ask Him for it, and plead for it. That does not mean that as you ask you are receiving; all you do is to ask and plead with Him to give the Spirit to you. This thought is found in many of our hymns. The following English translation of one of the hymns of William Williams is typical:

> *Tell me Thou art mine, O Saviour,*
> *Grant me an assurance clear;*
> *Banish all my dark misgivings,*
> *Still my doubting, calm my fear.*

Have you ever used such words as these in prayer? Or take Charles Wesley's way of expressing it:

> *O Love Divine, how sweet Thou art!*
> *When shall I find my willing heart*
> *All taken up by Thee?*
> *I thirst, I faint, I die to prove*
> *The greatness of redeeming love,*
> *The love of Christ to me.*

Tell Him that that is your heart's desire! Or again,

> *God only knows the love of God;*
> *O that it now were shed abroad*
> *In this poor stony heart!*
> *For love I sigh, for love I pine:*
> *This only portion, Lord, be mine,*
> *Be mine this better part!*

Charles Wesley was an Arminian, but he and his brother John did not hold the teaching of 'take it by faith'. Charles Wesley knew he could not 'take it by faith'. All he can do is to 'sigh' for it – 'For love I sigh, for love I pine'. The other teaching began to be taught only about 1873, and it has been popular ever since. But the Wesleys and their fellow Methodists did not teach it. They knew that they could not 'take' the blessing, that it had to be given, and that all you can do is to ask, to cry for it, to sigh for it. There is no need to roll on the floor, and no special merit in doing so; but if once you have a glimpse of what this means you may very well find yourself groaning and agonizing. Those who know what true human love is, know what it is to groan and to agonize when separated from the object of their affection, or when they are doubtful of the love of those whom they love. Love causes them to sigh, to plead, to cry in that way which the Scripture indicates.

Or take a verse with which I was not familar until I found Spurgeon quoting it:

> *If in my Father's love*
> *I share a filial part,*
> *Send down Thy Spirit like a dove*
> *To rest upon my heart.*

Is not that beautiful! Observe the argument: 'If in my Father's love I share a filial part'. I believe I have the Spirit, I believe I am led by the Spirit; very well, 'I share a filial part'. Then the prayer, 'Send down Thy Spirit like a dove, to rest upon my heart'! That is what we can do. Let the Father know that we desire it; let Him know our longing. Let us say with the Psalmist, 'As the hart panteth after the water brooks, so panteth my soul after thee, O God' (Psalm 42: 1). I want 'the living God'; I want to know Him.

This is what is possible for us as Christians. This is real enjoyment of the Christian life – having 'the Spirit of adoption, whereby we cry, Abba, Father'. Not merely believing it, and persuading ourselves! We know it, we can be more certain of it than anything else. Let no one persuade you that you have this until you know you have it, because to have this Spirit is to know that you have it. Your heart will be melted, you will be filled with a 'joy unspeakable and full of glory', and you will feel an irresistible desire within you to cry out like a child 'Abba, Father'. You cannot take this by faith, and do it when you will; it is given by God, and it is one of the most wonderful things that can ever happen to anyone in this life, and in this world of time.

Twenty-three

*

The Spirit itself beareth witness with our spirit, that we are the children of God.   Romans 8: 16

In this 16th verse the Apostle takes one further step in demonstrating the grounds on which we can be certain and assured that we are 'children' or 'sons' of God. The first step was in the fourteenth verse, 'As many as are led by the Spirit of God, they are the sons of God'. If therefore we have evidence that we are being 'led by the Spirit of God' we are *ipso facto* sons of God. The second step was that we should know something about 'the spirit of bondage and of fear'. The next step is the positive one of knowing that the spirit of bondage and of fear has been removed, and that we have received 'the Spirit of adoption, whereby we cry, Abba, Father'. We have emphasized that these last two grounds of assurance are not essential to salvation. You can be 'led by the Spirit' without having 'the Spirit of adoption, whereby we cry, Abba, Father'. This last, we have suggested, is one of the profoundest experiences one can ever know, and we should all seek and covet it, and never be satisfied until we are rejoicing in it.

So we come to this ultimate step in verse 16: 'The Spirit itself beareth witness with our spirit, that we are the children of God'. This is, beyond any question, one of the most glorious statements concerning Christian experience found anywhere in the Bible from beginning to end. Nothing is more important from the standpoint of experience, from the standpoint of happiness and joy in the Christian life, from the standpoint of enjoying our great salvation. If it can be said that any one verse constitutes the hallmark of the evangelical Christian I would say that it is this one. It has always been dear to the hearts of evangelical Christians ever since the Protestant Reformation, for there is no other verse

[285]

which shows so clearly the difference between Protestantism and Romans Catholicism as this particular verse. The Roman Catholic teaching is opposed to the doctrine of assurance of salvation. Their teaching is that a Christian can never be sure of his salvation. That is why he has to leave himself in the hands of the Church and the priests. Not only can he not be sure of it in this life, but according to their teaching there is even uncertainty beyond death, and he has to pass through purgatory still needing the assistance and the ministrations of the church and of the saints. This verse therefore reminds us in a striking manner of the essential difference between the slavish spirit of Roman Catholicism, and the 'liberty of the Spirit' which is, I say, the hallmark of true Protestantism.

Ever since Martin Luther had his crucial climactic experience, this verse has always been very prominent in Protestant witness, and therefore in true evangelical preaching and teaching. It is particularly important at the present time, in view of the teaching which goes under the name of Barthianism, which also denies the doctrine of assurance of salvation. There is no certainty, no assurance in the Barthian teaching; and it is at this point that we see most clearly that that teaching cannot be regarded as evangelical in the true Protestant and Reformed sense. Any teaching that denies assurance and the certain knowledge of salvation in this life automatically does not fit in with the traditional Reformed evangelical teaching. This verse was also in many ways the key verse of the great Evangelical Awakening of two hundred years ago. The great emphasis in that Awakening – and what I am saying is as true of Wesley's preaching as it was of Whitefield's and the rest of the Methodist – was on 'assurance of salvation'. Assurance was the peculiar note that they introduced; and they were not satisfied with anything less. If then we can get hold of this doctrine, and experience it in our lives, we shall not only be in the great Protestant Evangelical Tradition, we shall also have arrived at one of the highest heights, if not the highest of all, of Christian experience. This is what has been true of God's people always in every time of revival and reawakening. Whenever there is a revival in the Church there is always great certainty and assurance of salvation. At the same time there is much talk about the Spirit and about 'the witness of the Spirit'. The testimonies given by church members in a time of revival conform to a definite pattern. They say that they have been church members, perhaps for many years, and have hopefully deduced their salvation from the Scriptures. But, suddenly, in the revival they are given this inner assurance of the Spirit, which transforms the whole of their lives. For a while they even begin to question and to doubt whether they have actually been Christians before. The change is so marked, so striking, so moving, that it almost seems to them as if they have now been converted for the first time.

As we begin our exposition there are one or two preliminary, more or less mechanical points which we must take up. The Authorized Version reads: 'The Spirit itself beareth witness'. Those who do not believe in the Person of the Holy Spirit always point to this statement in defence of their position. They say that the Spirit is only an influence, and that if the Spirit were a person the translation would be 'The Spirit Himself'. The answer is that the word 'spirit' in the Greek is a neuter word, and it is a rule in the Greek language that the personal pronoun always must agree with its antecedent in gender. Therefore, as the word 'spirit' is neuter, so the personal pronoun becomes neuter also. And the translators of the Authorized Version, at this point adhering very closely to grammar, and not paying as much attention as they normally do to the sense and the teaching of other parts of Scripture, quite mechanically translated it as 'itself'. But while that is strictly accurate from the purely linguistic standpoint, it is actually wrong as a translation, for the Scripture everywhere speaks about the Holy Spirit as a Person, and He is indeed the third Person in the blessed Holy Trinity. We must not digress by quoting various Scriptures to prove this statement. Let it suffice to say that our Lord refers to the Spirit as 'another Comforter', and says: 'When he is come he will lead you into all truth'; he will convict the world of sin and of righteousness and of judgment'. In verse 14 we have already seen that 'As many as are led by the Spirit of God, they are the sons of God'. And in this sixteenth verse the Apostle is still dealing with the Holy Spirit. So a better translation would be, 'The Spirit himself beareth witness with our spirit, that we are the children of God'.

Next we must examine the expression 'beareth witness'. This brings us to the very crux of the exposition of this verse. The actual word used by the Apostle means 'the bearing of a joint witness' or 'the bearing of a joint testimony with some other person'. So what the Apostle is saying is that the Holy Spirit Himself bears witness with us, 'with our spirit'. The Person of the Spirit bears joint witness with us as persons to the effect that we are the children of God. I remind you that in verse 15 the Apostle has been telling us of the witness that is borne by 'our' spirits, which cry 'Abba, Father'. That is *our* side, the witness in *our* spirits that we are the children of God. We have that filial spirit, and we witness to it. But, here, Paul says that the Holy Spirit bears His witness alongside our witness. He comes alongside us and He bears His witness jointly with our spirits, 'that we are the children of God'.

But, to complete this mechanical part of the exposition, let us look at the word 'children'. We have seen in verses 14 and 15 that the term used is 'sons' – 'As many as are led by the Spirit of God, they are the sons of God'; and in verse 15 Paul talks about a filial spirit. But suddenly he changes the word, and in verse 16 it is not 'sons' but 'children'. Why did the Apostle make this change? What is the exact difference in connotation between the two expressions? 'Son' is more or less a legal term, as we saw when we were discussing the matter. The whole notion of adoption is concerned with the legitimacy of our filial position. The word 'children', on the other hand, represents the inner reality of the filial relationship which we enjoy. When we look at the relationship from the standpoint of feeling we say 'children'; and when we look at it in terms of our legal standing we say 'sons'. But – and I am concerned to make this plain – that does not mean that there is any essential difference between the two terms.

I emphasize the point because there is a teaching which has had a certain limited popularity in recent years to the effect that there is an essential difference between being 'sons' and being 'children'. It teaches that all Christians are 'children' of God but that all Christians are not 'sons' of God. What makes the difference is that some Christians become 'sons' of God through the exercise of a faith that fights and that conquers. The general run of Christians are only 'children', but those Christians, those children, who have been fighting the fight of faith truly, and who have been conquering and prevailing, become sons of God in addition. The advocates of this teaching base it partly on the Revised Version translation of Matthew 5: 9, which reads: 'Blessed are the peacemakers; for they shall be called sons of God.' All

Christians, they say, are not peacemakers, but if you become a peacemaker, then you become a 'son' of God. And again, in Matthew 5 : 45: 'That ye may be sons of your Father which is in heaven.' That is to say, if you, like your Father, 'love your enemies, do good to them that hate you' and so on, then you become a 'son' of God. If you do not, you remain as a 'child' of God only. They also quote Luke 20: 36, where we are told that Christians are 'sons of God, being sons of the resurrection'.

This fantastic teaching not only asserts that you can be a child of God without being a son of God; it goes further and says that it is only the sons who will be with Christ and take part in the first resurrection when He comes; and it is they alone who will be with Him in heaven. The children will be left on earth, but the sons will be with Him eternally in heaven. The teachers of this doctrine make an essential difference between being children and being sons; and they go so far as to say that it is a difference that will be maintained throughout eternity. They add various other elements also to their teaching. They say that in their churches (though they do not seem to believe in an organized church) certain portions of 'higher' teaching can only be given to the sons; the children are not fit to receive it. They make a cleavage between Christian and Christian, not only in time, but also in eternity.

The answer to such a teaching is found in this section we are studying. Very obviously in verses 14, 15, and 16, the Apostle is talking about precisely the same people. He says that all who are 'led by the Spirit of God' – and you cannot be a Christian without that leading – are 'sons of God.' He does not say that they are but children only, and that those who have this further assurance become 'sons'. He uses the term 'sons' of all Christians. Indeed it is clear that he uses these terms interchangeably. In verse 17 he actually says, 'If children, then heirs'. 'Heirship' is something that belongs to sons, but there he uses it about 'children', not about 'sons'. 'If children, then heirs; heirs of God, and joint-heirs with Christ.' It is clear that to the Apostle Paul the terms are interchangeable. In Ephesians 1 : 5 we find exactly the same thing; he talks about our receiving the 'adoption of children'. Not the 'adoption of sons', but the adoption of children. The only difference is, as I say, that between looking at it from a legal standpoint or from the standpoint of feeling and inner experience. In Galatians 3 : 26, again in the Revised Version, there is the same idea: 'For in Christ Jesus ye are all sons of God, through faith'. Here is a specific statement that all Christians are sons of God. Not merely some, not only certain exceptional people – all are 'sons of God'. We have exactly the same again in Galatians 4: 6 and 7. For a final proof of our contention we note that the Apostle John in his writings – in the Gospel and the Epistles – does not use the term 'sons' at all (in the Greek original), he only uses the word 'children'. So if we were to accept this curious teaching we would have to believe that the Apostle John did not know of this 'advanced' teaching about the difference between 'children' and 'sons'.

Such are the fatuities of which Christian people can quite sincerely and honestly be sometimes guilty. They go beyond the Scripture to such an extent that they ultimately deny the Scripture. All Christians are children of God, all Christians are sons of God. The Apostle changes the word simply to show that he is now looking at it from a more experimental standpoint instead of the more legal standpoint. In verses 14 and 15 he has his eye on the inheritance, as also is the case in Ephesians 1: 13 and 14, and in many other passages. But, here, he is concerned with our inner experience, our inner consciousness of all this. But in verse 17 he again links it up with the inheritance and our being 'joint-heirs with Christ'.

Having looked at the terms let us come to what is really the vital aspect of the teaching. 'The Spirit bears witness (a joint witness) with our spirit.' We must be most careful here, because if we adopt certain interpretations, I suggest that we shall be robbing this great verse of its central essential glory.

Let us start with the negative aspect. I do so by quoting certain authorities. I hope to quote certain other authorities on the other side after I have given the positive exposition. Dr James Denney, a well-known Scottish theologian of the end of the last and the beginning of the present century, says, 'In that we cry Abba, Father, the Spirit itself beareth witness with our spirit.' He adds, 'Our own spirit tells us we are God's children, but the voice with which it speaks is, as we know, prompted and inspired by the divine Spirit itself'. We cry 'Abba, Father', in our spirits; ah yes! but what makes us do that? Denney says that it is the Holy Spirit. In other words our crying 'Abba, Father' is 'the Spirit bearing witness with our spirit'. So according to Dr Denney, this 16th verse is simply an explanation of verse 15. It is the Apostle's explanation of how it is that any one of us should ever cry out 'Abba, Father'. There is nothing additional here; there is no independent witness of the Spirit. I suggest that such an interpretation is of necessity wrong, and that the Apostle is not simply telling us how it is that we come to cry 'Abba, Father'. He is actually saying that we, in our spirit, cry 'Abba, Father', but in addition to that, the Spirit Himself also bears witness with our spirits. There is something additional to our spirit, namely, the witness of the Holy Spirit. As we proceed we shall find that this is a most important and vital point.

Next, let us turn to Bishop Handley G. Moule, a contemporary of Dr Denney, and a well-known evangelical commentator. He says almost exactly the same thing. This is all he has to say: 'The Holy One, on His part, makes the once cold, reluctant, apprehensive heart "know and believe the love of God." He "sheds abroad God's love in it". He brings home to consciousness and insight the "sober certainty" of the promises of the Word; that Word through which, above all other means, He speaks. He shows to the man "the things of Christ", the Beloved, in whom he has the adoption and the regeneration; making him see, as souls see, what a paternal welcome there *must* be for those who are "in Him". And then, on the other part, the believer meets Spirit with spirit. He responds to the revealed paternal smile with not merely a subject's loyalty but a son's deep love – deep, reverent, tender, genuine love. "Doubtless thou art His own child", says the Spirit; "doubtless He is my Father", says our wondering, believing, seeing spirit in response.' That again, is surely inadequate for the same reason; that it is nothing but a statement to the effect that the Spirit enlightens us as to the way of salvation – as to our sinfulness, to the sufficiency of Christ, and to our being in Him. But that is not the Apostle's theme at this point. He has told us in verse 14: 'As many as are led by the Spirit of God, they are the sons of God', and the Spirit leads us to the understanding of verse 16, which is not just a repetition of verse 14, and does not refer merely to the enlightening, converting work of the Spirit, nor even to His work in regeneration. It is something further, something additional to the foregoing.

Take also the exposition of another famous expositor of last century, Dr Henry Alford. He writes: 'What is this witness of the Spirit itself? All have agreed, and indeed this verse is decisive for it, that it is something separate from and higher than all our own inferences and conclusions. But on the other hand it does not consist in mere indefinite feeling, but in a certitude of the Spirit's presence and work continually asserted within us.' I reject that for the same reason. Alford simply takes us back to verse 9, 'If any man have not the Spirit of Christ, he is none of his', and verse 14, 'As many as are led by the Spirit of God, they are the sons of God'. He only means that a man knows the Spirit of God is in him, he knows when he is led to prayer, he has joy in the reading of the Scripture, and responds favourably to the various tests we have suggested. So according to Alford verse 16 is nothing but a repetition of verse 14, and does not even rise to the level of verse 15.

A similar comment applies to the exposition of a famous German commentator of last century, Olshausen who writes: 'It is manifested' – that is to say this testimony of the Spirit with our spirit – 'it is manifested in His comforting us, His stirring us up to prayer, His reproof of our sins, His drawing us to works of love, to bear testimony before the world, etc. On this direct testimony of the Holy Ghost rests ultimately all the regenerate man's conviction respecting Christ and His work.' But that is simply to expound verse 14 again, and to be 'led by the Spirit'. It is a very good exposition of verse 14, and the 'leading' of the Spirit. But the Apostle is not concerned here with the leading of the Spirit but with 'the Spirit bearing witness alongside of our spirits that we are the children of God'. Olshausen evacuates this verse of its central glory.

A contemporary commentator, Floyd E. Hamilton, writes thus: 'Whenever we know in our hearts that we are trusting only in Jesus Christ and His atoning work of salvation, whenever we know that we love Him because He first loved us, then we have the inner consciousness given us by the Holy Spirit Himself that we are children of God because He has told us so in His Word.' I reject that for exactly the same reason, for it takes us back to the 9th verse, the 14th verse and the 15th verse. It makes of verse 16 nothing but an explanation of what the Apostle has already told us, and does not add anything to our knowledge of the truth.

The great Dr Thomas Chalmers who led the Disruption from

the Church of Scotland in 1843 to form the Free Church of Scotland, in his *Lectures on the Epistle to the Romans* – a most valuable work – is lamentably weak at this point. He says, 'It is He who hath brought the Word nigh and given it weight and significance to my understanding; and it is He who has manifested to me the thoughts and intents of my own heart and evinced some personal characteristic within that is coincident with the promise without, and it is He who sustains me in the work of making a firm and confident application.' Now all that is simply the Spirit's work in conviction of sin and in conversion; it is but to go back to the early chapters of this Epistle. The Apostle had dealt with that before we come to the beginning of chapter 5. Chalmers interprets this verse as going back to that original work of the Spirit in conviction and conversion. He continues, 'In all this He utters no voice. The Word of God made plain to my conviction, and His own work upon me made plain to my conscience – these are the vocables, and I do imagine the only vocables, by which He expresses Himself: but enough to furnish any Christian with a reason for the hope that is in him, and better than articulation itself to solace and to satisfy the inquiring spirit of its relationship to the family of God.' 'Just enough', he says, 'better than articulation to solace and to satisfy the inquiring spirit of its relationship to the family of God.' Again, this is quite inadequate, for the Apostle is speaking here of a degree of assurance that makes one more sure of this than of anything else in life. It is an absolute assurance, not a mere 'solace', not a mere something that 'satisfies the inquiring spirit of its relationship to the family of God'. Another excellent commentator and preacher of the last century, Dr Octavius Winslow, also falls into the same category of exposition. He quotes the passage from Chalmers and expresses his entire agreement with it.

My contention is that all these interpretations are utterly inadequate, that they do not add anything new, that they do not bring out the vital point that the Spirit 'comes alongside' our spirit to 'witness with us'. In other words they all simply say that it is the Spirit who enables us to believe and to live the Christian life. That of course is true, but it is not enough. The Apostle's statement goes much further.

Even Dr Charles Hodge is not very helpful. He is indefinite; and I find it difficult to know what he is saying. This is what he actually says: 'Beareth witness, together with our own filial feelings, to our spirit. "Beareth witness to" means *confirms* or *assures*.' Then he says: 'The Spirit of God produces in our spirit the assurance that we are the children of God.' There, I suggest, he is entirely wrong; for that is just to use verse 16 as an explanation of verse 15. But the Apostle does not say in verse 16 that 'the Spirit of God produces in our spirits the assurance that we are the children of God', for he has said that most definitely in verse 15; He is not repeating himself, but asserting that, in addition, 'the Spirit himself also' – in addition to this witness which we have in our own spirits – 'bears his witness to our relationship to God'.

Next we turn to Robert Haldane who at this point is altogether superior to Charles Hodge. He leads us to the door of entry to an understanding of this great statement. Haldane says that this statement about the Spirit bearing witness with our spirits 'is not merely the fruits of the Holy Spirit in the lives of believers which afford this testimony, but the Spirit Himself by imparting filial confidence, inspires it in the heart'. He says that this is not a mere statement that the Holy Spirit by producing the 'fruits of the Spirit' in us enables us to arrive at the deduction that we are the children of God, but that this is a testimony of the Spirit Himself. Here are further excellent statements by Haldane: 'We have the testimony of our spirit when we are convinced of our sinfulness, misery and ruin, and of our utter inability to relieve ourselves from the curse of the broken law, and are at the same time convinced of the righteousness of Christ, and of our dependence upon Him for acceptance with God. We have this testimony when we possess the consciousness of cordially acquiescing in God's plan of salvation, and of putting our trust in Christ; and when we are convinced that His blood is sufficient to cleanse us from all sin.' In all this, he continues, 'the Holy Spirit enables us to ascertain our sonship from being conscious of, and discovering in ourselves, the true marks of a renewed state. But to say that this is all that is signified by the Holy Spirit's testimony would be falling short of what is affirmed in this text, for in that case the Holy Spirit would only help the conscience to be a witness, but could not be said to be a witness Himself, even another witness besides the conscience, which the text asserts.' In that statement Haldane answers all the other expositions which I have quoted, and says in his own excellent manner what I have been trying to say. 'What we learn therefore from it', he goes on to say, 'is that the Holy Spirit testifies to our spirit in a distinct and immediate testimony, and also with our spirit in a concurrent testimony. This testimony, although it cannot be explained, is nevertheless felt by the believer. It is felt by him, too, in its variations, as sometimes stronger and more palpable, and at other times more feeble and less discernible.' Again, 'This witnessing of the Spirit to the believer's spirit, communicating consolation, is never His first work but is consequent on His other work of renovation'. The other expositions took us back to the first work of the Spirit. But, as Haldane says, this work is subsequent to regeneration. 'He first gives faith, and then seals.' Then Haldane quotes from Ephesians 1 : 13 : ' "After that ye believed ye were sealed with that Holy Spirit of promise". He also witnesseth with our spirit, graciously shining on His own promises, making them clear, assuring us of their truth, enabling our spirit to embrace them and to discover our interest in them'. In other words, Robert Haldane holds the view that the sealing of the Spirit is always subsequent to belief, and regeneration, and faith. It is a subsequent work of the Spirit to seal the faith of the believer. Thus Haldane confirms my suggestion that in Romans 8 : 16 we have another way of stating the doctrine of the 'sealing of the Spirit'.

So far we have only been able to clear the ground, or, as it were, to prepare the way. But we have already had a hint of what this glorious statement really means. We can now go on to expound it positively and I shall quote certain statements of some of the great authorities on this particular aspect of Truth. 'The Spirit beareth witness with [jointly with] our spirit, that we are the children of God.'

Twenty-four

*

The Spirit itself beareth witness with our spirit, that we are the children of God.

Romans 8: 16

As we come to our positive exposition of this great statement I suggest that we must do so in the light of two main considerations. First, we must follow a rule that should always be observed in interpreting Scripture, namely, that we should interpret Scripture by Scripture. We should always look for parallel statements. That is a sound and cardinal principle of exegesis and of exposition. If we are not quite clear as to the meaning of a statement we should look for parallel statements. In this case we find such a statement in St. John's Gospel chapter 7, verses 37 to 39, where we read: 'In the last day, that great day of the feast, Jesus stood and cried, saying, If any man thirst, let him come unto me and drink. He that believeth on me, as the scripture hath said, out of his belly [his inward parts] shall flow rivers of living water. (But this spake he of the Spirit, which they that believe on him should receive: for the Holy Ghost was not yet given; because that Jesus was not yet glorified.)' Dealing as we are, in this 16th verse, with the work of the Holy Spirit we go back to that statement in John chapter 7, where we find a prophecy concerning the coming of the Spirit, and His effect upon believers. They will know complete satisfaction. Not only so, but they will become the means of blessing to large numbers of other people.

Another important parallel statement is one which we have already met in this very Epistle in chapter 5, verse 5, where the Apostle said, ' . . because the love of God is shed abroad in our hearts by the Holy Ghost which is given unto us'. When we dealt with that verse we were at pains to emphasize the 'shedding abroad'. It is not a description of a man just managing to persuade himself that the love of God is in him. It does not mean our love to God, it means God's love to us. In other words it is a description of a man who is 'flooded' with a consciousness of the love of God. The term 'shed abroad' suggests a profusion, an amplitude.

The same emphasis is found in the account of what happened on the day of Pentecost (Acts, chapter 2). The disciples had been fearful, and apprehensive, and uncertain, after the death of our Lord, and even His resurrection appearances, though they had brought them comfort, and a certain amount of understanding, had not produced the vital transforming effect that obviously took place on the day of Pentecost. From then on they are entirely different men; they were 'baptized with (or by) the Holy Ghost'. The same thing is repeated in chapter 4 of Acts, where we are told that the place where they were assembled together was shaken and 'they were all filled with the Holy Ghost, and they spake the word of God with boldness' (vv. 23–33). Another illustration is found in Acts 8 in the account of what happened to the Samaritans who had believed after Peter and John had gone down from Jerusalem and prayed for them and laid their hands upon them. And again in chapter 10, we find the case of Cornelius and his household. Finally, there is the case of the 'disciples' at Ephesus on whom the Apostle Paul laid hands, and they were filled and baptized with the Spirit (chapter 19).

All these, I suggest, are examples of what we are dealing with here in Romans 8 : 16. Take also what we find in the Book of Revelation chapter 2, verse 17: 'He that hath an ear, let him hear what the Spirit saith unto the churches. To him that overcometh will I give to eat of the hidden manna, and will give him a white stone, and in the stone a new name written, which no man knoweth saving he that receiveth it'; which, I maintain, is only another way of saying what the Apostle says here in this 16th verse. The same idea is found in the 28th verse of Revelation chapter 2: 'And I will give him the morning star'. We need not here be concerned with the exact meaning of the symbolism which is used in the Book of Revelation. All I am indicating is that we are told in the verses I have quoted that the people who have obeyed and pleased the Lord, will be given tokens of His good pleasure represented by 'the hidden manna', 'the white stone', and 'the morning star'. Then in the 3rd chapter of the same Book, in the message to the Church at Philadelphia (verse 12), we find a similar idea: 'Him that overcometh will I make a pillar in the temple of my God, and he shall go no more out: and I will write upon him the name of my God, and the name of the city of my God, which is new Jerusalem, which cometh down out of heaven from my God: and I will write upon him my new name.' This further promise falls into the same category; it is given to believers, to members of the Christian Church. They will be given something extra, something special, 'the name of my God', 'the name of the city of my God', 'my new name'. They will be quite certain that they belong to God and to the Lord Jesus Christ, that their eternal destiny is secure, and that they will be given some very special assurance and seal of their position, and of their relationship to God.

Those passages help us to understand Romans 8: 16, and there are others. Is it not clear to anyone who reads the New Testament without prejudice, that the early Christians, speaking generally, had a spiritual experience, and insight and understanding, which distinguishes them in a very striking manner from the vast majority of Christians at the present time? Take, for instance, what Peter, writing to ordinary members of the Church, says in the first chapter of his First Epistle: 'Whom having not seen, ye love; in whom, though now ye see him not, yet believing, ye rejoice with joy unspeakable and full of glory' (v. 8). Those words were written to ordinary members of the Christian Church, and they seem to have been characteristic of the life of the members of the early Church. Such a background helps us to understand and to interpret this verse: 'The Spirit himself beareth witness with our spirit, that we are the children of God.'

Our second consideration must be the light that is thrown on this text by the subsequent history of the Christian Church. This again is a very valuable aid in interpreting a statement of Scripture. If we bring all Scripture down to the level of our own experience and understanding today we shall often rob it of some of its greatest glories. But if we look at the long history of the Christian Church, and pay attention to certain things that are to be seen in individuals, and in groups of churches, and perhaps in a whole country, at times, we shall be given an insight into what we have in this verse. In other words, if you are in doubt about the meaning of such a verse as this, do not reduce it to something that may be true in your own experience and limit it to that; read the lives of the saints, read the story of certain unusual people who have adorned the Church of God, and listen to what they have to say. I propose to give several quotations in order to illustrate what I mean. Some have had experiences of which they do not hesitate to say, 'At that moment the Spirit Himself bore witness with my spirit that I am a child of God'.

But in addition to individual experiences we have the phenomenon of great revivals. Revivals, and the history of revivals, are most important in this context. In such histories we read of people who have been members of churches, perhaps for years. They had believed on the Lord Jesus Christ and they had a measure of assurance of salvation; but when the revival came, when the Spirit of God was poured down upon them, what happened to them was so marvellous that they began to think that up to that time they had never been Christians at all. They were suddenly given an absolute certainty and assurance of their relationship to God which they had never had before. That, it seems to me, is the very thing we have in the verse we are studying. So, in addition to the Scriptures which point directly to this particular operation of the Holy Spirit, we have this extraordinary confirmation in the lives of saints, and in the whole history of the Church at periods of revival, when the Spirit of God is poured out in an unusual manner and in great profusion, and when numbers of people together suddenly come into this place of assurance and of clarity of knowledge and of understanding.

So taking these two great canons of interpretation, at what conclusion do we arrive? The first conclusion is that this is obviously something that is done by the Holy Spirit Himself. The Apostle chose to put it in this way: 'The Spirit Himself beareth witness.' Why did he not simply say: 'The Spirit beareth witness,' or 'The Spirit also beareth witness with our spirit'? He deliberately said 'The Spirit Himself beareth witness', as if to safeguard us against the very errors we have considered and to make it clear to us that he is not concerned here with the witness of the 'work' of the Spirit in us but with the Person of the Spirit Himself witnessing to us, and with our spirits – which is a very different thing. We have already seen, in verse 14, what the work of the Spirit is, and that it is a 'witness'. We have seen in verse 15, still more strikingly, that it is when the Spirit comes into our hearts that we in our own spirits have the Spirit of adoption. That again is part of the work of the Spirit. But here, Paul emphasizes that he is not dealing with such work of the Spirit, but with what the Spirit Himself does directly.

It is the witness and the testimony of the Holy Spirit Himself confirming the witness of our own spirits. Our own spirits cry 'Abba, Father', and they thereby witness to the fact that we are the children of God. We have a child-like spirit, a filial spirit within us. My own spirit tells me that I am a child of God, and I feel towards God as a child feels towards its father. But here, the Spirit Himself comes alongside the witness of my Spirit and Himself bears His witness and His testimony. In other words the peculiar characteristic of what is described here is that it is a direct and an immediate witness of the Spirit Himself.

I suggest that this is a part of the 'baptism with the Holy Ghost', or, if you prefer it, the 'baptism of the Holy Spirit'. That is why I referred to John 7: 37 to 39, and Acts 2 and so on. Indeed I go further and say that what Paul is describing is the most essential aspect of 'the baptism of the Holy Ghost'. We said, when dealing with verse 15, that the 'Spirit of adoption' is a part of the baptism with the Holy Ghost, but that, as I have just been indicating, is really a preliminary part of that baptism. We cannot be baptized with the Holy Ghost without having the Spirit of adoption, but we can have the Spirit of adoption without knowing this further experience. That is why I say that the most vital and essential part, the essence, of being baptized with the Holy Ghost, is that we have this particular form of assurance of our sonship of God.

I do not hesitate to say also that this is the same as the 'sealing' of the Spirit. There are three references to the 'sealing' of the Spirit in the New Testament. One is in the Second Epistle to the Corinthians, chapter 1, verse 22, where we are told: 'God, who hath also sealed us, and given the earnest of the Spirit in our hearts'. Another is found in Ephesians 1, verse 13, which reads: 'In whom ye also trusted, after that ye heard the word of truth, the gospel of your salvation: in whom also after that ye believed' – or, a better translation, 'in whom also having believed' – 'ye were sealed with that Holy Spirit of promise'. The third reference is in Ephesians 4: 30: 'And grieve not the Holy Spirit of God, whereby ye are sealed unto the day of redemption.' These statements have a direct bearing upon the interpretation of this verse, and I suggest that they refer to exactly the same thing. In other words, the Spirit Himself seals these promises to us and thereby testifies with our spirits as to our sonship.

There is obviously a difference between the 'sealing' and the 'earnest', and the difference helps us to understand our verse. Both the sealing and the earnest are concerned with the question of our inheritance, but they are interested in it in a different way. The sealing of the Spirit is that which assures me that I am a son of God, and therefore an heir of God. The earnest of the Spirit gives me an instalment of my inheritance, a first down-payment of what I am later to receive in its fulness. If you buy a house, for example, and you do not have sufficient money to pay for it, you pay the seller an agreed lesser amount saying, 'I give you this as an earnest that I will pay the remainder; I pay this on account, as a deposit'. That is to say, you pay him an earnest. It can also be thought of as a foretaste, or the first-fruits of a harvest, a portion of a fulness that is to come. The 'sealing' and the 'earnest' are both concerned with sonship, and especially with 'heirship', the earnest being that which is given to us 'until (the time of) the redemption of the purchased possession' (Ephesians 1 : 14). The sealing is more directly concerned with giving me assurance as to my sonship. So I assert that Romans 8 : 16 is just another way of stating the doctrine of the 'sealing of the Spirit'. Verse 17 goes on to speak of the inheritance.

What are the characteristics of this action of the Spirit Himself? The first is that the Spirit by a direct operation on our minds and hearts and spirits gives us an absolute certainty and assurance of our sonship. That is the great reality. It is not merely that He gives us a heightening of our understanding of the truth, neither is it merely that we are unusually conscious of being led in the direction of sanctification, or that the Spirit promotes our sanctification. We have dealt with that in verse 14. This particular action of the Spirit Himself must never be confused with sanctification. That, alas, was the error which was introduced by John Wesley, and which has persisted ever since. This is not sanctification. It helps in, and promotes our sanctification, but it is not sanctification itself. It is the Spirit telling us in this unusual way that we are the children of God. He lets us know in a way we have never known before that God loves us; as Romans 5 : 5 has stated it, 'The love of God is shed abroad in our hearts'. That is what the 'sealing' means, and we must never confuse it with sanctification. Obviously a man who knows this has the greatest possible stimulus to become sanctified; but it is not sanctification itself. This leads us to greater efforts in connection with our sanctification.

Yet again, this witness which the Spirit bears with our spirit is not only different from, and additional to, the 'Spirit of adoption', it goes well beyond it. That is the real crux of the matter; it takes us into a realm entirely beyond the other. Let me use an illustration from the realm of human love. It is a wonderful thing to tell someone whom you love that you love him or her, but still more wonderful is the experience of being told by the other that he or she loves you. That is the greatest desire and yearning of every lover, and it is the exact difference here. In verse 15 we tell God that we love Him. We have 'the Spirit of adoption, whereby we cry, Abba, Father', the child's cry of love to the Father. Ah, but here it is God, through the Spirit, telling us that He loves us, and doing so in a most unmistakable manner. It is personal and secret. Our quotations from the Book of Revelation emphasized the point that no one knows this but the one who receives it. It is a 'hidden manna', it is 'a white stone with a name that no one knows but the one to whom it is given'. He knows. 'I will give him the morning star' has the same message. It is a secret, known only to those to whom it is given –

> *The love of Jesus, what it is,*
> *None but His loved ones know.*

Furthermore, this is the highest form of assurance possible; there is nothing beyond it. It is the acme, the zenith of assurance and certainty of salvation! I emphasize my assertion by saying, negatively, that this is not a deduction. There is a form of assurance which is derived by deduction from the Scriptures. That is the form of assurance which most Christians seem to have, and many believe that it is the only form of assurance. They say, 'Are you troubled about your salvation? You need not be; it is quite simple. Do you believe that the Bible is the Word of God?' 'Yes, I do,' you reply. 'Very well, what does it say?' 'It says "He that believeth is not condemned".' 'Do you believe that?' 'Yes'? 'Well then, you are not condemned. The Word tells you so, and you have just to take God's Word for it.' They then take you through a number of similar passages which tell you that, if you believe, you are accepted and forgiven – 'Not condemned' and 'have passed from death to life'. They say, 'There the Scripture tells you plainly to believe, and if you do, you can have full assurance.' I am not concerned to criticize this method. As far as it goes, it is right. If we do not believe the Word of God we make God a liar. We must not listen to the devil and his accusations when the Word of God tells us a thing quite plainly. It is right to have that assurance of salvation which is derived by deductions from plain, explicit statements of the Scripture. But this is only the first, and the lowest form of assurance. Thank God for it; it will often hold your soul in times of satanic assaults. But you do not end there; that is only the beginning.

Secondly, what we have here in Romans 8 : 16 is also not what we deduce about ourselves when we apply to our lives, and our experiences, the various tests which are given us in the Scriptures. In our study of verse 14 we looked at ten such tests. They are summarized very clearly in the First Epistle of John. 'We know that we have passed from death to life, because we love the brethren' (1 John 3 : 14). In other words, I would say that if you enjoy meetings of Christian people above all others you must be a Christian. That is one of the tests. The next time the devil tells you that you are not a Christian, face him with this question – 'Explain to me how it is that I enjoy these things? Why do I prefer the society of Christian people to the best society I can find anywhere in the world which is not Christian? Why do I love the brethren? Why do I desire to keep God's commandments? Why do I desire to be holy? Where does it all come from?' You are deducing thereby from statements in the Scripture applied to your life and experience, the fact that you are a child of God. That takes you a step further than the first one; it is better than the first one. The first was merely believing the bare Word of God. But now you have examined your life and you are sure that you are not merely saying these things in a theoretical or intellectual manner; you are really living them. That is the second step.

But then there is a third step, that which we found in verse 15. I remind you of this, once more, in order to show how the Apostle is building up his argument. Having drawn these deductions, I now find in my own spirit something that makes me cry out,

'Abba, Father'. That is even better; it goes beyond the first two steps. But what we have in this sixteenth verse is still higher, and is altogether in a class of its own. This is entirely the action of the Holy Spirit Himself. I do nothing about this; it is entirely 'given'. It is solely and exclusively what He does to me. The illustration we found in Thomas Goodwin about the father and the little boy brings this out perfectly. What the father did when he picked up the child and kissed him explains Romans 8: 16. It does not change the relationship, it does not make that child a child. He already had an assurance of his sonship within himself. But he did not have it as he had it at the moment when he was enfolded in the arms of his father and the love was being poured out upon him. It is an extra assurance; and the child has done nothing; it has been done to him; it is all the action of the father. So is this! It is the Spirit Himself who does it. We do no deducing here. It is not the result of a syllogism, or of argumentation. It is the Spirit Himself doing it to me.

To what does this lead? As I have said, this is obviously the highest and the greatest form of certainty and assurance that one can ever have of the fact that one is a child of God. At the same time, of course, it gives a better understanding of the whole plan of salvation; there is a kind of luminosity with respect to the truth. I have referred to that already in the individual experiences I have quoted, and we shall find more later on. In times of revival Christian people often say, 'I have been reading my Bible, and books about the Bible for years. I felt I understood; but in a flash I seemed to see everything with a clarity and a luminosity that I did not think possible to any man while yet in the body.' Such a thing does happen; but that is not the essence of this experience. The essence is that He is telling you of His love for you – 'the love of God shed abroad in our hearts'. He is making absolutely certain to you, more certain even than the fact that you are alive, that you are His child. Naturally, that in turn leads you to love Him – 'We love him, because he first loved us'. The more you know about His love to you the greater will be your love to Him. This and other results follow. That, again, in turn, leads to a great desire to please Him in everything, to keep His commandments, never to offend Him in anything, to honour His law. It also leads to that which is seen so clearly in the apostles after the day of Pentecost, namely, a desire to witness to Him, accompanied by the power and ability to do so. 'We cannot but speak the things which we have seen and heard' (Acts 4: 20). The Apostles did so with great boldness and power; and their hearers were affected and convinced by it. They could not witness until they were absolutely certain of their position, until they were given this tremendous certainty. That is what happened on the day of Pentecost. That is what happens always when one receives 'the baptism of the Spirit'. We are given this absolute assurance of God's love to us, that we are His children, and that He has 'loved us with an everlasting love'.

Not only so; this experience may be accompanied by various gifts. It was so on the day of Pentecost. I say 'may be', however, for there are variations in this respect, and there is not an exact repetition each time. It is for this reason that those who say that if we have not spoken in tongues we have never been baptized with the Spirit are utterly unscriptural. The Apostle asks in 1 Corinthians 12: 'Do all speak with tongues?' The answer, obviously, is 'No'; as all do not work miracles, and so on. In the same way, when we look at the subsequent history of the Christian Church in the times of great revival when the Spirit of God has been poured forth and thousands have been baptized with the Spirit, there is generally no mention of their working miracles, no suggestion that they 'spake with tongues.' Similarly is this true of individuals who have experienced this baptism. There may, or may not be, accompanying gifts. These, then, are variable factors. What is invariable, what is an absolute, is the certainty and assurance of God's love to His own, this knowledge beyond any doubt or question that they are His children. He tells us that Himself: 'The Spirit beareth witness with our spirit, that we are the children of God.'

We move on to the last question. How is this experience given, how does it come to us, how does it happen? What stands out here so clearly is the absolute Lordship of the Spirit. It is His action; and therefore He can do it in various ways. So any teaching which tells us that we have but to do this or that, and it will happen to us, is of necessity wrong. The Spirit deals with individual Christians in different ways. False experiences – those which are psychological or mechanical – can be duplicated exactly, but operations of the Spirit cannot be duplicated. He is the Lord, and He dispenses His gifts according to His own sovereign will.

So He brings this certain knowledge of salvation to individual Christians in a variety of ways. The first answer to this question as to how it is given, therefore, is that we never know. It cannot be predicted; it cannot be controlled in any way, or received at will. No one can promise to give us this blessing. Certain people claim that they can give the gift of the Spirit. But it is not so. It is the Spirit Himself who does this, and we do not know how or when.

Another negative answer is that the blessing does not generally come through hearing an audible voice. There is no such indication in the Scripture nor in the subsequent history of men or churches. So when people claim to have heard an audible voice we have a right to be suspicious. It is not the Spirit's way of working. But though it is not through an audible voice, the assurance is quite as definite and as unmistakable as an audible voice. Many can testify that 'It was as if I had actually heard it with my very ears'. It is the Spirit speaking to the inner man, to the inner ear. But, thank God, it is not only as definite as the audible voice, it is even more sure because it happens in the highest part of our personality.

How does it come? Sometimes it comes when a Christian is alone, reading the Scriptures quietly; perhaps reading a passage which he has read many times before. Suddenly the passage seems to come out of the Book and to speak to him directly in this particular way. It does not give him some general knowledge, but it stands out and meets him, and impresses on his mind and heart and spirit in an unmistakable manner this personal message. It is as if it were written only for him, that he is a child of God. That is the commonest way in which it comes – through a word or a passage of Scripture. Sometimes this experience happens to a man when he is not reading. Suddenly a word of Scripture that he has read before is brought into his mind. He is not thinking about it – he may actually be thinking about something quite different – but suddenly it is impressed upon his inner mind, and he becomes convinced that God loves him, and that he is a child of God. The Spirit takes a word and brings it to him and impresses it upon him in an absolutely unmistakable manner. It may happen in a religious service, particularly in a preaching service. The preacher says something which means nothing to the vast majority of the people, but to one soul that had been unhappy, uncertain and doubting, and attacked by the devil, it is the very voice of God speaking and telling him that he is a child of God, and that God has loved him (or her) in particular. The soul never forgets what has thus happened.

But – and I must add this – the assurance does not always come through the Scripture. It has happened to many without any words at all; it is just an inner consciousness in the spirit given by the Spirit of God Himself, apart from Scripture. I am much concerned to emphasize this, and for this reason, that there are some who have disputed it. Some of the Puritans did so. They were so afraid of the Quakers who arose at the same time, that they went so far as to say that you can never have this experience of assurance apart from the Word. In my view that is quite mistaken. The Quakers were undoubtedly wrong in much of their teaching. Some of them said that the Word did not matter at all, and that what counted was the 'inner light', and the work of the Spirit directly and immediately. That is clearly unscriptural, because the Scripture has been given by the Spirit. But we must not go to the extreme of saying that He can never deal with us immediately and directly, and without the Word, for He has often done so. In any case, take the case of the Romans to whom Paul was writing. They did not have the New Testament Scriptures, most of which had not even been written, and certainly not in the form in which we have them. They were dependent upon preaching and exhortation. How then could they have known that the Spirit was testifying with their spirits if it happens exclusively through the Word? We must be careful lest, in our fear of a certain emphasis on the part of people who talk much about the Holy Spirit, we may become guilty of 'quenching the Spirit'. Normally, this testimony is given through the Word, but it can be given without the Word.

Let me quote a statement on this matter by Charles Haddon Spurgeon. In a sermon on full assurance, based upon Psalm 35 : 3, 'Say unto my soul, I am thy salvation', which he preached on April 28, 1861, he said:

'God has a way of speaking without the Word, and without the ministers, to our hearts. His Spirit can drop like the rain and distil like the dew, as the small rain upon the tender herb. We know not how it is, but sometimes there is a deep, sweet calm.

[1] C. H. Spurgeon, *The New Park Street Pulpit*, Vol. vii (1861), p. 294.

Our conscience says, "I have been washed in the blood of Christ", and the Spirit of God saith, "Ay, 'tis true! 'tis true!" In such times we are so happy – so happy that we want to tell our joys – so blessed, that if we could but borrow angels' wings and fly away, we would scarce know the change when we passed through the pearly gates, for we have had heaven below, and there has been but little difference between that and heaven above. Oh, I wish my whole congregation without exception consisted of men and women who had heard the Spirit say, "I am *thy* salvation". What happy hymns! what happy prayers! You might go home to some poor single room; you might to go a scantily furnished house, and to a table that has barely bread upon it; but happy men! happy men! Better would be your dinner of herbs than a stalled ox without confidence in Christ; better your rich poverty than the poverty of the rich who have no faith in Jesus; better all the griefs you have to endure, when sanctified by assurance, than all the joys the worldling has, when unblessed by faith and un-hallowed by love to God. I can say now,

> *Grant me the visits of thy face,*
> *And I desire no more.*

Ah yes, the Spirit can do this apart from the Word, without the Word, apart from and without a preacher. He can make the direct statement, 'I am thy salvation,' 'Tis true! 'tis true! thou hast been washed in the blood of Christ.

I cannot but repeat the words of Spurgeon. Oh that all Christians knew this and were able to use such words! It is meant for all; it is possible for all.

Twenty-five

*

The Spirit itself beareth witness with our spirit, that we are the children of God.   Romans 8: 16

The next question which we must ask concerning this testimony of the Spirit with our spirits, this highest possible form of assurance, is as to when it is given. This is obviously a crucial question. Those who identify this with the ordinary work of the Spirit, as if it were but a repetition of verse 14 concerning the general work of the Spirit in conviction and conversion and sanctification and illumination, say of course that it happens to all Christians, and that it happens at regeneration. All who hold that the 'baptism of the Spirit' takes place unconsciously at regeneration, also have to say that this happens to every Christian, and that it happens at that moment of regeneration. They say the same with regard to the sealing of the Spirit. They say that every Christian has been baptized with the Holy Spirit, every Christian has been sealed by the Spirit; otherwise, you cannot be a Christian. They are quite consistent in what they say, but, as I have been at pains to show already, their contention seems to me to do great violence to what is stated here in Romans 8: 16, and to the statements made elsewhere in the New Testament.

First and foremost, it is a totally inadequate explanation of what we are told here. The Apostle is reminding these Romans that they can have this absolute certainty that they are the children of God over and above the testimony of their own spirits. In dealing with the testimony of our own spirits we have seen that to be able to say from the depths of our being, 'Abba, Father', is an astounding thing. This crying 'Abba, Father' was the term used of our Lord in the Garden of Gethsemane, and it is a very powerful term. It is not just the use or repetition of the term as when we recite the Lord's Prayer and say 'Our Father, which art in heaven'. It is 'a Spirit of adoption'. We know, we have a filial feeling, we are certain that we are the children of God, and in that confidence we 'cry out'. But the view that all this happens to all Christians at regeneration does not do justice to the Apostle's statement. Here, we have something that goes beyond that, as we have seen. How utterly ridiculous, and how false to experience, it is to say therefore that every individual Christian believer experiences this witness of the Spirit with his spirit. If that is truly the case it raises acutely the question as to how many Christians there are in the Christian Church. No, that view is quite wrong! You can be a Christian without ever knowing the Spirit bearing witness with your spirit, as you can be a Christian without knowing the 'Spirit of adoption, whereby we cry, Abba, Father'.

In the second place, the exposition which regards this as something which happens to all at regeneration surely does great violence to what we read in the second chapter of the Acts of the Apostles where we are told that the disciples were baptized with the Holy Ghost. There are books which do not hesitate to say that the baptism with the Holy Spirit is 'not experimental'. That has been the popular evangelical teaching during this present century. But that teaching also means and implies that what happened to the Apostles on the day of Pentecost was non-experimental. It passes my comprehension as to how anyone can possibly say such a thing. It means also that what happened to Cornelius and his household was non-experimental. All I ask is, if it is non-experimental, how did Peter know that anything had happened to Cornelius and his people? The fact is that it just does not fit in with the accounts found in the Scripture.

Why should any be guilty of such a travesty? I have already given the explanation. It is their fear of excesses. To put it quite bluntly, they are so afraid of Pentecostalism that they are driven to some such exegesis; and I suggest that they are thereby guilty of 'quenching the Spirit'. Non-experimental! Look at the second chapter of Acts. If we say that every Christian receives the baptism of the Spirit, and the sealing of the Spirit, and the witness of the Spirit, the moment he believes and becomes regenerate, then we must also say that the Apostles were not regenerate until the day of Pentecost, whereas the Gospel of John makes it abundantly clear that they were already regenerate. Our Lord had said to them,

'Now are ye clean through the word that I have spoken unto you'; and in His high-priestly prayer He also says, 'I pray for them; I pray not for the world' (John 17: 9). He tells His Father that they are those He had given Him, and that they had believed His testimony, whereas the world rejected it. 'O righteous Father', He says, 'the world hath not known thee: but I have known thee, and these have known that thou hast sent me' (John 17: 25). Throughout that prayer He makes it abundantly clear that they knew Him, that they believed on Him, and that they believed His word. Furthermore we read in the 20th chapter that He put His seal upon that by 'breathing' upon them the Holy Spirit. Not baptizing them with the Spirit, but breathing upon them. He would never have done that were it not that they were already believers. Clearly they were believers and regenerate well before the day of Pentecost, but it was only on the day of Pentecost that they were 'baptized with the Holy Ghost' in fulfilment of the promise recorded in Acts 1: 8.

My third point, which follows from the second, is that that explanation does not do justice to the eighth chapter of Acts where we read of Peter and John going down to Samaria after Philip had already been preaching there. Under Philip's preaching many had believed, and Philip had baptized them; but they had not yet received the Holy Ghost. That only happened after Peter and John had prayed for them and laid hands upon them. The same applies in the case of Cornelius and his household. That the Holy Ghost had fallen upon them was abundantly clear to Peter, who had been dubious about the whole position of the Gentiles. He saw that they were baptized with the Holy Ghost and therefore he was ready to baptize them with water. Similarly the same is true of the case recorded in the 19th chapter of Acts of the disciples Paul found near Ephesus. The very question Paul puts to them, 'Did ye receive the Holy Ghost when ye believed?' shows clearly that it is possible to believe without receiving the Holy Ghost. These examples show clearly that we must not say that at the moment of belief, or regeneration, every Christian automatically, as it were, receives the baptism of the Holy Spirit.

Fourthly, consider the statement in the first chapter of the Epistle to the Ephesians, verses 13 and 14. In the Authorized Version it reads: 'In whom ye also trusted, after that ye heard the word of truth, the gospel of your salvation: in whom also after that ye believed, ye were sealed with that Holy Spirit of promise, which is the earnest of our inheritance until the redemption of the purchased possession, unto the praise of his glory.' We have agreed that the better translation is, 'In whom also having believed'. But does that make much difference? While it is the correct translation I suggest that it does not in any way change the meaning or the teaching. The point is that 'having believed, ye were sealed with that holy Spirit of promise', as Charles Hodge puts it so well. Though the translators of the Authorized Version were not strictly accurate they did nevertheless convey the sense and the meaning of the original. The Apostle says that not only had the Ephesians believed; but over and above that, they had been 'sealed with that holy Spirit of promise'.

Such is the evidence, the most striking evidence, in the New Testament with regard to this matter; and it all indicates clearly that believing is one thing, but being sealed with the Holy Spirit is another. They do not happen, of necessity, at the same time, and we must not say that anyone who believes, and thereby gives proof that he is regenerate, that he has life, has automatically, inevitably, been baptized with the Holy Ghost.

But an objection is frequently brought forward at this point in terms of what we read in Acts chapter 11, verse 17. There we are given an account of the Apostle Peter defending his action in admitting Cornelius and his household, who were Gentiles, into the Christian Church. Peter, in making his defence at Jerusalem in a council of the apostles and elders, says in verse 15, 'As I began to speak the Holy Ghost fell on them, as on us at the beginning. Then remembered I the word of the Lord, how that he said, John indeed baptized with water; but ye shall be baptized with the Holy Ghost. Forasmuch then as God gave them the like gift as he did unto us, who believed on the Lord Jesus Christ, what was I, that I could withstand God?' 'Ah yes,' say the objectors, 'but there once more the Authorized Version is not correct; the translators have done the same as they did in Ephesians 1: 13, where they said 'after that ye believed' instead of 'having believed'; and here they say that 'God gave them the like gift as he did unto us, who believed on the Lord Jesus Christ'. But they point out that in the Revised Version, in the American Revised Version, in the Revised Standard Version, and almost every other new Version you will find that it is translated thus:

'Forasmuch then as God gave them the like gift as he did unto us, *when* we believed on the Lord Jesus Christ.' There is no more argument, they say, for it was 'when' Peter and the others had believed that they received this gift, this baptism of the Spirit, therefore *ipso facto* it is the same with all others.

But unfortunately for those who use this argument, it is not quite as easy as that. No translator has a blank mind, or does his work in a state of 'scientific detachment'. No scientist is detached, still less Bible translators. We are all creatures of prejudice, and translators are apt to be governed by their beliefs. It is clear that this was the case with the Authorized Version translators; and it is equally clear that the same applies to modern translators. In saying dogmatically that it should read, 'when we believed', they but manifest their prejudice.

Let me quote as my authority for speaking thus, a great authority on these matters of grammar – the late Professor A. T. Robertson of the Southern Baptists in the United States of America. He says that we have a word here which is the first aorist active participle of this word in the dative case. He says that it agrees both with the 'unto us' and with the 'unto them'. That is an important point in and of itself. 'Forasmuch then as God gave them [or unto them] the like gift as he did unto us, who believed on the Lord Jesus Christ. . . .' Robertson says that this statement about the 'believing' may apply equally well to the apostles themselves or to Cornelius and his household, and that you cannot prove which is intended. From the standpoint of grammar alone you cannot know to which party Peter is referring. He may be referring to Cornelius and his household rather than to the apostles themselves. We must not be dogmatic about this. But then Robertson proceeds to suggest his own translation – 'Having believed on the Lord Jesus Christ'. He would translate the whole verse in this way: 'Forasmuch then as God gave them the like gift as he did unto us, having believed on the Lord Jesus Christ, what was I that I could withstand God?' His final comment is, 'Both classes, Gentiles and Jews, trusted in Christ, and both received the Holy Spirit'. That is all we are entitled to say. We have no right to introduce the word 'when'. All the verse tells us is that, having believed on the Lord Jesus Christ, both Peter and the other apostles received this gift, and also Cornelius and his household received this gift. What is common to both is that they had believed. 'Having believed', says Peter, 'it happened to us, and it happened to them'. So these modern versions are as faulty and as misleading as the Authorized Version. Indeed, that is an over-statement, and I suggest that the old Authorized Version after all is the more accurate of the two, and certainly conveys the sense and the meaning, even as Charles Hodge tells us it does in Ephesians 1 : 13.

Another objection is brought in terms of 1 Corinthians 12 : 13 where we read, 'For by one Spirit are we all baptized into one body, whether we be Jews or Gentiles, whether we be bond or free; and have been all made to drink into one Spirit'. It is argued that that statement says plainly that all Christians have been baptized by the Holy Spirit. But surely the answer to that is perfectly simple. 1 Corinthians 12 : 13 has nothing whatsoever to do with the 'baptism with the Holy Spirit'. The great theme of that chapter is the theme of the Church as the body of Christ, and the Apostle is simply saying in that verse that every Christian is a member in particular of the body of Christ. He says that specifically in verse 27: 'Now ye are the body of Christ, and members in particular'. Christ is the Head, and the Church is the body, and in verse 13 he says that we have all been baptized into that body, we have all been made members of, partakers in that body, sharers in that body, by the one and the self-same Spirit. He speaks thus in order to show how ridiculous it is for there to be any division or schism in the Church, for it is a body, and all have been put into the body in exactly the same way by the operation of the Holy Spirit. That is not 'the baptism with the Holy Ghost' at all. Paul is only concerned there to show us that we cannot be Christians at all without being united to the Lord Jesus Christ, and that it is as the result of the operation of the Holy Spirit that we are put into Christ in that way – baptized into Him, engrafted into Him. The same terms are used, as we have seen, in the sixth chapter of this Epistle to the Romans.

But there is a further difference. In 1 Corinthians 12 the Apostle is dealing with the operations of the Holy Spirit. The Spirit convicts, He enlightens us, He gives us new life, and He puts us, 'baptizes' us, into the body of Christ. But it is the Lord Jesus Christ Himself Who baptizes with the Holy Spirit – which is a very different thing. To baptize with the Holy Spirit is the operation of the Lord Jesus Christ. John the Baptist had said:

'I indeed baptize you with water, but one mightier than I cometh, the latchet of whose shoes I am not worthy to unloose. He shall baptize you with the Holy Ghost and with fire.' This is a baptism performed by the Lord Jesus Christ. He baptizes us 'with the Spirit', whereas in 1 Corinthians 12 we are taught how the Spirit Himself baptizes us into the Lord Jesus Christ and His body. I suggest that all this confusion has arisen simply because the word 'baptized' happens to be used. But this word is used in many different senses in the New Testament. Our Lord Himself says, 'I have a baptism to be baptized with', when referring to the suffering He would have to endure (Luke 12: 50). We must not be mechanical in our use of this term. I have previously said so in expounding the first six verses of the sixth chapter. 1 Corinthians 12: 13 is not a reference to the 'baptism with the Holy Ghost' but to the way in which the Holy Ghost baptizes us, puts us, into the body of Christ. That is true of every Christian, of necessity. The 'baptism with the Holy Ghost' is not only different, but you can be a Christian without it, as the Apostles were without it until the day of Pentecost.

That is the main New Testament and Scriptural evidence with regard to this matter. Now let me confirm what I have been advancing by noticing what we find in the history of the Christian Church. What we find in the records of the lives of the saints, and of men who have been greatly used and honoured of God, is confirmation of the fact that to be baptized with the Spirit does not happen inevitably and always when a man believes, or at the moment of his regeneration. There is sometimes a great time gap. Let me give some examples.

Take the case of John Flavel, the Puritan of 300 years ago. He was a godly, saintly man, a notable expositor of the Scriptures. He was not only a believer, he also had assurance of salvation. But he tells us in his *Treatise of The Soul of Man*[1] that one day, on a journey, he began to meditate on 'objects of faith and hope'. Ere long he felt as if he was lifted up into heaven. He was taken out of the world and out of time. He says that he even forgot his wife and children, and longed to be taken immediately to heaven. He was given a glimpse of the glory; the love of God was shed abroad in his heart in such a manner that he did not know whether he was in time or eternity. Flavel was a typical Puritan; not an

[1] *The Works of John Flavel*, Vol. III, pp. 57-8. Banner of Truth.

The Sons of God

excitable, emotional person at all, but a quiet, studious, pensive kind of man. But he says that as the result of that experience he 'understood more of the light of heaven by it, than by all the books he ever read, or discourses about it'.

The same is true of Whitefield. We find in his Journals that he had already believed and knew the truth before this 'sealing' took place in his experience. Everyone knows that it was true of John Wesley. The Methodist Church observes 24th May annually as some sort of festival, because it was on May 24th, 1738, that this happened to John Wesley in that little meeting in Aldersgate Street in London. He had already believed in Justification by Faith the previous March, but it was on the 24th May that the truth was sealed to him and his heart was 'strangely warmed' and he knew that Christ had taken away his sins. 'Yes', he says, 'even mine.'

The same is particularly true in the case of Howell Harris, one of the great men who were used by God in Wales in the Evangelical Revival of the 18th century. Howell Harris was convicted of his sin and really came to the truth on Palm Sunday March 30th and the following Sunday, 1735. He got his assurance of salvation on Whitsunday May 25th 1735. But it was three weeks later while he was reading the Scriptures and praying and meditating on these things in the tower of a little church by the side of a lake, in a place called Llangasty, that suddenly this happened to him. I shall give the detailed account of it later, I simply note now that there was this interval. He had not only believed the Gospel, he had had assurance, he knew that he was forgiven. But the Holy Spirit did not bear witness with his spirit until about three weeks later. Harris's case can be stated thus. Easter 1735 – Romans 8: 15a, 'spirit of bondage and fear'; Whitsun 1735, Romans 8: 15b, 'Spirit of adoption'; three weeks later, Romans 8: 16, 'The Spirit bearing witness with his spirit'.

In the autobiography of that mighty genius, that spiritual giant, Jonathan Edwards, of 200 years ago, who lived in Northampton, Massachusetts – one of the greatest brains and intellects the Christian Church has ever known – we find the same plain and unmistakable fact. To believe was one thing, and this 'sealing of the Spirit', this 'Spirit bearing witness with his spirit' was something different. In the life of another American, Edward Payson, of the 19th century, we find exactly the same. He was a saintly

[316]

and most godly man. He, again, tells us of his early struggles, and his long seeking, and of how a time came when this witness given him by the Holy Spirit confirmed the witness of his own spirit.

One of the most interesting aspects of this history is that, irrespective of their theological beliefs and the particular school of thought to which they belong, they all talk about the same thing. Hitherto I have only quoted the cases of men who were Calvinistic in their doctrine; but precisely the same experience is to be found in the life story of Charles G. Finney, a notable aggressive Arminian and opponent of Calvinistic doctrine. Finney tells us in his autobiography that he was converted on one particular day and came to know that he was converted and had assurance of his salvation; but it was not until the next day that the Holy Spirit bore witness with his spirit that he was a child of God. The case of Dwight L. Moody is well known and particularly clear. Moody had not only been a believer for a long time, but was, in addition, the successful superintendent of a Sunday School Mission, which was virtually a church, in Chicago. But on one occasion two ladies in his congregation indicated to him at the close of a service that there was something lacking in his ministry and that they were praying for him. He is honest enough to tell us that he did not like that, but the more he thought of it the more he knew that they were right. So he went back to them and pleaded with them to go on praying for him that he might be given great power. He also began to pray urgently for it himself. Some six months later as he was walking down Wall Street in New York City one afternoon the Holy Spirit came upon him mightily and testified to his spirit that he was a child of God, and filled him with love and power. It was the turning-point in his ministry, the event that turned him into a world-wide evangelist.

These are but some examples out of many more which I could give. In all of them the point that emerges is what we have already discovered from the Scriptures themselves, that there is this interval, as it were, between Romans 8 : 15 and Romans 8 : 16. It is to believers that this happens. 'Having believed, ye were sealed with that Holy Spirit of promise.' As it happened on the day of Pentecost to the Apostles, so it has happened to the others.

When does this happen? There are some instances in which it is almost simultaneous with conversion. Take the case of Cornelius and his household; 'while Peter was still speaking the Holy Ghost fell upon them'. But in the light of all the other examples and illustrations we realize that, even there, there must have been belief first – but the interval was a very short one. But in the vast majority of instances there is a clear interval, sometimes there is a long interval. The important principle is that the two things are always separable. And surely this is quite inevitable, for, if the Spirit confirms our own spirit, there must therefore have been something that has happened in our spirit first for the Holy Spirit to confirm. You cannot have 'the Spirit of adoption, whereby we cry, Abba, Father', without being a believer. Believing must come first. What the Spirit does is to testify with our spirit. If there was no testimony in our spirit, the Spirit could not confirm it. So it follows, of necessity, from every standpoint – from the plain teaching of Scripture, from the testimonies of men, and from an obvious deduction drawn from the very nature of what is happening – that believing must precede the testimony of the Holy Spirit.

That is the main argument. Let me now quote some of my authorities in support of my contention. It has often been said quite dogmatically that none of the Puritans held this view; so let us examine the evidence. To read one or two of the great Puritan writers and then make sweeping generalizations can be most misleading. We must be careful in these matters.

Let me start with one of the very early Puritans, John Preston. Here was a Court Chaplain to James I and Charles I, a very able man, a great intellect, a profound thinker. This is what he writes in his book,[1] *The New Covenant or the Saints' Portion* published in 1629:

'Now follows the testimony of God's Spirit which we see described besides the places named unto you in Ephesians 1, wherein after you believed you were sealed with the Spirit of promise. When a man hath believed and took Jesus Christ; secondly, when he hath washed and purified himself. That is, he hath gone about his work, and so his own spirit gathers a testimony hence, that he is in a good estate. After he hath thus believed, then, saith he, comes the Holy Ghost and seals the same things unto you; that is, the Lord leaves a man alone awhile, as it were to champ upon the bridle, as I may say. He lets a man alone to some

[1] Vol. I, p. 398.

doubts and fears that so he may purge himself the more carefully. But after a time, when a man hath put to his seal that God is true, then the Lord seals him again with the Spirit of promise. That is, the Lord sends the Spirit into his heart, and that Spirit gives witness to him; and when he hath put to his seal that God is true, then the Lord puts to his seal, and assures him that He hath received him to mercy.'

Could anything be plainer than that? The believer first puts his seal to the fact that God is true, and that what God has said is true, and when he has done that he may be left for a while to 'champ upon the bridle', but after a while, after the man has put his seal, God will put His seal on top of it through the Spirit. The Spirit will testify with his spirit that he is a child of God.

Let us now turn to John Owen. In John Owen's two volumes on the Holy Spirit you will find nothing about this, and because of that, some have said that John Owen does not teach this doctrine. But John Owen's works consist of some twenty-four volumes! In his treatise *Of Communion with God the Father, Son and Holy Ghost*[1] he tells us:

'Another effect we have of His, Romans viii, 16 [effect of the Holy Spirit is meant], "The Spirit itself beareth witness with our spirit, that we are the children of God". You know whose children we are by nature, children of Satan and of the curse, or of wrath. By the Spirit we are put into another capacity and are *adopted to be children of God,* inasmuch as by receiving the Spirit of our Father we become the children of our Father. Thence is He called (verse 15) 'the Spirit of adoption'. Now sometimes the soul, because it hath somewhat remaining in it of the principle that it had in its old condition, is put to question whether it be a child of God or no, and thereupon, as in a thing of the greatest importance, puts in its claim, with all the evidences that it hath to make good its title. The Spirit comes and bears witness in this case. An allusion it is to judicial proceedings in point of titles and evidences. The judge being set, the person concerned lays his claim, produceth his evidences, and pleads them, his adversaries endeavouring all that in them lies to invalidate them, and disannul his plea, and to cast him in his claim. In the midst of the trial a person of known

---

[1] *The Works of John Owen*, vol. II, p. 241. Banner of Truth.

and approved integrity comes into the Court and gives testimony fully and directly on the behalf of the claimant; which stops the mouths of all his adversaries and fills the man that pleaded with joy and satisfaction. So is it in this case. The soul, by the power of its own conscience, is brought before the law of God; there a man puts in his plea, that he is a child of God, that he belongs to God's family, and for this end produceth all his evidences, everything whereby faith gives him an interest in God. Satan in the meantime opposeth with all his might, sin and law assist him, many flaws are found in his evidences, the truth of them all is questioned, and the soul hangs in suspense as to the issue. In the midst of the plea and contest the Comforter comes and, by a word of promise or otherwise, overpowers the heart with a comfortable persuasion (and bears down all objections) that his plea is good and that he is a child of God. And therefore it is said of Him that "He bears witness with our spirit." When our spirits are pleading their right and title, He comes in and bears witness on our side, at the same time enabling us to put forth acts of filial obedience, kind and childlike, which is called "crying, Abba, Father". Remember still the manner of the Spirit's working before mentioned, that He doth it effectually, voluntarily and freely. Hence sometimes the dispute hangs long, the case is pleading many years. The law seems sometimes to prevail, sin and Satan to rejoice, and the poor soul is filled with dread about its inheritance. Perhaps its own witness, from its faith, sanctification, former experience, keeps up the plea with some life and comfort; but the work is not done, the conquest is not fully obtained, until the Spirit who worketh freely and effectually, when and how He will, comes in with His testimony also. Clothing His power with a word of promise He makes all parties concerned to attend unto Him and puts an end to the controversy.

'Herein He gives us holy communion with Himself. The soul knows His voice when He speaks; neither has He a mortal tone of voice. There is something too great in it to be the effect of a created power. When the Lord Jesus Christ at one word stilled the raging of the sea and wind, all that were with Him knew that there was divine power at hand (Matt. viii. 25-27), and when the Holy Ghost by one word stills the tumults and storms that are raised in the soul, giving it an immediate calm and security, it knows His divine power and rejoices in His presence.'

[320]

Let me quote another Puritan, Thomas Brooks, who writes on the subject of *'The unsearchable riches of Christ'*.[1] I quote from page 60:

'Before I come to the second thing premised, give me leave to give you this hint, namely, that there is no such way to joy, peace and assurance as this, to mind your work more than your wages. Ah, had many mourning, complaining Christians done thus, their mourning before this had been turned into rejoicing, and their complaining into singings. Christians, the highway to comfort is to mind comfort less and duty more. It is to mind more what thou shouldest do than what thou wouldest have, as you may see in Ephesians i. 13, "In whom ye also trusted, after that ye heard the word of truth, the gospel of your salvation: in whom also after that ye believed, ye were called with that Holy Spirit of promise". The original runs thus [Thomas Brooks is here correcting the Authorized translators who had produced their translation just a few years before] "In whom believing, ye were sealed". While faith is busied and exercised about Christ and those varieties and excellences that are in Him, the Lord comes and by His Spirit seals up the life and love and glory of them.'

Still the same teaching – believing first, faith engaged about Christ, and the Spirit comes and seals it up to us!

But now let us come to Charles Simeon of Cambridge, who preached and taught in Cambridge at the end of the 18th and the beginning of the 19th centuries. Charles Simeon writes thus on Ephesians 1 : 13:

'The blessings which we receive through Christ are innumerable; many are mentioned in the preceding part of the chapter. One of the last and greatest which we receive in this life is the sealing of the Spirit. This was vouchsafed to many of the saints at Ephesus. The experience of the individuals may vary with respect to it, but there shall always be some in the Church who possess and enjoy it. Nor are persons usually sealed at their first believing in Christ. This higher state of sanctification and assurance is reserved for those who, after having believed, have maintained a close walk with God. They must first be in Christ, and then for Christ's sake this benefit will be vouchsafed unto them.'

[1] Thomas Brooks, *Complete Works,* vol. III, p. 60 (Nichol edition).

To quote Robert Haldane once more, this is what he says in his Commentary on this very verse.

'This witnessing of the Spirit to the believer's spirit, communicating consolation, is never His first work, but is consequent on His other work of renovation. He first gives faith, and then seals (Ephesians i: 13).'

J. C. Philpot, one of the two men who really revived the Strict Baptist denomination last century, an able man who belonged to Worcester College, Oxford, in a sermon on Romans 8: 16 writes: 'But all the children of God have not this direct and immediate witness; many are longing for it.' A sermon by John MacKenzie, a friend and colleague of Philpot, on this subject has been reprinted recently; and it emphasizes the same truth particularly clearly both from the standpoint of exposition and also from his personal experience. Both the men were staunch Calvinists.

Let us turn finally to Charles Haddon Spurgeon. Spurgeon preached a sermon[1] on John 7: 37–39, and John 16: 7, on the morning of the 28th May 1882, and amongst other things, he said:

'Am I not so happy as to have in this audience some who will immediately ask [for this blessing]? I pray that some who have never received the Holy Spirit at all may now be led, while I am speaking to pray: "Blessed Spirit, visit me, lead me to Jesus".' [He is here referring to unbelievers who have not received the Spirit at all, and he is exhorting them to pray there and then as he was preaching.]

Then he goes on:

'But especially those of you that are the children of God, to you is this promise especially made.' [He is referring to the promise of having this blessing of the Spirit which will lead to rivers of living water, flowing out from the inward parts.] 'Ask God to make you all that the Spirit of God can make you, not only a satisfied believer who has drunk for himself, but a useful believer who overflows the neighbourhood with blessing. I see here a number of friends from the country who have come to spend their holiday in London. What a blessing it would be if they went back to their

[1] C. H. Spurgeon, *Metropolitan Tabernacle Pulpit*, vol. XXVIII (1882), pp. 311–12.

respective churches overflowing; for there are numbers of churches that need flooding; they are as dry as a barn floor, and little dew ever falls on them. Oh, that they might be flooded! What a wonderful thing a flood is! Go down to the river, look over the bridge and see the barges and other craft lying in the mud. All the king's horses and all the king's men cannot tug them out to sea; there they lie, dead and motionless as the mud itself. What shall we do with them? what machinery can move them? Have we a great engineer among us who will devise a scheme for lifting these vessels and bearing them down to the river's mouth? No, it cannot be done. Wait till the tide comes in! What a change! Each vessel walks the water like a thing of life. What a difference between the low tide and the high tide. You cannot stir the boats when the water is gone, but when the tide is at the full see how readily they move, a little child may push them with his hand. Oh for a flood of grace! The Lord send to all our churches a great spring tide! Then the indolent will be active enough, and those who were half dead will be full of energy. I know that in this particular dock several vessels are lying that I should like to float, but I cannot stir them. They neither work for God nor come out to the prayer meetings'

[Did you hear that?]

'nor give of their substance to spread the Gospel'.

[He regards them as Christians nevertheless.]

'If the flood would come you would see what they are capable of: they would be active, fervent, generous, abounding in every good word and work. So may it be! So may it be! May springs begin to flow in all our churches, and may all of you who hear me this day get your share of the streams! Oh that the Lord may now fill you and then send you home bearing a flood of grace with you. It sounds oddly to speak of a man's carrying home a flood with him, and yet I hope it will be so, and that out of you shall flow rivers of living water. So may God grant for Jesus' sake, Amen'.

I can but add my own 'Amen'. So be it with us individually, so be it with us as churches and gatherings of people.

Twenty-six

*

The Spirit itself beareth witness with our spirit, that we are the children of God.

Romans 8 : 16

We have seen that the 'sealing' with the Spirit, or this 'testimony' which the Spirit bears with our spirits that we are the children of God, does not always happen at the time of conversion. Indeed we can say that, on the whole, it but rarely happens at the time of conversion.

There is a final proof of this, it seems to me, which we can establish in two ways. If this does happen immediately, and of necessity, when a person is converted, and if you say that one cannot be a Christian without having this witness of the Spirit or this 'sealing' with the Spirit, then you are really saying that he cannot be converted and be a Christian at all without having assurance of his salvation. But we have seen earlier that that is condemned by most teachers and writers, and that, though some of the first Protestant Reformers tended to teach in this way, in their anxiety to correct the false teaching of the Church of Rome which denies assurance altogether, the Westminster Confession of Faith and the teaching of practically all the Puritans corrects it, and insists that we must differentiate between having salvation and having assurance of salvation. You can be a Christian without having assurance of your salvation. That is to say, if you are aware of your utter sinfulness, and realize that you can do nothing to commend yourself to God; if you rely entirely and solely on the work of the Lord Jesus Christ in His active obedience to the law on your behalf, and in His passive obedience in taking your punishment in His own body on the tree; if you are relying only on that, then I assure you that you are a Christian, though you may lack assurance of your salvation. If you can say

[324]

My hope is built on nothing less
Than Jesus' blood and righteousness;
I dare not trust the sweetest frame
But wholly lean on Jesus' name

then you are a Christian. The natural man does not believe that; he believes he can rely upon himself and his own good works. But if you can say that your trust is fixed in the blood and righteousness of Jesus Christ, you are a Christian though you may be assailed by doubts, and may not enjoy much happiness. What the Spirit does, we are told, is to come alongside and confirm what we are aware of in ourselves. He can only put His seal upon something which is already there: so there must be something present first before this seal can be added. Surely that should be sufficient in and of itself to prove my contention.

But there is a second argument which is a vital one. It is generally agreed by most, and even by Dr John Owen – who is not very clear in his teaching on this matter of the testimony and witness of the Spirit, and the sealing of the Spirit, and who admits that he is not very clear on it– that a parallel to this action of the Spirit in believers is what we are told in John's Gospel about our Lord and Saviour Himself – 'Labour not for the meat which perisheth, but for that meat which endureth unto everlasting life, which the Son of man shall give unto you: for him hath God the Father sealed' (6: 27). This is a most significant statement. Our Lord says about Himself that God His Father has 'sealed' Him, and it is generally agreed that He was referring to what happened to Him at His baptism. When our Lord was baptized in the Jordan by John the Baptist two things happened; the Holy Spirit descended upon Him in the form of a dove, and a voice came from heaven saying, 'This is my beloved Son; in whom I am well pleased'. That was the sealing to which our Lord refers; and this throws great light on what we are considering in Romans 8: 16. Our Lord was always the Son of God; and what happened to Him there, when the Holy Ghost descended upon Him, made no difference to His relationship to God. He was from eternity the Son of God. When He was born as a Babe in Bethlehem He was the Son of God. Not only so, the Holy Spirit was always in Him, always in Him from the very beginning. He gives indications of His awareness of His relationship to God. He did so as a boy in the temple. When upbraided by Joseph and Mary as to why He was not with them in the company going home, He said, 'Wist ye not that I must be about my Father's business?' And there are other indications of the same thing. But it was only at His baptism that He was sealed; and He was sealed by the descent of the Holy Ghost upon Him.

What happens when we are sealed by the Holy Spirit is comparable to that which happened there to our Lord. Obviously, therefore, it does not refer to our regeneration. It does not mean that we *become* sons of God when this happens. As believers we are already sons of God. The Holy Spirit is already in us, as the 9th verse has reminded us: 'If any man have not the Spirit of Christ, he is none of his.' A believer is a child of God and the Holy Spirit is in him, and he has a measure of understanding and an awareness of all this. It is in addition to that, as in the case of our Lord Himself, that the Holy Spirit comes in this special and peculiar manner as a 'seal'. Why? What was the reason in the case of our Lord? Obviously it was because our Lord was about to begin His public ministry. In order to enable Him to function in that ministry, which He was to exercise in the form of a man, He is given this special authentication of Himself and this special certainty of His relationship to God. In this way He is equipped and authenticated and empowered to exercise His ministry.

In other words, the coming of the Holy Spirit in this way to 'seal' or to bear this witness with our spirits is something additional, special; and its main function is to give us an absolute certainty of our position, and the power that will enable us to be witnesses to our Lord and to the kingdom of grace that has come in and through Him. So if you take what happened to our Lord at His baptism, and which can be described as His 'sealing' with the Spirit, as your standard or norm, there is only one possible conclusion, namely, that this is something that is given to, and done to, those who are already believers and regenerate, and who already have the Holy Spirit in them. If it is not kept to this special category there can be nothing but sheer confusion.

What is the nature of this witness which the Spirit bears with our spirits? The first answer is that it must obviously be experimental. It is an experience. I emphasize this because certain modern writers deny it. A title in a recent book on the Holy

Spirit reads, 'The sealing of the Spirit is not experimental'. Dr Lewis Schaffer in his volume on the Holy Spirit called 'Pneumatology', says, 'There is no experience or feeling related to the Spirit's baptism'. This has been the common evangelical teaching. Identifying the baptism with the Spirit with regeneration they have to say, of course, that it is non-experimental. The answer to this assertion is that what is described in the second chapter of the Acts of the Apostles is 'the baptism with the Spirit', the 'sealing' of the Spirit. The Apostles, who were already believers, already regenerate, and on whom our Lord had already 'breathed' the Spirit, were setting out upon their work and ministry. And as happened to our Lord Himself at His baptism at the beginning of His ministry, so it happened to the apostles on the day of Pentecost that the Spirit came upon them in this way. It was to give them an absolute certainty and assurance about their salvation and their calling, and to fill them with power that they might go out as witnesses unto their Lord.

To say that this happening was 'non-experimental' is simply to fly in the face of the facts, as I have shown earlier, not only in the case of the apostles but also in the case of the Samaritans and Cornelius's household and the disciples at Ephesus. If the object and the purpose of this assurance which we receive when the Spirit bears witness with our spirits, or when the Spirit seals us, is that we might be made sure and certain that we are 'children of God' and 'heirs of God and joint-heirs with Christ', how can it possibly do so if it is 'non-experimental'? Yet the Apostle's whole object is to show us how it does help us. Notice the context: 'If children, then heirs; heirs of God, and joint-heirs with Christ, if so be that we suffer with Him, that we may be also glorified together.' Then Paul goes on, 'For I reckon that the sufferings of this present time are not worthy to be compared . . .' Paul was writing all this, not as a theoretical disquisition on theology, but with a pastoral intent. His object was to encourage believers, to strengthen them, to enable them to go on triumphantly in spite of the fact that there were many things militating against them. But if this is non-experimental, why did he trouble to write about it? The answer is that the whole object of the 'sealing of the Spirit' is to give us certainty about our inheritance. It is an earnest, a foretaste, of good things to come. It is essentially experimental.

Secondly, it is an experience – and this follows, of course – which leads to great joy, and love to God. There is no instance of it in the Bible which lacks this feature. How obvious it is in the second chapter of Acts! One can almost feel the exuberant joy that was in Peter and the others, lifting them up above their circumstances and giving them holy boldness. I quote again the words of the Apostle Peter in his First Epistle: 'Whom having not seen, ye love; in whom, though now ye see him not, yet believing, ye rejoice with joy unspeakable and full of glory' (1: 8). Is this true of every Christian? We know well that it is not; but these words are not used accidentally, as a kind of hyperbole; it is not mere rhetoric on the part of the Apostle. It was the literal truth about those early Christians as it was of Peter himself. This witness or sealing of the Spirit always leads to great joy and to a great love to God. When we come later to contrast it with a false experience, we shall add further results which follow from it.

My third comment is that the Spirit's witness may, or may not, be accompanied by gifts and phenomena. Obviously in the case of the disciples on the day of Pentecost it was accompanied by very great gifts; it was a striking phenomenon. But not always! A man may receive this witness, this sealing, with no such phenomena. Sometimes it has been such an overwhelming experience that Christians have literally fallen down in a dead faint. But to others this has not happened. It may or may not be accompanied by visible or audible happenings such as 'the cloven tongues as of fire' and 'the rushing mighty wind'. These are the occasional concomitants; they are not essential parts of this experience. So we must be very careful not to limit the experience in terms of certain possible accompaniments.

A fourth, and a very important point relates to the intensity of this experience. There is a real danger that as the result of reading the New Testament concerning this matter, and also some of the most striking examples that we find in subsequent Christian literature, we may unwittingly tend to standardize the intensity of this particular experience. But we have no right to do so. All we have a right to say is that, though the intensity or the degree may vary considerably, the experience itself is always unmistakable. It is always distinct, and different from everything else we have known. This is true, of course, of all experiences – not only

Christian experience but ordinary experience of life. To use the obvious analogy, there are degrees and variations in the degree of our sensibility in the matter of human love. There is not always the same level or degree of intense feeling.

It is exactly the same with regard to Christian experience. Take the experiences of a number of converts and ask them to tell you exactly what happened to them. You will find all kinds of variations; some are much more dramatic than others. But, thank God, it does not mean that only some are Christians. Whether you come into the Christian life in a very dramatic manner, or in a very gradual manner, makes no difference; what matters is that you are in the Christian life. That is why some of us are not happy about the so-called giving of testimonies in public meetings; they can be very misleading. What matters is that we have 'life', and that we know we have life. It matters little as to how you were born, the vital fact is that you are alive and that you are giving evidences of having life. It is precisely the same with this experience. Let me use another illustration. When you receive a letter by post you look at the stamp on the envelope and also the postmark. You notice that the postmark is sometimes very clear, and at other times it is so faint that you can scarcely tell where the letter was posted. But though it is faint, it is there, and you can just make it out. That is the sealing that matters, the official stamp. So sometimes this 'witness of the Spirit with our spirit' is faint, but you know that it has happened. It is not very powerful but you know it has taken place, and you thank God for it. You may receive it later in a much greater intensity. So you must not say that it is not there at all because it has not the intensity that you sometimes read of in the great classic examples and illustrations.

I have found in my pastoral experience of over thirty years that many who have spoken to me about these matters, are unhappy about this point, so I put it in this form. It is wrong to standardize the experience. About thirty years ago I knew a man who was very much troubled about the spiritual state of his son. On my asking him for the grounds of his anxiety and worry he replied, 'He has not had the Damascus Road experience'. In other words because his son had not had the same very dramatic conversion as he himself had had he was doubtful as to whether his son was a Christian. But when, together, we applied the other tests of new life in Christ, the father became quite satisfied that his son was a Christian. The son is still alive and he has borne an excellent Christian testimony.

Or let me put the matter in another way. In books on medicine or surgery, you will find accounts of diseases, and of course in a textbook account it is necessary to have a description of all that may happen. All the possibilities are laid out in great detail – the severe and the mild forms of diseases. But when the medical student becomes qualified, and goes out into practice, he soon discovers that he rarely meets with what he has read in his text-book, that is to say, with classical examples of the various diseases. Obviously in the textbook the writer has to describe the classical picture; but the whole art of medicine is to be able to recognize the disease though it is not present in the glaring, obvious classical form. There are all kinds of possible variations and combinations of symptoms, but there is enough evidence for the practitioner to make his diagnosis. It is exactly the same in the spiritual realm. So, to use a Scriptural expression, never 'despise the day of small things'. If the postmark of the Heavenly Post Office is on you, thank God for it, even though it may appear to be very faint by contrast with other examples you may have come across in the Scriptures or in the literature of the Church throughout the centuries.

Another interesting point is the durability of this experience. There are some who think that once you have had it you have it for ever. There is no greater mistake than that! I have never heard of any case in which, once the Spirit came and bore this witness, the man continued in the same state ever after. Why is it not permanent? The answer is that the Holy Spirit is a Person; hence we have to be careful with all our illustrations. It is clear from the literature on the subject that this is an experience which comes and then goes. Indeed there have been instances where a man has known this witness of the Spirit once only, and never again. But – and thank God for this – once you have had it, the memory of it will remain with you as long as you live; you will look back to it as the greatest joy in your life. There are many such cases in history; and I have known such people personally. I have known people who had amazing experiences in the Welsh Revival of 1904–5. I think of one man, a minister whom I first met in 1927; he seemed to be of all ordinary ministers the most ordinary in every way conceivable, both in his own life and also in his ministry, which seemed to be quite barren and lifeless. Yet I shall never forget his account of how that Revival came to the college where he was studying as a ministerial student, and of how it came to him personally. He became quite transformed as he told me about it. The memory of the glorious experience, and the absolute assurance he received at the time, had remained with him. He had experienced much failure and discouragement since then, but the moment he looked back to that great day in his life he revived. In a sense he had lived on it.

Here is the danger – to live on past experiences! I have known many who have done that with experiences such as this, and especially in a time of revival. The point I am establishing is that this experience does not last for ever. You may get it; then it may go, and you may never know it again. The man to whom I have referred certainly had no repetition after the Revival, and he died without a repetition. In other words this experience can be lost as the result of the sin of 'grieving' the Spirit, or of 'quenching' the Spirit. The Spirit came on our Lord at His baptism in the form of a dove. The Spirit is very sensitive; He can be grieved, He can be hurt, He can be quenched. So however powerfully the Spirit may have come and borne this witness and testimony with a man's own spirit, if the man falls into sin he cannot expect that this testimony will continue. It would be unreasonable to do so; and it does not happen. So it is not 'once and for ever.' But, thank God, it can be repeated, and repeated many times. There are many illustrations of this. As far as I am aware, there is no man, no single person who had such repeated experiences of this as the great George Whitefield. The frequency of the repetition as recorded in his Journals is truly astonishing.

Let me now quote some of the authorities on this subject. J. C. Philpot, to whom I have referred previously, says, 'Those who enjoy it have it only at favoured moments and peculiar seasons. If once enjoyed, they cannot lose the recollection of it. But they may and do lose the enjoyment, and through temptation and desertion sink into those dark and miserable spots where nearly all seems lost and gone.'

An Independent minister named Joseph Smith of Charleston, South Carolina, preached a sermon in which he referred to a revival that had broken out in his church and neighbourhood as the result of Whitefield's visit. He was preaching on March 26th, 1740, and this is what he says about Whitefield: 'He renounced all pretentions to extraordinary powers and signs of apostleship – gifts of healing, speaking with tongues, the faith of miracles, things peculiar to the age of inspiration and extinct with these. He also allowed that these feelings of the Spirit were not in every person, or at all times and in the same degree, and that though a full assurance were attainable, and what everyone should labour to attain, yet not of absolute necessity to the being of a Christian.' Such was George Whitefield's teaching: everyone should have the experience, everyone should seek it; but it is not essential and there are many Christians who have never had it.

Similarly Philip Doddridge in a sermon[1] on this very verse Romans 8:16 says, 'And I judge it the more necessary to expatiate upon the thought because the devil sometimes takes an advantage to bring all into doubt, and to raise a storm in the soul merely on account of the cessation of those extraordinary experiences which were never intended as our daily food, but only as rich dainties with which our heavenly Father thinks fit now and then to delight the souls of His children and to make, as it were, a feast for them.' That is somewhat reminiscent of Thomas Goodwin's father and son walking along the road. Philip Doddridge says that it is like our heavenly Father giving us an occasional feast. You do not have a feast every day; if you did, it would not be a feast when you had it. You have your daily bread, you have your solid meals, but in addition your Father prepares an occasional party for you! That is a very good way of looking at this matter.

The next aspect of the experience to which we must turn is: To whom is this given? I have already supplied part of the answer. As my quotations have just been reminding us, it is open to all. But apart from the quotations, Acts 2:39 tells us that 'The promise is unto you, and to your children, and to all that are afar off, even as many as the Lord our God shall call'. Clearly it is not meant only for Apostles and certain exceptional saints. Indeed the New Testament Epistles seem to assume that it was an experience common to all Christians at that time. The quotations I have given from the New Testament show that. Peter in writing to the 'strangers scattered abroad' says that they 'rejoice with joy

[1] *Philip Doddridge: Sermons on various subjects*, vol. II, p. 391. London 1826.

unspeakable and full of glory' (1 Peter 1 : 8). He had never met them but he says that he knew that this was true of them. But someone may ask, 'How do you equate this statement with the statement you previously made that every Christian does not have the experience'? The answer is that the New Testament period was a time of intense activity on the part of the Holy Spirit. The New Testament era was the first of a series of out-pourings of the Holy Spirit. That is why the subsequent examples are called re-vivals, but it is doubtful whether any one ever again quite reached the height of the first. In the New Testament we have the first great sample, and there we see it in its fulness. It seems to have been the case therefore that most of those who were converted in those early days received this baptism of the Spirit almost at the time of their believing, as was clearly the case with Cornelius and his house. It is open to all; and not only for the apostles, but to the most ordinary believers. A man must be a believer before he can have it. It certifies his belief.

Let me quote another Puritan, Thomas Horton, whose book[1] of sermons on the eighth chapter of this Epistle to the Romans was published in 1674. He has interesting and quaint ways of putting the truth. 'The Spirit, it never seals but it first writes.' It is the Holy Spirit who first does the writing; in other words it is the Holy Spirit who brings us to conviction and to conversion. Paul states the same fact in 2 Corinthians 3 : 3 : 'Ye are our epistle written in our hearts, known and read of all men . . . written not with ink, but with the Spirit of the living God; not in tables of stone, but in the fleshy tables of the heart.' The Spirit does the writing first. He makes us Christians and starts the process of sanctification in us. That is the writing. Then He seals what He has already written. Horton continues, 'Never is a spirit of consolation where it is not first a spirit of renovation'. That is to say, it is only the regenerate man who can know the sealing; in other words, it can only be done to believers.

But let us remember that it is not given to all believers. A reason why some believers never know it is stated quaintly and tersely by Thomas Brooks, a Puritan whom I have already quoted. In one of his sermons[2] on Ephesians 3 : 8 he says, 'Mind your

---

[1] Thomas Horton: *Forty-six sermons upon the whole eighth chapter of the Epistle of the Apostle Paul to the Romans.* London, 1674.

[2] Thomas Brooks, *Complete Works,* vol. III, p. 60 (Nichol edition).

work more than your wages.' He states it again in this manner, 'The highway to comfort is to mind comfort less and duty more. It is to mind more what thou shouldest do than what thou wouldest have.' We must not keep our eye over-much on the comfort. In other words, those who set their heart on experiences are not likely to receive the true experience. They may have experiences, but not this! Our Lord had said the same thing in the Beatitudes: 'Blessed are they which do hunger and thirst after righteousness: for they shall be filled' (Matthew 5: 6). Not 'Blessed are they which do hunger and thirst after blessedness'! Seek happiness only and you will probably never find it; seek righteousness and then you are certain to find happiness. If you are always seeking sensations, experiences and comforts, and are not concerned about righteousness, do not be surprised if you never receive the Spirit.

This teaching is found repeatedly in the Scriptures. Take, for instance, John 14: 21: 'He that hath my commandments, and keepeth them, he it is that loveth me: and he that loveth me shall be loved of my Father, and I will love him, and will manifest myself to him.' This is the portrait of the man to whom Christ is going to manifest Himself in this way, of the man who is really going to know the love of God in this exceptional manner. He is the man 'who hath my commandments and keepeth them'; not the man who is looking for nothing but the feast. The same truth is found in the Book of Revelation, chapter 2: 17: 'To him that overcometh will I give to eat of the hidden manna, and will give him a white stone.' Again, in Revelation 3: 12: 'Him that overcometh.' And yet again in Revelation 3: 20: 'Behold, I stand at the door, and knock: if any man hear my voice, and open the door. . . . ' Remember that these words are written to Christians and not to unbelievers. All these letters are written to believing churches and to believers. It is to the man who hears, and who is listening for Him, and who opens the door, and obeys Him, that He comes. He comes always to the man who 'overcomes', to the man who 'keeps the commandments', the man who 'obeys'. That is why Charles Simeon says that this is the last and the highest experience which comes to those who have given a lifetime to promoting their sanctification and to hungering and thirsting after righteousness.

Are there any conditions? It seems quite clear from the literature that this tends to happen to a man who has made some special act of self-denial for the promoting of God's glory. It often happens, also, when a man has passed through some terrible conflict with temptation, and has obtained a victory over sin. He may have had an unusually hard and difficult time; I will go further, he may have been the subject of a veritable satanic attack, and may have felt that all the forces of hell were let loose upon him. He cannot understand it; he had never known this before; but suddenly he is tempted on all sides and attacked with a fury that almost takes his breath away. It not infrequently happens, either in the midst of such an attack, or after he has stood manfully, and resisted such an attack, that suddenly the Spirit bears witness with his spirit that he is a child of God. God says, as it were, to him, 'Well done, thou good and faithful servant'. Or again it sometimes happens when a person has shown some especial faithfulness or activity in God's service. Again, it is often given to those who have been mourning for it, longing for it, and seeking it. This is very clear in the case of Whitefield, and also in the cases of John and Charles Wesley. These three men became almost physically ill and sick while mourning on account of their sins, and longing after Christ. It is almost invariably given to people who have had a spirit of heaviness and of bondage, and who have mourned and grieved. It is given to such more frequently, perhaps, than to any other.

But then we also find that the experience is often given to people before some great trial. Whitefield tells us in his Journals that whenever he had this special visitation of the Spirit, he had come to feel that it was almost the harbinger of some unusual trial or difficulty, some terrible persecution or some such cause of distress. This has often happened, and not only to individuals but also to communities. You will often find that countries have had a religious revival just before a war or some great calamity. It so happened in the Congo before the terrible troubles of recent years commenced. It happened also in Korea before war broke out in that land just at the end of the second world war. God, as it were, in His love and Fatherly kindness gives this special assurance to enable His people to go through the trial. It certainly happened before the Mau Mau troubles in Eastern Africa. In the same way it often happens immediately after some such great trial or crisis. God, as it were, then rewards His people for having gone through the trial in such an excellent manner.

Lastly, you will often find that the experience is given to people just before they die. This is most remarkable and extraordinary. The case of a man named John Holland, reported in a book by Robert Bolton, a Puritan, illustrates this. And there is a striking example of it in the Journals of George Whitefield. It is the case of a Mrs Hugh Bryan found in Whitefield's Journals[1] for 1740-41, just after the entry for Thursday, January 1st, 1741. Mrs Bryan had recently died and her husband, Mr Hugh Bryan, in a letter to his niece telling her about the event writes,

'Dear Child,

Under written are the dying words of your aunt, which I send for your satisfaction and information. She died October 7 between the hours of nine and ten in the morning, being filled with the full assurance of faith in Christ, and a joyful hope of eternal salvation through His merits and mediation. As your aunt and I were praying to our Lord Jesus to give her the comforts of His Holy Spirit to support her under the agonies of death, she replied, "I see Him! I see Him! Now I see light!" After this she continued in prayer about half an hour; but her speech failing her we could not during that time understand what she spake, only we could hear the name of Jesus often and "Come Jesus! Come Jesus!" Then again she spake out plainly and said, "Who would die without God? Now I see light!" Then she lay in an agony about half an hour, and again spake out and said, "God has let me see great and glorious things which would not be believed if they were told". Then your uncle R—, coming into the room, spake to your aunt S—, and your dying aunt, hearing his voice, called him to her, and when he was come, she spake to us and said, "Mind what I say to you, for hereafter you must all give an account of what I now say to you. God has enabled me to speak to you before I go, for I am just going." Then she said, "God is a just God as well as merciful. Be diligent in searching your hearts. Brother, tell Mr (So-and-So) he is in the wrong. My pain is great, but Christ is sufficient for me." And she repeated that "God had let her see great things that would not be believed if they were told." She also said, "Follow Whitefield, God will bless him wherever he goes; do not speak lightly of him; bless him, bless him. God has enabled me to speak to you before I go. I am just

[1] *George Whitefield's Journals*, pp. 501-2. Banner of Truth 1960.

going. Farewell! Farewell! God be with you." Then she composed herself and lay about half an hour, and neither moved nor groaned, except her lips and tongue and the heaving of her breast in breathing, seeming to be in her perfect senses until about a minute before she died. She looked round at each of us that were about her bed, and then departed in quietness'. Whitefield adds, 'Thus far Mr Bryan. I shall only add, "O death, where is thy sting? O grave where is thy victory" over true believers? What fools are they who count their lives madness.' He is referring, of course, to the lives of true believers.

There are innumerable instances of happenings of this kind. Read the life of Edward Payson, a saintly minister who lived in America in the last century, and you will find that in a similar way he only knew and experienced the blessing just before he died.

These, then, are some of the conditions in which it comes; but none of these conditions guarantees that it will come. We cannot stereotype the event. The teaching of the Scripture, confirmed by the experiences of the saints throughout the centuries, indicates that these are the ways, and the times, in which this blessed experience of having 'the witness', the testimony of the Spirit with our spirits that we are the children of God, comes to those who already believe in our Lord and Saviour Jesus Christ.

Twenty-seven

*

The Spirit itself beareth witness with our spirit, that we are the children of God.
                                                           Romans 8 : 16

We have been describing, in general, the nature and the character of the witness of the Spirit with our spirits. We still have to consider other aspects of this teaching, such as how to differentiate between this and certain false experiences against which we are warned in the Scripture. The First Epistle of John warns us: 'Believe not every spirit, but try the spirits'. So obviously, when we are dealing with a spiritual witness and testimony such as this, we shall have to be careful to safeguard ourselves against a spurious or false experience. We shall also have to consider whether this witness is something that should be sought by God's children.

But before we pursue these matters, it will be well for us to look at further testimonies to this teaching which are to be found in the writings of prominent children of God in the 17th, 18th and 19th centuries. This is important because many imagine that what I have been saying in exposition of this verse is something new and strange. I want to show, therefore, that, far from being an innovation, it has been taught regularly throughout the centuries; and it is chiefly in this present century that it has dropped into the background, and has been neglected and forgotten. I do not hesitate to assert that the main explanation and cause of the present state of the Christian Church – and I am referring particularly to Evangelical churches – is the neglect of this doctrine, and the influence of the false doctrine which would have us 'take it by faith' and not be concerned at all about our feelings. The same applies to the teaching that all receive the baptism with the Spirit at regeneration, and that it is non-experimental.

The best way of handling these quotations is to take them

chronologically; so we start at the beginning of the 17th century. In *The Life of Robert Bruce*,[1] 1554–1631, a minister of the Church of Scotland and the successor of John Knox in St Giles Church in Edinburgh, there appears a letter he wrote to a friend in Edinburgh, after he had been exiled from that city:

'I never got such access in my time as I have gotten since I went from you. The treasures of His riches have been opened unto me. There was never such foul flesh has gotten a more gracious, more sensible, more powerful approbation of my ministry in Edinburgh, of my fidelity therein. His Spirit has testified to my spirit, not only by real joys, spiritual and elevated light, but by vocal speeches within me in the daylight, that I heard so sensibly with great effusion of tears, so far not only by approbation but to my commendation, that I admire how He should bestow such gracious speeches upon so wretched a creature as I was. Indeed, I grant the will was with me, but not so bent as it should have been neither, for I was over-timorous and laden with diversity of infirmities; the spirit in some measure ready, but the flesh was weak. Yet His Majesty, my gracious God, my God in Christ, accepts of it as it had been the most perfect and exact service in the world. Yea I admire how so true a mouth could speak so far in approbation of a silly poor wretch. My heart, howsoever Edinburgh has cast me off, rejected and banished me out of their parts, I leapt no sooner on my horse but the gates of heaven were cast open to me; I got such applause in my heart, with such floods of tears, with such real and constant approbation, that my heart could not wish for greater access. And on the second day of the same month I got another approbation in distinct terms, the Spirit testifying to my spirit so audibly, as it were, that I admired how His Majesty could make so much of so little doings and so mean service.'

That from a dour Scotsman! That is how he describes the Spirit bearing witness with his spirit, and you notice that it is full of emotion and of feeling – highly experimental!

My second quotation is from John Preston to whom I have previously referred. He was a man of great intellect, and again as

---

[1] D. C. MacNicol: *Robert Bruce, minister in the Kirk of Edinburgh*, pp. 169–70. Banner of Truth, 1961.

far removed as you can imagine from being an excitable, emotional, ignorant person. I quote out of the same book as previously mentioned,[1] entitled *The New Covenant or The Saints' Portion*. When he deals with the sealing of the Spirit in terms of Ephesians 1:13, he writes:[2]

'You will say, what is the seal or witness of the Spirit? My beloved, it is a thing that we cannot express; it is a certain divine expression of light, a certain inexpressible assurance that we are the sons of God, a certain secret manifestation that God hath received us and put away our sins. I say it is such a thing that no man knows but they that have it. You shall find it expressed by all these places of Scripture: Revelation 3 – "If any man will open unto me, I will come in and sup with him". That is, when the Lord enters into a kind of familiarity with a man, when he vouchsafes him so much favour as to come, and sup and dine with him, as it were, and to dwell with him.' [Then Preston quotes Revelation 2:17 as a verse of like import.] 'So John 14:21: 'If any man love me and keep my commandments, I will show myself to him'; that is, he shall have an extraordinary manifestation of myself; he shall have such an expression of love and peace that shall fill his heart with peace and joy, such a thing that no man knows but himself. Beloved, this is the testimony of the Spirit. I confess it is a wondrous thing, and if there were not some Christians that did feel it and know it, you might believe there were no such thing, but it were but a fancy or enthusiasm. But it is certain there are a generation of men that know what this seal of the Lord is. Indeed you must remember this, to distinguish it from all fancies and delusions. This Spirit comes after you have the water and the blood, after you are believers, after you have purged yourselves, and therefore if any man have flashes of light and joy, that witness that he hath received the promise, and that he is in the Covenant, and for all this he have not the things that go before it, he may well take it for a delusion. Saith Christ, "I will come and sup with him". But with whom? "With him that first openeth to me".'

Later in the same work[3] he says:

'Now when the Lord seeth a man believing thus, and trusting

[1] See p. 318.
[2] Vol. I, pp. 398–400.
[3] pp. 416–17.

[340]

him upon his bare word, then the Lord goes a step further with him and seals the same things to him with the Spirit of promise, as I showed before out of Ephesians 1.13. When you put to your seal that God is true, God then comes and puts to his seal. He gives you the Spirit of promise and assures you that it is so. That is, he doth by his own Spirit say to a man's soul, "I am thy salvation". My beloved, this is a certain expression of the Holy Ghost to the soul of a man, that we know not how to express to you; therefore it is called "the hidden manna", it is called "a white stone" . . . a certain manifestation of Christ to the soul, a certain divine light, a certain secret token of his love, whereby Christ manifests himself to the souls of man, that which the Scriptures call "supping with him". . . . This is the witness of the Spirit, that when the witness of our own spirit is somewhat obscure, we may then say, "Lord, thou now speakest plainly; now there is no question". My beloved, this is the witness of the Spirit'.

I have also referred previously[1] to another Puritan, Thomas Horton, who preached forty-six sermons on this eighth chapter of the Epistle to the Romans which were published in 1674. This is what he has got to say on verse 16:

'Whenever it comes in the reality and the fulness of it, and so long as it remains upon the soul, it silences all temptations, removes all scruples and doubts whatsoever to the contrary, and sets the heart at perfect rest.' He says, 'It is something secret and inexpressible; certain and at the same time infallible.'

I quote again also from the 17th-century Scottish preacher, William Guthrie, and from his famous book entitled *The Christian's Great Interest*.[2] This is how Guthrie expresses the matter:

'I speak with the experience of many saints, and I hope, according to the Scriptures, if I say there is a communication of the Spirit of God which is sometimes vouchsafed to some of His people that is somewhat besides, if not beyond, that witnessing of a sonship spoken of before.' [That corresponds with what we have been saying, that what verse 16 describes is over and above the matter dealt with in the 15th verse.] 'It is a glorious divine

---

[1] See p. 333.
[2] First published 1658. Banner of Truth edition 1969. See pp. 108–9.

manifestation of God unto the soul, shedding abroad God's love in the heart. It is a thing better felt than spoke of. It is no audible voice, but it is a ray of glory filling the soul with God, as He is life, light, love and liberty, corresponding to that audible voice, "O man, greatly beloved" (Dan. 9: 23); putting a man in a transport with this on his heart, "It is good to be here" (Matthew 17: 4). It is that which went out from Christ to Mary when He but mentioned her name – "Jesus saith unto her, Mary. She turned herself, and saith unto him, Rabboni, which is to say, Master" (John 20: 16). He had spoken some words to her before and she did not understood that it was He; but when He uttereth this one word "Mary!" there was some admirable divine conveyance and manifestation made out unto her heart, by which she was so satisfyingly filled that there was no place for arguing and disputing whether or not that was Christ, and if she had any interest in Him. That manifestation wrought faith to itself; it purchased credit and trust itself, and was equivalent with "Thus saith the Lord". This is such a glance of glory that it may in the highest sense be called "the earnest" or firstfruits "of the inheritance" (Ephesians 1: 14); for it is a present and, as it were, sensible discovery of the Holy God, almost wholly conforming the man unto His likeness; so swallowing him up that he forgetteth all things except the present manifestation. O how glorious is this manifestation of the Spirit! Faith here riseth to so full an assurance that it resolveth wholly into the sensible presence of God. This is the thing which doth best deserve the title of *sensible presence;* and is not given unto all believers, some whereof are "all their days under bondage and in fear" (Heb. 2: 15); but here "love, almost perfect, casteth out fear" (1 John 4: 18). This is so absolutely let out upon the Master's pleasure, and so transient or passing, or quickly gone when it is, that no man may bring his gracious state into debate for want of it.'

I go for my next quotation to another great Puritan, Richard Sibbes (1577–1635) who used to preach in Gray's Inn in London to the lawyers and the barristers and the solicitors. He was known as 'The heavenly Dr Sibbes', and was, again, a great intellect, and one who greatly helped many of the other Puritans. This is how Sibbes writes in his work entitled 'A Fountain Sealed':[1]

---

[1] *Works of Richard Sibbes,* vol. V, p. 440. (Nichol edition).

'But oft it falls out, that our own spirits, though sanctified, cannot stand against a subtle temptation strongly enforced. God superadds His own Spirit. Guilt often prevails over the testimony of blood; that of water, by reason of stirring corruptions, runneth troubled. Therefore the third, the immediate testimony of the Spirit, is necessary to witness the Father's love to us, to us in particular, saying "I am thy salvation" Psalm 35: 3, "thy sins are pardoned", Matthew 9: 2. And this testimony the word echoeth unto, and the heart is stirred up and comforted with joy inexpressible. So that both our spirits and consciences, and the Spirit of Christ joining in one, strongly witness our condition in grace, that we are the sons of God.'

Then shortly he goes on:

'The Spirit it is that witnesses with blood, and witnesses with water, and by water, whatsoever of Christ's is applied unto us by the Spirit. But besides witnessing with these witnesses, the Spirit hath a distinct witness by way of enlarging the soul; which is joy in the apprehension of God's Fatherly love and Christ's setting the soul at liberty. The Spirit doth not always witness unto us our condition by force of argument from sanctification, but sometimes immediately by way of presence; as the sight of a friend comforts without help of discourse. The very joy from sight prevents the use of discourse.

'This testimony of the Spirit containeth in it the force of all, word, promise, oath, seal etc. This is greater than the promise, as a seal is more than our hand, and as an oath is more than a man's bare word. The same that is said of God's oath in comparison with His bare promise, may be said of this sealing in comparison of other testimonies. That as God was willing more abundantly to clear to the heirs of promise their salvation, He added an oath (Heb. 6: 18); so for the same end He addeth this His Spirit as a seal to the promise, and to the other testimonies. Our own graces indeed, if we were watchful enough, would satisfy us. The fountain is open as to Hagar, but she seeth it not (Gen. 21: 17 *et seq.*) Howsoever the Spirit, if that cometh, it subdueth all doubts. As God in His oath and swearing joineth none to Himself, but sweareth by Himself, so in this witness he taketh in no other testimony to confirm it, but witnesseth by Himself. And hence ariseth "joy unspeakable and glorious" (1 Peter 1: 8), and "peace which passeth all understanding" (Philip. 4: 7); for it is an extract of heaven when we see our being in the state of grace, not in the effect only, but as in the breast and bosom of God.'

A further quotation from a 17th-century author is from Edward Elton, who again preached a series of sermons on Romans 8 and published them in a volume[1] in 1623:

'I take it therefore that the witness and testimony of the Spirit here spoken of is an inward secret and unspeakable inspiration of the Spirit; the Holy Spirit of God inwardly, secretly, and in an unspeakable manner, informing our hearts and inwardly persuading us that God is our Father and pouring into our heart a secret, wonderful and unspeakable sweet sense and feeling of God's love to us. Not of God's ordinary or common love, but of His special and Fatherly love, that God loves us with such love as He bears to His only begotten Son Christ Jesus in whom we are adopted to be His children. As the Lord Jesus Himself speaks in that excellent prayer of His (John 17: 23) that God loves us, we believing in Christ, as He hath loved Him, and to this purpose the Apostle speaks plainly (Rom. v: 5); the Holy Spirit of God given to us doth infuse and pour into our hearts a sense and feeling of God's love to us in Christ.'

For our last quotation from a 17th-century Puritan we turn to Thomas Goodwin. In expounding[2] Ephesians 1: 13, he writes:

'There is light that cometh and over-powereth a man's soul and assureth him that God is his, and he is God's, and that God loveth him from everlasting. . . . It is a light beyond the light of ordinary faith . . . the next thing to heaven; you have no more, you can have no more, till you come thither . . . It is faith elevated and raised up above its ordinary rate, it is electing love of God brought home to the soul.'

I could give many other quotations from Goodwin, but we must leave it at that.

Moving on to the 18th century we come to a number of great

---

[1] Edward Elton: *The triumph of a true Christian described, or an explanation of the eighth chapter of the Epistle to the Romans.* London. 1623.

[2] *The Works of Thomas Goodwin,* vol. I, pp. 233, 236, 237. (Nichol edition.)

names, and we start with George Whitefield. He says in his Journals[1]:

'Soon after this I found and felt in myself that I was delivered from the burden that had so heavily oppressed me. The spirit of mourning was taken from me, and I knew what it was truly to rejoice in God my Saviour; and for some time could not avoid singing psalms wherever I was. But my joy gradually became more settled, and, blessed be God, has abode and increased in my soul, saving a few casual intermissions, ever since. Thus were the days of my mourning indeed. After a long night of desertion and temptation, the star which I had seen at a distance before began to appear again, and the day star arose in my heart. Now did the Spirit of God take possession of my soul and, as I humbly hope, seal me unto the day of redemption. . . . Having now obtained mercy from God and received the Spirit of adoption in my heart, my friends were surprised to see me look and behave so cheerfully after the many reports they had had concerning me.'

Another quotation from Whitefield's Journals[2] reads:

'Was filled with the Holy Ghost. Oh, that all who deny the promise of the Father might thus receive it themselves! Oh, that all were partakers of my joy!'

But here[3] he is describing something that happened on November 5th, 1740:

'Mr Gilbert Tennent preached first and I then began to pray, and gave an exhortation. In about six minutes one cried out "He is come! He is come!" and could scarce sustain the manifestation of Jesus to his soul. The eager crying of others for the like favour obliged me to stop, and I prayed over them as I saw their agonies and distress increase. At length we sang a hymn and then retired to the house, where the man that received Christ continued praising and speaking of Him till near midnight. My own soul was so full that I retired and wept before the Lord under a deep sense of my own vileness and the sovereignty and greatness of God's everlasting love. Most of the people spent the remainder of the night in prayer and praises. It was a night much to be remembered.'

[1] *George Whitefield's Journals,* pp. 58, 59. Banner of Truth, 1960.
[2] Ibid., pp. 201, 205.   [3] Ibid., p. 487.

Another extract[1] November 22nd, 1740 reads:

'God's presence so filled my soul that I could scarce stand under it.'

On another occasion he tells us that he was so tired and exhausted that he went to lie down on a bed; but the Holy Spirit was so pouring the love of God into his heart that he could not sleep, though, physically, he was entirely exhausted.

The next witness is Jonathan Edwards who writes[2]:

'Once, as I rode out into the woods for my health, in 1737, having alighted from my horse in a retired place as my manner commonly has been, to walk for divine contemplation and prayer, I had a view that for me was extraordinary, of the glory of the Son of God as Mediator between God and man, and His wonderful, great, full, pure and sweet grace and love, and meek and gentle condescension. This grace that appeared so calm and sweet appeared also great above the heavens. The Person of Christ appeared ineffably excellent, with an excellency great enough to swallow up all thought and conception, which continued, as near as I can judge, about an hour; which kept me the greater part of the time in a flood of tears, and weeping aloud. I felt an ardency of soul to be, what I know not otherwise how to express, emptied and annihilated; to lie in the dust and be full of Christ alone; to love Him with a holy and pure love; to trust Him; to live upon Him; and to serve and follow Him; and to be perfectly sanctified and made pure with a divine and heavenly purity.'

So writes Jonathan Edwards, regarded by most as the brightest intellect that has ever appeared in the United States of America. Notice that he did not 'take it by faith'; he was overwhelmed, weeping, crying and overcome by the greatness of the glory that was revealed to him.

But, lest someone might think that this is only given to preachers or certain outstanding men, let me quote what Mrs Jonathan Edwards said[3] about what happened to her in 1742:

'I cannot find language to express how certain this [the ever-

[1] Ibid., p. 497.
[2] *Select Works of Jonathan Edwards*, vol. I, p. 32. Banner of Truth.
[3] Ibid., p. 38. See also *Works of Jonathan Edwards*, London, 1840, vol. I, p. cvii.

lasting love of God] appeared, the everlasting mountains and hills were but shadows to it. My safety and happiness and eternal enjoyment of God's immutable love seemed as durable and unchangeable as God Himself. Melted and overcome by the sweetness of this assurance I fell into a great flow of tears and could not forbear weeping aloud. The presence of God was so near and so real that I seemed scarcely conscious of anything else. At night my soul seemed to be filled with an inexpressibly sweet and pure love to God and to the children of God, with a refreshing consolation and solace of soul which made me willing to lie on the earth at the feet of the servants of God, to declare His gracious dealings with me and breathe forth before them my love and gratitude and praise. All night I continued in a constant, clear and lively sense of the heavenly sweetness of Christ's excellent and transcendent love, of His nearness to me and of my nearness to Him with an inexpressibly sweet calmness of soul in an entire rest in Him. My soul remained in a heavenly Elysium. I think that what I felt each minute during the continuance of the whole time was worth more than all the outward comfort and pleasure which I had enjoyed in my whole life put together. This exaltation of soul subsided into a heavenly calm and rest of soul in God which was even sweeter than what preceded it.'

I would emphasize that that happened in 1742, whereas the great Revival had broken out under her husband's ministry in Northampton in 1734 and 1735. She had been a believer, and had had great experiences, long before this.

But lest anyone should think that this experience is confined to those who belong to a particular theological school, let us now turn to John Wesley, the Arminian. Concerning this experience he writes[1]:

'Is not this something immediate and direct, not the result of reflection or argumentation? There may be foretastes of joy, of peace, of love, and those not delusive, but really from God, long before we have the witness in ourselves, before the Spirit of God witnesses with our spirits that we have redemption in the blood of Jesus, even the forgiveness of sins.'

[1] John Wesley, *Sermons on Several Occasions*, London 1824, vol I. Sermon XI, 'The Witness of the Spirit'.

The Sons of God

My next quotation comes from a book in Welsh on the beginning of Methodism in Wales by Richard Bennett.[1] It is about Howell Harris (1714–1773) one of the two great leaders in the Methodist Awakening and Revival in Wales 200 years ago, a great friend of Whitefield, who used to deputize frequently for Whitefield in Whitefield's Tabernacle, and who was also a great friend of both Wesleys. We have referred to him earlier but it is good to read what Bennett says[2] of him:

'After his conviction he recorded everything; he could do that without any offence to the reader at first because his heart was dancing in the warmth of his first love. After two to three weeks that love burst forth into a flame, a flame which melted his whole nature. The experience of forgiveness which he had had in the church at Talgarth was undoubtedly sweet, nevertheless it left in his heart an indefinable sense of some further need. But while he was engaged in secret prayer in the church at Llangasty, that secret place where he had given himself to God, God now gave Himself to him.'

Harris had gone into the tower of the church at Llangasty to read his Bible and to pray secretly so that no one should disturb him; and it was while he was there that, we are told, 'God now gave Himself to him'. And then the writer quotes two lines of poetry, which I have translated like this:

There was satisfied his longing – great and urgent plea,
Every need supplied completely – by the Godhead, One in Three.

The writer goes on, referring to Harris's own account of this in his diaries[3]:

'He piles the richest biblical phrases one on top of the other in an attempt to give adequate expression to what he felt and experienced that day. That was when his heart was cleansed from all idols and the love of God was shed abroad in his heart. Christ had entered in before, but now to sup. Now he had received the Spirit of adoption, whereby we cry, Abba, Father, and he began

[1] Richard Bennett, *The Early Life of Howell Harris* (English translation by Gomer M. Roberts) Banner of Truth, 1962.
[2] Ibid., p. 26.
[3] Ibid., Compare p. 27.

to desire to depart and to be with Christ. All fears were cast out for months and perfect love took their place.'

A later quotation[1] from Harris's diaries on page 54 of Bennett's book (Welsh edition) says:

'Were it not for that love I had experienced I would have drawn back, I would have given up. I could never have struggled against the flood. Love fell in showers on my soul so that I could scarce contain and control myself. I knew no fear and had no doubt whatsoever as to my salvation.'

A year later (1736) we find the following statement[2] in the same book:

'He refers frequently to a spiritual feast which he had about this time on a certain mountain while he was returning from Cwm Iau, when he saw God smiling upon him in such a manner that his heart was shattered under the powerful influences of the divine love. This place became for him ever afterwards a holy mountain.'

I have been fascinated to find, not in Bennett's book but in some of the extracts from Harris's diaries which have been recently printed, that on June 18th, 1746, when he was in London he wrote:

'London: A day to me memorable. This day eleven years ago I was sealed to the day of redemption.'

In other words on June 18th, 1746, he remembers what had happened on June 18th, 1735, in the tower of the church at Llangasty, when the Spirit for the first time bore witness with His Spirit that he was indeed a child of God. He keeps on referring to it every time that date comes round – 'A day to me memorable.' He never forgot it. It was the first occasion on which he had experienced this great effusion of the Spirit.

Let us now come right to the end of the 18th century and the beginning of the 19th. Primitive Methodism was really started, under God, by a man called Hugh Bourne. He is famous as the man who held great meetings on Mow Cop in Staffordshire where so many were converted and greatly blessed. He again describes

[1] Ibid., Compare p. 30.
[2] Ibid., Compare p. 52.

the same kind of experience. He also had retired for meditation and study of the Scriptures when suddenly the glory of God appeared to him in overwhelming power.

I must quote the experience of Christmas Evans, the greatest of all Welsh Baptist preachers, at the beginning of the 19th century. He had been in a dry arid state of soul for years as the result of adopting the Sandemanian teaching, but then he says[1]:

'On a day ever to be remembered by me, as I was going from Dolgelley to Machynlleth and climbing up towards Cader Idris, I considered it to be incumbent upon me to pray, however hard I felt my heart, and however worldly the frame of my spirit was. Having begun in the name of Jesus, I soon felt, as it were, the fetters loosening and the old hardness of heart softening, and as I thought, mountains of frost and snow dissolving and melting within me. This engendered confidence in my soul in the promise of the Holy Ghost. I felt my whole mind relieved from some great bondage, tears flowed copiously and I was constrained to cry out for the gracious visits of God, by restoring to my soul the joys of His salvation; and that He would visit the churches in Anglesey that were under my care.'

God answered his prayers abundantly.

Or take this from the biography of Edward Payson, an American Presbyterian minister at the beginning of the 19th century. On his death-bed he was asked, 'Do you feel reconciled?' 'Oh,' he said, 'that is too cold. I rejoice! I triumph! and this happiness will endure as long as God Himself, for it consists in admiring and adoring Him. I can find no words to express my happiness. I seem to be swimming in a river of pleasure which is carrying me on to the great Fountain.'

Merle d'Aubigné was a Swiss and is well known as the author of the famous *History of the Reformation*. But what happened to him and some of his friends is not so well known. This is the story:

'Several years after his conversion, when at Kiel in company with the Rev Frederick Monod of Paris and the Rev Charles Riell of Jutland, and Klenker, Biblical Professor of the University there, in the course of their conversation upon the Scriptures the

[1] Paxton Hood, *Christmas Evans*, p. 77. Hodder & Stoughton 1888.

aged Professor refused to enter into any detailed solution of difficulties presented, saying that the first step was to be "firmly settled in the grace of Christ", and that "the light which proceeds from Him will disperse all darkness". We were studying, says d'Aubigné, the Epistle to the Ephesians and had got to the end of the third chapter. When we read the last two verses, "Now unto him that can do exceedingly abundantly above all that we ask or think, according to the power that worketh in us", this expression fell upon my soul as a revelation from God. "He can do by His power", I said to myself, "above all that we *ask*, even above all we *think;*" nay "exceedingly abundantly" above all. A full trust in Christ for the work to be done within my poor heart now filled my soul. We knelt together in prayer. When I arose I felt as if my wings had been renewed as the eagle's. All my doubts were removed, my anguish was quelled, and the Lord extended peace to me as a river. Then I could "comprehend with all saints what is the breadth and depth and length and height, and know the love of Christ which passeth knowledge". Then I was able to say, "Return unto thy rest, O my soul, for the Lord hath dealt bountifully with thee".'

Another quotation from about this same time is most interesting. I have referred earlier[1] to the writings of a certain John MacKenzie who was acting as assistant editor or co-editor with J. C. Philpot of *The Gospel Standard* magazine from 1840 to 1849. Our friends the Strict Baptists are regarded as unusually serious and sober people, not given to emotionalism. But this is what John MacKenzie says in a sermon (recently reprinted) which he preached on Ephesians 1: 13 and 14. Here he is dealing with the sealing:

'As to the immediate act of this sealing of the heart and the peculiar feelings under it, they are better known and understood by the sweet experience of them than can be conveyed by words or conceived in ideas. I shall, however, endeavour to speak it briefly and plainly according to the manner that the blessed Spirit was pleased to impress upon my soul with it after He had prepared me for it. The Spirit is not confined to any particular means in giving this rich blessing, He may give it under the preaching or reading of the Word, or neither. But whatever outward means He may please to use, or should He, without any, come suddenly

[1] p. 322.

and sovereignly down upon the heart, the soul will feel fully assured it is the blessed Spirit within him. Nor is it anything in us, or done by us, that thus causes the blessed Spirit to descend upon the heart. It is the will and work of His own good pleasure (Phil. 2: 13) in His own set time to favour Zion. "Thus saith the Lord, I do not this for your sake, O house of Israel, but for Mine holy Name's sake". The sealing in the text is the earnest of the heavenly inheritance, which is a part and pledge of the immortal glory of God in Christ, sealed or impressed upon the heart by the Holy Ghost. And when the Spirit seals the heart with this blessed seal, He descends and softens and anoints it, and sheds abroad there the love and rich mercy of God, and the life and love and blood and death of Jesus, so that the heart will be dissolved and overwhelmed, the soul melted in the flames of love, mercy, grace, glory and heavenly blessedness and the eyes flowing with tears of love and joy. Every attribute of God is endeared to the heart till it bursts with love to Him; and this feeling contains a peculiar, heavenly and sacred delight and blessedness. And it will be so powerfully and sensibly felt on the heart that it will be enjoyed as the earnest of immortal glory, a part of that glory that the souls of the redeemed will enjoy to all eternity. And the feeling is so distinct and powerful that it bears evidence to the heart of its own divinity and that it is the blessed sealing of the Spirit, the earnest, pledge and foretaste of heaven. It brings with it assurance, pardon and peace with God, and "joy unspeakable and full of glory" rises out of it. He feels that the blessed Spirit has come down and taken possession of his heart and consecrated it as a sacred place to God, and sealed him up as His own property unto the day of redemption. He feels he is the temple of the Holy Ghost, and that the Spirit of God dwells in him, and the glory of the Lord has filled the house. He feels that part of heaven is let down into his soul, and oh! the peculiar, inexpressible, sweet feelings of love, gratitude, contrition and humility mingled together which fill the heart! He feels no sin, guilt, wrath or fears; these are all put away. A sweet peace and calmness rest in his mind. God the Father, God the Son, and God the Holy Ghost have taken up their abode with him. "We will come unto him and make our abode with him". It couches in it "the love of God shed abroad in the heart", "the Spirit bearing witness to our spirit that we are the children of God". And this causes the soul sweetly to rest in God, satisfied with His salvation and delighted with the abundance of His glory. He now understands in a sweet measure that precious Scripture, "Now he which stablisheth us with you in Christ, and hath anointed us, is God; who hath also sealed us, and given the earnest of the Spirit in our hearts" (2 Corinthians 1 : 21, 22). This sealing enlarges the heart, enlightens the eyes, instructs the understanding, and puts into the soul a meek independence of men and things.'

Charles Finney, about as far removed from John MacKenzie as is possible, in his Autobiography gives his account of how the experience came to him, and the results that followed.

But let me quote what happened in the case of D. L. Moody. He says:

'I began to pray as never before. The hunger increased, I really felt that I did not want to live any longer if I could not have the power for service. I kept on crying all the time that God would fill me with His Spirit. Well, one day in the City of New York – oh! what a day, I cannot describe it! I seldom refer to it, it is almost too sacred an experience to name. Paul had an experience of which he never spoke for fourteen years. I can only say God revealed Himself to me, and I had such an experience of His love that I had to ask Him to stay His hand.'

My final quotation comes from Charles Haddon Spurgeon. It is taken from his sermon[1] on Fellowship with God:

'But you know, brethren, the word "fellowship" not only signifies concord of heart, but *it implies a carrying out of that concord a little further, in converse or mutual communication.* May the Holy Spirit grant that we may not say a word which is not strictly verified by our experience! But I hope we can say we have had converse with the Divine Father. We have not seen Him at any time, nor have we beheld His shape. It has not been given to us, like Moses, to be put in the cleft of the rock and to see the back parts, or the train of the invisible Jehovah; but yet we have spoken to Him; we have said to Him, "Abba, Father"; we have saluted Him in that title which came from our very heart, "Our Father, who art in heaven". We have had access to Him in such a way that we

---

[1] C. H. Spurgeon: *New Park Street and Metropolitan Tabernacle Pulpit*, vol. VII (1861), p. 492.

cannot have been deceived. We have found Him, and through the precious blood of Christ we have come even to His feet, we have ordered our cause before Him, and we have filled our mouth with arguments; nor has the speaking been all on our side, for He has been pleased to shed abroad, by His Spirit, His love in our hearts. While we have felt the spirit of adoption, He, on the other hand, has showed to us the loving kindness of a tender Father. We have felt, though no sound was heard; we have known, though no angelic messenger gave us witness, that His Spirit did "bear witness with our spirits that we were born of God". We were embraced of Him – no more at a distance; we were "brought nigh by the blood of Christ". I trust, my brothers and sisters, you can each of you say – though you wish it could be more intense than it is – "I have in all these things had fellowship with the Father, for I have conversed with Him, and He has spoken to me".'

Then take a final word from Spurgeon in the volume of *Revival Year Sermons*[1]:

'Let me say now, before I turn from this point, that it is possible for a man to know whether God has called him or not, and he may know it too beyond a doubt. He may know it as surely as if he read it with his own eyes; nay, he may know it more surely than that; for if I read a thing with my eyes, even my eyes may deceive me, the testimony of sense may be false. But the testimony of the Spirit must be true. We have the witness of the Spirit within, bearing witness with our spirits that we are born of God. There is such a thing on earth as an infallible assurance of our election. Let a man once get that, and it will anoint his head with fresh oil, it will clothe him with the white garment of praise and put the song of the angel into his mouth. Happy, happy man! who is fully assured of his interest in the covenant of grace, in the blood of atonement, and in the glories of heaven. Such men there are here this very day. Let them "rejoice in the Lord always; and again I say, Rejoice".'

Like the Author of the Epistle to the Hebrews I am tempted to say: 'And what shall I more say? for the time would fail me to tell of . . .'

I have but given a few extracts from different centuries and

---

[1] C. H. Spurgeon, *Revival Year Sermons* (1859), p. 77. Banner of Truth, 1959.

different places from men and women of very different types and temperaments. Some were men of unusual ability and learning, men who kept a strict control over their feelings, and who were remote from excitability and superficiality; others were more ordinary, but with one accord they all bear the same testimony as to what happens when the Spirit bears witness with our spirits that we are indeed children of God.

Having thus reinforced what we have been trying to say by means of these great authorities, we shall proceed to consider further aspects of this great and vitally important matter.

Twenty-eight

*

The Spirit itself beareth witness with our spirit, that we are the children of God.

Romans 8 : 16

We have now arrived at a point at which we have seen something of the nature and the character of this great experience which comes to all who know what it is to have the Spirit testifying with their spirits that they are the children of God. In addition I have demonstrated that the apostolic teaching has been emphasized in various centuries of the Protestant era in particular, by men of different schools of theology, and by men of different types of character and of temperament. We have seen that there is a strange and curious unanimity with regard to the character of the experience of knowing the witness of the Holy Spirit with our spirits that we are children of God. There is one further bit of evidence to be considered. We have looked at the Puritans, and at the two sections into which Methodism divided in the 18th century. We have seen the testimony of the Baptists as represented by Charles Haddon Spurgeon, and of the Presbyterians in America and Scotland, and also Congregationalists such as Jonathan Edwards.

To make this evidence complete I now show that the early teachers among the people commonly known as Plymouth Brethren also taught this doctrine. Take for instance J. N. Darby, in many ways the founder of Brethrenism. In his book on *The Sealing of the Spirit* you will read the following: he says, 'That a person may be born again and not have received the Holy Ghost is perfectly certain according to the Scriptures'.[1] And then he proceeds to quote the various Scriptures in Acts and elsewhere which we ourselves have considered. Another famous teacher among the

[1] p. 18.

Brethren wrote a number of books which bear his initials alone to indicate the authorship – 'C. H. M.', which stand for C. H. Mackintosh. In his works known as *Things New and Old* we find this[1]: 'We consider Acts 19: 1–7 does most clearly show that persons may be disciples and believers and yet not be sealed with the Holy Ghost'. C.H.M. says that it is perfectly clear from Acts 19: 1–7 that to be a Christian is one thing, to be sealed is another; that you can be a Christian without knowing this sealing; you can be a believer, you can be a disciple, and yet not know the sealing of the Spirit.

The third, and the last, of the great teachers among the early Brethren whom I quote is William Kelly. He is still read extensively by the Brethren and others; they are republishing his works at the present time. One of his books on the New Testament deals with the doctrine of the Holy Spirit. It was first published in 1867, and in that edition,[2] you will find that he contrasts the reception of the Holy Spirit with belief and repentance. Belief and repentance, he says, are possible without receiving the Holy Spirit in this special sense. Of course, a man cannot believe the gospel without the Holy Spirit, he cannot be a Christian without the Holy Spirit being in him. We have seen that clearly in the 9th verse of this chapter: 'If any man have not the Spirit of Christ, he is none of his'. So when Kelly and the others write about the 'reception' of the Spirit, they mean the 'receiving' of the Spirit in the sense that the Apostles 'received' Him on the day of Pentecost, and the people in Samaria 'received' Him after Peter and John had visited them, and the disciples in Ephesus received Him after Paul, having already baptized them, laid his hands upon them. Kelly says specifically: 'It is a subsequent operation, it is an additional, separate blessing, it is a privilege founded upon faith already actively working in the heart. So far is it from being true that a man receives the gift of the Holy Ghost the moment that he believes, that it may well be doubted whether there ever was such a case since the world began. I do not mean to deny that the gift of the Holy Ghost may be practically on the same occasion but never in the same moment.' That is surely as explicit and as clear as anything can possibly be.

So, then, we have these three great teachers among the early Brethren – J. N. Darby, C. H. Mackintosh and William Kelly

[1] Vol. X, p. 198.
[2] pp. 161, 162.

– agreeing with the other authorities whom I have quoted and with what we have seen for ourselves from our study of the Scripture. Hence we are now in a position to sum up by saying that it is clear that this is a distinct and separate experience, that it is something intensely experimental, and that a man can know for certain whether he has ever received this witness of the Spirit, or the sealing of the Spirit. It is not something outside the realm of consciousness, not something non-experimental; indeed it is highly experimental, and as we have seen from the various accounts here in the Scriptures and from others throughout the centuries, it is something that, once a man has known it, he can never forget it. If it has only happened to a man once he will always look back to it as the highest point which he ever reached in his Christian experience.

I have referred again in passing to several clear statements in the Acts of the Apostles. There is one, perhaps, which I have not emphasized as much I might have done, namely, the case of the Apostle Paul himself. It is quite clear that he not only saw the Lord Jesus Christ on the road to Damascus, but that he also believed on Him, and in Him, on that occasion. But it is equally clear that he was not baptized with the Holy Ghost until three days later. We are told that 'he was three days without sight, and neither did eat nor drink' (Acts 9: 9). Then Ananias, a disciple living at Damascus, was told by the Lord to go to Paul (then Saul), and we read as follows in verses 17 and 18: 'And Ananias went his way, and entered into the house; and putting his hands on him said, Brother Saul, the Lord even Jesus, that appeared unto thee in the way as thou camest, hath sent me, that thou mightest receive thy sight, and be filled with the Holy Ghost. And immediately there fell from his eyes as it had been scales: and he received sight forthwith, and arose, and was baptized.' So even in the case of the great Apostle himself the same fact is evident as in the other cases. The case of Paul is often forgotten. Acts chapters 2, 8, 10, and 19 are considered, but the Apostle himself is as clear an illustration of this essential distinction between 'believing' and 'receiving the Holy Spirit', or being 'baptized with the Spirit', or being 'sealed by the Spirit', as any.

Another important scripture is Galatians 3: 2. The Apostle starts in verse 1 by saying: 'O foolish Galatians, who hath bewitched you, that ye should not obey the truth, before whose eyes Jesus Christ hath been evidently set forth, crucified among you?' Then he continues: 'This only would I learn of you, Received ye the Spirit by the works of the law, or by the hearing of faith?' Notice his question. He does not ask, 'Did you become believers, Christians, by the works of the law, or by the hearing of faith?' but 'Did you receive the Spirit?', clearly indicating that there is a difference between the two. If the Apostle had held that every believer of necessity receives the Spirit at his conversion, at his rebirth, on his becoming a Christian, then the question he would have asked would have been, 'Did you become Christians as the result of the works of the law, or by the hearing of faith?' If he had regarded these things as being invariably simultaneous, this would not have been the form that his question would have taken; he would have put it in the more general form. But he puts it here in exactly the same way as he did to the disciples whom he found at Ephesus: 'Did you receive the Holy Ghost when you believed?'

Indeed, the same thing is suggested by the fourteenth verse in the same third chapter of the Epistle to the Galatians. Paul says: 'Christ hath redeemed us from the curse of the law, being made a curse for us: for it is written, Cursed is every one that hangeth on a tree: that the blessing of Abraham might come on the Gentiles through Jesus Christ; that we might receive the promise of the Spirit through faith.' It is not merely that we become Christians, but that we Gentile believers, as well as those who were Jews, might receive this great 'promise of the Spirit', the 'promise of the Father', that which had been promised throughout the Old Testament, and which we find referred to again in John 7: 39, 'The Spirit was not yet given, because that Jesus was not yet glorified'. This great promise is of the coming of the Spirit in profusion, giving great clarity of understanding and insight, and a great feeling of assurance and of certainty with regard to our standing and our relationship to God. As I have shown, we find this teaching and experience not only in the Scriptures but also in numerous teachers in the Church whom God has honoured, and who belong to all sections of the Christian Church, cutting right across all the divisions and the distinctions, and all the theologies. Here they seem to be one – your Strict Baptist, your John Wesley, Jonathan Edwards and D. L. Moody. The list includes great intellects and men of much lesser intellects, outstanding people in the Church and quite ordinary people. We have seen that the experience is common to all, and this helps us to understand its unique character and its 'givenness'. It is not the result of what we do, it is something that God Himself does to us.

The next question we must consider is, How can we differentiate between this experience and counterfeit experiences? This has to be done because, the moment we emphasize the experimental or the experiential aspect of anything taught in the Scriptures, we at once expose ourselves to the danger of the counterfeit. The devil, the adversary, is always ready to take advantage, and particularly so when it is a matter of experience, and feeling and the sensibilities are involved. Therefore it is of urgent and vital importance that we should be aware of this and on our guard. The New Testament exhorts us to 'test', to 'try', to 'prove' the spirits, for the reason that certain of them are 'not of God'. There is a spirit of antichrist, a false spirit. These false spirits have manifested their activities from the early days of the Church, and it is as incumbent upon us as it was on Christians in the Apostle's days to apply the tests. But not only does the teaching of the Scripture urge us to do this, the subsequent history of the Christian Church shows it to be imperative. As you read the long story of the Church you will find that nothing has been a more frequent source of trouble than the tendency of certain people to go to excess, and to be guilty of extravagances which bring the entire Christian cause into disrepute.

This was seen at the time of the Reformation, and still more at the time of the Puritan Awakening of the 17th century. There were people on one edge of the Puritan movement who, starting very rightly by stressing the importance of an experience of the Spirit, tended to go too far, and ended in mysticism, and manifested certain excesses. This happened among many of the early Quakers who arose at that time. In other words, the moment you begin to emphasize experience, the devil will endeavour to drive certain people to extremes. Hence it is absolutely essential that all experiences should be examined and tested. Later still, the Evangelical Revival of the 18th century placed great emphasis on experience and assurance of salvation. Whitefield and the Wesleys emphasized the importance of assurance and of an active living experience of the Spirit. Christianity, they had learned from

Henry Scougal, is '*The life of God in the Soul of Man*'. The result of their preaching was that certain people tended to go off into extravagances and excesses. The same thing happened in the 19th century. A number of 'freak' religions and movements arose, particularly in the United States of America. An excellent account of these is found in one of Warfield's two volumes on *Perfectionism*,[1] and also more popularly in a book entitled *Group movements and experiments in Guidance* by Ray Strachey. It is therefore essential that we should carefully test ourselves. The devil knows that if he succeeds in giving us a counterfeit experience, and in persuading us that we have the true experience, we shall no longer seek the true experience. Not only so, but, as I am going to show, we shall be in a state of self-satisfaction which inhibits growth.

The moment a person begins to desire and to seek for the witness of the Spirit, the devil will do his utmost to supply him with a counterfeit experience. Because of that, some people say: 'Realizing that it is dangerous to seek this experience, the only safe position is to have nothing to do with experiences, but to hold to the Word, to be a man of the Word. If you start seeking experiences you never know what may happen to you.' But if you speak thus, then you are guilty of the terrible sin of 'quenching the Spirit'. That is exactly what it means. To say, in a spirit of fear, that you are not interested in experiences is to say that you are not interested in something which God is offering you, something which God teaches in His Word, and which He has demonstrated through His great saints. You may be content to live a nice little self-contained, respectable Christian life, but thereby you are 'quenching the Spirit', robbing yourself of one of the most glorious aspects of the Christian faith, and at the same time deliberately turning your back upon the teaching of the Scripture. And you will certainly suffer as a result. But still more important, perhaps, is the fact that you are helping to keep the Christian Church from revival, and thereby you are hindering the vital work of evangelism. What can be more serious? I emphasize this because I know that there are many such people. They do not want revival because they are afraid of excesses, and their slogan is, that 'Everything should be done decently and in order'. That is 'quenching the Spirit'. To refuse anything that is offered in the Word of God because you are afraid of certain possible conse-

[1] B. B. Warfield, *Perfectionism*. Presbyterian and Reformed Pub. Co. 1967.

quences is a most grievous sin, and it will undoubtedly receive the punishment it deserves. The way to face this problem is not to turn your back upon it; it is to be clear as to the difference between the true and the false. Because there is the real danger of false experiences you must not shut out all experiences. The right way is to seek the true experience, and to make certain that you know how to tell the difference between that and the false.

What then are the differences? I have decided to adopt the common Puritan classification. I borrow it because I cannot think of a better one. The Puritans taught that you can partly test the difference between the true and the spurious by investigating what they call the 'antecedents' of the experience. What they mean is that if you examine the person's life before this experience came it will be a good guide as to whether it is a true or a false experience. Of course, sometimes you cannot do so, for, as William Kelly has reminded us, the 'believing' and 'the receiving' of this experience may be almost simultaneous. Then you cannot say much about the antecedents. But that is exceptional. Speaking generally, in most cases there is a clear time-interval between becoming a Christian and knowing this testimony, or sealing, of the Spirit; and therefore you are able to concentrate on the antecedents.

The true antecedents are a sense of sin, and a sense of failure. If you have had a sense of sin and a sense of failure, a sense of weariness and emptiness, a sense of soul need; if you have known a longing for assurance, for power and ability, then it is very good presumptive evidence that the experience you have had is a true experience. If, on the other hand, you talk about some marvellous experience you have had, but have never known what it is to be grieved about yourself; if you have never known a spirit of heaviness, a spirit of mourning; if you have never been seeking; if you have never really had a deep hunger; then it is presumptive evidence that your experience is not a true one. It does not prove it, but it is very valuable evidence. Those whose experiences I have quoted are unanimous in saying that they had always known that preliminary stage. There had been much prayer, there had been much diligent seeking of this witness of the Spirit. In some shape or form, every one of them had been uttering the cry we have earlier quoted from the hymn of William Williams:

Tell me Thou art mine, O Saviour,
Grant me an assurance clear.

That had been their desire, the thing they had been longing for, and they had expressed it to God and to the Lord Jesus Christ in prayer.

In addition these souls have proved the genuineness of their seeking and their desire by holy living. They have done all they could to 'perfect holiness in the fear of God'. They have not gone on living carelessly, merely asking God to give them this blessing. They have realized that this experience comes as a kind of 'seal' upon the fact that we are the children of God, and therefore holy; in consequence they have realized that they must do everything they can to please Him. They have been careful about their lives, they have not been negligent and wayward. They have walked warily, they have 'walked circumspectly'; they have realized that if they are to receive this great boon and blessing from God, they must prove themselves dutiful children. It is not that they believe that, because they are living a good life, it is bound to happen. Let me use the obvious illustration again. When we were children, if we wanted some extra gift from our parents, we were very careful to be on our best behaviour; we knew well that if we had been mischievous, or had done something that was wrong, there was no sense in going to ask for an extra penny. We had sufficient common sense to know that if we wanted some special favour from a father or a mother we must have some kind of a right, as it were, to ask for it. It is the same in the Christian life. So if you find persons claiming some marvellous experience, but know, as the result of observation, that there is no effort after holiness or striving after godliness in their lives, it is right that you should have queries and questions in your mind concerning them, and be on your guard. The antecedents are most important. Universal experience teaches us that, and also the Word of God itself. The Holy Spirit seals His own work; and He is not likely to grant this sealing to a man who is behaving badly, and who is an undutiful child of God. He would be, as it were, almost contradicting Himself were He to do so.

But let us turn to the accompaniments of the experience, and consider first the false, the spurious experiences. We almost invariably find that those who have had a false experience say that it came to them quite independently of the Word of God. That is already a most valuable point for it indicates that you are probably dealing with the false. The matter became very clear in the 17th century. The Quakers, and certain others on the extreme wing of the Puritan party, tended to depreciate the value of the Bible. They claimed that they did not need it, that they had the 'inner light', that the Spirit was speaking directly to them. There are many such people today. I remember a man who had had a striking conversion, saying once in a discussion meeting that it mattered not at all to him what Paul or anyone else said; he knew! That is what tends to happen when people claim an experience that is independent of, and apart from the Word.

Another characteristic of such people is that they have much to say about visions or ecstasies or signs. They are always interested in phenomena. They have seen a ball of light, or they have seen a vision of the Lord Jesus Christ. There is great emphasis on the phenomenal aspect, on some striking dramatic incident that has happened in their experience; and the physical, or semi-physical element always comes in. The devil is never as clever as he thinks he is; he always makes the mistake of overdoing the counterfeit experience which he can produce. There is always the tendency to exaggeration. They may talk a lot about physical prostrations or curious physical sensations. They often talk graphically about sensations, as if a hot iron or an electric current were passing through them. The result is that they are always very excited about the experience itself, and always ready to boast about it, and to emphasize the physical aspect, the phenomenal side.

When we turn to the true we find the exact opposite. Here, the experience comes almost invariably with or through the Word. We have already dealt with this. It may come apart from it, but generally the Word is very prominent. If the experience does not come when a person is actually reading the Word, or listening to a sermon, it is probably the case that the Spirit reminds him of a portion of Scripture and brings it back to memory. In any case it always confirms the teaching of the Scripture; it is always directly in accord with it. It is the Spirit who gives the Word, and it is the Spirit who gives this testimony; obviously, therefore, they are in agreement and work together, and each points to the other. That is a very good test.

But there is a further point of central importance. The hallmark of the true experience is a sense of awe, and accompanying it, a sense of unworthiness. This is inevitable because the Spirit is the *Holy* Spirit; and when He comes in great power, as He does in this experience, He gives us some impression of the glory, the greatness, the majesty, and the holiness of God. This was clear in all the experiences we have quoted. It stands out in the 6th chapter of Isaiah. When Isaiah was given a glimpse of the glory of God he said, 'Woe is me! for I am undone; for I am a man of unclean lips'. The same was true of the Apostle John on the Isle of Patmos. He says that he was 'in the Spirit'. He says that because he was not always 'in the Spirit', though the Spirit was always in him. This was something exceptional, a peculiar operation of the Spirit. 'I was in the Spirit on the Lord's day' says John, who then proceeds to describe his experiences. But what was the effect? He says: 'And when I saw him, I fell at his feet as dead' (Revelation 1: 17). It was not so much in fear as in awe produced by the sight of the glory, the majesty, the wonderful character of it all. The moment a person has a glimpse or a sense of this – and that is invariably what the Holy Spirit gives – he is at once not only filled with a sense of awe, but also with a sense of utter unworthiness, and a deep feeling of sinfulness. All the witnesses are agreed about this. The first thing the Holy Spirit does is to make you see the blackness of your own heart, your own sinfulness. At one and the same time you are being given this great assurance, and yet you feel totally unworthy of it.

Accompanying this sense of unworthiness is a great sense of thankfulness that such an experience has been vouchsafed to you, and that God has been so gracious. Another element which is invariable is that the Lord Jesus Christ is glorified. He Himself said that He would send the Spirit, and that the Spirit would glorify Him. 'He shall glorify me', He said, 'He shall not speak of himself' – that is to say, that He does not speak out of Himself – 'but he shall take of mine and shall reveal it unto you'. This is a most thorough test, and it never fails. If what you have 'received' makes you think of the experience only, of what you felt, and sensed, and if it has no reference to the Lord Jesus Christ, then there is every reason to fear that it has been a spurious experience. The Spirit has been given to glorify Christ, and the greater the power with which He comes, the greater will be your knowledge of the Lord Jesus Christ and your desire to speak of, and to glorify Him.

This is always an interesting fact in connection with revivals. A revival means that a large number of people have this experience at the same time. The Spirit comes in great power upon a number of people and gives them this assurance. But what is so striking always at such times is that the people do not sing so much about the Holy Spirit as about the Lord Jesus Christ. That is the great characteristic of the hymns resulting from the Evangelical Revival of the 18th century. The great hymns of Charles Wesley are about the Lord Jesus Christ, as also are those of William Cowper, and of John Newton, and indeed all the hymns of that period. It was the same in the revival of 1859, and strikingly so in Wales in 1904 and 1905. The popular singing had reference to the Lord Jesus Christ and His blood and His death and His power to save. The outpouring of the Spirit leads to an outburst of praise which glorifies the Lord Jesus Christ.

Another good test is that I am given a great sense of God's love to me. 'The love of God is shed abroad in our hearts' (Romans 5: 5). I am amazed and astonished at it, and can scarcely believe it possible. Another test is a sense of the glory that awaits me and the inheritance for which I am being prepared. The Apostle, you notice, in this very context goes on to speak of this, and so he must: 'The Spirit itself beareth witness with our spirit, that we are the children of God. And if children, then heirs, heirs of God, and joint-heirs with Christ, if so be that we suffer with him, that we may be also glorified together'. It is an almost invariable accompaniment of this experience that one is given a glimpse of that inheritance, and of the glory, and that one becomes very much concerned about such matters. So you find many of the witnesses to this experience testifying that they felt that they were lifted right out of time, and that they did not seem to belong any longer to time. John Flavel, we remember, tells us that he even forgot about his wife and children; he forgot everything; all he knew was that he was a child of God, that he was destined for glory, and that he longed to get there. This is what the Apostle teaches here: 'If children, then heirs; heirs of God, and joint-heirs with Christ'. And this is true in spite of the most adverse circumstances! You may be desperately ill, as were some of whom we have been speaking; everything may be going against you, you may have lost all your goods, you may be persecuted, you may be dying; but still you are able to say with the Apostle, 'I reckon that the sufferings of this present time are not worthy to be compared with the glory which shall be revealed in us' (Romans 8: 18). You are made independent of circumstances and conditions; you are so certain that you are going to the promised glory that, in a sense, nothing else matters to you.

Let me say a word about the consequences of this experience, which are obviously, again, most important. In the case of the false experience the consequence is generally pride. This leads to constant talking about the experience, and boasting about it, with all the emphasis on the phenomenal aspect. Accompanying that, there is a glibness; and with that a sense of false security, and a negligence in the life. As the persons involved have had this great experience without seeking it, and without striving after holiness, why should they bother to follow after holiness now? They 'have it', it has happened to them, they are complete. There is always this glibness, and at the same time there is a hardness. There is no humility concerning it, no tenderness, either at the time of the experience or afterwards; but a carnal self-satisfaction, and a delight in boasting to others about this wonderful thing that has happened to them. The consequences of the true experience are altogether different. We have seen that D. L. Moody said that he scarcely ever referred to what had happened to him as he walked down Wall Street in New York City that afternoon when the Holy Spirit came upon him. He scarcely ever mentioned it, because it was too sacred. He was almost afraid to speak of it. All saints are agreed in saying that it is much more easily known than described. It is so transcendent that they cannot truly describe it. They know it; but 'The love of Jesus what it is, None but His loved ones know'; and they find it very difficult to put into words. But the man with the false experience knows no such difficulty. The artefact of the devil leads to exaggeration – the deluded person can describe the ball of fire, the electric current and the sensation of heat. But by definition, the genuine experience is very difficult to describe. The Christian does not go around boasting about it; it is the 'hidden manna', it is the 'white stone'.

The true experience is a secret transaction, as it were, between your heavenly Father and yourself, between the Son and yourself, between the Holy Spirit and yourself; and you do not talk glibly about it. You do not 'cast your pearls before swine', you do not parade your experience. In the natural realm those who experience true love for a person do not parade it. The people who address everyone as 'Dear' or 'Darling' obviously know nothing about true feeling, otherwise they could not use the terms so easily and freely. That is the false, the make-believe, the counterfeit, the spurious. The characteristic consequences of the true experience are a great love to God and a desire to please Him. When 'the Spirit bears witness with your spirit' you will of necessity at the same time be crying 'Abba, Father' also. You cannot have this without the 'Abba, Father', though you can have the 'Abba, Father' without this. But this always leads to that! God is telling you in this unusual way of His love to you, and it immediately stimulates your love to Him. Inevitably so! 'We love him because he first loved us'. And it leads to a deeper view of sin, and to a great hatred of sin. As you see the divine holiness and have a sight of your own ugliness and vileness, you feel undone, you feel the need of cleansing; and you do all you can about it. You also show a greater carefulness in the life, and have a desire to serve God and the Lord Jesus Christ utterly with your whole heart.

Moreover, the true experience always leads to a freedom in prayer that the Christian has never known before. He cannot know this 'witness of the Spirit with his own spirit' without being set free – free in prayer, free in worship, praise and adoration. It is true of private prayer, it is equally true of public prayer. There is no difficulty in getting people to prayer meetings during a time of revival; there is no difficulty in persuading them to take part in prayer; there are no long pauses between prayers in revivals because there is a 'freedom of the Spirit'. When a man is 'filled with the Spirit' he is full of a sense of 'wonder, love and praise'. Such a man also knows spiritual power, and is aware of a power in his conversation and in his testimony. If he is a preacher he is aware of a power in his preaching that he never knew before. He may have been preaching correctly before, and have known at times what it was to be given ease and freedom; but nothing like this! This is new! He is now looking on as it were; and he is aware that he is being used by the power of the Holy Spirit. In addition, he loses the fear of men, and the fear of death, as Paul goes on to say here. This is seen clearly in the case of the

Apostle Peter, the craven Peter who denied his Lord just before His death on the Cross, because he was afraid of death. But look at his boldness on the day of Pentecost and ever afterwards. And Paul, though he knew 'weakness, fear and much trembling', and fightings without and fears within, spoke with great boldness and authority.

Perhaps one of the most subtle tests of all is that a man who has ever known this true experience is one whose supreme desire is to know more of it. Think of it in terms of the Apostle's statement in Philippians 3 : 10, 11 where we read of his supreme desire. Sometimes it sounds surprising, but this is what he says: 'That I may know him, and the power of his resurrection, and the fellowship of his sufferings, being made conformable unto his death; if by any means I might attain unto the resurrection of the dead'. To know anything of this experience means that your supreme desire will be to know the Lord Jesus Christ still more intimately, still more personally, still more powerfully. In other words, the prayer of a man who has ever known this witness of the Spirit, this sealing of the Spirit, is the prayer that was so dear to the heart of that great man of God, Hudson Taylor, the founder of the China Inland Mission. It was found on a sheet of paper in his Bible when he died:

> *Lord Jesus, make Thyself to me*
> *A living bright reality;*
> *More present to faith's vision keen*
> *Than any outward object seen;*
> *More dear, more intimately nigh*
> *Than e'en the sweetest earthly tie.*

Once a man has known anything of this experience, he says, 'To me to live is Christ and to die is gain'. He says with Count Zinzendorf, 'I have one passion, it is He, and He alone'! To have a glimpse of Him, to have this knowledge of Him, and our relationship to Him, means that for ever after, that is the supreme passion and desire of the soul. Not to have wonderful experiences, not to be able to speak with tongues or to exercise some other gift, but to 'know him, and the power of his resurrection, and the fellowship of his sufferings, being made conformable unto his death'.

Twenty-nine

*

The Spirit itself beareth witness with our spirit, that we are the children of God.
                                                            Romans 8 : 16

We have been considering the ways in which the true experience of the witness of the Spirit can be differentiated from the false experience which the devil as an 'angel of light' is ever ready to produce. It is not at all difficult to understand why he should be particularly anxious to cause confusion over what I have suggested is the highest and perhaps the greatest experience open to a Christian in this world. Obviously the higher you go in spiritual experience, or in the spiritual realm, the more likely you are to be attacked by the devil. No one has ever been tempted in this world in the way in which our blessed Lord and Saviour was tempted; and it has been the universal testimony of the saints throughout the centuries that, the closer their walk with God, the more furious was the attack of the adversary upon them. Furthermore, the history of the Church demonstrates clearly that any central and vital doctrine has always been a special object of attack. Take, for instance, the confusion which has reigned over the whole question of the Lord's Supper. Because of its special character the devil has come in, and has invented many theories and introduced most extraordinary and fantastic views. In other words, it is virtually a law in the Christian life that, if a doctrine is particularly important, you can be certain that the attack of the enemy at that point will be unusually strong. It is particularly true in this matter of the testimony of the Spirit with our spirits that we are the children of God.

So we come now to another aspect of this matter, namely, the relationship between this experience and sanctification. It is most unfortunate that confusion has ever arisen concerning this. Throughout the centuries there have been groups of people who have fallen into confusion on this matter, and have taught a doctrine of perfectionism which they have based on this particular experience of the 'sealing of the Spirit' or the 'baptism of the Spirit', and unfortunately this is still the case. The modern confusion as between this experience and sanctification was started by no less a person than John Wesley. In the early 1740's he began to teach a type of perfectionism which he called 'perfect love', and it has persisted in various forms ever since. Most of the modern perfectionist groups in the Christian Church can be traced back to his teaching. He is the father of the tendency to identify these two things.

The teaching, more or less, is that it is possible for a Christian to have this 'baptism of the Spirit', and, having it, he is entirely cleansed from sin. He is given a new, a clean heart; he is given perfect love and has perfect love towards God. The teaching is that sin is entirely eradicated out of him, taken right out of his entire system, out of the whole personality; so that, as the result of this baptism of the Spirit, the believer is entirely cleansed from sin and becomes completely and entirely sanctified. The scriptural evidence they adduce to support and to substantiate this teaching consists of two main passages.

The first is Acts 15, verse 9, where the Apostle Peter is explaining to the council at Jerusalem his conduct in the case of Cornelius and his household. 'God', says Peter, 'which knoweth the hearts, bare them witness, giving them the Holy Ghost, even as he did unto us; and put no difference between us and them, purifying their hearts by faith.' 'You have already quoted part of that verse in establishing that this experience of the Spirit is separate from, and subsequent to, and additional to, the original belief and regeneration,' they say to me, 'so why do you not go on to complete the statement and quote the whole?' The final statement is, 'put no difference between us and them, purifying their hearts by faith'. They argue that the position is quite clear – 'purify' means 'entirely cleared'; and we are told that their hearts were 'purified by faith'. Such is the argument.

The second passage they quote is in the Acts of the Apostles, where our Lord gives the Apostle Paul his commission. He tells him that He is going to 'deliver him from the people', which means the Jews, 'and from the Gentiles, unto whom now

[371]

I send thee, to open their eyes, and to turn them from darkness to light, and from the power of Satan unto God, that they may receive forgiveness of sins, and inheritance among them which are sanctified by faith that is in me' (26:18). 'There,' they say, 'we find the same thing again. It is said that believers are "sanctified by faith".' On this basis they do not hesitate to teach that it is possible for a Christian to be entirely sanctified or purified; and there are people who claim that they have been entirely sanctified, entirely purified, so that there is no longer any sin in them. There is no need to say that they are generally most sincere, zealous, and often very able Bible-loving Christians.

Clearly we must examine these two statements most carefully. Invariably, the first thing to do when confronted by a verse or a statement of Scripture which is perplexing is to look at the statement in its context, in its setting. Never was that principle, that canon of interpretation, more important than at this particular point, for in both cases the context suggests that the doctrine of sanctification does not arise in either of the instances. Neither statement is concerned at all with the biblical doctrine of sanctification which, as we have seen earlier in this Chapter (verses 5–14), teaches a progressively increasing deliverance from sin, and a steady growth in holiness. I assert that in both these verses there is no reference whatsoever to that. Take the case of Acts 15. Peter was not at all concerned there to deal with the question of 'sanctification' as distinct from 'justification'. Neither was our Lord in Acts 26, in giving the commission to Paul, telling him that he would have to teach 'justification' and then 'sanctification'. That does not arise in either case.

The point at issue in the council of Jerusalem in Acts 15 was the position and the condition of Gentiles in relation to the Church. Peter had admitted Cornelius (a Gentile) and his household into the Church. There were certain Jewish Christians who were querying and questioning the rightness of such action. Their argument was that no one could become a Christian unless he became a Jew, unless he was circumcised. Circumcision, they urged, was essential to salvation. Their argument was that Peter was wrong in baptizing Gentiles who had never been circumcised. All that Peter is concerned to do, therefore, is to justify his action in baptizing, and admitting into the Christian Church, these Gentile believers. He is not concerned at all to deal with their state of sanctification, but simply to justify their admission into the Christian Church. He argues that, with the coming of the Gospel, the way to become God's people is no longer that of circumcision, but the way of faith. That is the only thing he wants to say, it is the only thing he needs to say, it is the only thing that he does say. He asserts that Christians must no longer think in terms of Jews and Gentiles, the Jews being God's people and therefore clean, the Gentiles being 'dogs' and therefore unclean. No! says Peter, that has gone; Jews and Gentiles are now both made clean and become Christians in the same way, namely, 'by faith'. 'Purifying their hearts by faith.' Moreover it is a statement about all Gentile believers, and not merely about those who have received a 'second blessing'.

In the commission given to Paul by the Lord on the road to Damascus precisely the same point is made. What is to be Paul's ministry to the Gentiles? He is 'to open their eyes, to turn them from darkness to light, and from the power of Satan unto God'. What for? 'That they may receive forgiveness of sins and inheritance' – a share, a possession. Where? 'Among them which are sanctified by faith that is in me.' In other words, it is the same point once more. The Jewish believers in Christ are set in this new position; but so also are the Gentiles who believe in Christ – 'by faith that is in *me*'. They are put into the same position as the Jews and there is no difference at all. Tell the Gentiles, says the Lord to Paul, that if they exercise 'faith in me' they will not only receive forgiveness of sins, but they will be put into the same position as the Jews who, like yourself, have already believed in me. That, surely, is the sole purpose of both statements. Sanctification does not arise at all; the biblical notion of sanctification as something distinct from justification is not considered in either of the two statements.

Looking at the two verses positively, we find that in both instances they remind us of what God had said to the Children of Israel just before He gave them the Ten Commandments. The account is found in Exodus 19, which the Apostle Peter quotes in his First Epistle, chapter 2, verses 9 and 10. God had said to the Children of Israel: 'Ye are a chosen generation, a royal priesthood, an holy nation, a peculiar people.' The Apostle Peter, writing to Gentiles who now had become Christians, tells them that that statement was now true of them. In other words, the meaning of the terms 'purified' and 'sanctified' by faith, in both cases is 'setting apart as God's people'. It does not mean anything further. It did not mean anything more than that in the case of the Israelites. We have but to read their story to know that it cannot have meant 'sanctification'. All it means is that while the other nations of the world were not God's people, God had put these people on one side as His own people. He made them for Himself, they were to be to Him 'a peculiar possession', so they are 'an holy people', the others being 'profane'. In exactly the same way, the mountain on which the law was given to Moses is referred to as the 'holy mount', in the sense that it was set apart. Similarly the Scriptures talk about purifying and sanctifying the instruments and the vessels of the sanctuary and of the temple. This is the meaning of the terms 'purify' and 'sanctify' in both instances. Sanctification is not even remotely introduced at all.

But that is only the beginning of the evidence. My assertion is that the context establishes that both statements are only concerned to say that the Gentiles become the people of God, a part of the holy nation, a part of this peculiar possession of God, 'by faith', and that they have been cleansed from that which kept them out hitherto. What kept them out before? There is a statement in the Epistle to the Hebrews which is very important in this whole argument: 'Take heed, brethren, lest there be in any of you an evil heart of unbelief, in departing from the living God' (3: 12). Unbelief comes from an 'evil' heart, which means a polluted heart, an unclean heart. The opposite of that is 'a believing heart'; and belief obviously comes from a heart that is no longer evil, unclean, and polluted. Peter argues in the council at Jerusalem, that this is precisely what had happened to the Gentiles: 'God put no difference between them and us, purifying their hearts by faith'. Their hearts were evil, and unclean; but, says Peter, As I was preaching they believed the Gospel. It is obvious, therefore, that their hearts had been cleansed from the evil unbelief that was in them. They had no longer 'evil hearts of unbelief', their hearts had been 'purified by faith'. And so Peter had baptized them. Peter is not arguing that these Gentiles had suddenly been completely sanctified. The other interpretation means that Peter is saying that Cornelius and his household, hearing the Gospel for the

first time, were not only made believers, but were entirely sanctified at one and the same moment, and never had any need to
grow afterwards. But all we are told is that their hearts were
delivered from that evil unbelief that was in them formerly,
and purified by faith. In other words, the way into the kingdom
and family of God is not through circumcision and ceremonial
ablutions, but simply 'by faith', by 'believing'.

We have still further evidence to support our interpretation.
Take for instance what the Apostle Paul says in the First Epistle
to the Corinthians: 'Be not deceived' – God is not mocked –
'neither fornicators, nor idolaters, nor adulterers, nor effeminate,
nor abusers of themselves with mankind, nor thieves, nor cove-
tous, nor drunkards, nor revilers, nor extortioners, shall inherit the
kingdom of God. And such were some of you; but ye are washed,
but ye are sanctified, but ye are justified in the name of the Lord
Jesus, and by the Spirit of our God' (6: 9, 10, 11). What is
important here, of course, is the order. Notice that 'sanctified'
is put before 'justified' – 'Ye are washed, ye are sanctified, ye
are justified'. Has the Apostle suddenly forgotten that 'justification' must come before 'sanctification'? The question is ridiculous in the case of a divinely inspired writer. There are no such
mistakes; and when he puts 'sanctification' before 'justification'
in this way, he does so quite deliberately. In other words, in
this context 'sanctification' does not carry the same meaning
as it does, for instance, in the first chapter of that same Epistle
in verse 30, where Paul says, 'But of him are ye in Christ Jesus,
who of God is made unto us wisdom, even righteousness, and
sanctification, and redemption'. In this latter text we have the
biblical theological order – righteousness (justification), sanctification (meaning progressive sanctification), 'redemption' (glorification). But in chapter 6 verse 11 it is a different order – 'Washed,
sanctified, justified'. So there it does not mean what sanctification normally means; it means exactly the same as in Acts 15: 9
and Acts 26: 18 – simply a setting apart, and delivering from the
'evil heart of unbelief'.

But take 2 Thessalonians 2: 13 also: 'But we are bound to
give thanks to God for you, brethren beloved of the Lord,
because God hath from the beginning chosen you to salvation
through sanctification of the Spirit and belief of the truth.'
Again notice the order. He puts 'sanctification of the Spirit'

before 'belief of the truth'. The only possible way of expounding that accurately is to say that it does not refer to sanctification in its general New Testament sense. The Apostle is thanking God that He has from the beginning chosen the Thessalonians to salvation, for He has separated them by His Spirit to belief of the truth. That is exactly what the Spirit does in the first instance. Imagine a crowd of people listening to an evangelistic sermon. At the close of the sermon some have believed and some have not believed. Why is it that some have believed? It is because the Spirit has 'sanctified' them, has set them apart, has called them out. It is the 'call' of the Spirit; it is the work of the Spirit in conviction, and calling out, and giving the power to believe. As Mount Sinai was set apart and is called 'the holy mount', so these are set apart by the Spirit, and belief of the truth is the outcome.

This is a vital matter because those people – honest and sincere – who misinterpret these two verses (Acts 15: 5 and 26: 18) and persuade themselves that they are entirely sanctified, when they subsequently may fall into sin, and people know that they have done so, then sometimes feel that they have never been Christians at all, or that they have sinned against the Holy Ghost. Other people look on and say 'There is your perfect person! There is the heart that was pure, and full of love, and entirely sanctified! Look at it!' Thus it does grievous harm to the Christian cause.

Take, further, the statement in 1 Peter 1: 2. Here the Apostle, as I have already reminded you, is writing to a number of 'strangers scattered abroad' whom he does not know personally. He says, 'Peter, an apostle of Jesus Christ, to the strangers scattered throughout Pontus, Galatia, Cappadocia, Asia, and Bithynia, elect according to the foreknowledge of God the Father, through sanctification of the Spirit, unto obedience and sprinkling of the blood of Jesus Christ'. Note the same order again. These people have become Christians 'through (by means of) the sanctification of the Spirit'. The Spirit puts them on one side, separates them, does His gracious work in them, in order that they may give 'obedience unto the truth' concerning the sprinkling of the blood of Jesus Christ, whereby a man's sins are remitted and he becomes a child of God. But notice that it is 'through sanctification of the Spirit, unto (belief and) obedience', whereas we know that

[376]

with the doctrine of sanctification, as generally expounded, you believe first and are justified, and then your sanctification follows and goes on progressively.

But to settle the matter once and for ever we have to go to the 22nd verse in the 1st chapter of Peter's First Epistle. Starting with verse 18 we read: 'Forasmuch as ye know that ye were not redeemed with corruptible things, as silver and gold, from your vain conversation received by tradition from your fathers; but with the precious blood of Christ, as of a lamb without blemish and without spot: who verily was foreordained before the foundation of the world, but was manifest in these last times for you, who by him do believe in God, that raised him up from the dead, and gave him glory; that your faith and hope might be in God. Seeing ye have purified your souls in obeying the truth through the Spirit unto unfeigned love of the brethren, see that ye love one another with a pure heart fervently.' The Apostle says that these Gentiles have 'purified their (own) souls' by believing. This is the very thing Peter was arguing in the council at Jerusalem (Acts 15) when he said that God had 'purified their hearts by faith'. But here he says that they had purified their own hearts and souls by believing the truth. Of course, it means exactly the same thing. He is saying in both instances that God has given these people the gift of faith, and in exercising it they have purified their hearts. What purifies the heart is the belief, the faith, the obedience to the truth. And so the Apostle is equally right in saying here that they have purified their own souls in obeying the truth – through the Spirit. It is always 'through the Spirit'. 'The natural man receiveth not the things of the Spirit of God; for they are foolishness unto him'. No man believes this truth except 'through the Spirit'. The Spirit does this separating work, this calling out; and then, in believing, our hearts are purified. We no longer have 'an evil heart of unbelief'. By believing you have 'purified' your heart. So it does not matter whether it is said that your heart is purified or that you have purified your own heart, for it comes to the same thing. So there is really no ground whatsoever for arguing that these two verses teach the possibility of 'entire sanctification by faith' at any moment. They are not intended to teach anything of the sort; and they most certainly do not do so.

Having dealt with the question directly in that way, I now call attention to a passage which supports my thesis indirectly. It is in the First Epistle to the Corinthians, chapter 7, verse 14. This is a chapter in which the Apostle deals with the married relationship of people who have become Christians. Some of these early Christians clearly thought that if one of them had become a Christian he or she should leave the unconverted partner. But the Apostle says; 'If any brother hath a wife that believeth not, and she be pleased to dwell with him, let him not put her away. And the woman which hath an husband that believeth not, and if he be pleased to dwell with her, let her not leave him. For the unbelieving husband is sanctified by the wife, and the unbelieving wife is sanctified by the husband: else were your children unclean; but now they are holy' – a very important statement! Our friends who teach Perfectionism say: 'When the Scripture says "purified" it means purified; when the Scripture says "sanctified" it means sanctified. So if it says that "their hearts were purified by faith" it means that they were absolutely cleansed from all sin.' The simple answer to such a claim is 1 Corinthians 7: 14, where the same word is used about 'the unbelieving husband', a man who is not a Christian at all, and yet we are told that he is 'sanctified by the wife'. If 'sanctified' means sanctified in the 'perfectionist' sense, then the unbelieving husband is entirely cleansed from sin. Such is the ludicrous, the ridiculous position to which the claim leads!

We must never base an argument on one word. The word must always be taken in its context. The same word may carry several different connotations, and if you pay attention to the context you will avoid trouble. We are told also in 1 Corinthians 7, that the children of the two parties – one a believer, the other not so – are 'holy', they are no longer 'unclean'. That can have but one meaning. It does not mean that they are 'entirely sanctified', it means that they are allowed to come into the church, they are allowed to come among God's people while they are worshipping in their churches, and to enjoy certain general benefits. And that is, of course, all it is intended to mean.

We deduce, therefore, that all we have in those two statements in the Acts of the Apostles – 15: 9 and 26: 18 – is a reference to 'setting apart'. According to the Arndt and Gingrich Lexicon the word means, 'To include in the inner circle of what is holy in both religious and moral uses of the word'. Nothing more! It means that the 'set apart' person is allowed to belong to this particular company. Indeed they go on to say: 'These words which are translated by either "purified" or "sanctified" or "make holy" are what are described as Cultic words'. That means, of course, that they have an association with the various mystery religions and other religions that were known in the world in New Testament days. The pagans had their various religions. The words in question always have this Cultic association; they invariably conjure up the notion of some ritual, or ceremony or some process of initiation into the circle of the devotees of a particular religion. Similar ideas are employed in the modern world; I am told that people who become freemasons have to be 'initiated' into that circle. In the same way people used to be initiated in ancient times; they could not belong to a particular religion unless they had been initiated according to its rites. An animal might be killed, and the blood put upon them and so on. So the words translated as 'purify' or 'sanctify' indicate that the way of initiation into the Christian Church, and into the kingdom and the family of God, is now 'by faith'. That is all they say – nothing more! As the result of believing the message the believer was no longer unclean; but not in the sense that he was now perfectly sanctified. Outside the kingdom of God we are all unclean. So to come into the kingdom of God we have to be cleansed in this sense – 'ye are washed, ye are sanctified'. Thus we are brought in; it is the 'initiation', that by which we are 'introduced'; and since the coming of our Lord and His perfect work it is a matter of 'faith'. Faith, and faith alone, admits into this relationship to God, which is found in and through our Lord and Saviour Jesus Christ.

We must note that in all these quotations and illustrations the reference has been to Christians in general. Peter, when speaking in the council at Jerusalem, was referring to all who had believed with Cornelius in his house, and to all other Gentiles who had believed subsequently. In exactly the same way it is stated of all the members of the Church at Corinth that they had been 'washed and sanctified and justified'. The Lord, in giving His commission to the Apostle, tells him that this will happen to all Gentiles who believe; all Gentiles who exercise faith will have a share in the inheritance among all who are sanctified. It is always universal. Peter in writing to the 'strangers scattered abroad' addressed his words to all the members of all the churches in all those countries. But according to the erroneous teaching, all Christians are not 'sanctified by faith', for this sanctification is regarded and taught as a second and a special blessing. It says that all Christians are justified, but it is only some who are 'sanctified by faith', namely, those who believe the teaching and therefore 'go in for' the second blessing. But the two verses on which they rely are universal, and all similar verses are equally universal in their application. So, from every conceivable standpoint, there is no evidence whatsoever for the teaching that the baptism of the Spirit means 'entire sanctification by faith'. Peter says: 'And God, which knoweth the hearts, bare them witness, giving them the Holy Ghost even as he did unto us' (Acts 15: 8). He is clearly referring to Acts 2 and the day of Pentecost, and the baptism with the Holy Ghost. So then, when he goes on to say 'purifying their hearts by faith' (verse 9), they put the two together and say that 'the baptism of or with the Holy Spirit' obviously means entire sanctification, purification of the heart, entire eradication of sin, complete holiness. How subtle this is! The only way to avoid such pitfalls is to pay careful attention to the context instead of isolating a phrase and establishing a doctrine on it; and at the same time to 'compare scripture with scripture'.

Let me produce some further proofs. Surely the state of the Church at Corinth, and elsewhere, proves that my interpretation must be correct. Who would care to say that the members of the Church at Corinth were 'entirely sanctified'? In that sixth chapter where the Apostle reminds them that they had been washed and sanctified, he also warns them to be very careful as to how they lived. 'Be not deceived', he says, God is not mocked. They still had need of much teaching about the way of sanctification. And so it is with all the New Testament Epistles. If the 'entire sanctification' teaching were true, as I have pointed out earlier, these New Testament Epistles would never have been needed. It would only have been necessary to address Christian people to the following effect: 'Now that you have believed the gospel and have become Christians, all you have to do is to receive a second blessing which will make you perfect and entire. You can have your sanctification at any moment; and then your hearts will be entirely purified and cleansed; you will be utterly delivered from sin.' But what we actually find in the New Testament is something very different. It is what we have already found in this eighth chapter of the Epistle to the Romans, verse 13, where the Apostle says: 'For if ye live after the flesh, ye shall die; but if ye through the Spirit do mortify the deeds of the body, ye shall live.' He does not tell them that they can be fully sanctified by faith in one act. They have to 'mortify' the deeds of the body; they have to go on being 'led by the Spirit' as he says in verse 14. And it is the same throughout. The New Testament is full of detailed exhortations. The very word we have been studying is used in James 4: 8: 'Draw nigh to God, and he will draw nigh to you. Cleanse your hands, ye sinners; and purify your hearts, ye double minded.' How important it is to compare scripture with scripture, and not isolate one verse or phrase such as 'purified by faith'! James exhorts believers to 'purify their hearts', which means, in part, that they must not be 'double minded', must not admit again that 'evil heart of unbelief'. They must not imagine that they can have Christ, and yet lust after sin at the same time. They must get rid of sin and purify their hearts. 'Cleanse your hands.' We have to do that; sin is not all taken out of us suddenly. Are not all the New Testament Epistles full of the same teaching? do they not all exhort us? 'Let him that stole steal no more.' 'Let no filthy communications come out of your mouth.' And such communications do not come only from the mouth. 'What comes out from the mouth', says our Lord, 'comes out of the heart' (Matthew 15: 17–20). We have to go on waging this battle. But these exhortations are all misplaced if there is such a thing as being cleansed entirely from sin, and given a pure heart, in one act of faith. It makes so much scriptural teaching and exhortation quite unnecessary; and therefore it must be wrong.

What then is the true relationship between this experience of the 'sealing of the Spirit', or 'baptism of the Spirit', or 'the testimony of the Spirit with our spirit', and sanctification? My answer is that it has no direct association or relationship; but it has a very important indirect relationship. This is seen clearly in the various experiences which have been quoted, as well as in the teaching of the Scripture. Those who have had this experience say that, when the Spirit bore witness with their spirit that they were children of God, they were aware that they were in the presence of the holy God. Everything was light, and pure, and clean, and holy; the whole atmosphere was 'light and holiness'. And yet, at the same moment, they felt that they were sinful. Not only so; they hated sin, and never wanted to sin again. They felt an utter, complete abhorrence of sin at that moment. Of course! In the presence of God, their hearts went out to Him in love, and they desired to live only to Him and to His glory and praise. They felt they must never sin again. But, alas, that does not mean that even at that moment their heart was entirely cleansed from sin. It was the presence of the Lord that made sin unthinkable! But in their heart, in their inmost being, they remained the same, there was still sin in their members, in this mortal body of which the Apostle has written so much.

It can be easily understood how people feel at the moment of the experience that they are entirely cleansed from sin. We all know something about this in the ordinary experiences of life. Do you not feel that you are a better person when you are talking to a saint? And have you not sometimes felt when you are talking to a very saintly person that sin is utterly unthinkable? It is certainly so! They have a cleansing, purifying effect upon you while you are with them, and you feel that you will never willingly sin again. But that has not changed your constitution, you are still the same person; and you may leave such a saint and in a moment you may sin. Is not that true to experience? It was the experience of these New Testament people, of the members of the Church at Corinth who had to be warned solemnly in a powerful exhortatory manner. Most New Testament Christians had probably received the baptism of the Spirit – hence their gifts – but that does not guarantee sanctification, does not guarantee holiness.

But the baptism of the Spirit does stimulate and promote sanctification, indeed it is the greatest possible help to it. This is so, partly because, as so many Christians have testified, it has given them a sense of the glory that is awaiting them; they have had a glimpse of it; and the result is as described by John in his First Epistle: 'Every man that hath this hope in him, purifieth himself, even as he is pure' (3: 3). Everything that brings us nearer to the Lord gives us a sense of His glory, of His love to us, of His holiness, and of what He is preparing for us. Nothing so stimulates us to be more sanctified, to cleanse ourselves, and to prepare for what is coming. So this testimony of the Spirit stimulates sanctification, and encourages us to seek it; but it does not guarantee it automatically; it does not *cause* it to happen within us.

Let me try to convey this truth in the form of an illustration. Imagine a farmer or a gardener sowing seed in the ground. He digs or ploughs and harrows, and then puts in the seed. He covers it over and flattens it out. Then he waits for some sign of growth. But weeks pass and nothing happens. There may be a particularly dry spell of weather. At long last the seed begins to sprout and just appears above the ground. Then growth seems to stop at that stage and there seems to be no development, so the man begins to wonder whether there is life or not. Then suddenly there comes a wonderful burst of sunshine and a good shower of rain. The man returns and looks at the plot which had seemed to be quite dead in the morning and finds that by evening all is green. He can almost see the shoots growing. What is the explanation? It is that life was there all along, but it was feeble. But there was life in the seed, though it did not seem to be much in evidence. But the sunshine comes and the shower comes, and the life springs up immediately. More happens in one afternoon than had happened in the previous weeks. That is a picture of the relationship. The sunshine and the rain are the Spirit 'bearing witness with our spirits', 'the love of God shed abroad in our hearts'. And some men have testified that they received more in one hour of this experience than they had felt and learned in fifty years. The effect of the rain and the sunshine on the seed in the ground is to stimulate, to draw out the life that is present in the seed. It is precisely the same in the Christian life. The moment we are born again the process of sanctification has started, the seed of life and of holiness is implanted in us, and nothing so causes that seed of life to spring up, to grow and to develop and to show itself in a manner that amazes everyone, as this baptism or sealing with the Spirit, this testimony that the Spirit bears with our spirits. Such, then, is the relationship between the testimony of the Spirit and our sanctification. It is not direct, it is not immediate: it is indirect. It is the greatest stimulus to sanctification, but it is not sanctification itself.

[383]

Thirty

*

The Spirit itself beareth witness with our spirit, that we are the children of God.
Romans 8 : 16

There is still one aspect of this all-important subject for us to consider, and it is the most practical. As Thomas Goodwin has reminded us, there is nothing beyond this except heaven itself; it is the highest point which we can ever reach in this world of time. So we now face the question that remains – Is this, then, something that we should seek?

I answer: Certainly, obviously, it should be sought, and for reasons which should be quite self-evident. If this experience is open to all Christian believers in this life, and any feel that they have not known it, surely they should seek it. Every Christian should always be seeking the best and the highest. We should never be content with anything less than what is described as possible to the Christian in the New Testament. One of the great troubles in the Christian Church today, as has often been the case before, is that so many Christian people are content to live complacently. They are anxious to know that they are saved and that they are not going to hell; but they seem to be content with that. But it should be our earnest desire always to enjoy all that is offered us of 'the exceeding riches' of the grace of God in and through our Lord and Saviour Jesus Christ. What happens on the natural level demonstrates this clearly. It is a characteristic of love always to demand certainty. Love not only gives, love also demands. Any hesitation, any doubt, any query in the love relationship leads to misery; love demands certainty. And it should be the same in our relationship to God. God is our Father, and we are His children. It is a relationship of love, and it is unnatural there-

[384]

fore, apart from anything else, for the child not to desire an absolute certainty and assurance of the love of his heavenly Father.

That argument should be more than sufficient in and of itself. But a contrary argument is frequently brought forward which sounds very spiritual and scriptural. It asks: 'Where do you find any teaching of the New Testament which tells us to pray for this?' We are reminded that we must always be scriptural; and as there is no specific injunction in the New Testament telling us to pray for this blessing of the Holy Spirit, it is surely wrong for us to seek it.

This seems to me to be not only a false argument, but also a most dangerous one. The same argument is brought by the same people against praying for revival. They do not find anywhere in the New Testament an exhortation to pray for revival, they say, so they do not pray for revival. How then do we answer such a plea? We do so by remembering always that the New Testament period, and all that is described for us in the pages of the New Testament, was a time of a great outpouring of the Spirit. I have already shown that it was taken for granted that the New Testament saints knew and enjoyed this experience. Take for instance Ephesians 1: 13, 'In whom also, having believed' – or as the Authorized version has it, 'In whom also, after that ye believed – ye were sealed with that Holy Spirit of promise, which is the earnest of our inheritance until the redemption of the purchased possession'. The Apostle takes it for granted that, 'having believed', the Christians had been sealed with the Spirit of God. That is indicative of the fact that at that time most, if not all, members of the Christian Church had received this great blessing, a state of things that is comparable to what happens in a time of revival, when this great blessing comes to a large number of people and seems to be the normal Christian experience. The Spirit descends upon a company of people, or upon a whole district, or a whole country of people, and almost everyone in the Church is rejoicing in the experience. And such was the state of affairs when these New Testament Epistles were written; hence one would not expect believers to be exhorted to seek the blessing. Instead, we find exhortations and injunctions addressed to people who are already filled with the Spirit and who are in danger as a consequence of various excesses. As I have often pointed out, there are not many churches today (1961) to whom it is necessary to write Paul's First Epistle to the Corinthians and especially chapters 12–14 concerning the spiritual gifts. But it was very necessary then because these people had been baptized with the Spirit. The problems of the New Testament churches were so often the problems of people in that state and condition. Obviously, therefore, they do not need a specific injunction to pray for this particular witness of the Spirit with their spirits in this matter of assurance; they were already rejoicing in it. Indeed, in a sense, that almost constituted one of their greatest dangers.

Furthermore, there is quite clear and specific teaching concerning this matter in Old Testament and New Testament alike. Take for example the fifth chapter of the Song of Solomon, where we find a typical statement of the experience of a believer desiring the loved One. At first the bride foolishly ignores the overtures of the Bridegroom, and does not want to be disturbed. Then, realizing what she is missing, she goes to open the door; but He has gone. She is frantic and begins to search for Him. She goes out into the night – a thing women rarely do – and is ill-treated by people in Jerusalem. But it all shows her intense desire to recover the Object of her love. She tells the keepers to tell Him if they see Him, that she is 'sick of love'. This is a typical statement of the believer's seeking this blessing. But if it be replied that it is but Old Testament teaching, then the difficulty is not so much failure to understand this doctrine of the Spirit as failure to understand the doctrine of the Scriptures. The relationship of the believer to his Lord is essentially the same in both Testaments; and what the believer desired in the Old is still what the believer desires in the New. So when the Beloved is not clearly and obviously present, and when the believer is not rejoicing in communion with Him, this search for Him begins.

But, coming to the New Testament, we find this exhortation in the Second Epistle of Peter, chapter 1, verse 10: 'Wherefore the rather, brethren, give diligence to make your calling and election sure.' I agree that these word pertain mainly to conduct and behaviour, but not exclusively so. We must with the whole of our being give diligence to make our calling and election sure, and there is no better way of doing so than by receiving this testimony of the Spirit with our spirits that we are the children of God. But still more specific than this, there is the statement in the eleventh chapter of Luke's Gospel, and in particular, verses 11–13, where the Lord uses a familiar picture and illustration beginning at verse 5: 'If a son shall ask bread of any of you that is a father, will he give him a stone? or if he ask a fish, will he for a fish give him a serpent? Or if he shall ask an egg, will he offer him a scorpion? If ye then, being evil, know how to give good gifts unto your children; how much more shall your heavenly Father give the Holy Spirit to them that ask him?' This is a plain statement to the effect that we are to ask God to give us the Holy Spirit; with the promise that, if we do so, He will grant us our request.

Why then should there be any difficulty about this? Here we are dealing with a difficulty which is very characteristic of this present generation of believers. The reply that is made is, 'Ah, but that was before Pentecost, and therefore it no longer applies. That was in the days before the Holy Spirit had been poured out upon the Church; but on the day of Pentecost the Spirit was poured out upon the Church once and for ever.' Some would even go so far as to say that it is sinful to pray such a prayer now, and to ask God to give us His Spirit. They say, 'But you have already had the Spirit, as a Christian. Does not Romans chapter 8: 9 tell us that 'If any man have not the Spirit of God, he is none of his?' I reply: If you are going to take that dispensational view of this verse, why do you not take a similar view of every verse in the Gospels? Of course, some people do so, and they say that the Gospels have nothing to do with present-day Christians; that they applied only to the Jews to whom our Lord was ministering before His death. They will also apply again, they say, at some future time. But not now! they have nothing to do with Christians! The Sermon on the Mount, they say, has nothing to do with Christian people, and the statement I have quoted from Luke 11 has nothing to do with Christian people. To be logical, therefore, that must be said of the whole of the Gospels, and Christian people should not read them and expound them and try to put their teaching into practice in their lives. But if such is the case, the position becomes obviously ridiculous. It is certain that these verses apply to us today as much as they did to the people to whom our Lord first uttered them; and we are to ask God as our Father for the Holy Spirit today as then.

An exact parallel in this context is supplied by the statement we have already considered in John 7. 37–39, where our Lord gives an invitation, 'If any man thirst, let him come unto me and drink', and then gives the promise and the explanation follows of what would become possible after the Spirit had been given in Pentecostal fulness. But He does not mean that from the day of Pentecost onwards all Christians would receive the Spirit in all His fulness always. It is certainly not true to say of *all* Christians that 'out of their inward parts' come 'streams of living water'.

The invitation of our Lord in John 7: 37–39 is as applicable today as it was in His own day while on earth. He is still saying, 'If any man thirst, let him come unto me and drink'. In other words, our Lord is saying, 'If you are conscious of the lack of the Spirit, and of this need, go to God as your Father and offer a petition to Him.' It is quite true that the Spirit is sometimes given to people without their asking, as in the case of Cornelius and others. But it is also true that some have obtained this blessing as the result of much seeking and asking. So the general exhortation is that we should pray for it. Indeed, our Lord emphasizes the element of importunity: 'Ask, seek, knock.' Go on, He says, be persistent. He uses His illustration in order to impress upon us the importance of not only asking but of asking urgently and of continuing with our asking until we have received the desired blessing.

But we need to ask a second question – How is the blessing to be sought? Here, again, there is much confusion even among those who agree that it should be sought. I start therefore with a warning against the teaching which says, 'Take it by faith'. We have already considered the matter in dealing with verse 15 and 'the Spirit of adoption, whereby we cry, Abba, Father'. But it must be repeated here as that teaching is so insidious. 'It is quite simple,' people say; 'ask Him, believing that He is your Father, and that therefore He has given it to you'. It is unbelief, they say, not to believe that you have already received it when you have asked for it. But if you say, 'I do not feel anything', they reply, 'Do not worry about your feelings, feelings do not matter. You must believe God's Word, and therefore you must believe that if you have asked, you must have received. Take it by faith, and thank Him for having given it you, and go on'. In my opinion there is nothing that better accounts for dryness, deadness, and the lack of a deep experience of the love of God than such teaching as this.

Why is it so wrong? One reason is that this is not something that we can 'take'; it is entirely 'given'. It is the Spirit bearing witness with our spirit. You cannot 'take' that witness. It is something that He does; it is the action of the Spirit. You cannot 'take' the action of the Spirit; you can only desire it, you can only ask for it. Faith does not mean that you persuade yourself that you 'take' something, that you have something; faith means that you believe the Word of God, that you believe in the possibility of this experience, that you believe the instruction which tells you to 'ask' and to 'seek' and to 'knock', and that, if you keep on doing so, it will be 'given unto you'. Faith does not lay hold on the blessing itself, it lays hold on the One who gives the blessing, and pleads with Him. The confusion is due ultimately to a misunderstanding concerning faith. Faith is that which produces the urge and desire in us, and leads us to pray without ceasing until we receive the blessed gift.

Furthermore, by definition you must not say that you can 'receive' this gift and feel nothing. We have seen that when the Spirit bears witness with our spirits, people are moved as they have never been moved before; they are lost in a sense of 'wonder, love and praise'; they are melted into tears, they are humbled. The idea that this highest form of assurance can be 'taken by faith' is a contradiction in terms. The Apostle is concerned here that we, as the children of God, should know that we are 'the children of God', and he is telling us how we can know it. If you have proof that you are being 'led by the Spirit' you have assurance that you are a child of God. But, beyond that, if you have within you a Spirit of adoption which makes you cry 'Abba, Father', you can be yet more sure. But you cannot cry 'Abba, Father' without feeling that you are a child. It is ridiculous to tell a man who is crying 'Abba, Father' not to trouble about his feelings. The man is full of the most glorious feelings. But the highest assurance of all results from 'the Spirit bearing witness with our spirit, that we are the children of God'. When that happens you will be overwhelmed by your feelings, you will be lost in the most glorious experience that you have ever had. This is essentially experimental, experiential; and so to tell people that they can take this, of all blessings, by faith and not to worry about their feelings, is sheer confusion of thought and a denial of the teaching of the Scriptures about the highest and the greatest experience possible to a human being.

But now we face another difficulty. There are those who agree with what has been said and emphasize the experimental character, but who then go on to teach that what we have to do is to go to one of their meetings and submit ourselves to 'the laying on of hands' by one of their leaders. They agree that sometimes one can be baptized with the Holy Ghost, apart from the 'laying on of the hands', by simply being in a meeting and in a certain 'atmosphere', and as the result of other people's prayers on your behalf. Again we have to test this primarily by the teaching of the Scriptures, but there are other tests also. It is remarkable to note that there is no talk about this in the history of the Church throughout the centuries apart from 'Catholic' teaching with respect to 'Confirmation'. The new teaching has arisen mainly during this present century, and has been popular only since about 1907. That is interesting in itself. The question we are entitled to ask therefore is, What happened to Christian people throughout the long centuries before these special teachings came in? Did they know nothing about these experiences? And the simple answer is that they did, as we have seen. The Apostles certainly had this power – they 'laid hands' on people, and the people received the gift of the Holy Ghost. The case of Simon the Sorcerer is interesting in this connection. We read of how he offered money in order to acquire this power, (Acts chapter 8, verses 18 and 19) which was clearly confined to the apostles for a specific object and purpose; for even Philip the evangelist did not possess it. It seems to have been given specially to Ananias in the case of the Apostle Paul (Acts 9: 17). Those who believe in the myth of 'apostolic succession', whether Roman Catholic or Anglo-Catholic, claim to have it, but 'by their fruits ye shall know them'. Their followers seem to know nothing about this 'testimony of the Spirit', and may not even believe in it.

Another teaching, not common now but very popular at the beginning of the 19th century, and particularly in America, and subsequently in this country, was the teaching concerning 'tarrying meetings'. It certainly had the merit of not teaching the 'take it by faith' idea, and of realizing that the blessing is 'given'. The teaching was that we should seek it, but especially that we should seek it together in meetings, and stay in the meeting until we received it. Sometimes they would even stay for days on end. The dangers that can arise from this practice are obvious from the psychological standpoint. And, again, there is nothing of this teaching in the New Testament. Indeed there is much in the New Testament that shows that it is erroneous. If you say that you are going to 'wait' and 'tarry' in a meeting until you have this blessing, what you are really saying is that you are the one who determines when it comes, and you are thereby denying the sovereignty and the Lordship of the Giver. He gives this in His own time and in His own way; and for us to lay down the condition that it must happen before we leave a meeting is not only verging upon blasphemy, but it also opens the door as widely as possible to the strange psychological, psychic, and even devilish powers that are ever ready to mislead the children of God and to give us a counterfeit and false experience.

How, then, does this blessing come? First and foremost, let us be clear in our minds as to the nature and the character of this experience. As we have seen, you can be a Christian without having this testimony of the Spirit, but you cannot be a Christian without having the Holy Spirit in you. We must be clear about the unique character of this blessing which is the fulfilment of John 7: 37–39, and of John 14, where our Lord makes the gracious promise which was afterwards fulfilled. It is what we have seen in the description of Christians given in the Book of Acts. It is what Peter means when he says, 'Whom having not seen, ye love; in whom, though now ye see him not, yet believing, ye rejoice with joy unspeakable and full of glory' (1 Peter 1: 8). Is that true to your experience? It should be, it can be. If, then, you recognize that it can be, give yourself no rest until you have it. Believe that it is possible for a Christian in this life to rejoice in the Lord Jesus Christ with 'a joy unspeakable and full of glory'. Realize that it is possible for a Christian to say, 'The love of Christ constraineth me'; realize that we are meant to know 'the breadth, and the length, and the depth, and the height, and to know the love of Christ which passeth knowledge'. We are meant to be 'filled with all the fulness of God' (Ephesians 3: 19). Do we know anything about such things? This is the starting-point. Get rid of all the objections, and all the fears which arise because of the fear of excesses. Realize that you are meant to be a rejoicing Christian, knowing the love of God as certainly as you know anything else, and even more certainly. Then having realized and having believed in that possibility, begin to seek it.

Secondly, be careful that you are seeking for the right thing. Do not merely seek an experience, or manifestations. Seek a knowledge of God, and of the Lord Jesus Christ. Do not seek 'balls of fire' or any 'sensation of electricity' going through your body. Seek Him! Say that you want 'to know him, and the power of his resurrection, and the fellowship of his sufferings'. Desire the knowledge of God and of Christ, in this intimate manner, and the knowledge of His 'love shed abroad in your hearts'. That is what we are to seek! Seek to be holy, seek God's glory. Do not merely desire a comfortable feeling, but say to yourself, 'Apart from this I can never be a true witness. I cannot witness truly for Him any more than those disciples could before the day of Pentecost'. Christ told them to stay where they were until the power came, and that they could not be witnesses to Him until it came. Say to yourself, 'Is it conceivable, then, that I can be a witness without that power, and is not its absence perhaps the reason why I am such a poor witness?' Seek His glory, not your own!

The third step follows; do everything you can to please Him. As the Apostle has told us in verse 13, 'mortify the deeds of the body through the Spirit'. Do your utmost to be holy. Do what Peter tells us in his Second Epistle chapter 1, verses 5–7: 'Beside this, giving all diligence, add to your faith virtue; and to virtue knowledge; and to knowledge temperance; and to temperance patience; and to patience godliness; and to godliness brotherly kindness; and to brotherly kindness charity'. Go on, give all diligence, work hard at it, keep on! Do not just relax, and 'take it by faith'; add to your faith, go on 'furnishing it out' – which is the real meaning of the word 'add'. That is the Apostle's teaching as it is the teaching throughout the New Testament. Do everything that the risen Lord said to the Church at Laodicea (Revelation 3: 14–22) – another New Testament example of an exhortation to seek this blessing.

Then give diligence to seek Him in the written Word. He has often met His people as they have been reading about Him. Read the Word. Spend time with it; meditate upon it. These are the ways the saints have always followed. And then, to crown all your endeavours, use importunate prayer. 'Ask, seek, knock.' Go on, and keep on; let nothing hinder you. Make your desire known to Him to the utmost of your power. And above everything else, do not give in; be urgent; be persistent. Ask, and if you do not get your reply, continue to seek it; and if you have still not received, keep on knocking, hammer on the door! As Isaiah says, 'Give him no rest till . . .' (Isaiah 62: 7) This is the teaching of the Scriptures.

In order to encourage such seeking and to show how Christians throughout the history of the Church have done this very thing, and have heeded these exhortations of the Scriptures, let me quote the teaching of certain men of God on this subject. We start with Thomas Goodwin (who lived 300 years ago). The first volume of his *Works*[1] gives us his Sermons on the first chapter of Ephesians. On verses 13 and 14 he writes:

'You that believe are to wait for this promise. As the Jews waited for the coming of Christ, so are you to wait for the coming of the Holy Ghost into your hearts. It is said that the fathers served God night and day, waiting for the promise, namely, Christ to come. Acts 26: 6. Serve your God day and night faithfully; walk humbly. There is a promise of the Holy Ghost to come and fill your hearts with joy unspeakable and glorious, to seal you up to the day of redemption. Sue this promise out, wait for it, rest not in believing only, rest not in assurance by graces only; there is a further assurance to be had. It was the last legacy Christ left upon earth (John 14: 16). He saith there that He would send the promise of the Father, this very promise of sending the Comforter. Read Luke 24: 49. Therefore sue out the will of Christ.' [You see it is like going to court. As you 'sue' a man in court for something, you sue Christ for this.] 'Sue out that last legacy of His. It was the fruit of His ascension. When He was ascended up and received this promise, then He poured it out.'

Again he goes on:

'The Ephesians had it, you see, they were sealed; for afterward, chapter 4: 30, he exhorts them not to grieve the Holy Spirit by which they were sealed. The Thessalonians had it (1 Thess. 1: 10) They received the Word with such joy that he saith they waited for the coming of Jesus Christ from heaven, for that is the next step; heaven is next unto it, and to wait for Christ when you are thus sealed. Those that Peter wrote to had it (1 Peter 1: 8). "In

[1] *The Works of Thomas Goodwin*, vol. I, pp. 248, 249, (Nichol edition).

[393]

whom believing, ye rejoice with joy unspeakable and full of glory." '

Then again, strikingly –

'Thus ordinary it was in the primitive times. Where the defect lies God knows, but certainly it might be more common if men would sue it out. Such a promise there is. He is therefore called the Spirit of promise, because He is promised as a sealer. Only, my brethren, let me give you a direction or two. First, believe this promise. Wait for it by faith.'

[Note the difference. Goodwin does not say, 'Take it by faith,' he says. 'Wait for it by faith, make it the aim of your faith.']

'We are said to "receive the promise of the Spirit through faith" (Gal 3 : 14). Believe there is such a thing, aim at it, wait for it and serve God day and night in all humility to obtain it. Rest in no other lower and under assurance, and in the end the Lord will give it. The reason why men attain it not is because they rest in other assurance, and they do not aim at this. They content themselves with bare believing and that their consciences are quieted. But, my brethren, there is such a work as sealing by the Spirit, if you have faith. There is a Spirit, and a Spirit of promise made to believers, which you may receive by faith. This is the first reason why He is called a Spirit of promise, because He is promised to believers as He is a sealer.'

Take now a brief extract[1] from George Whitefield, written on Thursday, December 20th, 1739:

'It is a dreadful mistake to deny the doctrine of assurances or to think it is confined to a time of persecution or to the primitive ages of the Church. Not only righteousness and peace, but joy in the Holy Ghost, which is the consequence of assurance, is a necessary part of the Kingdom of God within us, and though all are not to be condemned who have not an immediate assurance, yet all ought to labour after it. I really believe one great reason why so many go mourning all their life long is owing to ignorance of their Christian privileges. They have not assurance because they ask it not. They ask it not because they are taught that it does not belong to Christians of these last days.' [He might very well

[1] George Whitefield's *Journals*, pp. 374, 375. (Banner of Truth) 1960.

have been writing today!] 'whereas I know numbers whose salvation is written upon their hearts, as it were with a sunbeam. They
can rejoice in God their Saviour and give men and devils the
challenge to separate them, if they can, from the love of God in
Christ Jesus their Lord. Dear Redeemer, enlighten all Thy
followers to see their privileges and never let them cease wrestling
with Thee till Thou dost bless them by assuring them of their
eternal salvation.'

And there follows this portion of one of Isaac Watts' hymns –

> *Why should the children of a King*
> *Go mourning all their days?*
> *Great Comforter, descend and bring*
> *Some tokens of Thy grace.*
> *Assure each conscience of its part*
> *In the Redeemer's blood,*
> *And bear Thy witness with each heart*
> *That it is born of God.*

This is only one of many quotations I could give out of the
Journals of George Whitefield.

Let me end again with Charles Haddon Spurgeon. This is how
Spurgeon states the matter in a sermon[1] which he preached on
February 24th, 1861, on Solomon's Song, chapter 8, verses 6
and 7:

'She (the spouse) longeth that she may know the love of His
(Christ's) heart, and that she may experience the power of His arm.
Can we not, each of us, join the spouse in this prayer tonight:
"Oh, Lord, let me know that my name is engraven on Thy
heart! Not only let it be there, but let me know it! Write my name
not only *in* Thy heart but may it be as a signet *on* Thy heart that I
may see it." Doubtless there are the names of very many written
upon Christ's heart who have not yet been able to see their names
there. They are there but not written as on a signet. Christ has
loved them from all eternity, His heart has been set on them from
everlasting, but as yet they have never seen the signet, they have
never had the seal of the Spirit to witness within that they are

---

[1] C. H. Spurgeon: *New Park Street and Metropolitan Tabernacle Pulpit,* vol. VII
(1861), p. 130.

born of God. While their names may be in His heart they have not seen them there as a seal upon His heart. And no doubt there are multitudes for whom Christ has fought and conquered, and whom He daily keeps and preserves, who have never seen their names written as a seal upon His arm. Their prayer is that they may see Christ's love visibly, that they may discover it in their experience, that it may be beyond a question, and no more a matter of doubt, that His hand and His heart are engaged for their eternal salvation. I repeat it: ye can all join in this prayer, ye people of God. It is a cry that you would put up now and continue to put up till it is fully answered – "Oh, let me know, my Lord, that I am Thine, bound to Thine heart; and let me know that I am Thine, protected and preserved by Thine arm!" This is the prayer. I shall not say more upon it, because I wish to speak more at length upon the arguments with which it is here pleaded.'

Here is another quotation[1] from Spurgeon where we find the same thing once more. He says: 'These operations of the Spirit of God are easily to be obtained by the Lord's children'. And then he says:

'There is another thing to be done as well, and that is, to pray, and here I want to remind you of those blessed words of the Master.' [He then quotes the words I have already quoted from Luke 11.] 'You see, there is a distinct promise to the children of God that their heavenly Father will give them the Holy Spirit if they ask for His power, and that promise is made to be exceedingly strong by the instances joined to it. If there be a promise that God can break – which there is not – this is not the promise, for God has put it in the most forcible and binding way. I know not how to show you its wonderful force. Did you ever hear of a man who, when his child asked for bread, gave him a stone? Go to the worst part of London, and will you find a man of that kind? You shall, if you like, get among pirates and murderers, and when a little child cries, "Father, give me a bit of bread and meat" does the most wicked father fill his own little one's mouth with stones? Yet the Lord seems to say that this is what He would be doing if He were to deny us the Holy Spirit when we ask Him for His necessary working. He would be like one that gave his children stones instead of bread. Do you think the Lord will ever bring

[1] C. H. Spurgeon: *Metropolitan Tabernacle Pulpit*, vol. XXVIII (1882), pp. 310, 311.

Himself down to that? But He says, "*How much more* shall your heavenly Father give the Holy Spirit to them that ask Him?" He makes it a stronger case than that of an ordinary parent. The Lord must give us the Spirit when we ask Him, for He has herein bound Himself by no ordinary pledge: He has used a simile which would bring dishonour on His own Name, and that of the very grossest kind, if He did not give the Holy Spirit to them that ask Him. Oh then, let us ask Him at once, with all our hearts! Am I not so happy as to have in this audience some who will immediately ask? I pray that some who have never received the Holy Spirit at all may now be led, while I am speaking, to pray, "Blessed Spirit, visit me, lead me to Jesus". But especially those of you that are the children of God, to you is this promise especially made. Ask God to make you all that the Spirit of God can make you, not only a satisfied believer who has drunk for himself, but a useful believer who overflows the neighbourhood with blessing.'

My last quotation is taken from the volume of *Revival Year Sermons* by Charles Haddon Spurgeon which has been reprinted recently. It is found in a Sermon[1] on Romans 8 : 30 : Predestination and Calling. Spurgeon is talking about assurance and he has been saying that the believer may know it as surely as if he read it with his own eyes, nay, he may know it more surely than that. Listen to this –

'What would some of you give if you could arrive at this assurance? Mark, if you anxiously desire to know, you may know. If your heart pants to read its title clear, it shall do so ere long. [He does not say 'Take it by faith', but 'ere long'] No man ever desired Christ in his heart with a living and longing desire, who did not find Him sooner or later. If thou hast a desire, God has given it thee. If thou pantest, and criest, and groanest after Christ, even this is His gift. Bless Him for it. Thank Him for little grace, and ask Him for great grace. He has given thee hope, ask for faith; and when He gives thee faith, ask for assurance; and when thou gettest assurance, ask for full assurance; and when thou hast obtained full assurance, ask for enjoyment; and when thou hast enjoyment, ask for glory itself; and He shall surely give it thee in His own appointed season.'

---

[1] C. H. Spurgeon: *Revival Year Sermons* (1859), p. 77. Banner of Truth.

There we have quotations from the 17th century, 18th century and 19th century. They all teach the same thing. You do not 'take it by faith'; you ask for it, you plead, you seek, you knock, you groan, you wrestle – these are their terms. And you go on doing so until you have received it. The same truth is stated in the English translation of a hymn by William Williams:

> *Speak, I pray Thee, gentle Jesus,*
> *Oh how passing sweet Thy words,*
> *Breathing o'er my troubled spirit*
> *Peace which never earth affords!*
> *All the world's distracting voices,*
> *All the enticing tones of ill,*
> *At Thine accents mild, melodious,*
> *Are subdued, and all is still.*
>
> *Tell me Thou art mine, O Saviour,*
> *Grant me an assurance clear;*
> *Banish all my dark misgivings,*
> *Still my doubting, calm my fear.*
> *All my soul within me yearneth*
> *Now to hear Thy voice divine;*
> *So shall grief be gone for ever,*
> *And despair no more be mine.*

Do you know this? If I may borrow Spurgeon's language – 'Have you seen your name on the signet ring?' Has the Spirit borne witness with your spirit that you are a child of God? Have you heard these 'accents mild, melodious'? Have you had this supreme assurance? Or are you resting merely on saying, 'I believe the Scripture. It says that if a man believes, he is saved; I need nothing more than that'? Are you resting on deductions which you can draw about the characteristics and the marks of the Christian man? Are you saying that is enough for you? How can you speak in that way when He Himself is offering to give you the Spirit of promise, who will give you full assurance, the absolute certainty that you are a child of God, and that the inheritance is prepared for you? The Spirit is a witness, He is a seal, and an earnest. We have no right to remain uncertain; for as long as we are uncertain we shall to that extent be poor witnesses. The best witnesses of the Lord Jesus Christ that the world has ever known have always been men who had full assurance, and the consequent enjoyment of that fulness and certainty, and whose hearts were ravished at the sight of the glory to which Spurgeon refers. Christian people, do you know this? Have you got this highest, supreme assurance? If not, seek it, seek it in the way indicated, with your life, with your obedience, with your all, and especially with words. He delights to hear His children asking, as any parent worthy of the name likes to hear a little child asking for expressions of love. Plead with Him saying,

> *Tell me Thou art mine, O Saviour!*
> *Grant me an assurance clear.*

And go on doing so until you have that 'assurance clear'; then you will indeed 'rejoice with joy unspeakable and full of glory'.

Thirty-one

*

> *And if children, then heirs; heirs of God, and joint-heirs with Christ; if so be that we suffer with him, that we may be also glorified together.* Romans 8: 17

This statement is obviously a continuation of what the Apostle has been saying in the 16th verse: 'The Spirit itself beareth witness with our spirit, that we are the children of God.' In the light of this, it follows that, 'if children, then heirs; heirs of God, and joint-heirs with Christ'. We may well ask why exactly the Apostle amplifies what he has already said. We know from our past studies that the Apostle's main object in this section is to show the type of assurance and certainty Christians should enjoy as the children of God. Why was he not content to leave it with the statement that 'the Spirit itself bears witness with our spirit, that we are the children of God'? Why this addition?

We can adduce the first answer from something we find elsewhere in the Apostle's teaching. The mention of the Holy Spirit as the One who 'seals' us is generally joined by him with the fact that the Spirit also gives us an 'earnest' of the inheritance of which he assures us. And that is, surely, what he does here. It explains why he mentions our heirship. He does the same thing in 2 Corinthians 1: 22 where he says: 'Who hath sealed us, and given the earnest of the Spirit in our hearts.' And again in Ephesians 1: 13 and 14: 'In whom ye also trusted after that ye heard the word of truth, the gospel of your salvation: in whom also, after that ye believed, ye were sealed with that Holy Spirit of promise, which is the earnest of our inheritance until the redemption of the purchased possession, unto the praise of his glory.' It seems to be an established rule in the Apostle's thinking and writing that he never mentions the Spirit as the 'seal' without at the same time mentioning the Spirit as the 'earnest'. Sonship immediately conjures up the notion of inheritance; the two things are indissolubly linked together. So, having emphasized the Spirit as the One who 'seals' to us the fact that we are the children of God, he goes on to say that for that reason He is also the guarantee of the inheritance itself. This, incidentally, confirms our exposition of the first part of the 16th verse to the effect that the Spirit's bearing witness with our spirits is the sealing of the Spirit. The very fact that the Apostle goes on immediately to talk about 'inheritance' proves it. Here, as elsewhere, he deals with the Spirit in His dual capacity of 'seal' and 'earnest'. The witness of the Spirit to the fact that we are children tells us that we are in a position to be inheritors; and now he goes on to tell us something about the character of that inheritance. The purpose at the back of it all is to give us great assurance and certainty with regard to our ultimate, complete and final salvation. This is the theme of the whole of this eighth chapter of this Epistle, the theme Paul really began at the beginning of chapter 5 and which was interrupted by the digressions in chapters 6 and 7.

The authorities are agreed in saying that the Apostle probably had in his mind here a main characteristic of Roman law with respect to these matters. He was writing to Romans, to the Church at Rome, and he takes it for granted that they are familiar with their own laws. According to Roman law all the children of a man were his inheritors, and they were equally his inheritors. That was not the case in Jewish law, in which the first-born had twice as much as the other children. But not in Roman law! This is the point which the Apostle takes up here. He says, 'Because you are children, you are therefore all of you heirs of God'. This teaches clearly, therefore, that according to the Apostle all Christians are the heirs of God, and joint-heirs with Christ, not merely some Christians. There are those who teach that this is only true of some Christians, and that, though you are saved, if you do not live a good life, if you are not entirely sanctified, you do not become an heir. That is not the Apostle's teaching. He says that all believers are children of God, and because they are all children, they are all heirs – every one of them! There is no distinction made here at all. It does not follow from that, of course, that the exact inheritance is the same in each case. There is teaching in the Scripture which suggests that there may be a variation in the amount of the inheritance dependent upon our conduct and behaviour. But what is established here is that we are all heirs, that we are all going to the same glory. Though 'one star differeth from another star in glory' we are all inheritors of the same glory.

What is this? Once more I suggest that the Apostle is but elaborating on what he hinted at, and put in a brief statement, at the beginning of chapter 5, in verses 1 and 2: 'Therefore being justified by faith, we have peace with God through our Lord Jesus Christ: by whom also we have access by faith into this grace wherein we stand' – and especially – 'and rejoice in hope of the glory of God.' He is referring to this here, for he says immediately that it is one of the inevitable consequences of being 'justified by faith'. Then in that same 5th chapter, in verses 12 to 21, he began to give the great solid reason for the certainty of our ultimate arrival at that glory, the grounds on which we 'rejoice in hope of the glory of God', namely, that we are united to the Lord Jesus Christ. He now takes up that thought again and works it out more in detail. Let us follow him as he does so.

The Apostle starts by saying, 'If children, then heirs'. 'If children', which means 'now that we are children'. Of course, as we have already seen, that is not true of all human beings. We do not believe in the 'universal fatherhood of God', nor in 'the universal brotherhood of man'. That is not taught in the Scriptures. It is only those who are 'led by the Spirit of God' who are 'the children of God'. If you really are children of God then glory follows; if you are not children, it does not follow. Let us remind ourselves of this; our position as Christians is that we are the children of God. That is a most glorious and most thrilling fact. The Apostle John in the prologue to his Gospel brings out this very point. He says, 'He [the Lord Jesus] came unto his own, and his own received him not' (John 1: 11) 'but as many as received him, to them gave he power to become the sons of God, even to them that believe on his name'. Such is the position of every one who is a Christian. All who believe on His name have this power, this right, this authority to regard themselves as the sons of God.

The Apostle Paul, of all teachers, constantly reminds us of our sonship. For instance, in appealing to the Ephesians for good conduct, he says in chapter 5 verse 1: 'Be ye therefore followers

ot God, as dear children.' What an appeal! James has exactly
the same idea, and the same teaching, in his Epistle: 'Of his
own will begat he us with the word of truth, that we should be
a kind of firstfruits of his creatures' (1: 18). We have been
begotten of God by the Word, and thus become 'the firstfruits
of his creatures'. The Apostle Peter is still more explicit in his
Second Epistle chapter 1, verse 4: 'Whereby are given unto us
exceeding great and precious promises: that by these ye might
be partakers of the divine nature.' What a staggering statement!
We, as Christians, are 'partakers of the divine nature'. A Christian
is not only one who is forgiven, he is not merely a man who is
born again, he is a 'partaker of the divine nature'. As John says
again: 'Who are born, not of blood, nor of the will of the flesh,
nor of the will of man, but of God' (John 1: 13). This is what
John means in his third chapter by his teaching about being
'born from above', being 'born of the Spirit'. That is true of all
who are Christians. We must not think of ourselves merely as
forgiven; nor must we think of ourselves only as adopted. We
are adopted into the family of God; but there is more than that –
we are 'partakers of the divine nature'. We are made in such a
way that we become 'conformable to the image of his Son';
we have 'the life of God' in our souls. It is nothing less than that.

The very word the Apostle uses here, which is translated as
'children', brings out this whole notion of the similarity of nature.
Let us not misunderstand this; it does not mean that we are gods;
but in some marvellous sense it does mean that we are 'partakers
of the divine nature'. It is a great mystery, it is something that is
beyond our understanding; but we have to realize that in Christ,
who took unto Himself human nature, we 'receive', we become
'partakers of' the divine nature. And it is in that sense that the
Apostle reminds us here that we are 'the children of God'.
And then he says that, because we are children, we are heirs.
The 'if' does not raise any doubt; it means that 'because' we are
children we are therefore heirs.

The word 'heirs' means that there is a great inheritance awaiting
all Christians. This is one of the great themes in the Bible, and,
to me, it is a matter of increasing astonishment that it is such a
neglected theme. I want to emphasize it therefore. I think sometimes that there is no more important theme for the Church
at this present time than this very theme of our being 'heirs'

[403]

of God. This teaching, this notion, this truth influences our whole view of the Christian life. It is as important as that! It involves our whole view of this world, and of life in this world. This is going to be the Apostle's theme for the remainder of this chapter. He introduces it at the end of this verse: 'if so be that we suffer with him, that we may be also glorified together'. It is a very practical theme. The Christians in Rome were suffering so he gives an explanation of their suffering. He is writing to comfort them, and the chief comfort he has to give them is that they are 'heirs' of God. That is the controlling thought.

This should surely control even our evangelism; and to the extent that it does not, we engage in a false evangelism. Far too often evangelism takes the form of saying, 'Are you in trouble, are you unhappy, are you failing somewhere, do you need some help? Very well, come to Christ and you will get all you need.' Thank God, it is very true that, if you come to Christ, you will derive many benefits; but I do not find the Christian Gospel presented in that way in the New Testament itself. Another form of evangelism urges us to become Christians in order to solve the problems of the world, in order to make the world a wonderful place to live in. Similarly I do not find that teaching in the Bible. We must be careful never to present the gospel in a way that puts it into line with the cults. That is what the cults do. They say: 'Are you worried? Well, believe this theory and you will lose your worry. Are you suffering ill health? Just realize that there is no such thing as matter, no such thing as disease, no such thing as pain. If you but believe that, you will lose all your aches and pains, and you will be perfectly well.' That is typical of the cults. They come to us and offer to put everything right for us here and now.

But that is not what we have here; and it is not what we have anywhere in the Bible. The Bible, unlike the cults, does not seem at first to promise us very much in this life. What it does promise lies mainly in the future. The whole Bible points to that glorious future – to the 'promise', the 'hope', the 'inheritance'. And this teaching should govern our evangelism. The chief reason why men should believe on the Lord Jesus Christ is that they are under the wrath of God, and that if they die under the wrath of God they will go to hell, and their eternal future will be one of misery and shame. They must 'escape from the wrath to come'. That was the message of John the Baptist, and the message of our Lord Himself. They did not come to people and say, 'The gospel will solve your problem for you, and enable you to live a happy life while you are in this world'. They called for repentance, because, in their state of sin, men and women are under the wrath of God. The main thrust of New Testament evangelism is always in terms of this 'wrath to come', and the two great possibilities that face us for all eternity. Such is the theme we are dealing with here.

Why should I be concerned about knowing that I am a child of God? The answer is, that I may be certain that I am an heir and that I am going on to that inheritance. And this is not only very important from the standpoint of evangelism, it is equally important from the standpoint of the pastor and the need to help people in a pastoral sense. Popular evangelism too often comes to us and says: 'Believe on the Lord Jesus Christ and all will be well with you; you will never have any troubles or problems, the whole world will be changed. You will walk down the road of life with a light step, and all your problems will have gone.' People believe this and on they go for months and perhaps for a year or two. Then things begin to go wrong with them, and they pray to God. They say, 'I have only to ask God, and all will be well'. But nothing happens, things are not put right, and they are surrounded by trials and troubles and the malice of other people. The devil seems to be active, old temptations rise up and shake them, and they wonder where they are and what is happening to them. Then the devil comes and says: 'You have never been a Christian at all, because if you were a Christian, obviously these things would not be happening to you. Don't you remember what the evangelist said?' And so they think that they have never been Christians at all. Or the devil will come to them and say: 'Didn't I tell you not to believe it? The evangelist promised you that if you only believed in Christ you would never have any more troubles; but look at yourself now.' So if you have believed the message of that pseudo-evangelism you have no answer.

True evangelism does not offer some panacea for all the ills in our life in this world; it does not promise to make us perfect in a moment or set the whole world right. It says rather, 'In the world ye shall have tribulation; but fear not, I have overcome the world'. It is 'the promise', the 'inheritance'; it is the future. If you believe what the Apostle says here, you will be in no difficulty when someone tells you that the gospel is not true because you are experiencing trials. You say, 'Were we ever promised by the gospel that we would have no troubles?' 'If we suffer with him', says the Apostle, 'we shall also reign with him'. 'The sufferings of this present time' are real, and I cannot promise you that they are going to decrease, but what I can tell you is that 'they are not worthy to be compared with the glory' which is coming. Hold on, therefore, quit yourself as a man, carry on; because, whatever may happen to you in this life, that inheritance is absolutely certain. That is how the gospel speaks to us. So I emphasize that this is a vital doctrine from the standpoint of evangelism as well as from the standpoint of pastoral ministry.

This is a central biblical theme. The whole Bible points to this glorious future, to this 'promise'. The promise was made most clearly to Abraham, although it goes further back still. It is first found in Genesis 3:15: 'The seed of the woman shall bruise the serpent's head.' It is indefinite and indistinct at that point, but it is there. It is seen in the birth of Seth and then in Shem. But we see it most clearly when we read of Abraham; and then it begins to develop. God made His promises much more explicit to Abraham than He had ever done before. He made a covenant with Abraham that in his seed all the nations of the earth should be blessed; that in and through him He purposed to send this great blessing of final and ultimate salvation. That is the promise. And from that point the whole of the Bible looks forward to this grand consummation. It was a promise that was made only to the Children of Israel; and it remained their hope during the long centuries. Things went wrong with them, and often they did not understand what was happening, but there was always this promise. They had to live a different life from other people. They were not only given the Ten Commandments but a ceremonial law also. Why all this? Because they were God's people, and because as God's people they were God's heirs, and they were looking forward to the fulfilment of the promise. Things might go wrong with them and against them but they do not give up to final despair, because of the promise of the coming Messiah who would bring deliverance.

The Jews thought of that in terms of one great event. We

know that it can be divided into two parts; that He came the first time, then an interval, and that He will come again a second time. But in the Old Testament we are given a general picture of the work, the delivering work of the Messiah. This is the great promise. And the Children of Israel were looking forward to this promise; a great inheritance was to come. They were looking, as the author of the Epistle to the Hebrews puts it, 'for a city which hath foundations, whose builder and maker is God'. They were 'pilgrims and strangers in the earth', they were looking for that other city, that city of God that was to come. But it applied to them only, and the Apostle, in writing to the Ephesians who were Gentiles, reminds them of this. He says in chapter 2, verses 11 and 12: 'Wherefore remember, that ye being in time past Gentiles in the flesh, who are called Uncircumcision by that which is called the Circumcision in the flesh made by hands; that at that time ye were without Christ, being aliens from the commonwealth of Israel, and strangers from the covenants of promise.' And because they were strangers from 'the covenants of promise' he adds, 'having no hope'. The Gentiles had nothing to look forward to, they had no hope. It was to the Jews only that the promise had been made; all others were outside the 'covenants of promise', and had no hope. And it is still true. Christians are the only people who have a 'hope'. It is true of all unbelievers in the world to say that they are 'without hope, without God in the world'. I do not know how they managed to live. They do so, of course, by refusing to face facts. That is why they spend their time looking at television, listening to radio, running to football matches, drinking, taking drugs – anything to get away from it all.

So in the Old Testament the promise was only to Abraham and his seed, to no one else. All others were 'strangers from the covenants of promise'. But, and this is the marvellous thing, in Christ the position has been changed; the Gentiles can come into blessing. 'But now in Christ Jesus ye who sometimes were far off are made nigh by the blood of Christ. Therefore ye are no more strangers and foreigners, but fellow-citizens with the saints, and of the household of God' (Ephesians 2: 19). In all probability most of the members of the Church in Rome were Gentiles; but 'now', like the Ephesians, they have been 'made nigh'.

The Sons of God

This is the great theme the Apostle expounds so frequently. In Galatians 3: 28 and 29, he says that, as the result of the coming of Christ, 'there is neither Jew nor Greek, there is neither bond nor free, there is neither male nor female: for ye are all one in Christ Jesus. And if ye be Christ's, then are ye Abraham's seed, and heirs according to the promise'. Gentiles, who used to be outside, in Christ have become 'Abraham's seed', and therefore they have become 'heirs according to the promise'. This was the marvellous thing that had happened in Christ. We find it again in the first chapter of the Epistle to the Ephesians. In verse 10 Paul describes God's great purpose; then in verse 11 he says: 'In whom also we have obtained an inheritance.' The 'we' there stands for the Jews. 'We have obtained an inheritance, being predestinated according to the purpose of him who worketh all things after the counsel of his own will: that we should be to the praise of his glory, who first trusted in Christ'. Then in verse 13: 'In whom ye also trusted' – that is, you Gentiles – 'after that ye heard the word of truth, the gospel of your salvation.' Then he goes on to refer to the inheritance.

Again, in the 3rd chapter of the same Epistle, there is a very interesting statement. He is writing about himself and his own ministry, of which he says in verse 2: 'If ye have heard of the dispensation of the grace of God which is given me to you-ward: how that by revelation he made known unto me the mystery.' What is the mystery? In verse 5 he goes on: 'Which in other ages was not made known unto the sons of men, as it is now revealed unto his holy apostles and prophets by the Spirit'. Still 'the mystery'! What is it? 'That the Gentiles should be fellow-heirs, and of the same body, and partakers of his promise in Christ by the gospel.' This is the precise thing of which the Apostle reminds these Romans at this point – that this promise is no longer to the Jews only, but also to the Gentiles, in Christ. They have been made one, 'the middle wall of partition' has gone. This was not known before, it is now revealed. If a man believes in Christ he becomes an heir, and so all Christians are 'fellow-heirs' together with the Jews who had formerly believed, and who were true children of Abraham.

This is the key to the understanding of what is the great central message of the Bible. The Old Testament message is, in a sense, summed up perfectly in Hebrews, chapter 11. All those heroes of the faith lived in faith, by faith, and they died in the same faith. They did not receive fulfilment of the promise, they 'saw it afar off'. And because of that, they counted themselves as 'strangers and pilgrims in the earth'. Like Moses, they kept their eye on 'the recompense of the reward'; they preferred to 'suffer affliction with the people of God, than to enjoy the pleasures of sin for a season'. It was the promise of the inheritance that sustained them. They all lived by it, they looked forward; they did not belong to this earth; they were 'strangers' here.

When you come to the New Testament you find the same thing. Our Lord Himself stated this perfectly in Matthew 25 : 34, in His picture of the Son of man coming at the end of the age and sitting upon the throne of His glory: 'And before him shall be gathered all nations: and he shall separate them one from another, as a shepherd divideth his sheep from the goats: And he shall set the sheep on his right hand, but the goats on the left. Then shall the King say unto them on his right hand, Come, ye blessed of my Father, inherit the kingdom prepared for you from the foundation of the world.' That is the promise! that is what we should look forward to! – 'The kingdom prepared from the foundation of the world.' And when the Apostle Paul was given his great commission by the Lord on the road to Damascus, it was stated in the same terms: 'delivering thee from the people and from the Gentiles, unto whom I now send thee, to open their eyes, and to turn them from darkness to light, and from the power of Satan unto God, that they may receive forgiveness of sins, and inheritance among them which are sanctified by faith that is in me' (Acts 26 : 17 and 18). We are not surprised, therefore, at the character of the prayer which the Apostle tells the Ephesians he offers for them: 'that the eyes of your understanding may be enlightened, that ye may know what is the hope of his calling' that is to say, the hope of the inheritance to which He has called them. Then he mentions 'the riches of the glory of his inheritance in the saints'. That means, in part, God's inheritance in His saints – 'the Lord's portion is his people' – but it also means the glory of our inheritance in Christ in God (Ephesians 1 : 15–18).

In the Epistle to the Colossians we find the same truth. Paul had not seen them, he had heard of them, and he says that he gives thanks for them 'unto the Father, which hath made us

meet to be partakers of the inheritance of the saints in light'
(1: 12). That is what Christians really are! They are men and
women who are made 'meet to be partakers of the inheritance of
the saints in light'. Again, in Colossians 3: 4: 'When Christ,
who is our life, shall appear, then shall ye also appear with him
in glory.' In the 24th verse of that same third chapter we read:
'Knowing that of the Lord ye shall receive the reward of the
inheritance: for ye serve the Lord Christ.' The Apostle writes the
same thing to Titus: 'That being justified by his grace, we should
be made heirs according to the hope of eternal life' (3: 7).

It is the same throughout. The Apostle does not concentrate
on this life and this world, but on that which is to come. The
Author of the Epistle to the Hebrews expounds the same truth.
What are angels? In verse 14 of the first chapter he says: 'Are
they not all ministering spirits, sent forth to minister for them
who shall be *heirs* of salvation?' The Apostle Peter speaks similarly at the beginning of his First Epistle: 'Blessed be the God
and Father of our Lord Jesus Christ, which according to his
abundant mercy hath begotten us again' – Unto what? Unto a
life free from troubles? – 'unto a lively hope by the resurrection
of Jesus Christ from the dead, to an inheritance incorruptible,
and undefiled, and that fadeth not away, reserved in heaven
for you, who are kept by the power of God through faith unto
salvation ready to be revealed in the last time' (1: 3–5). And
again, in verse 13, he expresses the same thought: 'Gird up the
loins of your mind, be sober, and hope to the end for the grace
that is to be brought unto you at the revelation of Jesus Christ.'
The Apostle John re-echoes it all in his First Epistle where he
states the matter thus: 'Beloved, now are we the sons of God,
and it doth not yet appear what we shall be: but we know that
when he shall appear, we shall be like him: for we shall see him
as he is. And every man that hath this hope in him, purifieth
himself, even as he is pure' (3: 2–3).

I have selected these statements in the scriptural teaching in
order that we might realize that this 'hope of the inheritance'
is the great promise of the Scriptures from first to last. It is the
hallmark of the Christian, that his eye is upon the inheritance,
that he realizes he is a child of God, and because he is a child
he is an heir, 'an heir of God, and joint-heir with Christ'. This
should be our controlling thought. We should be looking for

'the coming of the great God and our Saviour'; 'looking for and hasting unto the coming of the great day of God, wherein the elements shall melt with fervent heat'; and when eventually there shall be 'new heavens and a new earth wherein dwelleth righteousness'. This is the Christian teaching: 'Teaching us that, denying ungodliness and worldly lusts, we should live soberly, righteously and godly, in this present world, looking for . . .' Such is the Christian outlook, and we must always test ourselves by that.

Is this your habitual way of thinking of yourself? Do you live rejoicing day by day in the fact that you are a child of God, and because a child, then an heir? What is your heart set upon? At what are you looking? Is it only at this present life and world? Are you like the heroes of the faith in Hebrews 11? Are you like the patriarchs and the saints? are you looking forward? Are you like the believers of the New Testament? They were all looking forward. We are only given the 'earnest of our inheritance' here; the great inheritance itself is to come. We are only tasters of the first-fruits here, the harvest has not yet arrived. So we look forward, and are waiting and looking unto and hasting unto the coming of this blessed, glorious day of God, the day of glory, the day of our glorification, the day of our ultimate, final, full salvation.

Thirty-two

*

And if children, then heirs; heirs of God, and joint-heirs with Christ; if so be that we suffer with him, that we may be also glorified together.

Romans 8 : 17

So far we have been concerned just to emphasize this one great principle, that we, as children of God, are of necessity 'heirs'. This doctrine which we have seen is such a cardinal and central doctrine in the realm of biblical teaching is, for some peculiar reason, neglected by Christian people at this present time. But the Apostle goes out of his way to say not only that we are heirs, and that we should be looking forward to a great inheritance, but he takes the trouble to define that inheritance in a twofold way. He says that we are 'heirs of God', and 'joint-heirs with Christ'. He works out this whole concept of our heirship in these two particular ways, and as he troubles to do so, we must follow him. Obviously he has some very special reason for doing this. His great object, as we have been noting all along, is to emphasize the absolute certainty of the Christian 'hope'. He is eager to give Christians a full assurance; so he is not content merely to say that, because they are children, they are heirs of God, but that, in addition, they are joint-heirs with Christ.

The Apostle's first emphasis, then, is that we are heirs of God. We might have thought that that was obvious in and of itself; that the whole statement, 'The Spirit itself beareth witness with our spirit, that we are the children of God: and if children, then heirs', makes it perfectly clear. But the Apostle does not take it for granted; he underlines it, he repeats it for emphasis. He wants to make quite sure that no one misses its significance. This is interesting because it throws light upon the great Apostle as a teacher, an incomparable teacher. One of the first and most important essentials in any teacher is never to take anything for granted. To do so is the most fatal mistake we can ever make. In other words, these things have got to be brought right out and underlined; and that is what the Apostle does here. Let me explain his meaning.

Heirship gives a man a very special position. This is something that we are all familiar with in ordinary life, in secular affairs, though perhaps these things are not as familiar nowadays as they used to be. In olden times in families there may have been a large number of children, but the first was the heir. It was not that the parents paid less than the requisite attention to the others, but that they paid more attention to him. The heir is the one who carries on the line, who keeps the name going; and therefore in every family, from the royal family downwards, he is always in a peculiar and special position, and receives special treatment and attention. That is common to all heirship, and what the Apostle seems to me to be saying is that, if this is true of every heir, we should realize the peculiar blessings that come to, and the exceptional privileges of those who are heirs of God.

What are these blessings and privileges? I cannot deal with the matter exhaustively, but merely intend to indicate certain lines. In the first place, because we are heirs of God, the things that have been promised us, and which are coming to us because we are heirs, are absolutely safe. There is no possible nor conceivable danger that we shall ever be robbed of this inheritance. Why not? The chief reason is that the One who has promised us these things is God. We know that, when we are dealing with human beings, we are dealing with men and women subject to change. History is full of illustrations of the matter. Someone might have been a favourite of a king or of some great man, and while he was the favourite, the king or the great man made great and lavish promises to him. But then, being capricious and changeable and sinful, the great man may suddenly turn against this favourite and dismiss him, and the man who had been promised much gets nothing. This is what happens in life so frequently. You can never be sure of anything promised by a fellow-man; he may become diseased, many things may happen to him, and a variety of influences may be brought to bear upon him. Great tragedies have resulted in this way. So the Apostle goes out of his way to emphasize that we are not only heirs, but heirs of God. Our inheritance is therefore absolutely certain, or, speaking in human terms, the 'Will' will never be changed! Why not? This same Apostle in writing to Titus puts it like this: 'Paul, a servant of God, and an apostle of Jesus Christ, according to the faith of God's elect, and the acknowledging of the truth which is after godliness; in hope of eternal life, which God, that cannot lie, promised before the world began' (1: 1–2). It is good for us that the Apostle broke his statement up and said that we are 'heirs of God'. 'God cannot lie', God cannot change. He is 'The Father of lights, with whom is no variableness, neither shadow of turning'. When God says something, it is eternally said, and there will never be any change. So as God has made these promises to us, as God has said that we are His heirs, there is never need to have any kind of fear that He may go back on his word, or change it, or modify it – never! 'Heaven and earth shall pass away', said His Son while He was here on earth, 'but my word shall not pass away'. And that is true of all these great promises of God to us.

In a notable statement by the Author of the Epistle to the Hebrews we find precisely the same point: 'For men verily swear by the greater: and an oath for confirmation is to them an end of all strife. Wherein God, willing more abundantly to show unto the heirs of promise the immutability of his counsel, confirmed it by an oath: that by two immutable things, in which it was impossible for God to lie, we might have a strong consolation, who have fled for refuge to lay hold upon the hope set before us' (Hebrews 6: 16 to 18). So 'we have this hope as an anchor of the soul, both sure and steadfast, and which entereth into that within the veil'. So, then, there is one great deduction which we can make at once – the immutability of the promise!

The Apostle is also concerned to bring out God's care for us. As I have already indicated, special attention is always paid to the heir. As the heir special care is bestowed upon him, and the father keeps his eye on him. He is proud of him, and sees the future as dependent on this one; therefore he gives him this exceptional amount of attention. All that applies to us as 'heirs of God' meets with abundant illustration in Scripture. Our Lord Himself on one occasion said that, because of this relationship, 'the very hairs of your head are all numbered'. That is the measure of God's care for us. What is the care of an earthly father for his heir in comparison with this? Another great statement by our Lord is: 'Fear not, little flock, for it is your Father's good pleasure to give you the kingdom.' There is no need for us to be troubled, though we may be surrounded by troubles and tribulations and trials. Having determined our destiny, and having pledged Himself to it, nothing which is necessary to our preparation for the inheritance will ever be neglected.

Let us work this out a little in detail. What does the man do who has an heir? He sends him to the best school he knows of, and sees to it that he gets the best training and the best preparation. And God does exactly the same with us. He does some extraordinary things to us. We are told in Hebrews, chapter 12, for instance, that He sometimes even sends us to rather a painful school. 'Whom the Lord loveth he chasteneth, and scourgeth every son whom he receiveth. If ye endure chastening, God dealeth with you as with sons; for what son is he whom the father chasteneth not? But if ye be without chastisement, whereof all are partakers, then are ye bastards, and not sons. Furthermore, we have had fathers of our flesh which corrected us, and we gave them reverence: shall we not much rather be in subjection unto the Father of spirits, and live? For they verily for a few days chastened us after their own pleasure; but he for our profit, that we might be partakers of his holiness.' There is no greater measure of God's concern for us than that; and nothing is more important for us than to realize it. The Apostle will elaborate the point when he adds at the end of the 17th verse: 'if so be that we suffer with him, that we may be also glorified together.' But here it is in principle. It is because we are His heirs that God puts us into this gymnasium where we seem to be having rough treatment at times. That is good for you, says that Author, and you should deduce from that your heirship and your sonship. It is because you are going to receive a great inheritance as the heirs of God that He takes all this trouble with you. He feeds you, He clothes you, He is concerned about everything that happens to you, and He shows it supremely in the matter of chastisement.

But in the next place, we can be quite sure that the care of us which is taken by God will continue. Here again we see the contrast between the human father and the divine Father. The human father does things by fits and starts. He for a while exercises discipline, then he becomes slack, with the result that the child does not know where he stands, because he does not know what the father is thinking at any moment. The child is confused by the father's changeableness and capriciousness. But God is not like that; He goes on with everything He starts; and never ceases until His purpose is achieved. The Apostle Paul, face to face with death, which might take place at any moment, says to the Philippians in the 6th verse of the 1st chapter: 'Being confident of this very thing, that he which hath begun a good work in you will perform it until the day of Jesus Christ.' What a comfort it is, and what a consolation, to know that the treatment, the preparation, will go on without ceasing until the day of Jesus Christ – the day for which we are looking! The Apostle tells them that it does not matter how changeable circumstances may be; he himself may be taken from them, and many other painful things may happen to them, but no matter! God will not abandon them; once He starts a work He continues it. God has never left anything incomplete, and He never will.

And I would say further – and it is a most comforting thought – that God will carry on His work even in spite of us. It is comforting because oftentimes, when we hear about the inheritance and the glory, we feel and we say, 'How can I ever get there? I am weak, I am frail, I am fallible, I am changeable, "I dare not trust the sweetest frame", I never know what I am going to be like tomorrow morning, and I wonder whether I shall falter and fall finally by the wayside. Have I sufficient strength and power to guarantee that I am going to arrive at the goal and enjoy the inheritance?' The answer is given by the Apostle, and this time in particular in Ephesians 1, verses 18 ff., to which we have referred already, but particularly in the third petition of the Apostle's prayer for those people, namely: 'What is the exceeding greatness of his power to us-ward that believe.' 'His power'! Our destiny does not depend upon our power but upon His! Paul assures us that it is 'according to the working of his mighty power which he wrought in Christ when he raised him from the dead, and set him at his own right hand in the heavenly places, far above all principality, and power, and might, and dominion, and every name that is named, not only in this world, but also in that which is to come'. In other words the power that is working in us is the power of the resurrection. He repeats it again at the end of the third chapter of the Epistle to the Ephesians: 'Now unto him that is able to do exceeding abundantly above all that we ask or think, according to the power that worketh in us, unto him be glory in the church by Christ Jesus throughout all ages, world without end'. Can anything be more comforting than that? We are heirs of God, and because we are heirs of God, this is the power that is working in us. It will perfect the work that has been begun, until eventually we shall be 'faultless and blameless, without spot or wrinkle or any such thing', standing before Him in the glory.

But this also entitles us to say that, because of God's ability and power, we can be sure that there is nothing outside us that will ever be able to rob us of this inheritance. Having seen that nothing within us can ever prevent our getting there, we may still fear that something outside us – the world, carnality and the devil – may rob us of it. What about all the forces that are so antagonistic to us? The world is full of them; we are set in an evil world of 'principalities and powers, the rulers of the darkness of this world, spiritual wickedness in high places', all of which are against us. Everything seems to be against us 'to drive us to despair'. Are not these things going to rob us of the ultimate inheritance? The answer is that we are the children of God, the heirs of God. Our Lord stated it very clearly in the Sermon on the Mount in Matthew 6, verses 19 and 20: 'Lay not up for yourselves treasures upon earth, where moth and rust doth corrupt, and where thieves break through and steal.' You cannot hold on to anything in this world; moth and rust insidiously come in. A process of decay is going on everywhere. You look at a solid block of wood and feel that it will last for ever; then you hear that the whole thing has suddenly collapsed. Why? It had been eaten up inside by dry rot or worms or something of that nature, and it is nothing but dust and powder. Such is the nature of the world, and that is why we should not 'lay up for ourselves treasures upon earth, where moth and rust doth corrupt, and where thieves break through and steal'. We should rather 'lay up treasures for ourselves in heaven, where neither moth nor rust doth corrupt, and where thieves do not break through nor steal'. There, they never will! There is no moth, no rust in heaven, there are no thieves in heaven, they can never make an entry there. Heaven is shut to them. And our Lord adds a further

word in John 10: 28 and 29: 'And I give unto them eternal
life; and they shall never perish, neither shall any man pluck
them out of my hand. My Father, which gave them me, is greater
than all; and no man is able to pluck them out of my Father's
hand.' That is the measure of our safety. It is absolute security.
We are heirs of God, and God, our heavenly Father, takes care
of us. No man – no power in earth or hell – will ever be able to
pluck us out of His hand.

When we turn to the closing verses of this eighth chapter of
Romans, we read: 'Who shall separate us from the love of Christ?'
In the light of all the Apostle has been saying – 'Who shall
separate us from the love of Christ? shall tribulation, or distress,
or persecution, or famine, or nakedness, or peril, or sword? Nay,
in all these things we are more than conquerors through him
that loved us. For I am persuaded', – he is certain! – 'that neither
death, nor life, nor angels, nor principalities, nor powers, nor
things present, nor things to come, nor height, nor depth, nor
any other creature, shall be able to separate us from the love of
God, which is in Christ Jesus our Lord.' We are heirs of God
and therefore we can never be robbed of this inheritance. The
Apostle Peter says the same thing in his First Epistle: 'Blessed
be the God and Father of our Lord Jesus Christ, which according
to his abundant mercy hath begotten us again unto a lively hope
by the resurrection of Jesus Christ from the dead, to an inheritance incorruptible, and undefiled, and that fadeth not away,
reserved in heaven for you, who are kept by the power of God
through faith unto salvation ready to be revealed in the last time'
(1: 3–5). You cannot add to that. The inheritance is being reserved
for us, kept for us, in heaven, by God Himself. We are heirs of
God, so we can be quite sure that nothing from within us, or
from without, or from any other conceivable quarter, shall be in
any way able to rob us of this inheritance which is ours because
we are heirs of God.

The final truth that emerges is that, because we are heirs of
God, we are given the enjoyment of God even while we are
in this life and in this world. It works in the following way.
An heir is always allowed to share in certain knowledge and
certain secrets that are not divulged even to other children in
the same family. It is a part of his training and instruction, a
part of his preparation for the day when he will enter into the

inheritance. All of us who are old enough to do so, looking back across life, treasure as perhaps some of the most wonderful moments in our experience the occasions when our parents or someone in that position began to tell us certain things. They said, 'Now that you are old enough I can tell you certain secrets' – they may be problems, worries, anxieties in the family, or perhaps certain prospects. We are let into the secret, given this intimate kind of knowledge, because of our position and relationship. This is equally true of us as heirs of God; God tells His heirs certain of His own secrets. No one else knows them. In this connection I have previously referred to 'the white stone' and 'the hidden manna' mentioned in the Book of Revelation, chapter 2 : 17. The world knows nothing about these things. One of our hymns puts it very well:

> *Behold the amazing gift of love*
> *The Father has bestowed*
> *On us, the sinful sons of men,*
> *To call us sons of God.*

> *Concealed as yet this honour lies,*
> *By this dark world unknown,*
> *A world that knew not, when He came,*
> *E'en God's eternal Son.*

But that is the glory of our position. The world does not know, the world does not understand; it regards us as fools for meeting together to study the Scriptures when we might be in a cinema or watching a football match, or with our eyes glued to a television set. 'What an utter waste of time!', they say. But here we are introduced into the secrets, our heavenly Father treats us as heirs, He reveals things about Himself to us, as the human father does, but on an infinitely vaster scale. He lets us into the secret of aspects of His own glory. And it happens to us in this life; the heirs are given a foretaste, are allowed to taste the first-fruits. We have already referred to this fact. The Holy Spirit is not only a 'seal' but also an 'earnest'. As one of Isaac Watts' hymns expresses it:

> *The men of grace have found*
> *Glory begun below;*

[419]

The Sons of God

Celestial fruits on earthly ground
From faith and hope may grow.

We are marching to Zion, and because we are heirs, we are
being given a foretaste of the glorious feast that is awaiting us
in the eternal inheritance. That is mainly a knowledge of God
Himself, realizations of His presence – all that comes through
the sealing of the Spirit. It is all designed to make us certain of the
inheritance, to give us this assurance 'until the redemption of the
purchased possession'.

Even the Old Testament saints knew something about these
things. Abraham, we are told, was 'the friend of God'. Enoch,
before him, 'walked with God', which means conversing, talking
with God. God was telling Enoch something of what He was
going to do, giving him a little pre-view of the coming of His
Son into the world. The Old Testament saints were given such
intimations of His secrets. And so the author of the seventy-
third Psalm is able to cry out in verse 25: 'Whom have I in heaven
but thee? and there is none upon earth that I desire beside thee.'
Nothing matters, he says, but this, that I know Thee. What has
the world to give?

> *Fading is the worldling's pleasure,*
> *All his boasted pomp and show;*
> *Solid joys and lasting treasure*
> *None but Zion's children know.*

Because we are His heirs, God speaks to us in this way, leads
us into the secrets, gives us an understanding, gives us glimpses
of what is going to be true of us, anticipates it all.

But we must also consider the second aspect of our heirship.
We are heirs of God, and secondly, we are joint-heirs with Christ.
Why did the Apostle trouble to say this? It was because he was
so anxious that these Roman Christians should understand and
enjoy the meaning of it all. The addition, in the first place, explains
how we become heirs. It is, in a sense, because we are joint-heirs
with Christ that we are heirs at all. Hebrews 1:2 reminds us that
God has appointed His Son 'heir of all things'. *He* is *the* heir.
The Apostle expresses this in the Epistle to the Galatians:
'Now to Abraham and his seed were the promises made. He saith

not, And to seeds, as of many; but as of one, And to thy seed, which is Christ' (3 : 16). The promises are really all made to Christ Jesus the Lord; He is 'the heir of all things'. And it is important that we should realize that we only become heirs because we are incorporated into Christ, because we are in Him. We are children of God through Him. We become the heirs of all things because of our union with Him.

The 5th chapter of this Epistle to the Romans has established the matter once and for ever. We are no longer 'in Adam', we are now 'in Christ'. We inherited the consequences of the action of the one man Adam; we are now inheriting the consequences of the action of the last Adam, the second Man, the Lord Jesus Christ. We have been 'crucified with him, buried with him, risen with him'. We are even now 'seated in the heavenly places in Christ Jesus'. In other words all blessing comes to us because of our relationship to Him. And He Himself also has made a promise to us. We find it in Luke 22, verses 29 and 30: 'And I appoint unto you a kingdom, as my Father hath appointed unto me; that ye may eat and drink at my table in my kingdom, and sit on thrones judging the twelve tribes of Israel.' Such is our Lord's specific and particular promise to us. As the Father has appointed to Him, He appoints to us. So our relationship to God is always in and through Him, and we are heirs because we are joint-heirs with Christ. This is stated again in the Book of Revelation in chapter 3, verse 21: 'To him that overcometh will I grant to sit with me in my throne, even as I also overcame, and am set down with my Father in his throne.'

I therefore stress the importance to us of realizing that, over and above the fact that we are heirs of God, we are joint-heirs with the Lord Jesus Christ. How does this take us further? Have you noticed how often the Apostle in his letters writes in the following way: 'Blessed be the God and Father of our Lord Jesus Christ'. Why does he not simply say, 'Blessed be our God and Father?' Why does he say, 'God and Father of our Lord Jesus Christ?' I recall what I heard an old preacher saying once in expounding this statement. He said, 'We should thank God that Paul did not just say, "Blessed be God who is our Father". There are', he said, 'certain poor, unfortunate people in this world to whom that sort of statement would not be a comfort at all. Their only idea of a father is a drunken brute who comes home many nights a week and who smashes things and ill-treats them. That is their idea of a father, the only kind of father they have ever known. So to tell them merely that God is Father is not enough. Ah', said the preacher, 'the Apostle was inspired to add that further statement, "Blessed be the God and Father of our Lord and Saviour Jesus Christ". How does that help us? In this way. Seeing the Lord Jesus Christ, reading about Him, we know what He is like. Well, "like Father like Son", "like Son like Father". Such a Son', said the old preacher, 'could not have the kind of father that some of these children have had. So Paul writes of the "God and Father of our Lord and Saviour Jesus Christ".'

So, then, we are not only heirs of God, we are joint-heirs with Christ. The statement has a rich content. The devil will come to us and tempt us, and will try to shake our confidence, and say, 'Ah yes, you say that God has pledged Himself by an oath that He is going to give you various things because you are His children, but God cannot give blessings to people who are sinners, and who fail, and who have broken their vows and their pledges so often'. The Apostle's answer to that is, that we are heirs of God because we are 'in Christ'; it all comes to us through Him. He is the only-begotten Son of God, the only One of whom God said, 'This is my beloved Son, in whom I am well pleased'. We have displeased God often in many things; but here is One who has never displeased Him. And the promise is to Him! All the promises are to Him, and therefore we can be absolutely certain of our position. We get all through Him. All the promises will be fulfilled to Him, and we are in Him, we are a part of Him, we are joined to Him; and therefore they will of necessity come to us. He is at the head of a great procession: 'Looking unto Jesus, the author (file-leader) and finisher of our faith'. He is at the head of the procession of the children of God. 'Behold me', He says, 'and the children which thou hast given me.' He is 'the first-born among many brethren'. We are walking after Him. He is going to enter, and we enter after Him. That is the argument.

Consider the One who is in this position. He is the One of whom it is written: 'All things were made by him, and without him was not anything made that was made'. Not only so, already all things have been put into His hands. Listen to Him saying after His resurrection: 'All power is given unto me in heaven and in earth' (Matthew 28: 18). Already! He has it! He is seated at the right hand of God in glory, 'waiting until his enemies shall be made his footstool'. 'The forerunner is for us entered, even Jesus'. He is already there! He said, 'Let not your heart be troubled: ye believe in God, believe also in me. In my Father's house are many mansions: if it were not so I would have told you. I go to prepare a place for you' (John 14: 1–2). So the joint-heirship is most important. It makes our inheritance absolutely certain in every way. He has already conquered every enemy that is set against us. He conquered the devil when he came to tempt Him repeatedly, defeated him utterly, exposed him and put him to an open shame upon the Cross, triumphing over him there. He has conquered death and the grave. The last enemy has been conquered. He has risen triumphant over all. And we are 'in Him', we are joint-heirs with Him. People who invest their money wisely are always careful to discover who guarantees the project. Multiply that by infinity! The Lord Jesus Christ is with you in this matter; He has underwritten it all. He has already received the inheritance, and we belong to Him, and are joint-heirs with Him. Our inheritance is certain and sure, 'nothing shall ever be able to separate us from the love of God which is in Christ Jesus our Lord'.

Let us thank God that the Apostle was not content just to say, 'if children, then heirs'; but went on to say, moved and led by the Spirit, 'and joint-heirs with Christ'. His Name is on the prospectus with ours, it is there on the document, He has sealed it with His own blood, He has conquered all the enemies that could ever rob us, and He is now seated at the right hand of all glory and power. All power is His, and He will exercise it on our behalf; and nothing and no one shall ever be allowed to stand between us and what 'God hath prepared for them that love Him'. Blessed be the God and Father of our Lord and Saviour Jesus Christ, who hath appointed us in Him, and through Him, as heirs of this indescribable glory!

Thirty-three

*

If so be that we suffer with him, that we may be also glorified together.

Romans 8: 17

The Apostle does something here which is very typical and characteristic of him. We have already seen how, in this short paragraph, each thought leads on to another. This verse starts, 'If children, then heirs'. In other words it follows on from what he had been saying in the 16th verse. And now in the second half of the verse he does the same again.

It is interesting to ask why the Apostle suddenly introduced the thought of suffering. From the beginning of verse 14 he has been talking about our sonship. He has been rejoicing in the fact that we have not been given 'the spirit of bondage again to fear', but 'the Spirit of adoption whereby we cry, Abba, Father', and, indeed, over and above that, 'The Spirit itself beareth witness with our spirit, that we are the children of God'. And not only so, but 'if children, [we are] then heirs, heirs of God, and joint-heirs with Christ'. He rises from one step to another; then suddenly he introduces this whole matter of suffering: 'If so be that we suffer with him, that we may be also glorified together.' But why did the Apostle suddenly introduce this question of suffering?

There need be no difficulty about the answer to the question. The Apostle undoubtedly introduced this matter here, first of all, because he was a man who had a great pastoral heart. Never think of the Apostle Paul as a kind of Professor of Theology. He was a profound theologian but he was also an evangelist and a pastor. He was never merely academic, never merely theoretical in his approach. He was a man who had a great heart of love, and was anxious to help all; so here at once, he foresaw a practical question, a practical difficulty arising. He had been building up this elevated and moving picture of Christian people and of their relationship to God through the Lord Jesus Christ; he had been talking about their great inheritance and the implications of their position as 'joint-heirs with Christ'. And then, it is as if he suddenly thought to himself: 'I wonder how these people will react to these truths, because their present position and circumstances are very different from the story yet to be revealed. They are having a hard time, they are suffering, they are in trouble, they are surrounded by distressing conditions; and it may very well be that they will say, Ah, it is all very well for Paul to write as he has done, but we find life hard and even bitter'. Therefore, in order to help them, and to deal with such difficulties as might arise in their hearts, the Apostle takes up this subject. He but introduces it in the second half of verse 17; then he takes it up properly at the beginning of verse 18, and continues to deal with it right to the end of the chapter.

Suffering was a very urgent problem in the early Church. There is a sense in which nearly all the New Testament Epistles are concerned with this one thing. People were tempted to say, 'We have listened to the preaching and we have heard about these great promises, these wonderful statements about the kingdom of God and what will happen to us if we believe the gospel; but our actual experience is that life is very hard and very difficult and very trying'. And the devil came in, of course, and tempted them at that point. He tried to shake their faith by saying, 'Didn't I tell you that you should never have believed it? It is but a fairy-tale, it is just a kind of phantasy and fancy; there is no substance in it. Why,' said the devil, 'if God were God, and if Christ Jesus was His Son, you would not be in such a plight'. The problem has continued from the apostles' days to our own, and it still troubles many Christian people in various parts of the world.

The problem is how to reconcile trials, troubles and tribulations with these 'exceeding great and precious promises', with this vista of glory which the Apostle has just been painting. The New Testament devotes considerable space to the matter, much more in fact than is generally realized. Many Christian people are unhappy because they have never understood the problem and its solution. The devil seems to attack almost all of us along this very line. We feel as if we are not being dealt with fairly, or we wonder whether we are Christians at all. We say: 'If I am really a Christian why is all this happening to me?' This is the theme so frequently dealt with in the New Testament. Take, for instance, the Book of Revelation; this is really its one great theme, its one great concern. It was written to encourage Christian people suffering in the days of the Apostles, and in every later period. It is a Book which is always up-to-date for that reason.

A second reason for the introduction of the problem of suffering is that Paul is continuing his discourse on assurance, and he argues that suffering for Christ's kingdom's sake is a further way of being certain and sure of our salvation. In other words, this verse is one of the links in a chain; it carries on the theme about sonship, and at the same time it introduces this other particular theme. And the Apostle is showing that this whole matter of suffering, if we understand it rightly, is one of the strongest and most profound arguments for the assurance of salvation and the absolute certainty of our ultimate arrival in glory that we can ever find. So he is doing two things at one and the same time. He is comforting and consoling suffering Christians, and he is adding, as it were, the final argument with regard to assurance and to certainty.

Mention must here be made of the mechanics of translation. In the Authorized Version we read: 'If so be that we suffer with him, that we may be also glorified together'. The whole exegesis, the whole interpretation depends upon a right understanding of this 'if so be'. The New English Bible seems to me to be entirely wrong at this point. It translates thus: 'We are God's heirs, and Christ's fellow-heirs if we share his sufferings now in order to share his splendour hereafter'. Let us pass by the reduction of 'glory' to 'splendour'; but let us take up this other point, which is much more important. 'We are God's heirs, and Christ's fellow-heirs, if we share his sufferings now in order to share his splendour hereafter.' I may be mis-reading it, but this translation seems to me to suggest that our 'heirship' and our 'joint-heirship with Christ' is conditional upon our suffering now in this present life. But that is not what the Apostle meant. We have a key to his meaning in verse 9: 'But ye are not in the flesh, but in the Spirit, if so be that the Spirit of God dwell in you. Now if any man have not the Spirit of Christ, he is none of his.' We have there the same expression 'If so be'. And we have seen that it can carry only one meaning. It means 'since' there; and it means 'since' here. What the Apostle is saying therefore is this: 'If children, then heirs; heirs of God, and joint-heirs with Christ; since we suffer with him, that we may be also glorified together'. So the translation should not be 'If' but 'Since'; or 'If, as is the fact'; or 'Seeing that', 'In view of the fact that'. There is nothing conditional about the expression. The Apostle is saying, 'As we are suffering with him now, we shall also experience the glory with him'. It is something, as I shall show, that is said in many places in the New Testament Scriptures. In other words, we must get rid of any notion that our heirship of God, and joint-heirship with Christ, is conditional upon our suffering here. The case is far different.

But we must also look at the word 'that' – 'If so be that we suffer with him *that*. . . ' Here, there seems to be general agreement that the 'that' means 'in order that' – 'in order that we may also be glorified together'. So we can read our sentence thus, 'If children, then heirs; heirs of God, and joint-heirs with Christ; since we suffer with him in order that we may be glorified also together'.

There are two main doctrines here. The first is that the sufferings of Christian people, far from raising any doubts about the truth of the gospel promises, or of their interest in the promises, should rather be seen as strengthening both the promises and our share in them. The two aspects are important. As I have already indicated, the devil comes to us and tempts us. He says it is one of two things: either the gospel is full of lies and of false promises which do not materialize; or else, if the promises are true, it is obvious that we are not Christians. 'It is one thing or the other', says the devil, 'and it may be both'. The reply to this is that, correctly understood, the statement tells us that sufferings, far from raising either of these doubts or questions, is rather a proof of the truth of the promises, and also establishes that we have a share in them.

How does it do this? Notice that the Apostle has just been saying that we are not only heirs of God but 'joint-heirs with Christ'. The Apostle is reminding us here, as he has done already in chapter 5 and elsewhere, of our union with Christ, our one-ness with Him. We are 'in Christ' and therefore sharers of everything that is true of Him – 'buried with him in baptism', 'raised again with him', 'seated with him in the heavenly places'. We are 'in him'; He is the Head and we are the body, and therefore we are sharers in the things that pertain to Him. This is the doctrine the

Apostle has been laying down; we are 'joint-heirs' with Him because we are incorporated into Him. But that applies to the suffering quite as much as it does to everything else, and this is what the Apostle is really saying.

We can therefore look at the matter in the following way. Look at the Lord Himself, and at what happened to Him when He was in this world. He was 'a man of sorrows, and acquainted with grief'. There is no record anywhere of our Lord having laughed aloud. We read of Him weeping, we read of Him saying that His soul was troubled. He was despised, He was 'rejected of men', He was buffeted, He was hated, He was persecuted. No one has ever suffered as the Son of God suffered when He was in this world. Suffering was His lot. He was the very incarnation of everlasting love, 'in the likeness of sinful flesh', living His life as a man in this world. But read the record in the four Gospels, and especially about His death upon the Cross and all that led up to it. It is summed up in the expression – 'a man of sorrows, and acquainted with grief', 'his visage was so marred more than any man'. That is the picture!

Here is the key to the understanding of this doctrine. This was the experience of the Head of the Church Himself when He was in this world. He suffered. The reason why He suffered, of course, is quite clear. He suffered because He was the Son of God. He Himself says so repeatedly. Look at John 5 : 43: 'I am come in my Father's name, and ye receive me not: if another shall come in his own name, him ye will receive.' He turned to people who were persecuting Him and about to throw stones at Him, and said, 'Many good works have I showed you from my Father; for which of those works do ye stone me?' There was no answer. He suffered as He did because He was the Son of God. The world, He said, recognizes its own, and it loves its own; but it hates Me. He said on one occasion to His followers: 'The world cannot hate you; but me it hateth.' Why? Because they belonged to the world, and He was 'not of this world'. He suffered in this world because this is a world which is evil; it is a world that is governed by 'the prince of the power of the air, the spirit that now worketh in the children of disobedience'. It is a world that is dominated by 'the god of this world'; it is 'this present evil world', as this Apostle describes it in writing to the Galatians. Hence it hates God, and hates His Son; and therefore, when He came into the world, 'his own received him not'. They cried, 'Away with him; crucify him!' They did not want Him. We have His own word for this: 'This is the condemnation, that light is come into the world, and men loved darkness rather than light, because their deeds were evil.' Light is that which always exposes the hidden things of darkness, and the darkness does not like that to happen. No one likes being found out, no one likes being exposed; but light always has that result. Christ is 'the light of the world', and He exposed the hidden things of darkness, and the darkness hated Him. They loved darkness and hated the light, instead of loving the light and hating the darkness. This is what happened to Christ; and He says that this is the general rule.

This is also the key to the understanding of so much that happens to us as Christian people in this world. We are given some very clear and definite predictions by Christ as to what will happen to His own people. Some of them are found in the 15th chapter of John's Gospel, as for example: 'If the world hate you, ye know that it hated me before it hated you. If ye were of the world, the world would love his own: but because ye are not of the world, but I have chosen you out of the world, therefore the world hateth you. The servant is not greater than his lord. If they persecuted me, they will also persecute you; if they have kept my saying, they will keep yours also. But these things will they do unto you for my name's sake, because they know not him that sent me' (vv. 18–21). This is a specific prediction that Christian people, because they are Christian, will suffer in this life. It is still more explicit in John 16: 33: 'These things have I spoken unto you, that in me ye might have peace. In the world ye shall have tribulation: but be of good cheer, I have overcome the world.' The reason why it must so happen is that Christians are His people. 'Like Master, like servant'; like Head, like body! You cannot belong to Christ without receiving the treatment He received. You must expect it, so do not be taken unawares, do not be troubled, do not be upset; it is bound to happen to you. Because you are His people the world will treat you as it treated Him.

Turn to the Acts of the Apostles and, in the light of this prophecy, note what did happen to His people. You find almost at once, at the beginning of Acts 4, that Peter and John were arrested and tried before a court. They had been preaching and teaching in the name of Jesus, and had healed a man at the

Beautiful Gate of the temple, saying, 'In the name of Jesus Christ of Nazareth, rise up and walk'. They were arrested and were straitly charged and threatened, we are told. They were told that they would be set at liberty on condition that they never again preached or did anything in the name of Jesus. Thus early was suffering for Christ's sake befalling them. They were described as 'ignorant and unlettered men'; they were not leading an insurrection, they were not gathering an army; they were doing nothing but talking about this Jesus, and healing a lame man; but opposition to them arose, as it had happened to Him. At the beginning of the eighth chapter of Acts we are told that there was a great persecution of Christian people in Jerusalem; and they all had to leave the city, apart from the apostles. Ordinary Christian people were being persecuted simply because they were followers of Christ.

But one of the most wonderful illustrations of all is found in the ninth chapter of Acts in connection with the call of Saul of Tarsus, later this Apostle Paul, on the road to Damascus. The first words he heard were, 'Saul, Saul, why persecutest thou me?' Whom was he persecuting? Christian people! Yes, but our Lord puts it in another manner, 'Why persecutest thou me?' The Head and the body are one, they are indissolubly linked together, so He says, 'Why persecutest thou me?' Here is the essence of this great doctrine.

Again, in chapter 12 of the Acts we find that James, the brother of the Lord, was put to death, and that Herod then proceeded to arrest Peter. They put him in prison, bound him to soldiers, and put four quaternions of soldiers to guard him, intending after Easter to bring him forth and to put him to death; and but for a divine interposition this would have happened to him. Next, in Acts 14: 22, we find a very definite statement made about the Apostle Paul. We are told that he went round the churches, 'confirming the souls of the disciples, and exhorting them to continue in the faith, and that we must through much tribulation enter into the kingdom of God'. The Apostle was repeating the message of his Master, that Christian people had nothing to expect and to anticipate but much tribulation; and that they would enter into the final glory via, along the route of, 'much tribulation'. There is much further evidence in the Acts of the Apostles to the same effect.

In the Epistles you find the same teaching almost everywhere.
I have selected certain passages. Take, for instance, what we find
in 2 Corinthians chapter 1, reading from verses 3 to 7: 'Blessed be
God, even the Father of our Lord Jesus Christ, the Father of
mercies, and the God of all comfort; who comforteth us in all
our tribulation, that we may be able to comfort them which are
in any trouble, by the comfort wherewith we ourselves are
comforted of God. For as the sufferings of Christ abound in us,
so our consolation also aboundeth by Christ. And whether we
be afflicted, it is for your consolation and salvation, which is
effectual in the enduring of the same sufferings which we also
suffer: or whether we be comforted, it is for your consolation
and salvation. And our hope of you is steadfast, knowing, that
as ye are partakers of the sufferings, so shall ye be also of the
consolation.' Again in 2 Corinthians, chapter 4, verses 17 and 18:
'Our light affliction, which is but for a moment, worketh for us a
far more exceeding and eternal weight of glory: while we look
not at the things which are seen, but at the things which are not
seen: for the things which are seen are temporal; but the things
which are not seen are eternal.' Then in chapter 11, beginning at
verse 23, he tells them something further: 'Are they ministers of
Christ? (I speak as a fool) I am more; in labours more abundant,
in stripes above measure, in prisons more frequent, in deaths oft.
Of the Jews five times received I forty stripes save one.' And on
and on he goes, giving a recital and a list of his sufferings and his
trials and his tribulations. That was the kind of life this great
Apostle lived; 'like Master like servant'.

In the Epistle to the Philippians we have further testimony.
The Apostle is in prison threatened with death, and not knowing
what was going to happen to him, and he writes: 'I would ye
should understand, brethren, that the things which happened
unto me have fallen out rather unto the furtherance of the gospel;
so that my bonds in Christ are manifest in all the palace, and in
all other places' (1 : 12–13). And that leads him to say explicitly in
verses 28 and 29 of that same chapter: 'In nothing [be] terrified
by your adversaries: which is to them an evident token of
perdition, but to you of salvation, and that of God.' He tells the
Christians that the adversaries think that, because they are suffering
in this way, it is a sign of perdition; but to them it should be a
proof of their salvation, and that of God, 'for [because] unto you

it is given in the behalf of Christ, not only to believe on him, but also to suffer for his sake'.

There is another statement about suffering – a very wonderful one – in the 3rd chapter and in the 10th verse. Indeed, there is much the same thing in the second chapter in verse 17: 'Yea, and if I be offered upon the sacrifice and service of your faith, I joy and rejoice with you all.' That is a way of saying, 'If I am going to be put to death because of all this, all is well'. But in chapter 3 verse 10 there is this wonderful statement: 'That I may know him, and the power of his resurrection, and the fellowship of his sufferings, being made conformable unto his death; if by any means I might attain unto the resurrection from among the dead'. Go on to Colossians 1:24: 'Who now rejoice in my sufferings for you, and fill up that which is behind of the afflictions of Christ in my flesh for his body's sake, which is the church.' What a statement! Then consider 2 Thessalonians chapter 1, verses 4 and 5: 'So that we ourselves glory in you in the churches of God for your patience and faith in all your persecutions and tribulations that ye endure . . . that ye may be counted worthy of the kingdom of God, for which ye also suffer'.

Go on to 2 Timothy 1:7: 'God hath not given us the spirit of fear, but of power, and of love, and of a sound mind.' Timothy seems to have been in trouble on this question of suffering; so the Apostle proceeds to say to him: 'Be not thou therefore ashamed of the testimony of our Lord, nor of me his prisoner: but be thou partaker of the afflictions of the gospel according to the power of God.' In the second chapter of that Epistle in verse 12 he says: 'If we suffer, we shall also reign with him.' It is exactly what we find in the seventeenth verse of the eighth chapter of Romans: 'It is a faithful saying; if we be dead with him, we shall also live with him: if we suffer, we shall also reign with him.'

But perhaps the most explicit statement of all is found in the third chapter of the Second Epistle to Timothy, in verses 10–12: 'But thou hast fully known my doctrine, manner of life, purpose, faith, longsuffering, charity, patience, persecutions, afflictions, which came unto me at Antioch, at Iconium, at Lystra; what persecutions I endured: but out of them all the Lord delivered me. Yea, and all that will live godly in Christ Jesus shall suffer persecution.' The Author of the Epistle to the Hebrews is equally definite, in chapter 2, verse 10: 'It became him, for whom are all things, and by whom are all things, in bringing many sons unto glory, to make the captain of their salvation perfect through sufferings'. It is also the theme of chapter 11 of the same Epistle. The Author is urging them to look at all the great heroes of the faith, to observe how they had to suffer, how they were maligned, how they were persecuted, how they were thrown into prison, sawn asunder, delivered to lions. . . . The whole of that glorious chapter devotes much attention to this question of suffering. And the same applies to the 12th chapter.

In the Epistle of James we have this same teaching in chapter 1 verses 2 and 3: 'My brethren, count it all joy when ye fall into divers temptations [trials]; knowing this, that the trying of your faith worketh patience'. In verse 12 he continues the theme: 'Blessed is the man that endureth trials.' He is a 'blessed' man, he is a man to be congratulated, as it were. The Apostle Peter has the same doctrine. In his First Epistle, chapter 1, verses 6 and 7, writing about the 'blessed hope' he says: 'Wherein ye greatly rejoice, though now for a season, if need be, ye are in heaviness through manifold temptations: that the trial of your faith, being much more precious than of gold that perisheth, though it be tried with fire, might be found unto praise and honour and glory at the appearing of Jesus Christ.' And the Apostle John in the Book of Revelation, chapter 1, verse 9, writes: 'I John, who also am your brother, and companion in tribulation, and in the kingdom and patience of Jesus Christ'.

What does all this mean? The doctrine is that, because we belong to Christ, this is what happens to us. It happened to Him, it happens to His people. He prophesied that it would happen. It happened in the early Church, it has been happening ever since. The followers get the same treatment as the Head. There is this unity in Christ; we share the blessings, but we share the sufferings also. It is the picture of the Head and the body once more. That, then, is the argument. If you are suffering as a Christian, and because you are a Christian, it is one of the surest proofs you can ever have of the fact that you are a child of God, and if a child, then an heir, an heir of God, and a joint-heir with Christ. Someone once wrote a wonderful phrase which sums up this teaching: 'All Christ's sheep are branded with a cross, and that not in the fleece only, but also in the flesh.' The cross is burnt in by a hot iron. Peter in the fourth chapter of his First Epistle writes: 'Beloved, think it not strange concerning the fiery trial which is to try you, as though some strange thing happened unto you: but rejoice, inasmuch as ye are partakers of Christ's sufferings; that when his glory shall be revealed, ye may be glad also with exceeding joy. If ye be reproached for the name of Christ, happy are ye; for the spirit of glory and of God resteth upon you: on their part he is evil spoken of, but on your part he is glorified' (vv. 12–14).

The argument is inevitable; if we are suffering as Christians it is an absolute proof that we belong to Him, that we are therefore joint-heirs with Him. So we must look at our sufferings in that way. We must not allow the devil to frighten us, and to say that the promises of God are not true, or that, if they are true, we are clearly not partakers in them because we are suffering. Turn on him and say, 'Thank you very much; you are not as clever as you think you are, because what I am enduring is a proof to me that I am a child of God. The world governed by you is treating me exactly as it treated Him. If I belonged to you I would not be having this treatment. Thank you; you are giving me a proof of the fact that I am a Christian.' That is the way to deal with the devil. Resist him, turn the Scriptures on to him; and he has nothing to say, he flees. 'Resist the devil, and he will flee from you.' 'Yea, and all that will live godly in Christ Jesus shall suffer persecution.' So the believer must not begin to grumble and complain and say, Why am I having such a hard time? I have believed the gospel, but I have trouble at home, and I am suffering in the office, nothing seems to go right. That is wrong; rather thank God and 'count it all joy'. It is a proof of the fact that you are a child of God, an heir of God, and a joint-heir with Christ. 'Since we suffer with him, we shall also be glorified together.'

But there is a second part to the Apostle's statement: 'Since we suffer with him, in order that we may be also glorified together.' The suffering that we undergo as Christians is a part of our preparation for the glory that is awaiting us. This very suffering is a part of my preparation for the inheritance which I am going to enjoy with the Lord Jesus Christ. The Author of the Epistle to the Hebrews tells us in chapter 2 and chapter 5 that our Lord Himself was 'made perfect' by His sufferings as our leader and as our mediator and redeemer. 'It became him, for whom are all things, and by whom are all things, in bringing many sons unto glory, to make the captain of their salvation perfect through sufferings' (chapter 2: 10). The same truth is taught in chapter 5: 8: 'Though he were a Son, yet learned he obedience by the things which he suffered.' He was thus 'made perfect', and 'the author of eternal salvation unto all them that obey him' (verse 9). It was because He endured even the death of the Cross that Paul says in Philippians 2: 9 to 11: 'Wherefore God also hath highly exalted him, and given him a name which is above every name: that at the name of Jesus every knee should bow, of things in heaven, and things in earth, and things under the earth; and that every tongue should confess that Jesus Christ is Lord, to the glory of God the Father'.

The argument is that the same process works in us. When we are expecting something really great and important to happen to us, we always prepare for it. We are never ready for the greatest privileges; we always need some extra preparation. Hard work is necessary if we want to pass an examination. Much practice is essential if we want to be perfect in any art. When we are attending an interview for some post we are careful to be clean and well dressed. Multiply all this by infinity and face the glory of our inheritance. As we are, we are not ready for it, we are not fit for it. But, thank God, He is preparing us for it; and it is He who is doing so. The Apostle works out the argument thus in 2 Corinthians 4: 17: 'Our light affliction, which is but for a moment, worketh for us a far more exceeding and eternal weight of glory.' The same point is the basis of the argument in 2 Corinthians 12 about 'the thorn in the flesh'. Paul could not understand at first why he should have the thorn, and he prayed three times that it might be removed. But it remained. Eventually the Apostle came to understand what was happening to him. He saw that he was in danger of becoming proud as the result of his experiences and the wonderful things he was enabled to do. He needed to be kept down, and so a 'messenger of Satan' was sent to buffet him for his good. 'It is good for me that I have been afflicted' says the Psalmist in the same way (119: 71). The Apostle was learning the meaning of the thorn in the flesh, and eventually he thanks God for it. For the same reason he says in Philippians 3: 10: 'That I may know him, and the power of his resurrection' – Yes! – 'and the fellowship of his sufferings, being made conformable unto his death'.

[435]

We learn things about the Lord Jesus Christ when we are suffering that we would never know otherwise. All Christians can testify to that. We can look back and thank God for things that have gone against us. I personally thank God for times when He has slammed doors in my face. I did not like it at the time, but I thank Him now. It is when you are in trouble and distress and tribulation that you begin to realize the glory of these wonderful promises. You have to be down before you can receive some of the best blessings. It is the pauper who knows what it is to receive; the self-sufficient man needs nothing. Look at the Pharisee in our Lord's parable of the Pharisee and the publican (Luke 18: 9–14). He just thanks God that he is not like others. He is not aware of needs; and he does not receive anything. No, it is through trials and troubles that God manifests Himself to us in some of the most tender ways; it is thus we appreciate some of the greatest glories of His love.

In Colossians 1: 24 the Apostle says that he is 'making up in his flesh that which remains of the sufferings of Christ'. It is difficult to understand fully what he means, but he indicates that he is entering intimately into the experience of union with his blessed Head; and he says that he did not know what it was really to know that unity until he discovered it through the sufferings involved in his work. He sees now that the Head and the body are one; and that his sufferings are part of the Lord's sufferings. Christ suffers it all as the great Head, and as he, Paul, participates in the ministry and the sufferings of Christ, he is making up 'that which remains of the sufferings of Christ'.

Let me use an almost ridiculous illustration. No child likes to be washed, but when he is going to a party his mother washes him, and is particularly careful. The child grumbles; he does not want her to clean out his ears, he does not want his neck to be washed. He objects to it all, but the mother insists upon it because he is going to the party, and the honour of the family is involved. The child does not like it, but it is done to him for his good and for his enjoyment of the party. God deals with us in that manner! We need to be washed and cleansed; God's purpose is to make us absolutely perfect, 'without spot or wrinkle or any such thing', faultless and blameless, holy, and fit for His holy presence. And in order for such a work to be accomplished, it is not sufficient that the gospel be preached to us. We do not listen as we should;

we are too busy and we forget. But God has His other methods; He puts us on a sick bed; He gives us a disappointment; there is a loss, there is a set-back. It is all a part of His preparation of us for the great glory that lies ahead. Hence James says: 'Count it all joy, my brethren', when these things happen to you. And it is Peter's meaning in the statement in his First Epistle to which I have already referred: 'That the trial of your faith, being much more precious than of gold that perisheth, though it be tried with fire, might be found unto praise and honour and glory at the appearing of Jesus Christ'. Very much alloy is mixed with the gold of our faith, and nothing will pass the heavenly examination but the pure unadulterated gold. How do men purify gold? They place it in a crucible and put a powerful flame underneath it, until everything is melted away and destroyed except the pure gold. A well-known hymn expresses it well in the words:

> *When through fiery trials thy pathway shall lie,*
> *My grace all-sufficient shall be thy supply;*
> *The flame shall not hurt thee, I only design*
> *Thy dross to consume and thy gold to refine.*

'Since we suffer with him, we shall be also glorified together.' The individual who needs to be troubled about his condition is the man who thinks that he is a Christian but who knows nothing about this suffering for Christ's sake. If you are not in some shape or form suffering for Christ's sake you need to examine yourself. It need not mean being thrown into prison, or into a concentration camp; but as certainly as you are a Christian you will have to suffer for it. It may be no more than to see people looking knowingly at one another when you enter the room, or to see a snigger or a sneer on their faces, or just to hear derogatory remarks made at your expense simply because you are a Christian. If you refuse to do certain things, not so much because they are wrong in and of themselves, but because you feel that they are not consistent with your position in Christ, and you suffer for it, you are suffering for Christ's sake. 'Yea, and all that will live godly in Christ Jesus shall suffer persecution.' 'If they hated me', our Lord says, 'they will also hate you.' And they do! The world hates the Christian because he is like his Master and Lord, because he belongs to Him, because they see in him what they saw in Him. They hated the light that was in Him, and they hate the light that is in us. So if you are suffering as a Christian for Christ's sake 'rejoice'; it is an absolute proof of the fact that you are 'in Christ'. It is more than that; it is an absolute proof that God is preparing you for the glory that He has prepared for all who are in His Son, all who are His heirs, and who are 'joint-heirs' with His only begotten Son. Thank God, then, that the Apostle added this further statement: 'If children, then heirs; heirs of God, and joint-heirs with Christ; since we suffer with him, in order that we may be glorified together.'

Blessed is the man, blessed is the woman who is aware of this process of preparation! Are the corners being knocked off your character? Do you know something about the chiselling? Are you being cleansed, and especially in those parts that are sensitive? Are you being hurt in this cleansing process? Do you know for certain that God is dealing with you and handling you? Are you aware as children that God as your heavenly Father is preparing you for 'that day', the day of the glory which is coming? Happy are you if you are aware of that! 'Rejoice and be exceeding glad'. 'Rejoice, inasmuch as ye are partakers of Christ's sufferings; that, when his glory shall be revealed, ye may be glad also with exceeding joy' (1 Peter 4: 13).

> *High is the rank we now possess,*
> *But higher we shall rise;*
> *Though what we shall hereafter be*
> *Is hid from mortal eyes.*
>
> *Our souls, we know, when He appears*
> *Shall bear His image bright;*
> *For all His glory, full disclosed,*
> *Shall open to our sight.*
>
> *A hope so great and so divine*
> *May trials well endure,*
> *And purge the soul from sense and sin,*
> *As Christ Himself is pure.*

(Scottish Paraphrases, 1781)